A CAPITOL JOURNEY

A CAPITOL JOURNEY

★★

Reflections on the Press,
Politics, and the Making of
Public Policy in Pennsylvania

VINCENT P. CAROCCI

The Pennsylvania State University Press
University Park, Pennsylvania

Library of Congress Cataloging-in-Publication Data

Carocci, Vincent P., 1936–
A capitol journey :
reflections on the press, politics, and the making of public policy in Pennsylvania /
Vincent P. Carocci.
p.   cm.
Includes bibliographical references and index.
ISBN 978-0-271-05857-3 (pbk : alk. paper)
1. Pennsylvania—Politics and government—1951– .
2. Press and politics—Pennsylvania.
3. Carocci, Vincent P., 1936– .
4. Journalists—Pennsylvania—Biography.
I. Title.
F155.C27 2005
320.9748—dc22
2004025003

Copyright © 2005 The Pennsylvania State University
All rights reserved
Printed in the United States of America
Published by The Pennsylvania State University Press,
University Park, PA 16802-1003

The Pennsylvania State University Press is a member of the
Association of American University Presses.

It is the policy of The Pennsylvania State University Press to
use acid-free paper. Publications on uncoated stock satisfy
the minimum requirements of American National Standard
for Information Sciences—Permanence of Paper for Printed
Library Materials, ANSI Z39.48–1992.

To Toni . . .

To Tommy and Patty . . .

To David and Steve . . .

*You always were and always will be,
each of you and all of you,
my most precious assets.*

*You made me
whole in so many ways.
Thank you.*

Contents

Preface ix
Introduction: Early Years 1

PART 1: THE PRESS

1. The Legislative Correspondents 12
2. Frank and Lindy: One Memorable Ride, One Memorable Coal Mine 19
3. The Divvy and a Pulitzer Prize 25
4. Reader Beware: Editorial Comment to Follow 32
5. Forks in the Road 36

PART 2: THE PENNSYLVANIA SENATE

6. The Pennsylvania Senate, 1970s Style 40
7. The Senators 47
8. Legislative Reorganizations and Strange Bedfellows 69
9. Transgressions 87
10. The Vince 106

PART 3: THE GOVERNORS

11. Chief Executive Officer 116
12. David L. Lawrence (1959–1963) 120
13. William Warren Scranton II (1963–1967) 125
14. Raymond Philip Shafer (1967–1971) 142
15. Milton J. Shapp (1971–1979) 161
16. Richard L. Thornburgh (1979–1987) 186

PART 4: THE CASEY YEARS

17. The Casey Pursuit 202
18. Reforming the Liquor Control System 212
19. Bouncing Around the Governor's Office on the Way to a Dream 219
20. The Budget from Hell 230

21. The Longest Week 236
22. Health: The Issue That Just Wouldn't Go Away 248
23. Reflections, Recovery, Reentry 266
24. The Final Year 278

Postscript 288
Index 293

Preface

A Capitol Journey had its genesis in a manuscript I wrote almost three years ago for Toni, my wife, and our four children, Patty, Tommy, David, and Steve. I called it "A Father's Life," a purely personal memoir intended for a purely family audience. I wrote it to share with our four children some insights (important insights, I thought) into their father's life—life as a child growing up in an Italian family on the south side of the city of Scranton, life as a collegian and a young adult charting his course and career, life as a new husband and new father striving to establish a reputable and comfortable environment for his family, and life as a professional whose course took him to careers in journalism, politics (to a lesser degree), and public service (to a larger degree). Those who read my story came back to me and said, "You have two stories here; one personal, the other professional. You might want to separate them someday down the road." That's what I have attempted to do here.

A Capitol Journey is the story of a lifetime, one man's lifetime, in and around the people, politics, and public policy-making processes of Pennsylvania over forty years leading to the new millennium. It is a story of Pennsylvania journalism on Capitol Hill forty years ago and an era long gone by, a story of the journalists who called the Capitol newsroom their workplace, a story of their work ethic and work habits, and a story of the liquor divvy and one Pulitzer Prize.

The book is also the story of the Pennsylvania Senate as an institution of public policymaking, of the members who gave the chamber its life and personality and its public-policy direction. It is also, in its way, a story of politics, the political machinations of Senate reorganizations and the political transgressions of individual members that, collectively, cost one political party its political majority and consigned it to minority status, possibly forever. *A Capitol Journey* also is a series of reflections, reflections about five Pennsylvania governors who served the people of the Commonwealth over a quarter-century between the early 1960s and the mid-1980s—reflections on their personalities, their politics, their governance style, their agendas, their successes, their failures, and their legacies.

Finally, *A Capitol Journey* is a series of recollections about a man whom I admired without reservation—Pennsylvania Governor Robert P. Casey of Scranton, whose commitment to public service in spite of three electoral setbacks led him on a steadfast pursuit of the Commonwealth's pinnacle of public office. I tell the story of a particularly bitter and prolonged fight to balance one nasty state budget, and one about the mean-spiritedness and disingenuousness of the Democratic National Convention of 1992. The book is, finally, a recollection of a governor's valiant struggle against a series of health problems that plagued him throughout his tenure: heart bypass surgery, amyloidosis, and, above all, the life-saving dual heart and liver transplant that disabled him temporarily but ultimately gave him the lease he needed to finish his gubernatorial term with a flourish and live out his life with his still-growing family.

Why is this book necessary? Because the story has never been told before, certainly not from the unique, insider perspective of one who traveled the corridors of the Capitol for almost half a century, first as a journalist, then as a senior legislative aide, and, finally, as a senior aide to a Pennsylvania governor. The people and events chronicled here deserve to be recorded and preserved for future generations and the lessons they might take from them. I believe I have done them justice. But let's be clear: *A Capitol Journey* is not a history, or a record, or a transcript (notarized or otherwise). It is a narrative—a narrative of people, places, and events as I saw them, lived them, and remembered them. The book is admittedly and distinctively subjective. Any factual imprecisions are mine and mine alone. But I make no apologies for the conclusions I draw from the stories I tell. They are as I saw them from the tiny corner of my world. They are, above all, accurate portrayals from my perspective.

To those who ask, "Why now?" I answer, "What better time." To those who ask, "Why you?" I say, "If not me, then who?" Others are certainly welcome to try their hand. The subjects I write about are not my exclusive domain. To borrow from "A Father's Life": the stories, I hope, are complete; the reflections, I know, are accurate as I remember them; and the prose, I pray, is better than merely pedestrian.

Enjoy, please.

Vincent P. Carocci
January 2005

Introduction

★★★★★★★

Early Years

The sun was setting on a cool, clear evening in April 1961 when I drove over the Harvey Taylor Bridge for the first time into the city of Harrisburg, Pennsylvania, the capital of the Commonwealth. I had just completed a two-year tour with the U.S. Army Intelligence Corps in Washington, D.C. I was arriving in Harrisburg to join the United Press International (UPI) bureau to begin what I envisioned would be a professional career as a political journalist.

The trip from the nation's capital had not gone well. Not well at all. Some forty-five minutes south of Harrisburg, in the quiet country town of Emmitsburg, Maryland, the radiator on my 1958 Dodge sedan had overheated and required immediate service. Now Emmitsburg and the people who call it home are pleasant enough, without question. But for a stranger on the road on an April Monday morning, a stranger in a hurry to reach his destination in pursuit of a career, it was not where I wanted to be. Fortunately, a mechanic's shop was nearby. The problem was fixable, but it would take time . . . six hours, in fact. I had no alternative but to wait. It was not an auspicious start to a new career path.

I was twenty-four. Harrisburg, in my set of professional aspirations, was to be but the first stop on a road to national political reporting. I wanted to go back to Washington where folks like Jack Bell of the Associated Press and Merriman Smith of United Press International, James Reston and Tom Wicker of the *New York Times,* Marquis Childs of the *St. Louis Post-Dispatch,* Peter Lisagor of the *Chicago Tribune* were the headliners of the national press corps. And a new president, John Fitzgerald Kennedy, and prominent politicians like Vice-President Lyndon Johnson, Speaker of the House Sam Rayburn, Senate Minority Leader Everett Dirksen, Senator Hubert Humphrey of Minnesota were the newsmakers. My hope that day was to return to the nation's capital to work and walk among them.

Harrisburg is only 125 miles north of Washington, D.C., but my journey really had its origin another 125 miles further to the northeast in Scranton, Pennsylvania, my birthplace. What is it they say? You can take the boy out of Scranton, but you can't take Scranton out of the boy. On that old saw, I am decidedly Exhibit One.

I was born December 5, 1936, the first child of Roy and Sophie Carocci, in St. Mary's Hospital in the south side section of the city. The building still stands today, structurally pretty much as it was sixty-odd years ago but now it's a day school for Jewish children. I was christened Vincent Roy Carocci, the first grandchild of the proud Ivo and Elizabeth ("Lizzie" to the family) Carocci; the first great-grandchild of Marie Antoinette and Vincenzo Carocci. Great-grandfather Vincenzo was deceased by the time of my birth, but his wife, Marie Antoinette, "Nona Tota" to us children, was the undisputed matriarch, the commanding presence, the elder, the glue that bonded our family (immediate and extended) as one.

"Space" was not a part of our lexicon or culture at the time. Ivo and Lizzie ("Nono and "Nonie") and their two children, Roy and Alva, shared the homestead at 519 Ripple Street with Nona Tota, Nona's older daughter, Adrienne, her husband, Tommie Preno, and their two children (Russell and Joanna). Just half a block down the street, Nona Tota's youngest daughter, Alice, lived with her husband, Bernie Mascioni, their three girls, and Bernie's mother (Nonie Mugs, we called her). On the second floor of that house lived Bernie's sister, Rose, her husband, John Barbini, and their two children.

We came together as family often—every Sunday, every holiday, and many days each week in between. What values I learned in life, I learned on Ripple Street. And I'm a much better person for it. Nona Tota ruled the roost in that stern yet elegant manner of hers. She and Vincenzo had migrated to this country from the Perugia region of Italy. I'm told she was a maid for an aristocratic family. Vincenzo was a shoemaker and a musician. They met at a town festival. They courted and they married. Her family was not pleased. For some inexplicable reason, they thought she had married beneath her station. Legend had it that her family disavowed her. That may account for their migration from Italy to America and, ultimately, Scranton.

I knew my great-grandmother for but a short time. She spoke little English, but she was beloved by her children and grandchildren. I remember them whispering about how beautiful a woman she was in her younger days. For as long as she lived (I was eight when she passed), she was the unquestioned mistress of the Ripple Street house, the command post, if you will. She had the unwavering love and devotion of her family. She commanded that by her mere presence. She never had to demand it once.

South Scranton was a neighborhood in the classic definition of the word. It covered a thirty-or-so square-block area, fifteen or twenty minutes removed first by trolley, then by bus from downtown Scranton. It was a neighborhood of modest, middle-to lower-income family homes, most of them Italian families. It had a drugstore (Notari's); three family-run grocery stores (Bartoli's, Bucari's and Constantini's); two family bakeries (Notari's and Schiavi's); a barbershop (Curcio's); a movie theatre (Favini's); our church (St. Francis of Assisi with a pastor by the name of O'Malley); a public elementary school and two Italian American social clubs, the Dante Literary Society and the 20th Ward Social and Athletic Club. The latter two, most assuredly, were misnamed because there was nothing literary or athletic to either. But they served their purpose as evening and Sunday afternoon gathering places for the men of the neighborhood. Cards and shuffleboard and, at the Dante, bocce were the activities of choice. As a child and a teen, I saw plenty of the inside of both in the company of my father.

When I was growing up, my father, Roy, was my best friend. My grandfather, Ivo, was my hero. I had a special bond with both, though for different reasons.

Roy Carocci was a beer-truck driver for most of his adult life. He worked hard to support his wife, son, and daughter by doing the heavy lifting on that beer truck of his. I never heard him complain once about his lot. He made do with the little he had . . . his ever-present cigars; his easy chair; bowling on Friday nights with the Dante gang, followed by pasta and an all-night card game; family gatherings at Ivo and Lizzie's; a little Vaughn Monroe on the radio and three-handed pinochle with his wife and son on Sunday evenings before he retired for the night to begin the workweek once more.

As I grew older, my time came to help my dad deliver beer, particularly on my holiday vacations from college when he needed help the most. We talked a lot in that truck on those occasions. Nothing momentous or profound, usually sports and politics, often how I was doing and where I hoped to go with my life. It was time well spent, a time for a young man to learn first-hand from his father the literal meaning of physical labor and to witness how hard a father would work to make his way in life to make a life for his family.

Some moments stand out more than others. One in particular was when my father took me on a Dante bus ride to old Shibe Park in Philadelphia in 1948 (or was it 1949?) for my first major-league baseball game, a doubleheader between the Philadelphia Athletics and the New York Yankees. Joe DiMaggio, in the twilight of his illustrious career, played the first game that day. He hit a home run high in the left-field upper deck the first time I saw

Dad, Roy (*left*), "Nono," Ivo (*right*), and I gather circa 1940–41 in the yard of the 519 Ripple Street homestead in South Scranton for our traditional Easter Sunday photo. Easter was the time each year that I received my new suit, shirt and tie, shoes and, lest we forget, a sporting chapeau to mark the occasion. Roy and Ivo were then and remain to this day my best friend and my hero.

him swing a bat. I also got to shake hands with Yankee first baseman Joe Collins, a South Scranton boy of considerable baseball talent who made it to the "Bigs" and was kind of a hero around our town.

Young boys tend to remember those moments and cherish them as they grow older. I remember the Yanks won the doubleheader. I remember Herman Buscarini, Roy's best friend and organizer of these twice-a-summer Dante rituals, pulling out his accordion for the final leg home after our dinner stop. I remember the men, most of them Italian, gathering in the back of the bus for lusty choruses of songs from their native land. I remember I was exhausted with excitement. I fell asleep shortly thereafter, somewhere in the second stanza of "Oi, Marie."

Ivo Carocci also was a very special man to me, but in a different sort of way. I still remember him each and every day. Always a smile on his face and a pleasant word on his tongue; always immaculately dressed, white shirt and tie; a straw hat in the summer ("skimmers" we called them) and Hamburgs in the winter. His hat, his cigar (like father, like son), and his smile were his trademarks.

Ivo came to this country at age three with his immigrant father and mother. As an adult he also labored hard to provide for his family, always in the beer business but never on the truck. His special qualities attracted the attention of the city's Democratic political leadership and in the 1940s he was invited to run as a candidate for City Council, probably to add ethnic and neighborhood balance to a political ticket in what was largely an Irish town. Scranton also was a Republican town at the time. Ivo lost his first race by fewer than three hundred votes. But the party's candidate for mayor, "Friendly" Jim Hanlon—he became known as the "Friendly Mayor of the Friendly City"—won. Political power in Scranton was shifting. Two years later, Ivo was endorsed again for council by the Democratic City Committee. This time he won handily. The Democrats assumed political control of both the mayor's office and the council. I was just in grade school at the time. But my grandfather's electoral experience introduced me to politics at a very young age, and my appetite for the process never diminished through the years.

My grandfather took his public duties seriously. If I heard him ask the question once, I heard him ask it countless times. "What's the right thing to do?" he'd inquire of his colleagues as he contemplated his vote on issues before the council. Not a bad road map for public service, when you think about it. The first years of Scranton's new Democratic regime were marked by paved roads for the adults to travel on their way to and from their labors and neighborhood park development for the children to play in. Ivo was a proud supporter of both. He recognized immediately how good roads and developed playgrounds would improve the quality of life in Scranton for young and old. In later years he led the fight against rising utility rates and for protection of homes threatened by coal-mine subsidence throughout the city. His effort was rewarded by the party and the voters. He subsequently was elected to two more four-year terms. When he died after the first year of his third term, my father was selected to replace him. He won a special election to fill the remaining two years of his father's term and then won a four-year term in his own right.

Ivo Carocci was the first person of Italian ancestry to be elected to public office in the city of Scranton. That was important to him. Just how important I never realized until that Sunday in September 1954, when I was departing for my freshman year at Penn State. I remember that day as if it were yesterday: my mother, tearing up at each goodbye during the obligatory visits to the aunts and uncles. Her first-born was leaving home . . . my grandmother Nonie fretting that I would never get enough to eat on the just plain American dormitory cooking I would find in college . . . my father, proud that his son would have the opportunity to receive a college education (the first of the family so enabled), but eager to get started on the three-and-a-half-hour trip to State College . . . my aunts and uncles, happy for me but not quite certain I was cut from the stuff to make it on my own . . . and their sons and daughters, my cousins, envious that I was breaking the traces, anxious for their time to come as it surely did . . .

My grandfather stood off to the side that morning, calm and serene, but ever so aware of what was happening around him. He loaned us his car, the Chrysler New Yorker, to make the trip. I suspect he gave my dad the money to buy the lunch and the dinner we would have that day. Just before we were about to leave, he called me aside. We stood in the upstairs hallway, alone for a brief moment. And he said to me, "I've worked hard to make the Carocci name a good name in this city. I expect you will do nothing to change that in any way." With that, he kissed my forehead, shook my hand, slipped me ten dollars, and sent me on my way.

That was almost fifty years ago. But the message of that plain-spoken, wise, and generous self-made man was not lost on me. He was telling me that I was about to embark on a wonderful opportunity, but that opportunity was not free of responsibility to myself, my family, and my family name.

Family was not a word I merely learned. It was a word I literally lived. Family taught me values, it nourished my traditions, it reminded me of my responsibility to others in my family. Through the years, as Ivo cautioned me that day, I came to learn that the worth of our lives will not be measured merely by the number of days we live, but rather, by the quality of the lives we lead, and the quality of the legacy we leave behind for our children and theirs to come. Ivo taught me that, and I am forever grateful that he did.

My grandfather died of a heart attack one Sunday during my junior year in college. Reflecting on his life, an editor of the *Scranton Times* wrote,

> In public and private life there was nothing of sham and pretense about Ivo Carocci.
>
> He was a kindly, charitable man, most of whose contributions to the welfare of his neighbors and to the needy orphans of Italy, his native land, were known only to himself and his recipients.
>
> His character and personality made it easy for him to win and hold friends. In his private business dealings, his word was his bond.

Those who had been fortunate enough to enjoy his friendship will mourn his passing. His family can be comforted by knowing that his life has been a rich one, and that as a private individual and a public official he represented the highest type of American citizen.

Roy Carocci died in his sleep in 1985. There were no editorials for him. But neither he nor we needed any. He had lived a long and full life, long enough to see his children grow into self-sustaining adults, to see them marry and have children of their own. Though he knew them for only a few years, he came to know all seven of his grandchildren, and they him. He loved them beyond expression, and they returned his affection. He was a good father and a good grandfather. That would have been epitaph enough for him.

It's strange, indeed, how one's life path can be charted more by happenstance than premeditation. It happened twice in my career. The first occasion occurred in my senior year at Scranton Central High School when my English teacher, Miss Jordan, asked me to write an article for the high school literary magazine, though "literary" may be too strong a characterization. I did, and because I did, I walked the first step on this journey that would take me to Harrisburg that April evening some seven years later.

"You write beautifully," Miss Jordan told me on publication. "You should pursue it."

"Beautifully" was without doubt an overstatement. To this day, I can't even remember the subject of the article. What I do remember is that when I saw the byline, "By Vince Carocci," well, I was hooked. But good! For the first time I began entertaining seriously the thought of going to college to pursue a degree in journalism, which is how events ultimately played out.

The second crossroad came as I was winding down my active duty tour as an Army Intelligence photo interpreter in Washington, D.C. There were three options to consider:

The first was to return to the Johnstown *Tribune Democrat,* my first employer, where I spent nine months between college graduation and active military service as a general assignment and sports reporter. I had an offer to go back in that same capacity. Johnstown and its people were both rock solid, but it was not the place for me. One option easily discarded.

The second was to stay in Washington, D.C., as a civilian employee of the Central Intelligence Agency, with whom I had collaborated in my Army Intelligence activities. It was not an unattractive offer. Washington was a place of great social opportunities for a young bachelor, and, politically, with the exciting 1960 presidential election just concluded and a new administration inaugurated, it was, in the vernacular, hot to be there. This offer I could not dismiss so casually.

The third option was to head up to Harrisburg to restart a career in journalism, this time political journalism with the UPI capital bureau. I never had lost the bug to write professionally and my interest in politics was as strong as it was when my grandfather and father were running for election to Scranton City Council. I never entertained the notion to run for public office myself. But the opportunity to write about those who did had more than limited appeal to me.

What to do, what to do? I, frankly, was conflicted—so much so that I accepted an invitation from one of my Army housemates, who also was being separated from active service, to visit Atlanta, Georgia, our first week out of the military, where I hoped to clear my head. We were in Atlanta only a day or two when an urgent call came from my prospective CIA supervisor, who told me, without going into detail, that I was needed back in the city the next day. I told him I wasn't quite ready to return. He said if I didn't come back, he couldn't promise me the job would still be waiting. I said, Well, if that's the way it must be, then it must be. I'd have to pass. End of story. Washington and the CIA were out. Harrisburg and political journalism were in. That's how I found myself driving over the Harvey Taylor Bridge when I did.

Before the month was out, I learned the reason for the rushed call from Washington. The newly inaugurated Kennedy administration had inherited a secret plan from the departed Eisenhower administration to unseat Fidel Castro and his Communist regime in Cuba. The plan called for an attack on the island by a troop of anti-Castro Cubans which, it was predicted, in turn would spark an anti-Castro upheaval among the general Cuban population. I was to be one of a team of photo interpreters conducting prelaunch photo analysis of the targeted landing sites and surrounding environs.

The mission became known as the Bay of Pigs. It was, of course, a colossal failure. The sentiment of the Cuban people was badly misread by the U.S. Intelligence apparatus and badly misrepresented by the anti-Castro Cubans who pressed the Eisenhower and Kennedy administrations so aggressively for the attack. In hindsight, this serious political and operational miscalculation undoubtedly created the climate for the more threatening Cuban Missile Crisis a year and one-half later which set the United States and Russia on a nuclear collision course. My presence and participation in the Bay of Pigs preparation certainly would not have altered the course of events. But it certainly would have altered the course of my life and career. It's not something I spent a lot of time . . . any time, frankly . . . wondering about through the years.

So this is how things ultimately come to pass in one's roadmap to a career. Harrisburg by way of Scranton, with stops in University Park, Johnstown, and Washington, D.C., in between. AAA could not have mapped this route in advance.

Harrisburg, clearly, was not the city of Kennedy, Johnson, Nixon, Humphrey, Rayburn, and Dirksen. But it was the city of Governor David Lawrence, Senate President Pro Tempore Harvey Taylor, and Republican State Chairman George I. Bloom, with visits by U.S. Congressman William J. Green and U.S. Senators Joseph Clark and Hugh Scott (Philadelphians all) thrown in for good measure. Each of these politicos in his own right was a major player in Pennsylvania politics, and Pennsylvania at the time was a major player in the national politics of their respective parties. It was not a bad place at all for an aspiring young journalist to begin his pursuit of a career as a national political reporter.

I was to report the next morning to the Harrisburg UPI office under the watchful eye and steady hand of Bureau Chief Lloyd Rochelle to man the UPI Pennsylvania radio desk from 6:30 A.M. to 2:30 P.M. daily. It was not a challenging assignment, mostly rewriting the overnight copy of the UPI Capitol Hill staff every hour on the hour for transmittal to UPI's several radio clients across the state. But it was a beginning.

Little did I know that I would spend forty years of my forty-two-plus-year professional career in the state capital region nestled in the quiet and family-friendly environs of Central Pennsylvania . . . that during my reportorial travels on Capitol Hill I would meet a scheduling secretary in the office of Lieutenant Governor Raymond P. Shafer . . . that we would marry and raise our family of four children in suburban Harrisburg . . . and that, ultimately, we would call it home for good. All I knew that night was that the next day would be the first day of my new life, my Capitol journey. I was ready.

Part 1
★★★★★
The Press

Chapter 1

★★★★★★★

The Legislative Correspondents

When you get right down to it, there's really only one significant difference between the way politics is played in the nation's capital and the Pennsylvania state capital. That's the size of the stage. The same can be said about the way politics is reported from the two cities: The only real difference is the reach and the power of the microphone.

To be sure, news coverage out of Washington in the 1960s was (and in large part still is) driven by the nation's most prestigious media outlets. In that era, it was the *New York Times*, the *Washington Post*, the *Washington Star*, the *Chicago Tribune*, and the *St. Louis Post-Dispatch*, the *Los Angeles Times*, and the *San Francisco Chronicle*, plus the Associated Press (AP) and United Press International (UPI), the two national wire services that were the CNN of instant news transmission in that generation.

Though on a slightly less celebrated scale, in the context of news coverage from the state capital, Harrisburg was no second-class citizen. Six major newspapers had permanent bureaus working out of the Capitol newsroom—the *Philadelphia Bulletin*, the *Philadelphia Inquirer*, the *Pittsburgh Press*, the *Pittsburgh Post-Gazette*, the *Harrisburg Patriot*, and the *Harrisburg Evening News*. AP and UPI each had their own six-man staffs. The *Press*, the *Inquirer*, and the *Bulletin* would add a second correspondent each legislative week, and a couple of other papers, most notably the *Allentown Morning Call*, the *Reading Eagle*, and the *Easton Express*, would send reporters regularly to the Capitol on legislative days. If the news outlets covering state government and state politics in that day were not quite as prestigious on a relative scale as their Washington counterparts, their coverage nonetheless was every bit as extensive.

Newspapers were the principal information medium of that day. As a society, we learned about new developments in public policy and politics and about current events and current affairs (foreign and domestic) by reading our morning and evening newspapers. Radio had a relatively minor role at the time. Television was in its infancy as a news purveyor. Talk radio and cable (mercifully, perhaps) were nonexistent. It was, by comparison to contemporary standards, a relatively tranquil but no less competitive era in the gathering and dissemination of news. That had certain advantages for citizens who wanted to be informed. Readers had time to educate themselves on what was happening around them. They had time to digest what they had learned and to come to their own conclusions about the merit or demerit of events. They were spared the instant and constant 24/7 analysis and counteranalysis they are subjected to (if not bombarded with) today on virtually every major news event from a limitless cadre of "experts" . . . many so-styled simply by virtue of their mere presence on the analytical stage.

When I arrived in Harrisburg in 1961, the Pennsylvania capital press corps was organized—loosely, but still organized and remains so today—in what was named the Pennsylvania Legislative Correspondents Association, the oldest organization of state house reporters in the nation, dating back to 1895. It also was manned at the time by an impressive array of capital reporters—crusty Duke Kaminski of the *Philadelphia Bulletin;* suave Lindy Lindgren of the *Pittsburgh Press;* curmudgeonly John Scotzin of what was then the *Harrisburg Evening News,* the "Dean, Old Pro" of the Correspondents Association; Carmen Brutto, Scotzin's colleague but still competitor with the *Harrisburg Patriot;* inscrutable Frank Matthews of the *Pittsburgh Post-Gazette;* cranky, solitary Joe Miller of the *Philadelphia Inquirer;* Dick Graves, Fred Walters, Jack Lynch of the Associated Press; and Gene Harris, Cy Siglin, and Marty Sikora of United Press International—prestigious names all in Pennsylvania political journalism in the early '60s. No one who followed the affairs of Pennsylvania state government and the machinations of Pennsylvania state politics was unfamiliar with their daily bylines and news reports. Now was my opportunity to work, if not exactly at their side, at least in their company. Virtually every one of the elders I met my first morning on the job greeted me as "kid" or "kiddo"—as in "Pleased to meet cha, kid!" I was to remain "kid" for the next several weeks, until the seniors determined that this young man was serious about his work and his profession. Then, and only then, did they decide to remember my name.

Becoming a working member of the state capital press corps was rather heady stuff at the time for tender young rookies. I, frankly, was thrilled to be starting my career there. And while I confess I was a bit in awe as I walked through the portal of the Capitol newsroom just off the Capitol rotunda for the first time, I was not overwhelmed. Nor did I consider myself journalistically unprepared.

My pre-Harrisburg training, first as a student journalist for the Penn State *Daily Collegian,* the campus newspaper, and then for almost a year as a sports and general assignment reporter for the *Johnstown Tribune-Democrat,* had been good for me. As sports editor of the *Collegian* covering a Penn State–Penn football game at Franklin Field in Philadelphia, I sat next to the famed Jesse Abramson of the *New York Herald Tribune*. He wore a hat cocked on the back of his head, smoked cigars, as I recall, loosened his tie when he started to write, and also called me "kid." I twice served as a spotter for Lindsey Nelson of NBC Sports on national telecasts of Penn State football games. As a game against Syracuse was coming to a close, Nelson acknowledged me by name on the air, just as my dad was making a beer delivery to the home of a customer. He almost dropped the case, he told me later.

In Johnstown during my brief stay there, I interviewed, among others, native son Frank Oceak, a coach under manager Danny Murtaugh and the world champion Pittsburgh Pirates. Oceak and I were seated in the third-base grandstand of the city's Point Stadium when we talked. He was in town on a Pirates off day to watch a game in an annual Triple ABA baseball tournament which brought teams from all parts of the East Coast to Johnstown. What makes the interview worth recalling is that a young first baseman of some future baseball prominence was playing for the team (Brooklyn, I believe it was) on the field. His name was Joe Torre. His only claim to fame at that moment, however, was that he was the younger brother of Milwaukee Braves first baseman Frank Torre. I must confess, I spent more time talking to Frank Oceak than I did watching Joe Torre play ball. Little did I know. . . .

My most important preparation for a career in journalism took place at Penn State. Thanks to the *Collegian,* I had the opportunity to build running (even if only temporary) news relationships with a number of prominent collegiate coaches and athletes, including head coach Rip Engle and a young assistant who was one of my most cordial and cooperative sources on Penn State football by the name of Joe Paterno. I also learned what it was like to be brushed off by prominent news personalities. Two incidents in particular are worth recounting, both involving U.S. military academies.

The first encounter, if you can call it that, came with Coach Eddie Erdelatz, the rather successful head football coach of the Naval Academy Midshipmen. In 1955 Navy came to Penn State to play the Lions at old Beaver Field (lest it be forgotten, then located on the main campus virtually next door to Recreation Hall with a seating capacity of approximately 30,000—big crowds in those days). My assignment for Penn State's legendary sports information director Jim Coogan was to man a field telephone located behind the visiting team bench in case of injuries or other inquiries from the press box as the game progressed. But my first and, perhaps, most important duty was to relay the visiting team starting lineup to the press box for the benefit of the assembled football writers. Thus it was that I, with game program in hand, approached Erdelatz during Navy's pregame warmups.

"Coach," I said by way of introduction. "Vince Carocci of the *Daily Collegian*. I need your starting lineup for the press box." Coach Erdelatz wasn't impressed. He never uttered a sound in response. Rather, he simply glared at me, turned, and walked away. He had his game face on early, I suppose. Fortunately some forgiving naval officer traveling with the team came to my rescue. He reached for my depth chart and marked off the starting Navy players. I was forever grateful to him. As for Erdelatz, I hoped he never won another game.

It was a hope that went unanswered that day. Navy handled Penn State rather easily, 34–14, before a homecoming crowd of 32,209. Middie quarterback George Welsh of the Pennsylvania coal regions (later a key Penn State assistant to Joe Paterno and an outstanding head coach in his own right at Navy and Virginia) set a Beaver Field passing record with his All-American wide receiver Ron Beagle. As the game was coming to a close with Welsh resting on the bench, his play done for the day, I approached, tapped him on his shoulder pads and said, "Great game, George."

"Thanks, kid," he replied. There was that moniker again.

My second encounter came with the legendary Red Blaik, who gained his coaching renown with the Army powerhouses of the mid-1940s featuring "Mr. Inside and Mr. Outside," Doc Blanchard and Glen Davis, Heisman Trophy winners both. In the fall of 1957, when the Cadets came to University Park, they still were a team of national reckoning. I was now sports editor of the *Collegian*. Dutifully, I went up to Beaver Field (still located on central campus) to watch the Cadets in their Friday afternoon walk-through. When they finished, I approached Blaik as he was making his way to the locker room.

"Coach, Vince Carocci, sports editor of the Penn State *Daily Collegian*," I said, again by way of introduction. "Who are you starting tomorrow?" Seemed like a reasonable opener to me. Turns out it still needed a lot of work.

"Nice to meet you," Blaik responded. (He was, at least, in a much politer mood than Erdelatz.) "The same eleven who started last week." With that, he was off and running (jogging may be more like it), never to be accessed by me again, that weekend or any other time. Now, I knew Army had beaten Vanderbilt the previous weekend, but I had no idea who started for them at every position. So I recall writing around the subject by making some passing reference to Army's "usual" starting lineup with particular focus on its featured players. (For the record, Army proved as difficult for the Lions to handle as Navy had three years earlier, winning, 27–13.)

Admittedly, as news encounters go, these were surely minor in nature. Certainly nothing close to the time U.S. Senator Joe Clark testily challenged Joe Miller of the *Philadelphia Inquirer* to step outside to settle matters when Miller asked him a particularly pointed question that he didn't care to answer following a leadership meeting of the state Democratic Party. (Incidentally, Miller didn't take him up on the offer.) Still, encounters with men like Erdelatz and Blaik have a way of staying with you. And as time went on, I came to the conclusion that covering sports was good training for covering politics. Coaches, like politicians, learn the art of spin control very early in their careers. Coaches, like politicians, can be as accessible and as cordial to reporters as they choose to be; or they can be as evasive and as hostile as the occasion demands or the mood strikes. (Bobby Knight of Indiana and, later, Texas Tech is one who comes to mind. And remember when, during a celebrated national television interview at baseball's annual All-Star extravaganza, Pete Rose wanted to take NBC's Jim Gray for the same walk Joe Clark wanted to take Joe Miller.) Coaches, like politicians, also know how to mouth words in response to questions, but still say nothing in the process. And finally, coaches, like politicians, like winning a whole lot better than losing.

The Pennsylvania Legislative Correspondents Association was not only the oldest organized assembly of state capital reporters in the nation; it also had developed, at least in that era, the reputation of being the most nasty collection of state house reporters among the fifty states . . . very, very critical of the politicians, public officials, and public policymakers (elected or otherwise) they covered so regularly.

After former congressman William Scranton was inaugurated as governor in 1963 and had a chance to settle into his office, he was asked at a press conference what was the most significant difference he defined between the Washington press corps and the Pennsylvania press corps. "Well," he responded, "you fellas have the reputation for being really tough to deal with. I think I'm about to find out for myself."

There was also the time in 1966 when Ray Shafer, Scranton's lieutenant governor seeking the governor's office in his own right, happened to pass by Duke Kaminski of the *Bulletin* in a restroom somewhere on the campaign trail. I was a witness to the exchange. "Duke," Shafer said, innocently enough in his own mind, I suppose. "I want to tell you I was warned you could be very hard on me during this campaign. But I want to say I've found you to be nothing but fair."

Kaminski was not pleased. "Don't tell me that," he snarled. "It makes me wonder if I'm doing my job." So went the mindset of the capital press corps about their working relationships with the people they covered.

The Associated Press Capital Bureau staff, mid-1960s, pose for a team picture in the bureau offices located at the time just off the *Harrisburg Evening and Patriot News* newsroom: *(front row, left to right)* Harrisburg correspondent Harry Ball and senior reporter Dick Graves; *(back row)* Dave Leherr, Jack Lynch, John Taylor (later to be my chief deputy press secretary in the Governor's Office), and myself. I was honored to work with such an able cast of reporters. Courtesy of John L. Taylor, Harrisburg.

What follows is not intended to be a classic treatise on the legislative correspondents association or the folks who toiled in the Capitol newsroom in the 1960s. Former *Pittsburgh Post Gazette* capital reporter Gary Tuma did an excellent job of that in his publication, "Covering the Capitol—A Century of News Reporting in Pennsylvania," published in 1996 commemorating the Association's centennial birthday. What is intended here is to paint a word picture of an era in Pennsylvania journalism long-gone, and the Pennsylvania political reporters who worked their beats, and how they did it.

Needless to say, the Columbia or Medill Schools of Journalism might not hold that generation of reporters up as working models of the contemporary profession. But they must be given their due. They had style and they had verve. They loved newspapering. They worked hard and were always highly competitive with each other. They practiced their trade in an era of "scoop" journalism, where the challenge always was to get the story first (the so-called scoop); but equally compelling was the responsibility to get the story right.

Fair to say, the folks who inhabited the Capitol newsroom in the 1960s were more likely to be characters than have character. They were often crotchety, crusty—even cranky. They also were all guys. Women, like television and talk radio, had yet to crack the business in a big way back then. Hell, in the 1960s, women weren't even allowed to attend the PLCA's annual Gridiron Show, the Association's traditional and usually much anticipated roast of Pennsylvania politicos. Political correctness had yet to make its debut in polite society, and the capital correspondents were hardly a polite lot. The Gridiron roast was a stag event at the time. No questions asked, no litigation filed.

The culture of journalism in the Capitol also was entirely different forty years ago. This was pre-Vietnam and the Gulf of Tonkin resolution; it was pre-Watergate and break-ins to the headquarters of the political opposition. Reporters and their news sources had an adversarial relationship for sure. It was understood, if unspoken (except, perhaps, if you were talking to Duke Kaminski). But when the working day was done, reporters and their news subjects could and frequently would make it a point to drink a beer or two together and trade stories, most of them off the record. Neither felt compromised in the process, nor should they have. There were priceless stories to be told and, at the right moment, at the right time, in the right setting, they were. Here are just some of them.

Chapter 2

★★★★★★★

Frank and Lindy: One Memorable Ride, One Memorable Coal Mine

Frank Matthews of the *Pittsburgh Post-Gazette* was a taciturn fella by nature. A newsroom veteran, hard-working, probing, smart. But, in the main, Frank went about his business in a quiet, unobtrusive way. Frank, however, also liked a frequent nip or two of bourbon (usually Jim Beam) as his workday was coming to an end. And when he nipped, he sometimes shed his normally solitary ways and could be a spellbinder in recounting his long experiences in the news business.

He told me this story one evening as he was unwinding at his desk in the Capitol newsroom. During the 1950 Pennsylvania campaign for governor, Frank had to travel to an out-of-the-capital appearance by John Fine, the Republican candidate for governor. So did Joe Miller of the *Philadelphia Inquirer*, and he asked Frank if he could ride along. Now, you have to understand. Joe Miller, by any measure, was a different kind of bird: short and stumpy; squinty-eyed, a penguin shuffle for a footstep. Joe mumbled more than he spoke and, secretive and shifty as he was, generally kept to himself. That was all right with most of the guys because Joe was not the kind of guy you buddied with over a drink after work. But he was a hard worker and he could trail a story with the best of them.

How good was he? Jack Conmy, Governor Scranton's press secretary from 1963 to 1967, told me of the time he went to New York for the annual Pennsylvania Society Dinner and had to be transferred from the Waldorf to another hotel because the Waldorf had slipped up on his reservation and was booked solid for the night by the time he arrived to check in.

"Nobody, not even the governor, knew where I was that night," Conmy recalled. The next morning the phone in his room rang unexpectedly. Conmy answered.

"Jack? Joe! Whatta ya know?" the voice at the other end of the line demanded. It was Joe Miller.

"Joe, you sunuvabitch," Conmy replied. "How'd you find me? If you were able to track me down overnight like that, then I'm going to tell you what you want to know if I can."

That was vintage Joe Miller. He could reach his sources like no one else in the business. That certainly was to his credit. The problem was that too often he only reached out to the sources he believed would reinforce the story line he was working on. Joe Miller had a dark side, and he and his *Inquirer* under Walter Annenberg's ownership were not at all hesitant to put it on display. One notable example involved the *Inquirer* and its coverage of Democratic gubernatorial candidate Milton Shapp in the 1966 race for governor. Word made its way through the press corps traveling with Shapp that the *Inquirer* was on the verge of breaking a story that Shapp had been treated for mental illness. But days passed without it appearing in print. One evening, as the campaign was winding down, Shapp appeared at a public forum at St. Joseph's College just outside the Philadelphia city limits. In the question-and-answer phase of the program, a young man popped up in the audience. "Were you, Milton Shapp, ever treated or committed for a mental illness?" he demanded of the candidate. If you were a betting man, you had a pretty good idea the question was a plant. Joe Miller was in the audience, so you also had a pretty good line on just who the source of the plant might be.

Shapp recognized the setup immediately. The *Inquirer*, he responded, had been trying to nail him on that for quite a while, but had no success because it just wasn't true. Next question. No one in the traveling press party made even passing reference to the incident that I recall. But the story was out there now, on the record. Shapp was forced to issue a public denial a few days later. Joe Miller wrote the denial story under the headline "Shapp Denies Rumor He Had Psychiatric Treatment in 1965."

So what's this have to do with Frank Mathews taking Joe Miller to the Fine campaign appearance? Well, to appreciate the tale Frank Mathews had to tell, you have to know something about Joe Miller. Frank agreed to take Joe along and lived to regret it. "Joe was such a pain in the ass," Frank recounted. "All the way up, all the way back, it was Joe complaining: 'Open the windows, it's too hot in here; close the windows, it's too cold in here; turn the radio on, it's too quiet in here; turn the radio off, it's too loud in here.'" Frank concluded, and with good reason, "When we got back, I swore to myself I'd never take Joe Miller on a trip with me again!"

What is it they say about the road to hell being paved with good intentions? Two weeks or so later, there was another Fine campaign event, this time in the Scranton region, and Joe asked Frank for another ride. Believe it or not, Frank said, "Okay."

As Frank told the story, he and Joe were riding along without incident or aggravation when, without warning, the car became difficult to steer. Frank immediately recognized the "bump, bump, bump" motion that comes with a flat tire. "Joe," he said as he eased his car to the side of the road, "we've got a damn flat and we have to change it."

With that, Frank slid out of the driver's seat, walked to the trunk, removed the spare and the jack, and immediately began replacing the tire. Five or ten minutes later, it dawned on Frank that Joe wasn't helping. In fact, he wasn't anywhere to be seen. Frank craned his neck around the rear of the car and, lo and behold, up the road about a half mile, he saw Joe Miller thumbing a ride. Sure enough, a car stops, the passenger door opens, Joe Miller gets in, and the car drives away, leaving Frank to fend for himself.

"I was right all along," Frank remembered thinking as Joe made off with his newfound driver. "Joe Miller *is* a no-good sunuvabitch." There was no word on how Joe Miller got back to Harrisburg that night. I do know he did not ride back with Frank Matthews.

Lindy Lindgren of the *Pittsburgh Press* was a tall, big-boned man with a stoic demeanor. Of Scandinavian origin, he was immediately recognizable with his graying, tightly clipped crewcut and his trademark horn-rimmed glasses. In his day, he was quite a good reporter. And, by his own admission, as a younger man, he could raise hell with the best of them.

He told me a story about a night he went out drinking after work. He found himself in the Democratic Club in downtown Harrisburg about 2 A.M., one sheet this side of sober, when it was time for the place to close. Fine with Lindy. He had to stop by Western Union anyway to wire his copy to the *Press* for the next day's editions. Problem was when he got to the street, he reached for his copy in his suit-coat pocket but couldn't find it. Thinking he may have dropped it upstairs, he buzzed to regain entry to the Democratic Club. Problem was, the staff upstairs wasn't about to let him back in; they were ready to call it a morning. Lindy argued that it was critical for him to find his misplaced copy. They could have cared less. As Lindy told it, the stalemate went on for fifteen or twenty minutes when he finally decided to take matters in his own hand. He found the nearest garbage can (they were heavy metal then) and proceeded to throw it through the glass door.

His timing couldn't have been worse. Just as the can was leaving his hands and shattering through the glass, one of Harrisburg's finest was cruising by in his squad car. To make a long story short, Lindy spent the rest of the night in a jail cell. What's worse, while sitting on his bunk lamenting his situation, what should he find in his inside jacket pocket but his copy? It never did make the next day's edition of the *Press*.

By the time I met Lindy in 1961, he was starting to coast as a reporter. He had been reporting from Harrisburg for the *Press* for about twenty-five to thirty years. His name and his reputation were legendary in Pittsburgh. His work habits, though slipping in his later years, still were beyond question in his city room. Lindy got his story; it didn't particularly matter to his editors in his later years that he just didn't work too hard to get it, or even necessarily get it right.

Sometimes he even reported on events that he had not witnessed personally. That I learned first hand, much to my consternation. During the 1966 gubernatorial campaign between Republican Ray Shafer and Democrat Milton Shapp, I traveled for the first time with the candidates, this day with the Shafer campaign, as a reporter for the Associated Press. Lindy and a number of other capital correspondents also were on this particular leg of the trip. As the schedule would have it, we were in Luzerne County in the northeast Pennsylvania coal region just a week or so out from the election. Shafer was to go several hundred feet down the shaft of a deep anthracite mine to greet miners as they were coming off their shift. My only instructions from the AP Philadelphia control bureau as I went on the road were to go wherever the candidate went, whenever he went. Period! So, if Shafer was going down a mineshaft, by damn, so was I.

The mine crew chief took Shafer, some of his assistants, and the traveling press into a large shed where we all were fitted with coveralls and a hard hat. When we emerged from the shed, there was Lindy, standing outside, prim as ever in his suit and tie.

"Lindy," I asked, "aren't you going down with us?"

He looked at me with a "poor boy you have so much to learn" look, pursed his lips as he often did, and replied, "Lad, I was down a mine shaft several years ago. With John Fine, I believe. I can't imagine it's changed all that much since then. I'll pass if you don't mind."

The traveling party was loaded on a large elevator and lowered 300 to 400 feet down into the shaft. We debarked at the bottom and the elevator started its way back up. Suddenly we heard a frightening rumble from the top. One of the miner escorts yelled, "Get back, get back!" Which we did without argument. Immediately, there was a loud thud from the bottom of the elevator shaft and a big cloud of dust flew up from the pit near where we were standing. We were, to say the least, quite shaken . . . if not in a state of panic, pretty close to it. The candidate's campaign manager looked as if he had wet his pants. But we were unharmed and the episode was over almost as quickly as it had erupted.

The miners were totally undisturbed by the rumble. Shafer stood by to greet them as they made their way to the elevator shaft to end their shift.

The miners were clearly unimpressed about who was there to shake their hands; they were more interested in getting topside so they could clear the dust out of their throats with their usual shot and a beer (ok, maybe two or three) before calling it a day. While Shafer was trying to connect with the miners, I saddled over to our mine escort and asked about what had happened in those few electric minutes. "Were we in any danger?" I wanted to know.

"Not at all," he explained. "That happens almost every time the elevator goes up or down. A rock or two in the shaft breaks loose and falls very quickly. I just pushed you back so you wouldn't get covered with dust when the rock landed. That's all. It's a very routine thing in these mines. No problem whatsoever."

Our visit to the bottom of the mine ended in about a half-hour. We took the elevator back to the top, changed out of our coveralls, and headed for our next stop, which is where Lindy and the candidate's press secretary caught up with the traveling party. (I don't know if the press secretary had been down that same mine shaft with Lindy and John Fine a few years earlier. I do know that for the time I spent with Shafer at the bottom of that mine, Lindy and the press secretary spent it at a nearby bar.)

I told Lindy the story pretty much just as I have just related it and we both had a good laugh. Since we were in no danger, I didn't even refer to the incident in my AP story that night. (The facts, ma'am, just the facts. That was the code of the profession in those days.) I thought no more of the event until 6 A.M. the very next morning when I was rudely awakened by my control desk in Philadelphia. "The [Pittsburgh] *Press* is running a story of how disaster almost struck the Shafer campaign at the bottom of a mine shaft!" he shouted at me through the phone. "Where the hell were you?" he demanded.

"Mine Rumble Shakes Candidate" was the eyebrow over Lindgren's story. "En Route with Shafer" was his dateline. And he wrote: "It was the case of another candidate going down into another mine—but it could have ended in disaster."

My man on the desk proceeded to read to me the rest of Lindy's "first-person account" of the incident that appeared in that day's first edition of the *Press*. It was more vivid than even what I had related to Lindy. "Only minutes after the visitors arrived at the working level [750 feet below ground, he reported], a thunderous roar rumbled through the mine. . . . The roar continued for a few more seconds and then the area was filled with coal dust. A rock dislodged up in a shaft and took coal and dust down with it. This was a dangerous situation because when the air is filled with coal dust, the smallest spark can ignite it and cause an explosion. It turned out well, though. Nobody was hurt—but everybody was scared stiff."

It took me about fifteen minutes to persuade the desk that what he wrote was what I had told him from my first-person vantage point. I must say, it was not an easy sell. But now that the incident was in print, we decided to protect ourselves with our AP paper members by adding a paragraph or two to my overnight copy. I told the desk just to pick up as much as they wanted from Lindy's piece because after hearing it read to me, it was as accurate as I could describe

I bumped into Lindy at breakfast an hour or so later. "Lindy," I demanded, "What the hell are you doing to me?"

"Well, lad," he replied, "in this business we write what our reliable sources tell us, and I consider you a reliable source." Whatever his faults, Lindy sure had style.

Chapter 3

★★★★★★

The Divvy and a Pulitzer Prize

Let's talk a bit about "the Divvy."

There's no other way to put it. It was a shakedown of the Pennsylvania political community by the capital press corps, pure and simple. Harmless, to be sure, but a shakedown nonetheless. The Divvy was very much a part of life in the Capitol newsroom when I arrived in 1961, and it manifested itself every Christmas season. This is the way it worked.

The Divvy was the cornerstone of the newsroom's annual Christmas party. Without it, there might have been no Christmas party. The concept was very basic. Each December, the Correspondents Association invited the governor and his cabinet to join the press corps for a holiday lunch in the newsroom. State legislators and leaders, the chairs of the two political parties, leaders of business and labor, and major state regulators like the State Liquor Control Board and the Pennsylvania Turnpike Commission were invited to pop in after the lunch to join the correspondents for a beverage or two marking the season. The only problem was that the invitees (not including the governor and the cabinet, of course) were expected to provide the alcoholic beverages that were to be drunk that day. (The newsroom, generously, put up the soft drinks.) The liquor would begin to arrive about a week before the Christmas party, sometimes by a bottle or two, sometimes in clusters of cases. The cases usually were with the compliments of the Pennsylvania Liquor Control Board. Gary Tuma, in his 1996 newsroom chronicle, reported of the time one correspondent "opened a case shipped over from the LCB on the morning of the party, saw that it contained 12 bottles of cheap scotch, and had it sent back with orders that it be replaced by a better brand." I imagine it was.

The president and officers of the newsroom had the responsibility to put the donated liquor (if that's the right word?) under lock and key until the designated day of the party, when all reporting would cease about noon and the socializing would begin. The food menu was fairly sparse—a rather common cold plate lunch for the governor and his cabinet, cheese, crackers, chips and pop, maybe some ring baloney if the newsroom treasury was unusually solvent, for the festivities to follow. But the camaraderie was plentiful and, usually, enjoyable.

The drill was pretty well understood by the guests. They were to stop in and mingle for a while over a drink or two, but they were not to overstay their welcome. And, surely, they were not to drink too much because the next day any remaining bottles of liquor were to be divided—hence the term "Divvy"—among the newsroom press corps. And, oh yes, did I mention that it was standard practice for the newsroom elders to keep the best liquor stored under lock and key for as long as possible? Well, it was. Bar whiskey always . . . always . . . *always* . . . was dispensed with first.

The liquor that remained on the day of the Divvy was carried from the file cabinets to a desk in the center of the newsroom. Then the ritual began. The most senior member would circle the assembled bottles until he made a selection of his choice. The next most senior member then would take his turn . . . and down the ladder the process went until the most junior member had had a pick. Then the cycle would repeat itself and continue until all the bottles were gone.

It was not unusual, if the harvest had been particularly bountiful that year, for the veteran members to walk off with four, five, even more bottles of Christmas cheer. The younger members usually went home with a bottle or two less than the senior take. Even in so-called slim years, the press corps seldom carried less than three bottles per member home each December.

Was this an acceptable practice under today's standards? Certainly not. But this was a different era, a different climate in the relationships between reporters and politicians, a time when reporters and their sources were more collegial and more trusting of each other than they are today. I'm certain those who contributed booty to the Christmas solicitation fully recognized they were being hustled. But it was a subtle hustle, conducted in a subdued and understated sort of a way. And clearly, the donors understood there would be no quid-pro-quos for their generosity, nor was any given by the press corps.

I really don't know to this day how the Divvy got started, or when. It was part of Capitol life long before I arrived on the scene. But I do know when the practice was brought to a halt. The *Philadelphia Inquirer*'s Bill Ecenbarger, later to become a successful freelance writer and author in his own right (and my roommate in our bachelor days), was one of the first to publicly attack the Divvy. In a January 1972 column he vowed in print never to attend the newsroom Christmas party as long as the newsroom hustled politicians for the liquor that made the event possible in the first place.

Ecenbarger only memorialized in a public way the momentum that had been building among the younger members for years. Several motions at the biennial newsroom reorganization meetings to do away with the Divvy had been defeated by narrow margins in prior years. By November of 1972, just months after Ecenbarger took the issue public, the newsroom reformers had secured a majority among the membership. The Correspondents Association voted officially not to accept liquor contributions in the future in the name of the Association.

The vote did not sit well with the veterans, current and former. One biting critique uncovered by Gary Tuma in his newsroom research was written by Dick Graves, a senior member of the AP Harrisburg Bureau when I joined the staff in 1962. Even though the demise of the Divvy came years after Graves left Harrisburg, he lamented in a letter to a former AP Harrisburg colleague, John Koenig:

> A few years after I left, a new generation of fundamentalists took control of the newsroom and changed the rules, ambiance and perspective. Jack [referring to the late Jack Lynch, another AP colleague of Graves] said they were a self-righteous lot who saw journalism as a cause, not a culture. The first reformist rape centered on the banning of liquor gifts. Free loads were shunned. More witch burning followed. Duke Kaminski, Sambo [Tom Snyder of the *Pittsburgh Post-Gazette*] and Sticky Bun [John Scotzin] and others of the Ancien Regime were out-voted and ultimately—in my view—literally bored to death.

While the newsroom attempted to make the ban on liquor contributions known to all, certain traditions were hard to break. Tuma's history cited an instance the very December following the vote when Governor Milton Shapp showed up for the Christmas lunch with a bottle of vodka under each arm. Newsroom supervisor Jack Nagle, a state employee and, theoretically, a Shapp subordinate, had to remind the governor of the new policy. Governor Shapp, according to Tuma, demurred.

"Oh, I heard something about that, but this is just a little cheer," Governor Shapp said.

"I'm sorry, governor, but we can't accept it," Nagle had to insist, somewhat nervously, I suppose.

Shapp reportedly handed the bottles to an aide before entering the party. One year later, the new majority in the Correspondents Association voted to do away with the Christmas party altogether, though Tuma noted it was resurrected in miniaturized fashion in the 1980s.

Was the Divvy inappropriate both in concept and practice? The answer would be yes. Was it corrupting in execution? The answer would be no.

"Some of the old-timers would drink your liquor one day and stick it to you the next if they had a good story," my former AP associate John Taylor told Gary Tuma. Truth is, there was a certain élan to the tradition. It was an occasion when newsmen and news sources came together almost like a fraternity once a year. And neither felt themselves compromised in the process.

I remain, to this day, ambivalent on the subject. While I cannot defend the Divvy (I probably would have voted with the "reformers" on grounds of appearance if nothing else had I been an active member of the Association at the time), neither can I condemn it, even after all these years. Virtue, then as now, was in the eye of the beholder. And I never remember a member, young or old, ever passing on his turn to make a pick when his name on the Divvy roll was called.

To a journalist, there is no more valued an award than the Pulitzer Prize. It is the Oscar, the Emmy, the MVP wrapped into one, the pinnacle of one's professional pursuits. Many an illustrious journalist has won that coveted award. I am privileged to have known one personally. His name was Paul Vathis, the legendary photographer for the Associated Press bureau in Harrisburg for all of my forty-plus years in the state capital.

Paul was a very good photographer. But he gained additional exposure in his trade because of our proximity to Gettysburg, the post–White House country home of former president Dwight David Eisenhower. When a host of political and international dignitaries would visit Ike at "The Farm," as they regularly did to seek his counsel or political blessing, Paul would without fail get the photo assignment from New York. He was in Gettysburg so frequently that he was on a first-name basis with Ike, Mamie, and Ike's irrepressible aide-de-camp, General Schultz. (In my infrequent reportorial visits to Gettysburg, usually in Paul's company, I always called him General Schultz. The general, Germanic to his core, would have had it no other way. I suspect Paul was on much friendlier terms with him, however, and he with Paul.)

In any event, in the days immediately after the failed Bay of Pigs Cuban invasion in 1961, President John Kennedy met Eisenhower at the Camp David presidential retreat in the Cactoctin Mountains, just miles below Gettysburg and the Pennsylvania/Maryland state line. The meeting was called to reinforce national political unity in the wake of the failed attempt to overturn this Communist foothold so near American shores. Given Paul's relationship with Eisenhower, it was no surprise that Associated Press Photos gave him the assignment, even though Camp David was about as close to Washington as it was to Harrisburg. It wasn't until next year that we realized just how momentous the assignment really was for Paul.

"AP, Carocci," I dutifully responded from my seat at my desk in the AP corner of the Capitol newsroom when the telephone rang this one summer day in 1962. Paul was just a few feet away at an empty desk playing a routine game of hearts with three other correspondents.

"Yeah, this is AP Photos in New York," the voice on the other end of the line said. "Is Paul Vathis there?"

"Sure is," I related. Turning in Paul's direction, I shouted, "Paul, it's for you, New York Photos."

"Okay," Paul replied, nonplussed and certainly in no hurry to take the call. "Tell 'em I'll be with them in a minute." Expecting another assignment, he wanted to finish his hand before taking the phone. Which he did.

"Vathis," I heard him say as he took the call. "What! You're kidding? You're not. Wow, that's just great! Thank you. Thank you very much." That's essentially the way the conversation went.

"What's up?" I asked when he finished. "Everything okay?"

"I just won the Pulitzer Prize," he announced to no one in particular.

Paul had taken a picture of Kennedy and Eisenhower walking up the path at Camp David, their backs to the cameras, after the perfunctory photo opportunity with the assembled press corps. It was that picture that won the Pulitzer Prize. "I don't know what made me take that shot," Paul explained in an interview I did for the AP story I wrote on the award. "It was a very solemn time for both men, and they looked so alone as they walked away. I just shot the picture. I don't think I knew exactly what I had until I saw the prints. That's how these things happen, I guess."

The Vathis picture started what became a national vogue in photojournalism. For the next year at least, every photographer was shooting principals at news events from the rear. Thirty-seven years later, another Associated Press photographer, Robert Borea, out of the Baltimore bureau, won an AP Pulitzer Prize for photography. It was a picture taken of President and Mrs. Clinton, separated by their daughter Chelsea, walking across the White House lawn to a helicopter en route to a Martha's Vineyard vacation the day after Clinton's televised confession of an affair with Monica Lewinsky. It also was snapped from the rear. Some techniques, it seems, never die . . . even in news photography.

I had a different take on Paul's version of the events leading to him shooting the picture he did. I kidded him through the years that the only reason he got that shot was because he arrived late for the assignment. He demurred in that good-natured way of his. Still, I asked him for a print of his Pulitzer Prize winner and, autographed as it was, it adorns my office wall to this day.

What better and more typical way to spend a quiet hour or two in the Capitol newsroom in the mid-1960s than with the correspondents' card game of choice, Hearts. The players (*left to right*): Billy Zeidler of the *Harrisburg Evening News;* Duke Kaminski of the *Philadelphia Bulletin;* the AP's Jack Lynch, and lobbyist Dick Wall. John Taylor (*rear right*) appears to be checking out his copy while I'm reviewing an early edition of the *Harrisburg Evening News*. Incidentally, the desk John Taylor is sitting at is the same desk I was sitting at when I took the call from AP Photos in New York alerting Paul Vathis that he had just won the Pulitzer Prize. Vathis, not so coincidentally, was playing Hearts at the time. Courtesy of John L. Taylor, Harrisburg.

One other incident, on a lighter note, is worth recalling here about Paul's award. He was certainly a celebrity, at least for the day, and he responded cordially to a series of requests for local radio interviews. One exchange went like this.

"What does the Pulitzer Prize mean to you, Paul?" radio broadcaster Pete Wambach (of whom we shall hear more later) asked in the last of a string of conversations Paul had that day. By now, with the others behind him, I would have expected Paul to respond with the same gushy stuff about the prestige of the award, what it represents in journalism, how proud and humbled he was by the honor . . . you know, something along that line.

Instead I heard Paul, in an unusual display of candor, answer, "$1,200, Pete, $1,200 dollars! " Quickly, he caught himself and added, "Oh, and, of course, the honor and prestige of it all."

That was Paul. Let the elites of the business gush on about what the Pulitzer symbolizes. Paul would take the cash, thank you.

Paul was a relatively young man in his late thirties or early forties when he won his Pulitzer. He was still practicing his profession in the state capital when he died at age seventy-seven in his sleep at home in December of 2002.

"One more, Governor. Thank you," was his stock in trade as the Capitol's foremost photojournalist. And when Paul Vathis asked for one more shot, he usually got it.

Chapter 4

★★★★★★★

Reader Beware: Editorial Comment to Follow

I'm sorry. I just can't resist. I just can't resist the temptation to comment (pontificate, perhaps, but not too much) about the dramatic changes that have taken place in journalism over the last half-century. Not because I presume to be the final word on the subject, but because, as a student and former practitioner of the profession, I'm not certain the changes have been necessarily for the better. That's something those of us who think about these things ultimately will have to decide, each for him- or herself. For what it's worth, here are my thoughts.

I start with an acknowledgment that today's generation of journalists ("reporters" we used to call them), are as a class much smarter, much better educated, much better read, and much more probing than my peers of the 1960s. For a society so dependent on them for the information we receive, that's clearly a large plus for them and for us.

There is a downside, however, to the contemporary generation of journalists, as articulate and erudite though they may be. Too many of them, at least to these eyes and ears, tend to take themselves and their positions much too seriously (more so in Washington than in Harrisburg, but endemic to some degree to both). Because of their easy access to talk radio and talk television, they fall prey to the trap of seeking personal celebrity as much as they seek a story. And most distressing of all, there seems to be a growing tendency for their view of the world more than the facts of a situation to dictate their story line. That's clearly not so good.

I'm not the only one to hold to this view, incidentally. No less than Carl Bernstein, one half of the celebrated Woodward/Bernstein investigative reporting team for the *Washington Post* in the Watergate era, said as much in discussing lessons to be learned in journalism thirty years after Richard Nixon's fall from the presidency: Bernstein put it this way:

> The lessons have to do with being careful, with using multiple sources, with putting information into context, with not being swayed by gossip, by sensationalism, by manufactured controversy. All of which (meaning gossip, sensationalism, manufactured controversy) I think has come to dominate our journalistic agenda

much more in the past 30 years. We've adopted, young reporters especially, a combative role that doesn't really look at the question of what is the important news and how you get it. We have moved very far into the area of manufactured confrontation rather than illumination.

His point is well taken. I point to the ascendancy of television as the root cause of the problem. Television's domination of our current culture, both in the entertainment we enjoy (that's usually good) and the news we get (that's not so good), is indisputable. In this mobile, fast-paced society, we get our news from television and we get it in tightly framed sound bites and images. Our news sources know that and have honed their skills to fit the medium where style takes precedence over substance, where glibness and wit can substitute for expertise.

In addition, the giant technological advances over the last half-century have made the instant transmission of information commonplace. The Associated Press, once the undisputed king of this turf, has become virtually irrelevant. United Press International, which once gave AP a good run for its money, long has been laid to rest in that growing graveyard of once-celebrated media outlets. CNN, MSNBC, Fox News, and CNBC now rule the roost in the transmission of instant news.

With the advent of cable television and the introduction of daily television and radio talk shows to our instant information stream, society suffers from an information overload because the appetite of this electronic beast is insatiable. Not only do we get our information immediately, but also the information we get is subjected to instant, constant, and repetitive analysis from the press and any number of pundits, all of whom, hour by hour, day by day, are only too willing and too eager to put their face and their insight on public display (the celebrity factor, as Carl Bernstein called it.) The babble is unbearable, and the volume has shortened our attention span, our focus, and our tolerance levels considerably.

Another problem with the instant news transmission we receive is that while it may be essentially accurate, I question whether it's as complete and as balanced as it should be. I see more ideology in story lines. Journalists become opinion-makers rather than reporters, and when that happens, the credibility and the quality of journalism and journalists must inevitably suffer in the process. Reporters of my generation, with rare exceptions like Joe Miller, really did try to deal in facts. Our treatment of the news contained a premium on accuracy and balance. We were less ideologically driven, and we trusted the general public to come to its own conclusions, informed or otherwise, without any undue prompting. Our first and most important mission was to *inform;* we left opinion-making to the editorial page. And what editorial views we might have held, we reserved for column or commentary pieces, clearly identified for what they were. I wonder how reporters who today so regularly put their personal views and opinions on public display can report objectively on the news they must cover daily.

Another concern raised by the supremacy of television is that today the news business seems to be driven more by a mission to entertain than to inform. Newspapers are no less driven to compete with their electronic brethren in their entertainment value. In the process, the line between news and entertainment has become blurred. In the process, so, too, has the line between reporting and editorializing. Try to remember the last story you heard on network television news that didn't take you to a conclusion consistent with the tone or the theme of the piece.

Is the American public better served or better informed in this climate? More informed, undoubtedly. Better informed, I think not. Public policy at any level has virtually no time to set in and demonstrate its merit or demerit. The pundits of the press (not to mention the pundits of academia) are omnipresent. The electronic airwaves get suffocated by all this point and counterpoint because radio and cable television have too much time to fill. And too often, there are too few new developments worth reporting. So the time is filled with opinion, analysis and repetition, more opinion, analysis and repetition, and, yet, still more *ad nauseum*. In the words of Linda Ellerbee, a former network correspondent and current documentary producer (no Rush Limbaugh she),

> It may not be the end of conversation in America, but it is the end of conversation on television because the rule is, if it's not combative, it does not get ratings and it does not get on the air. That's sad, but it's the truth and it's feeding the demonization of whoever doesn't think like you. Instead of conversation we get confrontation. There's no real exchange of ideas going on.

At some point, the American people get either confused, overwhelmed, or a little bit of both and they turn the cacophony off. The inevitable result is indifference, the worst affliction to confront purveyors of the news and a serious threat to an informed democratic society.

If you accept my notion that the primary purpose of news reporting should be to inform society, then you also should mourn along with me the diminishment of the newspaper as society's primary information source. Newspapers were born to inform. Television was born to entertain. Newspapers, in my view, suffer immeasurably when they attempt to compete with television for the entertainment attention of their audience.

I know I am in a distinct and rapidly declining if not totally extinct minority on this point, and the focus groups newspapers employ across the country undoubtedly would tell me I'm wrong. But I do believe good days should start with a good cup of coffee and a newspaper—preferably a good newspaper. Coffee and a newspaper prepare one to take on the day. I don't need a Katie Couric and Matt Lauer, a Charlie Gibson and Diane Sawyer, or any of a host of morning imitators, for that matter, to tell me what the day will bring, or what's important in the world, and why. When properly informed, I can make those judgments for myself, thank you.

To this point, most of the views expressed here were largely mine—my point of view, my words. Imagine, then, how gratified I was to come across in the bookstore at Notre Dame University a book by James Fallows, entitled *Breaking the News: How the Media Undermine American Democracy.* Fallows was the editor of *U.S. News & World Report* and a former Washington editor of the *Atlantic Monthly*. He also was a thoughtful weekly commentator of National Public Radio's "Morning Edition." Fallows wrote:

> Any organization works best when the behavior that helps an individual get ahead is also the behavior that benefits the organization as a whole. Any organization suffers when what is good for the individual is bad for the group.
>
> As journalism has become more star-oriented, individual journalists have gained the potential to command power, riches and prestige that few of their predecessors could have hoped for. Yet this new personal success involves a terrible bargain.
>
> The more prominent today's star journalists become, the more they are forced to give up the essence of real journalism, which is *the search of information of use to the public.* The effects of this trade-off are greatest at the top of the occupational pyramid, which is why the consequences are so destructive. The best-known and best-paid people in journalism now set an example that erodes the quality of the news we receive and threatens journalism's claim on public respect.

Fallows, Linda Ellerbee, and Carl Bernstein framed the issue much more eloquently and precisely than I. But they're all correct. And, I don't mind telling you, on this particular subject, I enjoy being in such distinguished company.

Chapter 5

★★★★★★★

Forks in the Road

Okay, you might ask, if I'm such a student and devotee of journalism as a profession, why then did I leave the news business in 1968 when I did? Fair question . . . deserves as answer. I am, you see, a disciple of that preeminent philosopher from St. Louis, one Lawrence "Yogi" Berra, by name. And Berra had this advice to offer about what he called forks in the road. "When you come to one," Yogi counseled, "take it!"

Well, this was one career, particularly in the early years after my arrival in Harrisburg, that came to any number of forks in the roads—crossroads, if you prefer. And I took every one of 'em as I came to them.

Certainly, the most important fork came in 1968 when I was offered a transfer to the Associated Press Washington Bureau, the point of return to which I had been aspiring so earnestly since I first drove over the Harvey Taylor Bridge that evening some seven years earlier.

I discussed the transfer at length with Washington Bureau Chief Marvin Arrowsmith at the Republican National Convention in Miami, Florida, where I had been assigned to cover the Pennsylvania delegation. The decision should have been a no-brainer for me. But it wasn't.

Marriage in 1964 to my wife, Toni, and the birth of our first child, Patty, in 1968, had reordered my life's professional ambitions and personal priorities. I wasn't certain anymore that I wanted to work the national political landscape as a journalist. The convention experience convinced me I did not.

I looked around the Miami convention with a sense of awe and fascination as the leading political journalists of the time—the Wickers, the Restons, the Lisagors, and a rising younger cadre of reporters like David Broder of the *Washington Post* and Walter Mears of the Associated Press—worked their beat. It got no better for political reporters than covering a national presidential election. Most of them, the role models I once so yearned to emulate, had been in Miami covering the party platform hearings at least a week before I arrived. They stayed the second week to cover the convention proceedings themselves. And when Miami concluded, they headed home for a change of clothes before journeying to Chicago and

Round Two of the 1968 presidential cycle, the Democratic platform hearings and convention. Once Chicago was history, they probably had another week or two at home before hitting the road again to crisscross the country covering the campaign itself. Essentially, they would be traveling from Labor Day through Election Day. And once the election was decided, it was full-time attention to the formation of a new administration, wherever that took shape.

The life of national political reporters certainly had more than enough challenge, celebrity, excitement, and prestige for anyone with those aspirations. But now I had to ask myself if that's what I really wanted out of life for my family and me. Moving to Washington would, in essence, be starting all over again—crazy hours, split shifts, split days off. The "rock pile," it was called in wire service lingo. And for what? The opportunity to spend time on the road, away from home for days and weeks at a stretch covering the antics and activities of national politicians? Subtly, if not suddenly, over the last seven years, the fire in my belly for national political reporting had subsided considerably without me ever recognizing what was happening. I turned the transfer down. At least this was a career decision made not by default, but by careful, calculated consideration. Scratch one potential byline in national political reporting. I doubt it was missed.

With Washington now out of my future, there really was no good reason for me to stay with the Associated Press in Harrisburg. So when an offer was extended to join the public information staff at my alma mater, Penn State University, I accepted. Fork Number Two encountered and taken in very short order. Truth was, I never did envision the shift to Penn State later in 1968 to be a permanent career move for my family and myself. Word at the time was that State Senate Minority Leader Ernest P. Kline was to make a bid in 1970 for the Democratic nomination to the U.S. Senate. I had been approached very preliminarily by one of his chief aides about joining his campaign staff when that candidacy was launched. I would have been interested. But in politics, as we know, a year can be a lifetime. Kline's campaign for the Senate never materialized. He ended up, instead, as Milton Shapp's running mate for lieutenant governor on the Democratic gubernatorial ticket, and candidates for lieutenant governor had no need of large, independent staffs of their own.

That same year, 1970, the *Philadelphia Inquirer* came calling, however. The Knight newspaper syndicate, nationally renowned and well respected within the profession, had just bought the paper from Walter Annenberg. I was invited to join my old roommate, Bill Ecenbarger, to open a new two-man bureau in the state capital. I accepted, Fork Number Three taken. My time with the *Inquirer* lasted only a year and a half, but it was an eventful experience in my professional learning process nonetheless. I got to cover the 1970 Democratic gubernatorial primary campaign between the aforementioned Milton Shapp and his party nemesis, Robert P. Casey of Scranton; and later that fall, Shapp's successful general election campaign against Republican Lieutenant Governor Raymond Broderick. After Shapp's election and inauguration, there was the prolonged 1971 budget fight to cover, and that occupied most of my time and attention. It was challenging work, professionally gratifying. But for a host of reasons not really relevant here—let's just say one of the principal among them was adequate compensation—I left the *Inquirer* in 1971 to accept the position of press secretary to the new Senate Democratic majority caucus. My interest in public service, first tweaked by my grandfather's and father's service on Scranton City Council, had been dormant all these years, but never fully abated. Now I would find out if I was a good fit in the process of public policymaking. Fork Number Four . . . come to and taken. Thanks, Yogi.

Part 2

★★★★★

The Pennsylvania Senate

Chapter 6

★★★★★★★

The Pennsylvania Senate, 1970s Style

If you happened to be a Democrat with an interest in public service, public policymaking, and politics, Pennsylvania was a good place for you to be in 1971.

The 1970 general elections had been particularly kind to the Pennsylvania Democratic Party. Its candidate for governor, Milton Shapp, was elected the state's new chief executive, ending eight years of Republican rule in the governor's office. The State House of Representatives remained in Democratic control, and for the first time in almost a half-century, since 1937–38 to be exact, Democrats won majority control of the Pennsylvania Senate. As political trifectas go, they don't come any better.

Now came the hard part. It was called governing. "More important than winning the election is governing the nation," Democrat Adlai Stevenson had said in accepting the presidential nomination of his party in July 1952. "That is the test of a political party—the acid, final test." Pennsylvania Democrats were about to find out for themselves how they would meet the Stevenson test because governing in 1971 was not going to be easy, certainly not going in.

First on the plate was the state budget. Not just one budget, but two. The preceding Republican administration under Governor Raymond P. Shafer had failed to pass a full twelve-month budget for the fiscal year 1970–71. Politics and intraparty GOP strife over Shafer's proposal to enact a standby state income tax—the very notion of a state income tax, standby or not, long had been a third rail in Pennsylvania political discourse—all but doomed the 1970 election year budget deliberations to failure and prolonged stalemate.

So it was left to the new state administration of Milton Shapp and his Democratic majorities in the House and Senate to not only propose and enact a new state budget for fiscal year 1971–72, which was to begin in a short six months—always, in itself, a daunting task for any new administration—but it also fell to them to bring the existing state budget into balance for the remaining six months of the current fiscal year as well. Eighteen months of budgeting for an administration just thirty days in office. Needless to say, that's about as difficult a debut as a new chief executive can confront. Welcome to Harrisburg and the state capital, Governor.

Fortunately for Shapp, he had excellent leadership in the General Assembly. In the House, Speaker Herb Fineman of Philadelphia and Majority Leader K. Leroy Irvis of Allegheny County still were very much in command of the Democratic majority there. More important, in the Senate, Martin L. Murray of Luzerne County was elected president pro tempore and Thomas F. Lamb of Pittsburgh was named Senate majority leader (replacing newly inaugurated Lieutenant Governor Ernest P. Kline as the party's floor leader in the chamber). Neither Shapp nor the Senate Democrats could have asked for a better leadership tandem.

Marty Murray was coal region and old school in so many ways—a devoted family man in his private life, a committed Democrat in the tradition of Franklin Roosevelt and Harry Truman in his political life. He believed deeply in the political philosophy of his party and he placed a very high premium on party loyalty. Marty Murray's word was his bond. And though he could be as partisan as the next senator if the circumstances demanded, he seldom if ever made it personal.

Larry O'Brien, a former Democratic national chairman and longtime confidant of President John F. Kennedy, wrote a book entitled *No Final Victories, No Permanent Defeats*. Marty Murray was a living testament to the wisdom of that credo. Essentially, in the Murray/O'Brien school of politics, alliances were never necessarily permanent. As issues arose, you took your allies where you could find them. Once resolved, you moved on to other matters and, if necessary, other alliances, wiping the slate clean for most everyone, but all the time remembering those who stood with you throughout. Marty Murray also gave life to another political dictum, the one that held politics often made for strange bedfellows. He was an exemplary practitioner of the theory, and, as the ranking member of the Senate in the 1970s, he honed it to a fine art.

Senator Murray adhered to another tenet of political life that could be applied just as easily and wisely to other professions. "Don't get mad, get even" was his rule, and he seldom failed to follow it. John Kennedy put it another way: "Forgive your enemies . . . but never forget their names." Though with different words, their counsel was profound in its simplicity. In politics, as in many of life's endeavors, to the Murray/Kennedy school of thinking anger most often is not an asset because it can color your judgment to a fault. It is a good lesson. But then again, if you watched Senator Murray in action, there was a lot you could learn about people, about life, and about professional relationships. Marty Murray of Luzerne County in northeast Pennsylvania was not only a good man, he was also about as good a teacher as one could find.

There was also a lot to be learned from Tom Lamb. If ever there was a principled gentleman in politics, congenial Tom Lamb would be that person. Like Senator Murray, he was very proud of his Irish heritage and no less devoted to his family. The two also pursued their political careers in similar ways. Senator Lamb and Senator Murray had risen through the legislative ranks from their home bases—Ashley in the northeast and Pittsburgh in the southwest—to serve first in the House of Representatives and then in the Senate. Lamb's word also was very much his bond. His collegial and conciliatory manner made him a majority leader who was respected and befriended on both sides of the aisle. He was steadfast in his convictions about and loyalty to the principles of his party, And, most important, Tom Lamb was another practitioner who never made his politics personal.

Senators Lamb and Murray settled on a simple formula for leading. Senator Murray took responsibility for the care and feeding of the troops in his narrow (26–24) Democratic majority. He left the strategy and timing of the Senate agenda (in consultation and, most often, in cooperation with the new Democratic state administration) largely to his majority leader. It made for a very successful arrangement for the Senate and the new governor for the next four years.

In mid-1971 I accepted an offer to join the staff of the Pennsylvania Senate as press secretary to the Democratic Caucus. Initially, there was a slight question of whether I would make my entry into public service with the Senate or the State House of Representatives. About the same time I was approached by Ernie Kline's chief of staff, Pete Coleman, to join the Senate Democratic staff, I also received a call from Speaker Fineman. Herb Fineman was a very skilled lawyer from Philadelphia (as opposed to a "Philadelphia lawyer"). He also was a brilliant legislative tactician, probably as good as they came. He wanted to talk to me about joining the House Democratic staff in a press relations capacity and, he said, I could name my salary, within reason. It was, to be honest, flattering to be recruited by him; needless to say, the compensation consideration had some very strong attractions as well. But there also was reason to pause, a reason relating to the political chain of command in the House leadership.

Technically, the position I was asked to consider was, for table-of-organization purposes, on the staff of Majority Leader Roy Irvis, another respected legislator who in later years would become the first person of African American descent to be elected Speaker of any state House of Representatives in the country. While Fineman and Irvis seemed to work well together, and clearly were compatible in their political philosophies, I had a question. "Who would I report to?" I asked Fineman. "You or Roy?"

Fineman said he saw no problem because of their long and successful relationship as the two most influential leaders in the House. But, he added, the Speaker of the House was the ranking officer of the chamber. I didn't need to hear more. I understood that even though I would be on the payroll of a House majority leader who didn't hire me, my ultimate responsibility would be to the Speaker who did. That arrangement just didn't sit well with me. So I opted (for less money) for the Senate where the chain was more precisely linked. Another fork in the road, another path taken. With, I thought, good reason.

If there were any two state officials Governor Milton Shapp should have been indebted to in his first half-year in office, it would have been Marty Murray and Tom Lamb. To bring the state's fiscal affairs in balance, the governor had to propose a state income tax—at a rate of 5 percent, and this time a permanent tax—as the keystone of his fiscal recovery package. Without the skilled and steady leadership of Senators Murray and Lamb, it's doubtful he would have succeeded as quickly as he did—not once, but twice in seven months.

The political condition was much different in the House of Representatives than it was in the Senate when the 1971 session opened for business; most pressing was the business of the budget. House Democrats had been in the political majority in the previous biennium and frequently enough before that so they were sufficiently experienced in playing the role of the governing party in their chamber. They also had the benefit of seasoned and effective leadership in the persons of Speaker Fineman, Majority Leader Irvis, and Majority Whip Jim Manderino of Westmoreland County (who was to emerge a few years later as a legislative leader certainly the equal if not more so than Fineman in his tactical skills). Most important, Fineman, Irvis, and Manderino held a healthy 112–90 margin in the House, with 102 votes necessary for passage for any legislation, including the Shapp income tax. "Breathing room," they call it.

Such was not the case in the Senate. The Democrats' political majority in the chamber was bare to the bone. There were no votes to spare, and not all members of the Democratic caucus could be expected to embrace Shapp's call for a state income tax, and for good reason. For the Democrats to win political control, they had to win in Senate districts that traditionally voted Republican. In the 1970 elections, they did in three: Senator Joseph Ammerman of Centre/Clearfield counties; Senator Henry Messinger of Lehigh County; and Senator Pat Stapleton of Indiana/Armstrong counties. To ask these freshmen to vote for the first state income tax in Commonwealth history in what was essentially the first and certainly the most important act of the new legislative session was not a vote likely to enhance their electoral job security back home. In addition, two other Democrats—Senator Tom Nolan of Allegheny County and Senator William Duffield of Fayette County—were elected on avowed anti-tax/anti-government spending platforms. Nolan and Duffield would take some persuading to support the Shapp tax plan.

While Senators Murray and Lamb were seasoned legislators and influential voices in their caucus, they were new to their roll as leaders of a majority caucus. "Being in the minority can be fun," Ernie Kline used to observe from his minority leader's chair in the Senate. "Being in the majority is always hard work." Messrs. Murray and Lamb certainly had their work cut out for them. They had little historical experience to rely on because in the first seventy years of the twentieth century, Pennsylvania Democrats had only held majority status in the Senate twice before. For a brief two-year span in 1937–38 under Democrat Governor George Earle they held a 34–16 margin (it quickly reverted back to its Republican traditions, 25–23, in the subsequent election), and in 1961–62 under Democrat Governor David L. Lawrence the membership was split 25–25, but Democrats had organizational control by virtue of the vote of Lieutenant Governor John Morgan Davis of Philadelphia. To get a 1970–71 and 1971–72 budget passed, Senators Murray and Lamb simply would have to learn how to steer a majority as they went along. They proved to be pretty adept at it.

Their mission was simplified to some degree by the fact that the electorate had bought into Shapp's campaign theme that it would take an outsider with private sector business experience to put an to end the political squabbling and stalemate in Harrisburg. Still it was left to politicians like Murray, Lamb, and Lieutenant Governor Kline (as the presiding officer) in the Senate and Fineman, Irvis, and Manderino in the House to sell the Shapp program to their members.

This proposition couldn't be taken for granted. After all, Shapp had established his political bona fides four years earlier as a maverick Democrat in his first (though unsuccessful) run for governor. Murray, Lamb, and most of their caucus, for that matter, were party regulars. Their political loyalties could have been divided, but it never came to that. Senators Murray and Lamb worked their caucus hard. In the face of solid Republican opposition, they had to hold their twenty-six members, including Nolan and Duffield, in the fold. Shapp's 5 percent income tax proposal was trimmed back to 3.5 percent. The Senate and House also scuttled the business tax relief contained in Shapp's original plan and told the business community they could thank their Republican friends in the General Assembly for that. That was enough to win over Nolan and Duffield. The Senate passed the first income tax in state history at 12:30 A.M., March 4, just about a month after it was proposed, on a straight party line vote of 26 Democrats for, 24 Republicans opposed. Governor Shapp signed it into law the next day. A semblance of fiscal stability had been restored to the Commonwealth, but not for long.

No sooner had the tax been enacted than a Republican-inspired taxpayer suit was filed challenging the constitutionality of the original state income tax on the ground that it violated the uniformity clause of the State Constitution. The challenge was upheld by the Pennsylvania Supreme Court so Shapp, Murray, Lamb, and the House as well, had to do it all over again. This time Nolan and Duffield were not about to be swayed in support of a restorative tax. They said they objected to the spending levels that would accompany it.

What's more, lame-duck Philadelphia mayor James H. J. Tate got into a public fight with Governor Shapp over the amount of money the city would get in the final budget. Tate had requested an additional $106 million for Philadelphia and $53 million for the Philadelphia school system. The Shapp budget would provide only $28 million and $33 million, respectively. By Tate's count that would be only $7 million more than the city would have received from the previous administration. "I see no reason for the tax," Tate told the governor. "If you want the votes, go to the Republicans."

Despite Tate's public opposition, the Democratic-controlled House of Representatives (with limited help from the Republican minority) passed Shapp's 2.3 percent alternative income tax at 4:01 A.M., August 27, on a bare constitutional majority vote of 102–93. In the Senate, three Democrats from Philadelphia—Tom McCreesh, Herb McGlinchey, and Joe Smith—absented themselves from the vote . . . just disappeared, if you will. They were believed to be acting at Tate's direction, though he and they denied it. With $153 million in combined business tax relief having been restored to the tax mix, Murray and Lamb were able to secure five Republican votes—R. D. Fleming of Allegheny County, Dick Frame of Venango County, Frederick Hobbs of Schuylkill County, T. Newell Wood of Luzerne County, and Wilmot Fleming of Montgomery County—to make up for the missing Philadelphia trio, and Nolan and Duffield. At 10 P.M. the night of August 27, the Senate sent the 2.3 percent substitute income tax bill and the elements of tax relief it held out to Pennsylvania business to the governor for his signature. Another period of prolonged fiscal instability had been averted.

Balancing the state budget for the next eighteen months was, unquestionably, Senators Murray and Lamb's most immediate leadership challenge, perhaps the most serious of their four-year partnership. But the episode was to frame the pattern of quiet, steady, persistent, loyal, and successful leadership that they together brought to the Pennsylvania Senate from 1971 through 1974.

Tom Lamb retired from the Senate at the conclusion of the 1973–74 legislative session. (Principled man that he was, when I interviewed for the job as caucus press secretary three years earlier, he told me that he probably would not seek re-election. He wanted me to know that before I decided whether to accept the offer. He didn't have to, but he did. That says as much of the man as you need to know.) With Lamb's retirement, Marty Murray had to form a new leadership alliance within the Democratic caucus, this time, principally, with a new majority leader.

No one could have known it at the time, but Lamb's departure would mark the beginning of the end to Democratic control of the Senate. It would take six years, but Republicans won back the political majority in the Senate in the 1980 elections. Whether that would have happened in any event is a matter of legitimate debate. But there is no question Tom Lamb's retirement certainly accelerated the pace and probability of the political turnover because of some serious political misjudgments by his successor. Almost a quarter of a century later, Democrats are still consigned to a minority status in the Senate with no potential for breakthrough in sight. There's more to say on this particular subject. But for the here and now, there's no debate: Between 1971 and 1975, first-term governor Milton Shapp had no better allies than Marty Murray and Tom Lamb. Pennsylvania was the ultimate beneficiary because the quality of governance in the Commonwealth was much improved by their service. As politicians (in the best sense of the word) who participated in making public policy work in the public interest, there may have been others their equal, but certainly none came better.

Chapter 7

★★★★★★★

The Senators

The Senate of Pennsylvania, for all its protocols and traditions, is what it is because of the members who serve there. They give it its life and blood, they chart its course at every moment in its history. Some members, like Marty Murray and Tom Lamb, are to be remembered for the influence they exerted on the body simply by the way they conducted themselves as public officials. Others who served in the three-decade period between 1970 and the turn of the twenty-first century deserve recognition for other reasons, such as the contributions they made to public policy, or their unique personalities or political style. Senators like Franklin L. Kury of Sunbury, Northumberland County, and H. Craig Lewis of Bensalem, Bucks County; Henry Messinger of Allentown, Lehigh County, and Gene Scanlon of Pittsburgh, Allegheny County; Joseph Ammerman of Curwensville, Clearfield County, Ed Zemprelli of Clairton, Allegheny County, and Buddy Cianfrani of Philadelphia. Each stood out in his own way.

Senator Franklin L. Kury

If government is to function truly and totally in the public interest, it can use more people like Frank Kury.

My first encounter with Frank came not as a member of the Pennsylvania Senate staff, but as a reporter for the Associated Press. I was traveling with Republican gubernatorial candidate Ray Shafer in the 1966 general election campaign. We were in Sunbury for a courthouse rally of several hundred Northumberland County GOP workers and other assorted party loyalists. The event was moderated by the renowned but not always lauded Northumberland County Republican chairman, Henry Lark.

If the program was intended to energize the troops behind Shafer and the GOP gubernatorial ticket, Lark quickly went off message. As master of ceremonies, he hardly mentioned the nominee and the campaign for governor. Instead he spent most of his time, energy, and remarks railing angrily about some young upstart Democratic lawyer who had the temerity to challenge

State Representative Adam Bower (a Northumberland County Republican fixture and the most senior Republican member of the House of Representatives at the time) at the ballot box. The lawyer's name was Frank Kury.

To hear Lark harangue, Kury was the living personification of Satan, Attila the Hun, Hitler, Stalin, and others of that ilk in one and the same living body. The more Lark lashed out at Kury, the louder the assembled Republican loyalists hooted and howled in support of their chairman. Gubernatorial candidate Shafer looked frustrated by the turn of events but there was little he could do about it.

"Who is this Kury fella?" I remember asking myself at the time. "What is it about him that can put Henry Lark in such an apoplectic state?" I was soon to find out.

As the rally ended and the crowd began to disperse, I started making my way to the awaiting campaign cars that would take us to our next stop when what should I spy but a neatly dressed young man and woman working the departing crowd, smiling, shaking hands, and passing out what appeared to be campaign hand cards (cards with a picture and brief bio of the candidate).

The couple was Frank Kury and his wife, Beth. They had stationed themselves silently on the fringe of the crowd and remained there even while Lark worked him over time and again. When the event ended, Frank and Beth mingled among the crowd, introducing themselves to those who didn't know them, smiling and shaking hands with those who did, and passing out "Kury for the House" cards to any and all takers. I was struck by the fact that many of the folks who had been hooting him only moments earlier were smiling as they took his hand and his campaign literature.

"I don't know this Kury fella, but Adam Bower ain't got himself no patsy," I said to no one in particular. "He sure looks like he could be one helluva an opponent."

He certainly was. Democrat Frank Kury won that race in Republican Northumberland County and went on to serve four terms in the state House and two more in the Pennsylvania Senate, carving out a most credible and laudable niche for himself in the legislative process.

Early on he established that he was a hard worker. Though very much aware and always sensitive to the personalities, the egos, and the politics of the legislative process, he nevertheless focused his energy and intellect on issues of substance throughout his legislative career. In the House he played a major role in shaping and passing a landmark Clean Streams Act for Pennsylvania. He also began his work on a major flood plain management bill, a project he would carry with him six years later to the Pennsylvania Senate, ultimately culminating in its enactment into law.

One time, as a member of the House, he traded his vote and publicly told his constituents about it. The incident involved a controversial bill to provide additional magistrates for the Philadelphia court system. It was a controversial measure because the way the Philadelphia magistrates court conducted business . . . well, let's say they hardly were the models of repute in most juris prudence circles. For an upstate Democratic legislator like Frank Kury, representing a fundamentally Republican district, it was a tough political vote. But the party pressure from his House leadership, dominated by Philadelphians, and the governor's office under Milton Shapp was equally intense. The matter had all the dimensions of a lose-lose.

Kury was called into a personal meeting with Governor Milton Shapp before the House vote. "Magistrates may be important to you, but they don't mean a thing to me or my district," he recalled telling the governor. But, he added, there was something important to his district, and maybe, just maybe, he could help on the magistrates legislation. The matter of importance was a new bridge at Sunbury over the Susquehanna River. Before he left that meeting, Kury had obtained a personal commitment from the governor and his transportation secretary, Jacob Kassab, to release $20 million for the design and land acquisition of the bridge.

Blackmail? Not at all. Call it a tradeoff—a new bridge, which meant something for his legislative district, in exchange for a vote for Philadelphia magistrates, which didn't. It was an impressive exercise in legislative and executive bartering. When Kury walked into the governor's office, the Sunbury bridge was lost somewhere on the Transportation Department's long list of long-range construction projects. When he walked out, it wasn't. What's more, he was quick to issue a press release to inform his constituency of the deal he had made (they were, frankly, impressed) and to put the deal on the record in case there was a sudden lapse of memory in the Shapp administration. Today, there's a new bridge over the Susquehanna River between Sunbury and Shamokin Dam, and Frank Kury, if not the father, was most certainly the moving force behind that project.

My professional association with Frank began when he was elected to the state Senate in 1972. Over the next eight years, we would work together, he as a committee chairman, I as a member of the staff, on a number of projects, but two in particular that truly could be classified as notable reform.

The first was reform and modernization of the Senate confirmation process. Senate confirmation of gubernatorial appointees was a sham at the time. In fact, it was nonexistent. The Pennsylvania Constitution required that every nominee of the governor's, be it for a vacancy in some justice of the peace position in Podunk or a vacancy on the Pennsylvania Supreme Court, had to be confirmed by a two-thirds vote of the Senate (meaning at least thirty-four of the fifty members).

There were over 2,000 gubernatorial appointments at play. It was rare that either party had thirty-four members in its ranks to reach that two-thirds level. So it was often impossible for governors to get their nominees confirmed. And governors, in turn, most often responded by simply delaying their appointments until the Senate had adjourned for the session. Then the positions would be filled, as provided in the Constitution, with interim appointments, who would serve either until a successful confirmation vote or the adjournment of the Senate. Then the process would start all over again.

Tom Lamb, leading a new Democratic majority in the Senate, decided to take the issue on as a matter of institutional improvement for the Senate itself. He proposed creation of a select, bipartisan committee to review the confirmation process and make recommendations for change. I was press secretary to the Democratic caucus at the time and I believe I suggested to him that Senator Kury be designated chairman of the committee. I didn't know where the study would go; but I was confident Kury would give it the substantive review it deserved.

Kury and his committee—senators Joseph Ammerman and Henry Messinger for the Democrats and Richard C. Frame and Stanley Stroup for the Republicans—did just that. The Report of the Special Senate Committee on Senate Confirmation Reform was submitted in the mid-1970s. It proposed a constitutional amendment to permit a majority of twenty-six votes instead of a super majority of thirty-four votes to confirm all but a handful of gubernatorial appointments. It also proposed to do away with the interim appointment process entirely.

The referendum was adopted overwhelmingly by the voters of Pennsylvania. As a result, public hearings on major appointments such as the governor's Cabinet became the norm for the Senate and a vote of the full chamber on every nominee within a specified period of time became guaranteed under law. The Kury report put that reform in place.

The second major reform that Frank Kury spearheaded came in the mid-1970s and resulted in the first wholesale rewriting of public utility law in forty years. By this time, Kury had become chairman of the standing Senate Committee on Consumer Affairs. The era of cheap energy was disappearing rapidly from the national and state landscape. Kury decided to look at how the state utility regulatory process, set in place in the mid-1930s, was equipped forty years later to cope with that changing landscape.

Two visits Kury made during the course of his review to two states reputed to have the most effective utility regulatory system in place at the time illustrate the constructive and thoughtful approach he brought to public policymaking. With both majority and minority staff, he spent two days in Madison with the Wisconsin utility commission and its staff. Upon his return, Kury invited the chairman of the Wisconsin commission to come to Harrisburg and publicly testify before his committee. The chairman did. I overheard him call his office after his testimony and tell his staff, "These fellas are really serious about this." Kury took that as a compliment and rightly so.

The second trip was to San Francisco for a three-day visit with California regulators. San Francisco being a great place to visit, Kury decided he would publicly notify the press in advance that a five-member contingent of the Pennsylvania Senate (he, ranking Republican Senator Wayne Ewing, and three staff) was going to the Golden State on this fact-finding mission. Not only did he identify the travelers by name and position, but he also offered to brief any reporter on his findings upon his return. When he got back, he repeated the offer. There were no takers. Announcing the trip in advance apparently had taken the news element out of the trip.

My former roommate Bill Ecenbarger, in one of his regular *Philadelphia Inquirer* columns, publicly labeled the study the best piece of legislative work in at least a decade and perhaps longer. Two developments of note emanated from the Kury Report. The most lasting was that it proposed to create in law the state's first Office of Consumer Advocate to represent consumer interests in utility regulatory matters. Today, the Office of Consumer Advocate is very much an integral and important part of the utility regulatory process in Pennsylvania. It also barred *ex parte* conversations (those held outside the formal regulatory process) in pending rate cases between the commissioners, their staff, and the regulated utilities.

Another consequence of the Kury Report was that the two lawyers who served as Democratic and Republican counsel to the committee, my close friend Jim Cawley and his minority counterpart, Susan Shanaman, eventually were appointed by Governor Richard L. Thornburgh as members of the Public Utility Commission. Their role in the preparation and implementation of the Kury reforms was what most qualified them for the nominations. (They were confirmed by the full Senate, incidentally, under the Kury reform procedures.)

There was much to recommend Frank Kury as a standard for high public service: His intellect, his political skills, his focus on the substance of public policymaking. But what was most impressive about him as much as any single factor in his character, in my judgment, was that he never forgot his roots.

Frank Kury received an undergraduate degree from Trinity College in Connecticut and a law degree from the prestigious University of Pennsylvania. He was a successful lawyer and a successful candidate for public office. But Frank Kury always remembered—first, last, and always—that he was the son of a Polish shoemaker named Barney Kury. He spoke of his father often in many of our conversations. He was proud of his heritage and he was true to the core values instilled in him by his father and mother. He wore them as a badge of honor, and they, in turn, served him well.

Frank Kury made two runs for higher public office—the Democratic nomination for auditor general in the 1980s and the party nomination for state treasurer in the 1990s. But in both instances he lacked the political base and the financial wherewithal to attract the political support of major party leaders that was critical to both campaigns. That was unfortunate, because Pennsylvania would have benefited from his service. He went on to a successful private sector career in law and lobbying in Harrisburg. We stay in touch.

Senator H. Craig Lewis

For public service to prosper and progress, it must periodically find a way to reenergize and reinvigorate itself. Most often, the principal way to do that is through the introduction of new, talented leaders, usually but not always young people who shine and rise to the top of their class. H. Craig Lewis of Bucks County was one of those people.

A native son of Hazleton, Lewis at twenty-eight was the youngest elected member of the Senate when he took his oath of office in January of 1975. The district he represented originally crossed between lower Bucks County and northeast Philadelphia. Self-assured and self-confident, he came to public service full of energy, ideas, and, it must be admitted, political ambition. It wasn't long after we first met that he shared with me his intention to one day run for the U.S. Senate. I immediately marked him as someone to watch, if only for his chutzpah.

I joined Craig's staff in 1979 as executive director of the Senate Local Government Committee, which he chaired. I had a lot of learning to do in cutting through the maze of what was and remains the convoluted structure of local government in the Commonwealth. Craig, however, took to the assignment of local government oversight with his customary zest and enthusiasm.

He authored a report that ultimately established in law the Local Government Retirement Study Commission. Prior to creation of the commission, bills changing local government pension laws were enacted by the General Assembly virtually by whim or whimsy. Cost implications seldom were a factor in their disposition. At the same time, local government pension systems across the state were finding themselves increasingly burdened by a growing mass of unfunded liability. The function of the newly created Local Government Retirement Study Commission was to bring some order and forethought to a system that heretofore had precious little of either. Henceforth, however, no bills affecting local government retirement programs would be considered by either the House or Senate without first having been analyzed for impact and cost by the commission. The act Lewis sponsored creating the commission was a distinct improvement to the process, not to mention a substantial cost-saver to local governments across the Commonwealth.

Thanks to the able services of some very dedicated staff on the Local Government Commission, a bipartisan research arm of the General Assembly, Craig also authored a new law dealing with the disposition of tax-delinquent property. It essentially required due notice to property owners and the public before property could be disposed of at sale for outstanding taxes. Before the statute, the system was rife with the potential for sweetheart arrangements, particularly when attractive tracts of real estate were involved. The Lewis law was designed to level the playing field for both the property owner and potential buyers. In a quiet, unheralded way, that's exactly what it did.

Lewis was an activist sort of senator who would have made his mark on the chamber in any number of ways. One major imprint he left came in the realm of Senate ethics. The first half of the 1970s had been very good to the Senate Democrats. Midway through the decade, the party's political majority reached an unthinkable margin of 30–20. That was because over the course of three election cycles (1970, 1972 and 1974), a number of Democrats—Democrats like Frank Kury, and Pat Stapleton (Indiana County), Henry Messinger (Lehigh County), Joe Ammerman (Clearfield/Centre counties), and John Sweeney (Delaware County)—were elected to the Senate in what had been traditionally Republican districts. The ranks of the Democrats swelled beyond imaginable proportions because of their election victories and remained that way through the decade because these members were re-electable. (John Sweeney was the only one of the group to lose his bid for re-election.)

But there was a price to pay for these electoral successes, which unfortunately manifested itself in the latter half of the decade in careless institutional governance and indefensible misconduct in personal matters. (More on all of this later.)

The cumulative effect of these misdeeds, and the surrounding uproar in the press, public, and, understandably, partisan political circles (particularly Senate Republicans), was to have the Senate establish within the formal committee structure of the body a standing, bipartisan committee on ethics. Craig Lewis was named its first chairman. This spoke volumes of his standing on the character and integrity fronts, not to mention his intellectual and political skills in assuming such a challenging assignment. Given their transgressions in the latter half of the decade, Senate Democrats needed someone of this stature to assume the chairmanship. It should also be acknowledged that for someone with Lewis' political ambitions, the appointment didn't hurt his potential for future political advancement.

His chairmanship of the Senate Ethics Committee was a major contribution to an improved legislative process. But it was only after Senate Democrats lost political control of the chamber in the 1980 general election that he made his most lasting legislative mark. A number of newer members were unhappy with the old guard leadership of the caucus during the troubled times and wanted to send a message to that effect. They asked Craig to be the messenger by challenging veteran senator Joe Smith, an entrenched Democrat from Philadelphia, for the minority chairmanship of the Senate Appropriations Committee. Lewis took on the campaign and won. Given the nature of internal caucus party politics, it was no small victory.

Lewis invited me to come along as the new chief of staff for the committee. What had once been a closed preserve of the chair (always a Philadelphian) and his single staff director was to take on a whole new dimension under Lewis's leadership. His first charge to me was to recruit and build a staff of young professionals who would not only analyze state fiscal affairs in depth, they would also share that information on a regular, continuing basis with other members of the caucus. For a Pennsylvania Senate fairly fixed and guarded in its ways, this was no small innovation.

Frankly, our staff model was not of our own making. It duplicated in many respects the Appropriations staff structure created in the House Democratic caucus largely under the leadership of Messrs. Fineman and, later, the now House Majority Leader Jim Manderino. Both had an eye and a respect for able (and loyal) staff talent. Under both, a very bright young man by the name of Michael Hershock served as the Democratic executive director of the Appropriations Committee. Mike Hershock a decade later would go on to serve as a very able budget secretary for Gov. Robert P. Casey. He was the first person I conferred with after Lewis unseated Joe Smith. His counsel on how to recruit staff and assign responsibilities on clear and direct departmental lines was a very helpful to start to our staff building process. It was to pay unexpected political dividends two years later.

The other counselor I turned to was former Shapp administration budget secretary Charlie McIntosh. McIntosh had been a career analyst in the state budget office when Senator Murray and then–Senate Minority Leader Ernie Kline wooed him to become director of the Democratic Appropriations Committee staff. Two years later, as Shapp's lieutenant governor-elect, Kline persuaded the new governor to name Charlie as his budget secretary.

It was a very wise move on Shapp's part. Charlie was as knowledgeable about state budgeting as anyone in the Capitol. What's more, he was well respected across party lines for his professionalism. And his word was golden. When Charlie told you something about the fiscal affairs of the state, you could take it to the bank. So I welcomed the opportunity to probe him for pointers. I remember he shared some tips about budget analysis, but he gave me one piece of advice that held me in good stead, not only in my service with the Appropriations Committee, but throughout my career. "Never lose sight of the big picture," Charlie counseled in that very serious way of his. It was a point well taken. Details count, to be sure. But without goals and objectives—some might call it an agenda or a vision—details can lead to nowhere.

The changes in the operating style of the Minority Appropriations Committee under Craig Lewis were noticeable almost immediately. He hired five budget analysts and their direction was very clear: Probe the state budget and state spending in as much detail as they could and share their findings with the Democratic caucus on a regular basis.

The members were surprised by the access they had to information that previously had been generally unavailable to them, and they welcomed it. Democratic members of the Senate Appropriations Committee went into state budget hearings with a treasury of information from which to formulate their lines of inquiry. Whether they chose to use it or not was their decision.

The system was such an operational improvement and innovation for the Pennsylvania Senate that I later learned Republican members complained to their leadership that the Democrats were much better prepared than they were going into the budget hearings. It reached a point that the incumbent Republican Appropriations chairman was threatened with a challenge at the next Senate reorganization unless he mended his ways along the lines of the Lewis operation. He did, and the challenge never materialized. But Lewis took the incident as the best testimony to the value of the work his staff was doing, and he was right.

Craig Lewis served in the Senate until 1994. He did pursue his ambition of running for the U.S. Senate in 1980. Alas, he finished seventh in a field of eight for the Democratic nomination. The winner was former Pittsburgh Mayor Pete Flaherty (who lost to Arlen Specter the following November). Flaherty pulled 771,000 votes in the primary. Lewis pulled a paltry 68,000. Like Frank Kury, he had the political and policymaking skills to move on to higher office. But he also lacked the political and fundraising base so necessary to advance his ambitions. In 1994 Craig was the Democratic nominee for auditor general against incumbent Republican Barbara Hafer. General Hafer had been overwhelmed two years earlier in her race for governor against incumbent Robert P. Casey. But her predictions of fiscal peril in that race, magnified by the depths of the 1990–91 economic recession and the prolonged budget fight and massive tax hike that ensued in the General Assembly, had rehabilitated her reputation. She beat Lewis by 280,000 votes.

Lewis spent another two years in the Senate. As a member of the Senate Judiciary Committee, he participated in the Senate trial of a Pennsylvania Supreme Court jurist, Rolf Larsen, after Larsen's impeachment by the House of Representatives for malfeasance in office. Not a bad cumulative record for a young unknown out of Bensalem in Bucks County. He retired at the still-tender age of forty-eight in 1995 after five terms in the body.

Lewis returned to the private practice of law. Later, he became a vice-president of Norfolk Southern Railroad. Since we both left public service our paths crossed only infrequently as the years passed by. But I enjoyed my partnership with him in the Senate and valued the work we attempted to do together. He was a credit to the institution, and I was a better person and professional from my association with him.

As noted at the top, there were other Democrats who served in the Senate of Pennsylvania who made their mark, mostly for the better, in the course of their tenure. I should acknowledge here and now that senators worthy of recognition in my view certainly crossed party lines. Republican senators like Senate President Pro Tempore Bob Jubelirer of Blair County and Majority Leader David "Chip" Brightbill of Lebanon County, former majority leaders John Stauffer of Chester County and Joe Loeper of Delaware County, Senator J. Doyle Corman of Centre County, each and all (and the list is not all-inclusive) made the Senate a better place by their presence and their service.

But I write here only of Democratic senators because, after all, it was as a member of the Democratic Senate staff that I came to know and observe them from close quarters. Let me start with two of the tide-turning class of 1970, Senators Joseph Ammerman and Henry Messinger.

Senator Joe Ammerman

Joe Ammerman was a rugged, outspoken, often stubborn individualist befitting his Curwensville roots in Clearfield County. He spoke his piece whenever he was of the mind to say something; and that was just about any time. Politics was his lifeblood, and he applied his profession with great zest. A life-long bachelor, he had just three purposes to his being—his mother, politics, and public service. His blunt, straight-spoken style didn't win him any popularity contests. But then, Joe Ammerman was the kind who didn't really care.

More important, Senator Ammerman was honest to his core. To my knowledge, his commitment to public service in the best sense of the phrase never wavered. He was one of those rare birds who loved the game of politics and the way it was played. Still he never permitted pure political considerations to subordinate the public interest.

Ammerman was one of the Shapp administration's sharpest critics, though he voted with the administration on a number of important issues like the 1971 state income tax and, later, no-fault auto insurance. He also was an important and outspoken (those who knew him would not have expected less) member of the Senate Confirmation Reform committee. Joe's bluntness would cost him dearly in 1974 when he was a candidate to replace retiring Tom Lamb as Senate majority leader. (There's more to say on this later.) With the benefit of hindsight, it is not off the mark to suggest that his loss in that leadership race might well have been the most single important event that ultimately resulted in Republicans regaining political control of the chamber three election cycles later. The unseemly activities that ultimately were so fatal to the Senate and its Democratic majority never would had been tolerated if Ammerman had been serving as majority leader at the time.

Joe Ammerman was to be respected for his plainspoken, straight-from-the-shoulder ways. You never had to wonder where you stood with him. Verbally, he could be like a bull in a china shop. But his candor held him in good stead back home. Before his election to the Senate, he had served a stint as Clearfield County district attorney; he left the state Senate to serve a term in the U.S. Congress; after he lost his re-election bid to Congress, he returned home to practice law and later serve on the Clearfield County Court of Common Pleas. He died while on the bench. He was a good man and a good public servant. There is no better way for him to be remembered.

Senator Henry Messinger

If Joe Ammerman was blustery, Henry Messinger was the "Quiet Man" of the Senate. Truth be told, nobody outside of Lehigh County knew who Henry Messinger was when he shocked the political establishment with his election to the body. I was writing the legislative election story for the *Philadelphia Inquirer* in 1970 as the results came in showing that some Democrat named Henry Messinger was defeating the veteran Republican Senate majority whip, John Van Zant, in the Lehigh Valley.

"Who the hell's Henry Messinger?" I asked aloud. "My God, he's giving the Democrats political control of the Senate for the first time since 1936!" A call to Senate Democratic offices in Harrisburg did little to shed more light on this mystery man. "All we know is that he's a school teacher from Allentown," I was told.

Unknown or not, Allentown's Henry Messinger was about to become a member of the new Senate Democratic majority, and that was a major political development for Pennsylvania. That bare majority made it possible for the new Shapp administration to resolve not one but two budgets in one sitting; it moved Pennsylvania into the twentieth century with a more modernized tax structure keyed to a state income tax and set the stage for some major public policy successes, not the least of which was a landmark program of property tax relief for Pennsylvania seniors funded by proceeds from a state lottery.

Unlike Joe Ammerman, Henry Messinger most often kept his own counsel. He was not much for speech making or political posturing. His approach to governing was very basic, but very important to the process. "What's the right thing to do?" seemed to be his underlying question to difficult problems. My grandfather used to ask that question a lot when he served on Scranton City Council. I certainly never thought of Henry as a grandfather figure, but his style of public service did remind me of Ivo Carocci in many ways.

Henry was elected Senate majority whip in 1974 because he was rock-solid honest and dependable. Joe Ammerman and he would have made a good leadership team in terms of the public agenda. Senator Messinger would later serve an abbreviated term as Senate majority leader when Tom

Lamb's successor, Tom Nolan of Allegheny County, resigned abruptly in another tax fight with his governor and his caucus. I served as special assistant to the majority leader under Henry Messinger. He was a man of great inner strength and unassuming confidence. He came to the leader's office in a time of great political turmoil within the Democratic caucus. He steered it through turbulent waters, though it was too late to avoid the inevitable political consequences of the misdeeds that had occurred.

When Republican Dick Thornburgh recaptured the governor's office for his party in 1978, and two years later the GOP regained political control of the Senate, Henry was replaced as Democratic floor leader by Ed Zemprelli of Allegheny County. The more politically sensitive members of the caucus thought it was time to have someone more vocal, visible, and rhetorical as their leader. Ed Zemprelli certainly fit that bill. I remember asking Henry before the reorganization vote if he was making calls to members for their support. "I wrote them a letter," he said. "That should be enough." That was vintage Henry Messinger. If his service didn't warrant the support of his caucus, he wasn't going to spend a lot of time worrying about it. He took his defeat for leader in stride. He once said to me, "If I have to worry every time I cast a vote about how it might affect my chances to be re-elected, then I'm in the wrong business and shouldn't be here." Coming from a man who spent the piddling sum of $1,200 (unheard of, even in an era of comparative cheap political cost) to defeat one of the most entrenched and senior Republican members of the Senate, that was not surprising. Henry Messinger was a decent man with few airs about him. The Senate was a much better place for his presence.

Senators Gene Scanlon and Ed Zemprelli

There was something about most of the legislators (not all certainly, but most) from Allegheny County that made them instantly likeable. Perhaps it was because they acted like *real* people—much more human, much more genuine, and certainly with fewer airs about them than their counterparts from Philadelphia.

Pittsburghers seemed to appreciate the fact that they were privileged to serve in state government. Philadelphians, on the other hand, seemed to have an attitude that said, for them, the state capital was just a training ground, a learning station on a route to higher political or professional achievement, usually back in the city. In their view of the world, Philadelphia, as the state's cosmopolitan center, was where the action really was, and where the best of the lot would find their higher calling. A recent illustration: When Governor-elect (and former Philadelphia mayor) Ed Rendell prepared to take his oath of office in January 2002, one Philadelphia newspaper wrote that he was about to be transformed from a "Philadelphia slick" to a "Central Pennsylvania hick." It was written only half tongue-in-cheek, if at all. To Philadelphia elitists, there is Philadelphia and the Philadelphia suburbs, and then the rest of the state, the hinterlands.

Not so with most Pittsburghers. Pittsburgh has always struck me as a *real* city with *real* people. Its culture and its political figures were much like what I came to know in my formative years in Scranton and northeast Pennsylvania. That was my frame of reference and it undoubtedly explains why I related better to Allegheny Countians than I did to Philadelphians. But I generally found Pittsburgh politicians to be comfortable with who they were and where they came from.

Tom Lamb certainly was that way. Two others were Senators Gene Scanlon and Ed Zemprelli. Scanlon was what I called a straight shooter. He was proud to be a Democrat, loyal to his caucus and his leadership. While he usually was a dependable "team player," he always could distinguish between right and wrong; and, when the occasion commanded, he always did. Most important, you also could take his word to the bank.

Scanlon was elected to Tom Lamb's seat in the Senate in 1974 after serving four terms in the House of Representatives. A big man physically, he was congenial, but not one prone to back-slapping or glad-handing. Neither was he given to political machinations that might lead to his own personal advancement.

I wasn't particularly close to Senator Scanlon. But I did work with him on occasion in a staff capacity. One such occasion involved a senator from Fayette County, William Duffield. Duffield had been disbarred by the Pennsylvania Supreme Court for the misappropriation of a client's funds in his private practice of law. The issue before the Senate was whether a private-sector act such as that warranted or required a public-sector reprimand from the Senate as well. Gene Scanlon, because of his reputation for even-handedness, fairness, and objectivity, was named chair of the special Senate Committee to review the matter. Craig Lewis served with him on the committee, and Scanlon asked me to assist in press relation matters.

After a round of public hearings during which Duffield testified in his own defense, the committee ultimately recommended that Duffield be censured for his conduct and stripped of the committee chairmanship and vice-chairmanship he held for the balance of his elected term. It was a very difficult pill for the volatile Duffield to swallow. He was a combative person by nature and it was not in character for him to be passive on the recommendation. But he knew it would serve no purpose to challenge the finding of a committee headed by Gene Scanlon, a senator who was held in high regard by members on both sides of the aisle. The recommendation was adopted by the full Senate. Duffield was censured formally and removed from his committee chairman and vice-chairmanships.

It was on the Duffield committee that Scanlon and Craig Lewis found and formed their common bond. When Scanlon was elected majority whip in 1977 and 1978, and minority whip in 1980 and 1982, Craig Lewis supported him. When Lewis ousted Joe Smith from the Appropriations position in 1982, Scanlon, in turn, supported him. It was a bond that never was broken, even when tested.

Four years later, when Lewis was challenged for the Appropriations post for a second time (by Philadelphia's Vince Fumo), one of his early supporters in the original contest against Joe Smith approached him in advance of the caucus balloting. Senator Bill Lincoln, who had replaced the troubled Duffield in the Senate, advised Craig he was going to contest Gene Scanlon for the minority whip's position and wanted Lewis's support in return for his vote against Fumo. Lewis declined. He told Lincoln that Gene Scanlon had been a friend and ally throughout his tenure in the Senate, and he would not betray that relationship—even if it meant losing Lincoln's vote in the reorganization. Lincoln, on the other hand, was just as straight with Lewis. In that case, he said, he would be voting for Fumo.

Lewis lost to Fumo in that reorganization and Scanlon lost to Lincoln. But they went down together, and neither, that I ever knew, had any second thoughts about their support for each other.

Gene Scanlon fell ill toward the end of his last term in 1994. He died before his term was over. Lewis retired the same year. Though they were different folks from different regions, their political philosophies and political styles brought them together and held them there throughout their service in the chamber. Fate would have them close, though in different ways, their Senate careers together. It seems only fitting that it did.

Ed Zemprelli, on the other hand, was a different study in personality. If you were going to describe Ed Zemprelli in a word, it would probably be "style." Because, above all else, stylish was what he was. He relished in his Italian heritage and his appreciation for fine wine, food, art, Italian opera, and other things cultural. Though he was never particularly aligned, politically or personally, to the senators with whom I tended to most associate, I liked him because his outgoing and gregarious nature made him instantly likeable.

An attorney by trade, he, like so many of his other Allegheny County colleagues, had worked his way up the legislative ladder. He served five years in the state House of Representatives before being advanced by the party elders back home in 1969 to fill a Senate vacancy representing little towns like Clairton and Duquesne and similar bedroom communities outside Pittsburgh.

When the Senate Democratic dissidents decided in 1980 to challenge Henry Messinger for floor leader as they did, "the Zemper" was a logical candidate for them. He was seasoned, smart, and well spoken. He did have a run-in with federal prosecutors a few years before, abuse of office allegations, as I recall. But the investigation failed to substantiate any wrongdoing, and he was exonerated. It was the only transparent blemish on his service in the General Assembly. He tended to indulge more than most in the restaurant scene and nightlife of Harrisburg. But that certainly not a disqualification for a leadership position.

I was completely in the Messinger camp, though that did not translate into caucus votes for Henry. But I also could understand the rationale to the Zemprelli candidacy. In many ways, his election was a preferred choice given the political position of the Senate Democratic caucus. Zemp was as expressive as Henry was stolid, and as a minority party, the caucus needed someone who could represent them rhetorically both on the floor and in the press. Zemp qualified on both counts.

My issue with him was that most of his support came from essentially the same group of Democratic senators who by their careless conduct had caused the loss of the political majority in the first place. I was still in charge of the Democratic press office though my title on Henry Messinger's staff was special assistant to the majority leader. When Zemprelli defeated Messinger, he and I had to confront a couple of immediate questions: Would I fit in a Zemprelli staff structure; where might that be, and was it right for either of us?

Senator Zemprelli apparently had the same concern. Shortly after his election, he approached me in a Capitol corridor. "What," he wanted to know, "did Joe Smith [the Philadelphia Joe Smith who Craig Lewis would challenge for the Appropriations Committee minority chairmanship two years later] mean when he told me to take a look at the Press Office operation?"

I knew the answer immediately. "He probably wants me out of there. He and I don't work on the same wavelengths." I offered to explore other potential opportunities in Senate staff structure if that would make his transition to the leader's office less complicated. He told me not to do anything until he got back to me.

I appreciated the exchange. Zemprelli certainly was under no obligation to broach the subject with me. He could hire and fire his staff at will, and I was one of those "at-will" staffers. Nor had I worked particularly closely with him prior to this point. A couple of times during the federal grand jury inquiry, he asked for my advice in how to handle press inquiries, which I gave without hesitation or reservation. That was about it. I was pleased for him when, after a couple of difficult years of investigative scrutiny, he finally received a letter informing him he was no longer a target of the prosecutors. It was a very difficult period for him personally; I can only imagine how hard it was on his wife and his daughter.

My brief corridor encounter with Zemp persuaded me that it was probably time to move on. That's when Lewis and I discussed my joining his staff. The deal was secured and I told Zemp about my intentions. I did, however, offer to assist him in recruiting his leadership staff, if he wished. Prior to that point, as chairman of the Senate Banking Committee, Zemprelli had no personal staff support except for his loyal secretary, Charlotte.

I did, in fact, introduce him to his ultimate choice for chief of staff, Mike McLaughlin. McLaughlin had served as press secretary to Milton Shapp in the final years of that administration. He came from an active political family in Philadelphia. His brother, Joe, had served as press officer/director of communications to the House Democratic caucus while I served in the same capacity for the Senate Democrats. Mike was a seasoned hand in Harrisburg, and, if he and Zemp hit it off, could jump-start the leader's staff organization with no difficulty. They did. Mike was hired. And I could move on to other Senate responsibilities without leaving Zemprelli in a lurch, which I really didn't want to do.

Zemprelli was still serving as Democratic Senate minority leader when the Casey administration took office in 1987. My direct contact with him was renewed when I joined the Casey administration as deputy secretary for legislative affairs. It was an easy reconnection to make.

What I remember most about Senator Zemprelli was personal. My dad, Roy, died in 1985 while I was serving as director of government affairs for the State System of Higher Education. I had been two years removed from the Senate by this time. One of the notes of condolence I received came unsolicited and unexpected. It was from Ed Zemprelli. I don't even know how he came to know of my father's passing. But it was a thoughtful gesture on his part. I appreciated it very much, and I never forgot it.

Buddy Cianfrani

Name me one profession—business, entertainment, athletics—that doesn't have its share of lovable rogues. Politics certainly is no different. Okay, perhaps *rogue* is too esoteric a word to apply to a street-wise guy like Philadelphia's Henry "Buddy" Cianfrani. But he certainly was roguish. And if not lovable, he certainly was likable. And I confess up front: I liked Buddy Cianfrani.

Buddy, too, had style. But it came naturally, it was not acquired for show. Gruff, graveled-voice, a combat U.S. Army Ranger with the famed Merrill's Marauders who also did a little boxing in his early years, Cianfrani was the consummate Philadelphia pol. His roots and his habits ran deep in South Philadelphia politics, and he parlayed his family's political connections and his innate street smarts into seats first in the state House of Representatives and then the Pennsylvania Senate. He was, in Philadelphia and the State capital, what in politics you call a "player."

The most admirable trait about Buddy Cianfrani, at least from my distant view, was that he never pretended to be anything other than who and what he was. He was straight talking. He was engaging. He was cocky without being arrogant. And once given, he was good to his word. If you were in a political fight, you wanted Buddy in the foxhole with you.

Buddy also had what the ladies call "sex appeal." I thought that strange because he was prematurely bald, only of medium stature, and of just average features. But he exuded an electric magnetism about him that women apparently found exciting and attractive. "That's one sexy man," one lady whose opinion on such matters I respected told me. Unfortunately, it was his relationship with women that led to his downfall. And, inadvertently, one of the most important women in his life—a woman he ultimately married—paid a very heavy price for her association with him.

I would never claim to have been close to Buddy. Buddy didn't need someone like me to attract the considerable publicity he did. We ran in different circles, no question. But there were two Cianfrani stories to which I was personal witness that are worth relating here.

The first was a serious matter. It occurred early in my tenure as press secretary to the Senate Democratic Caucus in the 1970s. As was my habit, I arrived at my third-floor office in the Senate wing of the Capitol about 8:30 A.M. I was surprised, and more than curious, to find two calls from Senate Appropriations Chairman Ben Donolow awaiting me, even at that early hour. Donolow, also of Philadelphia, was one of Buddy's mentors in the ways of the Senate. But, as Philadelphians in the Senate were wont to do, he kept his counsel pretty much to himself and seldom called on me (or the other Senate leadership, for that matter) for assistance. Very early into the Democratic reign in the Senate, for example, he called a press conference on the Shapp budget without bothering to advise either Senator Murray or

Senator Lamb of his intention, if only as a courtesy. They had to call me to learn what I knew. But I knew nothing. So when Ben Donolow made two very early calls to me that morning, it set me to wondering what in the world this was about.

I immediately walked the few short steps it took to reach the Appropriations Committee suite of offices. "He's waiting for you," Donolow's receptionist said as I entered. I went right in to the chairman's private office where I found two people inside. One, of course, was Donolow, a tiny man, prim and nattily dressed as always. He was seated behind his desk. The other person was Buddy, puffing his always-present cigarette and pacing about as he often did. Buddy wasn't one much for sitting.

"Have you seen the *Inquirer*?" Donolow asked me almost immediately. I had to confess I hadn't since I came right over when I found his call waiting.

"Read this," he said handing me the paper.

"Good mornings begin with the *Inquirer*" was the paper's slogan. But this was not a good morning for Henry Cianfrani. Buddy had been accused by a Philadelphia area woman of having paid for her abortion. As I recall, accompanying the front-page story were photos of a canceled check with Buddy's signature, and medical records from her doctor's office.

This was big time news for a couple of reasons. Abortion as a political issue had not reached the emotional crescendo of the 1980s and '90s, but it still was an attention-getter. An abortion involving as prominent a political figure as Buddy Cianfrani, someone who usually voted against the emerging feminist agenda on family planning social issues, only doubled the news value.

"Does this go away on its own, or do we have to answer it?" Donolow wanted to know.

"This may go away in couple of days," I responded. "But even if it does, if it isn't answered, people will always believe it's true, and it'll be too late to refute it later. I'd answer it immediately." I never asked whether the charges were true or not.

With that, Donolow dismissed me as he reached for the telephone on his desk. As I was walking out, I heard him admonish Buddy: "Jesus, Buddy, didn't your father ever teach you to deal only in cash?"

Buddy replied, "Ben, she told me she needed the money to buy a bus ticket to visit her mother in Ohio."

As I reached the door of Donolow's office, I heard him bark into the phone: "I need to know everything about her, and I need to know it soon."

It turns out Donolow, in private life a very successful defense lawyer, was talking to one of his investigators in Philadelphia. This investigator did his work very well and very quickly. By the time the Senate went into session about midday, Donolow had garnered enough critical information about Cianfrani's accuser as to challenge her character and her veracity. He led the assault on the Senate floor in a special order of business.

When he finished, the other members of the Philadelphia delegation rose individually to testify about their personal and political relationship with Buddy. This was particularly problematic for one Philadelphian, Senator Lou Hill. Hill, a former Marine, was as straight-laced as Buddy was a corner-cutter. Buddy was from the streets of South Philadelphia; Hill was a patrician from the city's Society Hill section. Though they came from the same city, they were worlds apart politically and personally. Buddy loved to play the game of politics. Hill, the stepson of the renowned Philadelphia reformer Richardson Dilworth, was straight and narrow. All ears in the Senate perked to hear what Senator Hill would have to say about his Senate colleague.

Hill was brief and to the point. "In all the years I've been associated in this Senate with Senator Cianfrani, I've never known him to tell me a falsehood," Senator Hill testified. With that, he sat down. It was, I thought, very skillfully done.

Throughout the discourse, Buddy paced very prominently about the Senate floor. I seem to remember him signaling his Philadelphia colleagues when it was their turn to rise to his defense. He wasn't about to go in hiding. He puffed and he paced in his typical mano-a-mano style. That was Buddy. What you saw was what you got. It was a large part of what endeared him to so many people on both sides of the aisle.

My second lasting memory of Buddy up close and personal came in the mid-'70s during the second major budget fight of the Shapp administration. Ben Donolow had died unexpectedly and Buddy had replaced him as Appropriations chairman.

The Democrats learned very early in the process that this stalemate was not going to be resolved quickly or easily. House Republican Appropriations Chairman Jack Seltzer of Lebanon County had walked into the first meeting of the joint House/Senate Budget Conference Committee, took off his jacket, sat down, and served notice: "Fellas," he said, "I'm ready to sit here until I get this settled the way I want." Since Seltzer's vote was essential to any conference committee agreement, that was as close as one gets to drawing a line in the sand with no sand at hand. It certainly had "deadlock" written all over it. And deadlocked the process was.

As days passed into weeks and weeks passed into months, the stalemate showed no signs of ending. Tempers in the Senate Democratic Caucus started to fray and patience was wearing very thin. At one caucus where the members were briefed, Senator Jeanette Reibman of Northampton County stood up in a moment of frustration, looked at Senators Murray and Cianfrani, and exhorted, "Marty, we should take the conferees, put them in a room, lock them up and not let them out until they get this thing settled."

Buddy, who was renowned for his distaste of staying overnight in Harrisburg, never missed a beat. "Jeanette," he responded in that gravel voice of his, "With all due respect. If anybody's going to lock me into a room, I'm going to pick my roommates and they're not going to be the conferees." It was Buddy at his best.

Buddy ran afoul of the federal government in the late 1970s. He was charged with mail fraud related to padding the Senate payroll with at least two ghost employees. One of the suspect employees was reputed to be his "significant other" of the moment; the other was her sister. Their compensation was peanuts by any standards, in the neighborhood of $12,000, as I recall. But they received their checks by mail, hence the mail-fraud charges. Buddy ultimately resigned from the Senate and accepted a negotiated plea from the federal government. He did his time in the federal minimum-security prison at Allenwood, about a two-hour drive from Harrisburg. He took his medicine and he didn't take anyone down with him. That was Buddy Cianfrani as well.

There was, however, one inadvertent victim to this saga. As Buddy's problems started to surface publicly, the *Philadelphia Inquirer* assigned a woman reporter by the name of Laura Foreman to cover his travails. Somewhere in the process, the two began to keep company. By the time Buddy had resigned and began to serve his sentence, Foreman had moved on to the *New York Times*. However, when her relationship with one of her news subjects, as controversial a news subject as Buddy Cianfrani, came to the *Times'* attention, she was forced to resign. She and Buddy ultimately married, and the marriage was still in place at the time of Buddy's death in 2002.

Buddy had re-established himself as a player in Philadelphia politics after his sentence was served. He was a consigliore and a connection of sorts to political candidates whose fortunes needed help in the city's Byzantine political culture and structure. As fate would have it, he suffered the stroke that ultimately claimed his life on primary election day in 2002. One might say he died with his boots on.

My take on Buddy Cianfrani is very fundamental. There is, I know, no way to condone some of Buddy's political conduct. But I also know this. He was one of the most engaging personalities I encountered in my many years in Harrisburg. Buddy was always Buddy, unadulterated and unadorned.

Our paths rarely crossed after he left the Senate—a chance encounter or two in the Capitol during one of his visits. Our association was such that I would never presume to consider myself Buddy's buddy; nor would he ever have considered me in that context. But his Italian heritage and his pure unembellished élan certainly captured my fancy from afar. As I said at the beginning, I liked Buddy for who he was. I had a lot of company.

Chapter 8

★★★★★★★

Legislative Reorganizations and Strange Bedfellows

American editor and essayist Charles Dudley Warner had it exactly right. Politics makes for strange bedfellows, he opined over a century ago. It certainly does. No more so, perhaps, than in contested reorganizations of the Pennsylvania legislative caucuses where the machinations that come into play in contests for leadership positions would make even Machiavelli proud.

I was involved in four contested reorganizations of note. The first I covered as a reporter for the *Philadelphia Inquirer*. For the second I was an interested though unaligned press secretary to the Senate of Pennsylvania Democratic caucus, and for the final two I was serving as chief of staff for Senator H. Craig Lewis, ranking Democratic member of the Senate Appropriations Committee. Each was different in its own way. Each involved peculiar activities and strange alliances worth recounting here if only for the record.

1970: Senate Democrats Organize as a Majority

When the Senate Democrats assembled after the 1970 legislative elections to select its leadership for the 1971–72 session of the Pennsylvania General Assembly, they met for only the second time in the twentieth century (1937 being the other) as the true majority party of the chamber. They had true political control, control in the ability to organize the standing committees, control of the committee process itself, and control of the agenda and the timeline to pass legislation on the party's own initiative. It was a new experience for most of the Democratic members.

It was preordained early that Senator Murray, the senior Democratic member, was going to be elected Senate President Pro Tempore, the ranking office of the chamber. The real decision the caucus had to make was who would be elected Senate majority leader, the leader who directs the flow of business on the Senate floor.

Murray and Shapp's lieutenant governor-elect, Ernest P. Kline (the retiring Democratic floor leader), aligned themselves behind congenial Tom

Lamb of Allegheny County. The eight-member Philadelphia delegation, always a power in such matters if only by virtue of their sheer numbers, had other ideas. It usually did.

Philadelphia mayor James Tate, one of the top two or three Democratic political powers in the state at the time, made noises from City Hall that he was supporting Philadelphia's own, the crafty Benjamin Donolow, for the floor leader's position. It appeared a significant reorganization battle was looming.

Because of the Philadelphia stakes in the reorganization, the *Inquirer* took a major interest, and I was assigned to cover it—blow by blow, if possible. I came to know Marty Murray in my prior reportorial life with the Associated Press, and I suppose, in truth, my coal-region heritage had me rooting sentimentally and privately for him to whip Mayor Tate in this reorganization contest. But, fundamentally, reporters are not supposed to take sides in such matters. So it was really not material to me who won. Given the Philadelphia role in the reorganization meeting, I had a good story brewing either way.

Mayor Tate personally traveled to Harrisburg the day of the reorganization meeting to address the Democratic caucus. While that was obviously significant, it was not unusual in itself. In fact, it was routine at the time for the political powers of both the state Democratic and Republican parties to appear before the four legislative caucuses to tell the members who their leaders would be for the new session. In those days, the rank-and-file were so dependent on the Party leadership for their political existence and survival that there were few if any objectors.

So while Tate's presence wasn't necessarily unusual for the era, it certainly added a noteworthy dimension to the drama of the political events unfolding that day, a struggle that on the surface pitted the powerful Democratic mayor of Philadelphia against the Democratic lieutenant governor-elect and the senior Democratic member of the Pennsylvania Senate. With Donolow from Philadelphia and Lamb from Pittsburgh, the reorganization also had the elements of a Pittsburgh versus Philadelphia intraparty fight. Things could get pretty interesting in a number of ways.

Marty Murray was never one to back away from a political fight. But neither was he one to engage in so public an internecine warfare. His preference in most matters of this sort was to settle the issue peacefully and, if at all possible, in private. There was no way of knowing exactly how many calls were exchanged between Philadelphia and Harrisburg before reorganization day. But there certainly were many. What's more, the governor-elect appeared to be sitting this one out in spite of his close ties to Philadelphia if only by virtue of his Montgomery County residency. Shapp, it appeared, had decided to let Ernie Kline, a veteran of Senate reorganizations, take the lead for the new administration in this main event.

As so often happens in such cases, the fight never lived up to its billing. Pay-per-view subscribers would have been disappointed. The vote for majority leader took only one ballot. Tom Lamb was elected without opposition. Murray emerged from the closed caucus to announce the result and praise Mayor Tate for his political statesmanship in averting a damaging intraparty fight on the advent of a new Democratic state administration and Senate Democratic majority. And, oh yes, Murray added: Ben Donolow would be named chairman of the Senate Appropriations Committee.

In many ways, this was even a more important position than floor leader because of the commanding role the Appropriations chairman plays in preparation and enactment of the annual state budget. With a new Democratic governor, and a Democratic House and Democratic Senate, Donolow would be a major player in determining the spending priorities of state government for at least the next two years. Donolow was a good Democrat, but he was a Philadelphian first. With him as chair of the Appropriations Committee, Philadelphia and Mayor Tate had their hands directly on the state purse strings. In a sense, they had control of the checkbook, always a priority in matters political. Philadelphia's interests were fully protected in a way that, to the city, was even more important than who served as Senate majority leader directing the flow of business on the Senate floor.

The press corps, myself included, failed to grasp the point immediately. Once again, we were not as perceptive as we presumed ourselves to be. The general story line the next day, certainly in the *Inquirer*, was that the city had been thwarted in its efforts to name the Senate majority leader and had to settle (almost as a consolation prize) with the Appropriations chairmanship. The storyline missed the point.

The full reach of the concessions Tate obtained in that reorganization began to unfold days later when Senator Murray announced other committee chairmanships (filled by appointment rather than election). Chairman of the tax-writing Senate Finance Committee: Henry Cianfrani of Philadelphia. Chairman of the highways building, mass transit financing Senate Transportation Committee: Herb McGlinchey of Philadelphia.

Philadelphia had used the Donolow candidacy for majority leader as a straw man to lay claim to the three most important committee chairmanships in the Senate: Appropriations, Finance, and Transportation. (Four other Philadelphians were named committee chairs. Not bad for a day's work, by any standard.) Murray and the Senate Democrats, meanwhile, elected themselves a rational and respected voice of the party in Tom Lamb, one who had a broader political view of the world than simply Philadelphia's stake. It was a quite acceptable negotiated settlement from both perspectives. But my press corps colleagues and I were slow to grasp the full implications of what had transpired that day. It was not one of our finer reportorial moments. I, at least, learned a good lesson. In politics, things are not always as they seem to be.

1974: A Fight for Majority Leader That Actually Was a Fight

When Tom Lamb retired in 1974, his departure confronted the Senate Democratic caucus with its most serious reorganization decision in four years—who would replace him. The stakes were a little higher this time because the November elections had been very good again to the party. Pennsylvania Democrats not only retained political control of the chamber, but their majority grew to 30–20. As political riches go, this was an unheard-of alignment for the time, one that is probably never achievable for this party in this state again. But the first consequential business with this unprecedented political prosperity was to select a new Senate Democratic floor leader for the 1975–76 session.

By this time I had left the *Philadelphia Inquirer* and signed on as press secretary to the Senate Democratic Caucus. Lamb's retirement came as no surprise since he had shared his intentions with any number of people over the course of his tenure. The question was who from Allegheny County or elsewhere would emerge to replace him. And in this pre-reorganization maneuvering, Senator Murray found himself at odds with the two most powerful delegations in his caucus—Philadelphia and Pittsburgh.

There was no pre-eminent favorite to replace Lamb but western Pennsylvania had, by this point in time, come to regard the floor leader's position as its domain. Allegheny County's John Devlin and Beaver County's Ernie Kline had preceded Lamb as floor leader. Philadelphia, with the three most powerful committee chairmanships under its control, had no inclination to challenge that arrangement.

The one western senator who, initially, seemed to lay out the most claim to the leader's job was Frank Mazzei of Pittsburgh. It was, to many, an unlikely candidacy for a number of reasons. The floor leader's position was, by its very nature, high profile and high visibility. Frank Mazzei, who was elected to the Senate in 1967 filling a vacancy created by John Devlin's death, was much more a back-room operator. He clearly lacked Lamb's oratorical and public relations skills. But he related in his quiet, private, one-on-one way very well with most other members of the caucus, and he was seasoned politically. What's more, he was perceptive enough to recognize his personal limitations and wise enough to know he needed to have good people around him. That's what he did when he authored and floor managed Senate approval and ultimate enactment of the Pennsylvania lottery into law in 1972. (A quarter of a century later, the lottery Frank Mazzei fathered was providing $560 million annually in benefits to senior citizens.) All things being equal, no one—not even Senator Murray—was likely to challenge his claim on the majority leader's position.

But all things weren't equal. Frank Mazzei had a considerable obstacle in his path. His name was Richard L. Thornburgh, an aggressive U.S. Attorney from western Pennsylvania. Thornburgh had just begun to earn himself a fast-growing reputation as a crime-fighting, corruption-busting prosecutor. And by 1974, Richard Thornburgh had Frank Mazzei in his sights.

The target was a kickback scheme in which Mazzei was allegedly involved. He ultimately was convicted in federal court and was sentenced to a medium-security federal prison. Thornburgh's pursuit of Frank Mazzei was fairly common knowledge among the political community and the press. While criminal investigations of this sort theoretically were to be confidential, prosecutors throughout the country have never been shy about this kind of publicity. And Richard Thornburgh was not a shy man.

The fact that the Thornburgh probe was a matter of public record took Mazzei out of the running for the leader's position. The question was, who would emerge to replace him.

Mazzei marshaled his home-base support and formed a coalition with Philadelphia. Together, the two largest delegations in the Senate Democratic caucus joined forces behind a surrogate candidate from Allegheny County named Tom Nolan. Nolan was an electric personality, at one and the same time outspoken, impulsive, combative, and unpredictable, true to his roots in the organized labor movement in western Pennsylvania.

Nolan won his Senate seat in 1971 as an antispending, antitax political maverick, a posture that played well in the blue-collar communities of McKees Rocks and others that he represented outside the city of Pittsburgh.

Nolan was one of the few Senate Democrats to oppose the tax program Milton Shapp had to enact to balance the 1970 and 1971 state budgets. Now here he was, an antigovernment Democrat, yet a viable candidate seeking to lead an activist-inclined Democratic caucus under an even more activist Democratic governor. Strange bedfellows, indeed. Even Charles Dudley Warner might have been surprised at this turn of events.

Nolan was as combustible a personality as he was unpredictable and outspoken. He had a hair-trigger temper and a simplified view of the world: Either you were for him or you were against him. And that was pretty much the world's view of him. Either you liked him or you didn't. It was hard to be neutral where Tom Nolan was concerned. Whether Frank Mazzei liked Nolan or not was not the question, however. He obviously trusted him enough to support him as his surrogate for leader.

Philadelphia city chairman Pete Camiel, after receiving certain assurances from Nolan (and probably Mazzei) on conditions like committee chairmanships and other matters (which ultimately involved payroll), lined the bulk of the Philadelphia delegation behind Nolan's candidacy. Lou Hill may have been the lone exception. Others, as events unfolded, would go along, but only most reluctantly.

Murray, if he was anything, was a good judge of political character. He understood instinctively that the temperamental Nolan as floor leader was trouble for his caucus, his governor, and his party. Murray's problem was that he had no one in Tom Lamb's mold to offer as a clear-cut alternative to Nolan. To be sure, there were one or two eager beavers among the younger members of the Senate who approached Murray for his support. But Murray wasn't comfortable that they were seasoned enough or heavy enough politically to be acceptable to the majority of the caucus. Ultimately, he settled on Senator Joe Ammerman as his candidate against Nolan.

Ammerman and Nolan were members of the same freshman class of 1971. The problem was that Ammerman was as prone to be as electric and outspoken as Nolan. He was not just a bull in the china shop; he could be a bull and a bear at the same time. Joe Ammerman would have won no degree from the U.S. Foreign Service school of niceties.

But Ammerman was this: He was clean politically (a former district attorney); he had character; he was smart, he was committed to sound public policy, and in his plain-spoken country way, he could more than hold his own in fulfilling the public role of Senate majority leader. He also understood that an effective leader for his party had to serve a greater role than just his narrow view of the world. Murray trusted Ammerman to be loyal to his caucus, his party, and his party's agenda. That's why he went with him, I'm sure.

I was not directly involved in the politics of the reorganization. As press secretary to the Democratic caucus, my loyalty to Marty Murray and the elected leadership was clear to all. My personal preference was Joe Ammerman for all the same reasons Murray gravitated to his candidacy—integrity, strength of character, conviction, and a commitment to sound public policy.

But, frankly, except for one or two conversations with individual members of the caucus, my opinion was not sought out. I was not asked by either Senator Murray or Ammerman to campaign with any individual members, nor did I presume to do so gratuitously.

Reorganization day arrived and, by everyone's count, the vote was going to be close, the outcome still unpredictable. It was. It took several secret ballots—as many as four, maybe five—for the winner to be determined. Ammerman, I was told, always was ahead in the tally, but never received the necessary majority because each ballot contained three or four abstentions.

As the event was recounted to me, after the fourth ballot—or was it the third?—Ammerman finished just one vote shy of the necessary majority. Senator Lou Coppersmith of Cambria County saddled up to Murray and asked for a recess so the two could talk privately.

Murray recessed the meeting and went to his office, where Coppersmith slipped in discreetly to talk with him. Coppersmith acknowledged to Murray that he was one of the abstentions in the balloting. He said he wanted to hire his son on the staff of the Public Health and Welfare Committee he chaired. He wanted Murray's assurances that the leadership would not object.

"You dumb son-of-a-bitch," Murray later recalled replying. "Is that all you wanted? If you had told me that before the meeting, we'd have had this wrapped up hours ago. Let's go in and settle this."

Murray quickly reconvened the meeting, confident that the next ballot would result in a victor. He was right about that. But it was not the outcome he anticipated. While he was meeting with Coppersmith, the Mazzei-Nolan forces went on a counteroffensive of their own, ably assisted by Buddy Cianfrani.

Mazzei and Cianfrani were reported to have strategically placed themselves around the conference tables in the majority Caucus Room where the balloting was taking place. Buddy was at the same table where two black members from Philadelphia, Herb Arlene and Freeman Hankins, sat. Nolan was not exactly an equal-opportunity kind of politician, and he was outspoken on the subject of public welfare reform. Arlene and Hankins understandably were not enthusiastic about him representing their views on the Senate floor. They immediately were suspected of being two of the abstentions.

"We're all friends, here," Buddy was reported to have said as the balloting began. "Here's my vote," he smiled as he flashed his ballot. "Let's see yours." The tactic worked, at least with Arlene and Hankins. They showed themselves to be two Nolan votes.

Mazzei and Nolan, meanwhile, were reported to have worked their table in a similar if not identical fashion, with the same success. There were no more holdouts. Nolan achieved the majority. He was the new floor leader of the Senate Democratic caucus. I wasn't satisfied with the result. Little did I or anyone else in the caucus know at the time that Lou Coppersmith's abstention would lead in just a couple of years to the downfall of the Democratic majority under Tom Nolan's leadership.

I remained in the press secretary position after Nolan's election. I had not pursued any other options, so it wasn't much of a calculated decision on my part. But where I had quickly aligned and identified myself as a member of Tom Lamb's staff, I kept my distance from Nolan. His style wasn't mine; mine wasn't his. I concentrated on serving the needs of the members of the caucus. Unless specifically called upon, I left the activities of the majority leader's office to Nolan's personal staff.

It was not the most pleasant of times for me, professionally. At one point in his second term as leader, Nolan ordered me to dismiss a member of my press office staff, ostensibly for personnel cost-cutting purposes. I knew the order was not directed at her, but, by indirection, at me. I prepared a letter of resignation and shared my intention with Senator Murray. He was quick to advise me against it. "You have what, a wife and three, four children?" he counseled me in that common sense way of his. "Never leave a job unless you have a job," he said. It was good advice.

I never submitted the letter. Instead, I spent the next two weeks trying to find a place for the innocent staffer who was taking the blow. Fortunately, the new Office of Consumer Advocate just had been established thanks to the Kury Report on the Public Utility Commission. The Advocate, a Harrisburg attorney by the name of Mark Widoff, was in the initial stages of hiring a staff. I knew him well enough to recommend my dismissed staff member to him. He interviewed her and hired her. I was relieved that one of my staff members wasn't victimized innocently by the political high jinks at play within the majority leader's office.

The incident was enough motivation, however, for me to conclude I would never be compatible with Tom Nolan and his methods. I began (discreetly but aggressively) to explore other possible staff options within the Senate when Nolan suddenly resigned as majority leader in 1977. His tenure as the voice and face of the Democratic caucus became untenable when he, again, was an outspoken opponent of another budget and tax program advanced by Governor Shapp. Under considerable pressure from the caucus to relent, Nolan chose to step down instead. Henry Messinger, then the majority whip, replaced him for the balance of the session. I remained on Messinger's staff. He was a decent, honest, honorable man. It was a privilege to be associated with him professionally.

1980: The First Appropriations Committee Fight

Every reorganization within the legislative caucuses presents its very own unique set of circumstances. There are no set formulas to apply, very few precedents to guide. This is particularly true when an incumbent caucus officer is challenged by a member of the rank-and-file. In most cases, the caucus leadership, if they've been effective and choose to get involved, can prevail in favor of the incumbent. Sometimes they do not.

This was the case in 1980 when Craig Lewis ousted Philadelphia's Joe Smith as minority chairman of the Senate Appropriations Committee. Smith had replaced Buddy Cianfrani as the minority chair when Buddy was forced to resign in 1977 in the wake of his payroll-padding plea. Joe Smith may have been from Philadelphia but he was no Buddy Cianfrani—or Ben Donolow, for that matter. His standard modus operandi was to keep fiscal information and strategies very, very much to himself—so much so that he became known as "Whispering Smith" to many members of the caucus.

His old-school style rankled a lot of the newer members of the Senate. Senators like Fayette County's Bill Lincoln and Philadelphia's Jim Lloyd were principal among them. It was Lincoln, I believe, who was, if not the first, certainly among the first to approach Lewis about challenging Smith for the Appropriations post. Others, while not drivers behind the challenge, supported it nonetheless. And new freshmen like Senator-elect Mark Singel of Johnstown were wooed to Lewis's corner very aggressively—and with some success.

Contested caucus elections are very much like political campaigns for the inside maneuvering and horse-trading that goes on. But on occasion, the issue is very fundamental. This was one of those occasions. Those who encouraged Lewis to make the run, and those who ultimately supported him, really had only one objective in mind. They believed the Democratic Party in the Senate had to present a more substantive and aggressive alternative to the policies and priorities of the Senate Republican majority and the Republican Thornburgh administration. They also wanted someone who could articulate the case in public forums like the Senate floor and the press.

Smith, an insular politician, could not. Lewis could. So the choice was very clear.

It was the very reason the caucus had replaced very quiet but steady Henry Messinger as floor leader two years earlier with outgoing, rhetorical Ed Zemprelli. And, now, it was the principal argument for Lewis to replace Joe Smith.

Going into the reorganization, the vote was thought to be close, perhaps closer than it should have been. Conventional wisdom held that if the leadership supported Smith, the challenge would be turned aside. Conventional wisdom was wrong.

Lewis won by a narrow margin—a vote or two, as I recall. It's always been questionable in my mind how energetically the leadership worked the members on Smith's behalf. Both Senators Murray and Zemprelli ostensibly were committed to Smith. But if they were applying the traditional pressures available to leadership—such as committee assignments, office space, staffing—we in Lewis's camp certainly didn't hear about it. And we most certainly would have.

Lewis calculated that every critical vote would have to break his way for him to win. In a secret ballot, each did. He was the new Democratic chair of the Senate Appropriations Committee. His campaign to win a majority in the caucus was very much a behind-the-scenes effort. Reorganization campaigns are never won by press release. It also was a very intense internal political struggle that proved good training for what was to come. Two more challenges, this time to Lewis's incumbency, would follow.

1982: Having Been Won, It Was Worth Fighting to Keep

No sooner had Lewis been installed as minority appropriations chairman than it became very clear that he would be challenged at the reorganization two years hence by the very formidable person of Vincent Fumo, also of Philadelphia. Fumo had been elected to Buddy Cianfrani's seat in the Senate from South Philadelphia and had been a key Joe Smith ally in the Lewis challenge. When Smith lost, Fumo set out almost immediately to reclaim the Appropriations position for Philadelphia (and, not so coincidentally, for himself). His intentions were common knowledge within the Democratic caucus.

This time, I was not just the interested bystander I had been in prior caucus reorganizations. I viewed the contest with Fumo to be more than just an election between two political personalities with different political styles and objectives. I viewed it to be a test of whether good job performance could be vindicated and rewarded in a political environment. If Lewis put in place a staff that served the Democratic caucus professionally, consistently, competently, and faithfully, then this contest would tell us how much job performance and delivering on a promise truly mattered.

All considerations being equal, Fumo should not have been a serious challenge to Lewis. He was new to the Senate. He had been under a serious legal cloud. As patronage czar for the Philadelphia Democratic City Committee, he was a codefendant in a federal court trial on charges of patronage abuses in Tom Nolan's majority leader's office. Senator Fumo was smart and as politically savvy (some might say cunning) as any member of the Senate. But he also was a creature of the Philadelphia political system. His challenge to Lewis would be a transparent power play, as much for himself as for his city. Nor had he the time to sufficiently establish his legislative credentials, articulate his public policy priorities, or even put his indisputable political skills on display in the legislative process for goals that exceeded his narrow, personal political interests. In short, he had yet to earn the trust of the Senate Democratic members. That alone should have minimized his threat.

But in politics, particularly in Democratic politics, more particularly in Philadelphia Democratic politics, it was understood that not all things are equal. When the 1984 reorganization rolled around, everyone accepted the reality that with Philadelphian Fumo in it, this would be a closely contested challenge once again. The prospect was very real that just the reach of Philadelphia's political influence in a twenty-three-member minority caucus could construct a coalition large enough to put Fumo in the Appropriations chair.

That it never happened largely was due to the political courage and conviction of another young Democratic senator from Philadelphia. Jim Lloyd came from a rock-solid Philadelphia rowhouse neighborhood in the Northeast section of the city. A graduate of St. Joseph's College, Jim ran the family's sporting goods business in private life before he was elected to the Senate. He had a lovely wife and two handsome young sons. Elected to the Senate in 1979, he and Lewis were age peers. They also were soulmates philosophically, politically, and personally.

Jim Lloyd was at the time a bright light on the Pennsylvania political scene in so many ways. He had a strong commitment to public service on behalf of others. He held strong public policy convictions and was true to them and to the district he represented in the Senate with an equally strong sense of public purpose. He, as much as any single legislator, persistently and successfully badgered a recalcitrant Republican Thornburgh administration into supporting an expansion of the Pennsylvania lottery to provide prescription drugs for senior citizens. His political future seemed very promising. He, in fact, did run a creditable though unsuccessful campaign as Congressman Allen Ertel's running mate for lieutenant governor in the 1982 gubernatorial race against Republican incumbent Richard Thornburgh.

Jim was one of those young mavericks who supported Lewis in his challenge of Joe Smith two years earlier. I'm certain he must have been under a ton of pressure from Philadelphia politicos then. And he certainly was under a ton of political pressure now to break with Lewis and support Fumo. But he never wavered. It was to cost him politically, as we shall learn, but he stayed solid again in the Lewis corner.

Because he did, Jim made it possible for Joe Rocks, another young, ambitious Philadelphia senator, to back Lewis as well. Where Jim Lloyd was strong and confident in his convictions, Rocks was more of a hold-your-finger-to-the-wind-to-test-how-events-are-going kind of politician. He is the only member in the history of the General Assembly to have served in all four legislative caucuses. He was a Republican when first elected to the House; he later converted to Democrat. He was a Democrat when first elected to the Senate; he later converted to Republican. If you get a picture of a political opportunist, you got the picture.

Because Lloyd was committed to Lewis, Rocks had the political cover he needed to oppose Fumo. In my view, Rocks's opposition to Fumo had more to do with competing political aspirations than any other single factor. The higher Fumo rose in the ranks of the Senate, the less of a role there would be for Rocks to play. For the moment, he was a Lewis vote and, motives aside, Lewis took his votes as he could find them.

With the Philadelphia delegation split, the pressures on other Democratic senators to join the traditional Philadelphia-based coalition in support of Fumo were relieved considerably., Essentially, they were free to vote as they saw fit. With two Philadelphia senators in opposition to one of their own, there was no price of any serious political consequence for non-Philadelphia senators to pay if they supported Lewis.

Left to their own devices in a secret ballot, they did. Lewis won by a three- or four-vote margin among the twenty-three Democratic senators who participated in the reorganization. The bloc that had formed in the Lewis-Smith contest two years earlier remained essentially intact in the Lewis-Fumo faceoff.

From a performance perspective, Lewis's victory certainly was testimony to the good work he and his staff had done with the Appropriations Committee and the value the members of the caucus placed on that effort. From a political perspective, it was one of the rare public defeats Fumo suffered. He did not take it in good form.

We were told by a staff witness that after the reorganization vote, he stormed back to his office and angrily began slamming things around on his desk. Somehow he had managed to gather the ballots used in the election and began reviewing them, one by one, to match handwriting to individual votes. Apparently, he believed he had commitments from members who did not vote for him as promised. It certainly wasn't an error-free process but he had to satisfy himself on this point. One senator, who shall remain nameless because I have no way of verifying this first-hand, was reported to have gone to Fumo's office and voluntarily provided a sample of his handwriting to affirm he did, in fact, keep his commitment to him.

The seeds of a second Fumo challenge two years hence were planted right there in Fumo's office at that very moment. That Fumo intended to challenge Lewis again was not in itself surprising. That he began to lay out his strategy in earnest within minutes of his defeat was. The depth of Fumo's persistence in pursuit of his political objectives was simply undeniable. You might deter him momentarily, but you did not deter him permanently.

There is no question in my mind that Lewis turned Fumo back because of the presence and unwavering open support of Jimmy Lloyd. Without Lloyd, Lewis would never have gotten Rocks. Without Lloyd and Rocks, it would have been difficult if not politically impossible for Lewis to put a majority together in the face of the inevitable pressures on the other members that would have come from the Philadelphia bloc.

Jim Lloyd would pay for his defiance of Fumo two years later when he lost his Senate seat to a Republican. Word on the street had it that Joe Smith and Vince Fumo had a discreet but very critical role in Lloyd's defeat. Difficult as his loss in the Senate was to accept, Jim was to pay a much dearer personal price after his departure, a price having nothing to do with Philadelphia politics. At a very tender age (early forties) he fell victim to a pervasive brain tumor that ultimately claimed his life. It was a painful chain of events to witness.

At the time of his death, Jim was serving the Casey administration as the governor's representative in southeastern Pennsylvania. I was privileged to be on the Casey team with him. Jimmy Lloyd was a stand-up kind of guy. He was in politics and public service for all the right reasons. He deserved mention among the outstanding senators whom I came to know. I saved that for here to give him the special mention he deserves.

1984: He's Back . . . and with a Vengeance!

Vince Fumo also must have read Larry O'Brien's book on politics and no final victories, no permanent defeats. If there is a truism in politics, it is that while you win some and you lose some, there are always other battles waiting to be fought. There's no resting on your laurels.

Round Two of Lewis versus Fumo was fought when the Senate Democratic caucus met after the 1984 general elections to organize for the 1985–86 biennial session. This caucus had a decidedly different look than its predecessor of two years earlier, and the new look was not in Lewis's image. The principal difference was that his good friend and steadfast ally, Jim Lloyd, was gone from the ranks.

That was step one in the Fumo strategy. Lloyd had been beaten in his bid for reelection by a likable beer distributor named Hank Salvatore who was fairly well known in the Northeast section of the city. Vince Fumo and Joe Smith were two of Salvatore's best though covert allies.

Remember Marty Murray's counsel of not getting mad, get even, or John Kennedy's about forgiving your enemies but remembering their names. Well, in the case of Jim Lloyd, Vince Fumo and Joe Smith did get mad; they neither forgave nor forgot; and they most certainly got even. Call it payback, I suppose. It goes with the territory in politics. It's just unfortunate that a good guy like Jim Lloyd had to be victimized politically because he held to his convictions.

I tried to help Jim in what little way I could, principally by promoting his candidacy with some Roman Catholic nuns who had taught our children at Good Shepherd Elementary School in Camp Hill before being transferred to a Philadelphia parish in Jim Lloyd's senatorial district. It was one of the largest Roman Catholic parishes in the city, and Jim knew that every vote counted. So I called the nuns to tell them about Jim and urge them to spread the word in the parish and with the families of the children enrolled in the parish school. They said they would. Jim may even have visited with them personally. He told me after the election he did very well in the parish, and I was certainly grateful to Sisters Janice and John Michael for their efforts on Jim's behalf. It was, as I said, the most tangible support I had to offer. It just wasn't enough.

Without Jim Lloyd, the foundation of Lewis's base in the caucus suffered a very serious crack. Joe Rocks, never a profile in courage in the best of times, began to waver under the Philadelphia pressure. With Jim Lloyd out, Rocks's cover was gone. He ultimately voted for Fumo. He told Lewis in an aside prior to the reorganization that his wife was furious with him. But stacked against his own political future, the alleged wrath of his wife just had to be endured, I suppose. He wasn't going to risk having the Fumo political reach in the city consign him to the same fate as Jim Lloyd. Joe could be charming in his way, but if you're going to war, he's not your first choice for your mate in a foxhole. (As a footnote, before the 1985–86 legislative session concluded, Rocks surveyed the political landscape and his own political future and decided to switch from the minority Senate Democratic caucus to the majority Senate Republican Caucus. It didn't save him, however. He made an unsuccessful run as the Republican candidate for city controller in Philadelphia. The next year, he lost his seat in the Senate to a Democratic woman activist, Allyson Schwartz, who served in the Senate until her election to the U.S. Congress in 2004. Vince Fumo was not of her political ilk but he was among her most ardent and active political supporters. Strange bedfellows, again. Meanwhile, there were few in the chamber, certainly on the Democratic side, who mourned Joe Rocks's political passing.)

With Lloyd gone and Rocks wavering, it was fairly obvious that Lewis wasn't going to muster the majority he needed to win Round Two. But there were two encounters in his reelection bid worth recounting. They both serve to further reinforce how fickle and unpredictable legislative reorganizations can be and further validate that there are no standard formulas to apply when members of a legislative caucus gather in private to elect their leaders.

The first involved Bill Lincoln, a young, energetic, combative and, at times, combustible senator from Fayette County. The Lincoln saga was pretty straightforward. Either by his own design, or at Fumo's urging, Lincoln decided to challenge Lewis's good friend Gene Scanlon for the position of Democratic whip. He asked Lewis for his support. Lewis declined for reasons explained earlier. In that case, Lincoln advised, he wouldn't be supporting Lewis this time around. It was just that direct a proposition, quid pro quo.

Lincoln certainly was entitled to pursue his own ambition to move up in the Senate leadership ranks. I suspect very strongly that Fumo encouraged him to make the race against Scanlon under the old divide-and-conquer political tactic. To Lincoln's credit, he was straight with Craig about the condition of his support and what would transpire if Lewis could not reciprocate. (I never verified it, but neither would I have been surprised if Fumo had approached Scanlon with the same offer. Fumo always touched all bases, and an overture to Scanlon was not beyond the realm of possibility, though Scanlon's answer to Fumo would have been the same as Lewis's was to Lincoln.)

Lincoln's defection certainly compounded Lewis's position going into the reorganization. But at least he wasn't blindsided in his vote count. Often the ability to count accurately where the votes stood was the most critical step in the reorganization process. Lewis went into this one knowing exactly where he stood. He was short.

The second event involved the senator from Erie at the time, Anthony "Buzz" Andrezeski. A frequently impulsive man, Andrezeski was at times a bit spacey and usually unpredictable from day to day. He and Lewis were hardly soulmates, political or other wise, yet in 1984 there was good reason to believe his vote could go to Lewis. Andrezeski had parlayed his deep roots with organized labor in Erie and its very strong political base in a successful effort to unseat a Democratic incumbent in a 1980 primary. He went on to win the seat in the fall. Andrezeski was pretty much a political loner in the Senate. If not a mystery, he certainly was a puzzle to most around him. Lewis and he exchanged pleasantries, but that essentially was the nature of their political and personal connection.

So it was something of a surprise when a few weeks before the 1984 general election Lewis either was asked or offered to help in Andrezeski's reelection campaign. Buzz was facing a very strong challenge from his Republican opponent. Heading into the homestretch, the outcome appeared very much in doubt. Whether on request or at his suggestion, Lewis committed to take his Appropriations Committee staff to Erie for a day. With Buzz as host, we would conduct a workshop for local government officials on state finances and the state budget and counsel how they somehow might tap into the process.

Buzz's introduction of Lewis and the staff was so glowing you would have thought the two were political pals of long standing. The event, itself, was a media attention-getter, which, after all, was the purpose of the visit in the first place. Lewis was knowledgeable; so was the staff. I was the staff moderator, wisely leaving the details to the others more versed in the dotted *I*s and crossed *T*s of the discussion. There's no doubt, the dog-and-pony show was informative and helpful for the attending officials. There's no doubt the show was helpful politically to Andrezeski. While the program was evolving, Buzz was benefiting from a series of newspaper, radio, and television interviews. He was getting the media attention he wanted as his reelection campaign entered the final, critical last two weeks.

The Sunday before the election, the Erie newspaper endorsed Andrezeski in print. The paper had to this point been sitting out the campaign. But they said in their endorsement editorial that if Andrezeski could bring someone of Senator Lewis's stature into the county for a serious discussion with local government officials on state finances and fiscal affairs, he demonstrated his ability to serve the region effectively and ably and deserved to be reelected. Buzz won that election. I was told by his top staff aide that the newspaper endorsement probably made the difference.

Lewis was delighted, obviously. If Andrezeski's support ever was within grasp, this was the time. With Buzz, however, nothing was that simple. This is a paraphrase, but this is how I remember Lewis recounting the conversation at their first meeting following the election:

Lewis: Buzz, congratulations. A great victory, and I'm glad I could help. I look forward to serving with you again in the Senate.
Andrezeski: Craig, I can't thank you enough. What you and your staff did was very important, and it came at just the right time. I really appreciate your help.
Lewis: Glad to be of service, Buzz. It was important for the caucus to keep you in that seat. Now, I need to ask a favor of you. I'd like your support in the reorganization for the Appropriations Committee. Can I count on it?
Andrezeski: Craig, I'd like nothing more than be able to support you. But I can't, I really can't. Vince [Fumo] has been lending me use of his place at the shore for a couple of years now, almost any time I needed it. I can't forget that. I have to support him. You can understand that, I hope. I really do appreciate what you did for me, and I really am sorry.
Lewis: So am I, Buzz. So am I!

End of conversation. End of Lewis's prospect for reelection as minority chair of the Appropriations Committee. Jimmy Lloyd's loss in his reelection campaign was critical, Bill Lincoln's defection was a serious loss, and the inability to reach out to other potentially supportive members like Andrezeski essentially sealed the deal.

Andrezeski, Lewis was to learn, was not the only beneficiary of Fumo's hospitality with his shore property. At least one other, Sen. Leonard Bodack, offered Craig the same excuse about access to Fumo's ocean retreat when he was approached about his possible support. One thing about Vince: He certainly used all the considerable personal and political resources at his command to achieve his ends. I guess that's to be respected in a political context where winning and losing are so important. After all, politics "ain't beanbags," as one practitioner I respected put it. And it certainly is no profession for the faint of heart. Whether that's good or bad, I'm not sure. But I am sure that's the way it is.

The outcome was preordained before Lewis entered the caucus room. He was three votes short, and that's the way the count ended: 13–10, Fumo. With Lloyd, he probably would have had Rocks. He could have withstood the Lincoln loss and still won, 12–11. But that was not to be.

Change in the political leadership of the legislative caucuses is not necessarily a bad thing. In fact, change is probably to be encouraged if the process is to remain alert, disciplined, and focused on a purpose larger than one's mere political survival.

Craig Lewis had a good run as minority chairman of the Senate Appropriations Committee. He assembled a staff committed to professional and careful analysis of state fiscal affairs, and because he did, the legislative process in the Senate was opened considerably. That, at least, created an environment that was conducive to careful, informed decision-making if the caucus wished to take advantage of it. Was the budget and fiscal analysis process depoliticized? Not completely, nor should it be. The political parties, after all, should stand for something rather than simply mimic each other.

The threat of a Fumo takeover of the Democratic Appropriations process was not a threat posed by Fumo personally or politically. It was a threat that the process would revert to its prior form when Appropriations almost solely was the private preserve of the Democratic chairman, a few but not all of the caucus leaders, and only selected members of the rank-and-file.

Fumo himself put that issue to rest almost immediately after his victory. In his first meeting with the staff, he opened the session by congratulating them on the good work they had performed the last four years. "You guys are legends around this place," he acknowledged. "The only way I could get the votes I needed to win was to commit to keep you and this operation in tact. Rest assured, I am."

I heard all this because my office was immediately adjacent to the conference room where the meeting was held. To his credit, Fumo not only took the staff structure that was in place, but he built on it through the years to such a degree that twenty-some years later it was widely and universally regarded as "the best" in the Capitol. At the time, however, I took Fumo's remarks as the best testament—vindication, if you will—to the value and productivity of the process and the staff that Lewis and I had set in place. It was time for Lewis and for me, each in our own way, to move on. We did.

Chapter 9

★★★★★★★

Transgressions

There I was . . . in the witness chair . . . testifying before a federal grand jury in Philadelphia, no less. I didn't have to ask myself how a nice boy like me came to find himself in a situation like that . . . I knew the answer. This particular grand jury was convened to investigate probable payroll fraud and abuse in the office of the Pennsylvania Senate majority leader. I was a link, indirect but a link nonetheless, in the federal prosecutor's chain of evidence.

But there was more to what brought me there that day than just that—much more. The Senate Democratic majority was being held to account for more than a half-decade of political missteps and misjudgments—I call them transgressions— by its leadership and its members. A time of accounting was all but inevitable. When one crosses the line of acceptable conduct in most professions, there usually is a price to pay. This is particularly true (as it should be) in politics and public service where the public trust is so critical to and the public interest so inherent in the public policymaking process.

Senate Democrats in the latter half of the 1970s endured more than their share of line crossings or transgressions. Some were individual in nature; others reflected on the body as an institution. Taken cumulatively, however, over time, they inevitably lost the party its public trust and, with it, its majority status in the chamber. A quarter-century later, Pennsylvania Democrats were consigned still to minority party status in the Senate, with no apparent light at the end of this political tunnel.

The laundry lists of Democratic woes that brought the party to such a perilous point in the short span of five, six years was almost as exhausting as it seemed endless at the time. Consider this:

Senator Frank Mazzei (Allegheny County) was indicted by a federal grand jury in a kickback scheme involving state leases. Disposition: Convicted in a federal court, expelled from the Senate and imprisoned.

Senator William Duffield (Fayette County) was disbarred from the practice of law by the Pennsylvania Supreme Court for misappropriation of client funds. Disposition: Censured by the Senate, stripped of his committee chairmanship and vice-chairmanships for the balance of his elected term, eventually lost his bid for reelection.

Senator Buddy Cianfrani (Philadelphia) was accused by federal prosecutors of mail fraud for Senate payroll padding. Disposition: A plea-bargained agreement with his federal prosecutors; resignation from the Senate, sentenced to a minimum-security federal prison.

Senate Majority Leader Tom Nolan (Allegheny County) and Senator-elect Vincent Fumo (Philadelphia) were indicted along with Philadelphia Democratic chairman Peter Camiel by a federal grand jury for Senate payroll padding. Disposition: Tried in federal court and found guilty by a jury of their peers; verdict overturned at time of sentencing by presiding federal judge.

The collective missteps of the General Assembly as an institution, but particularly the Democratic-controlled Pennsylvania Senate, prompted a mid-1970s several-part, investigative report from the *Philadelphia Inquirer* entitled "Pennsylvania General Assembly: Out of Control."

The *Inquirer* thought so much of the series that it submitted it to the Pulitzer Prize committee as an entry in its public service category. It didn't win the Pulitzer, but it still was as impressive a piece of investigative journalism as the Capitol had seen in modern memory. I was serving as press secretary to the Senate Democratic caucus at the time the series was published. I also happened to play racquetball a couple of mornings a week with one of the series authors. My critics in the Senate Democratic staff accused me of serving as a principal if not the primary source for the reports. Would that I had known so much as the series reported.

Because of my position on the Senate staff, I had some direct involvement in the way the aforementioned events were addressed. The Mazzei and Duffield cases were the subjects of major press coverage, which brought me into the matters as press secretary to the caucus. In the Cianfrani case, I was serving on Senator Craig Lewis's staff, and Lewis was serving as chairman of the new standing Senate Ethics Committee created in the wake of the Mazzei and Duffield cases. In the Nolan/Fumo investigation and prosecution, I was called as a witness before both a federal grand jury and the trial itself. None of this, individually or collectively, was a pleasant personal or professional experience. But each is worth recounting here for the lessons to be learned.

Case One: Frank Mazzei

Once a federal jury found Senator Mazzei guilty in his kickback trial, the issue was how long he should be permitted to remain a member of good standing in the Senate. There was no applicable precedent. Republicans, understandably, were demanding that he be removed immediately. Democrats weren't quite sure what to do, so they played for time. Appropriately so, as it turned out. But politically, the GOP had a winning hand either way.

The Democratic majority referred the case to the Legislative Reference Bureau for review and counsel. The bureau is a nonpartisan legal service agency to both the House and Senate. In this case, it served as independent legal counsel to the Senate. The critical question for the lawyers was what would happen if Frank Mazzei was expelled and an appeals court ultimately overturned his conviction. What recourse would he or any aggrieved party have then?

Contrary to the common assumption that a guilty verdict from a jury is a conviction, Reference Bureau attorneys determined otherwise. After extensive research, they concluded that under the law a conviction is not formalized and finalized until a judge renders a sentence. As we shall see, the opinion would have profound implications in the Nolan case years later. But it offered no relief for Frank Mazzei.

No sooner had the judge in the Mazzei trial handed down his sentence (jail time) than the clamor to remove him from the Senate started up immediately again in the press and from the Republicans. Mazzei's attorneys filed an immediate appeal. Instantly, they, and his allies in the Democratic caucus, asked the Senate to delay disciplinary action (expulsion) until the appeal was heard and decided, so as not to prejudice the issue before the appellate court.

Senate Republicans weren't buying the argument. Neither were many Democrats, some of whom had read the trial transcript and were convinced that the grounds for a reversal from the appellate court were minimal at best. The case had dragged on for what seemed an eternity. The political damage individual Democratic members were suffering in their districts was considerable and seemed to grow with each passing day. A vote on an expulsion motion was scheduled.

The day of the vote, Frank Mazzei made one last gasp to remain in the Senate. He sent a letter to the body pledging to absent himself from all legislative matters except constituent services during the course of his appeal so as not to color or taint the deliberations of the chamber in any way. I wrote the letter for him. Buddy Cianfrani read it into the record. But it wasn't enough to save him. The request was rejected. He was expelled.

I felt bad for Frank Mazzei. We weren't close, but I saw in him many of the traits I had seen in many of the Italian men I knew growing up in South Scranton. There was something godfatherly about him, not in the Mario Puzo sense of the word, but in the best sense of a gentleman who, at least in my presence, always treated other people with courtesy and respect. One trait of his particularly registered with me, though I never understood why. I can't ever remember being in an elevator with Frank Mazzei when, as some woman entered, without fail, he immediately took off his hat. And I also remember how he always deferred leaving an elevator until the women on it had left first. It was old-school courtesy that I found warm and genuine.

In our professional dealings, Senator Mazzei always appeared approachable, rational, and, I thought, sincere. He was in many ways a good man. His friends attempted to minimize his offense by rationalizing that nothing he had done was ever done to enrich himself. Rather, he used any money that had exchanged hands to benefit others who had no political fundraising apparatus of their own to sustain them.

Mitigating? Perhaps. Exculpatory? No!

Senator Mazzei had betrayed a public trust and he was about to pay an ignominious price for that: Expulsion from the Senate as well as a term in prison. The longer the matter dragged out in the Senate, the more tense the atmosphere in the Senate became. At one point, anonymous threats of "porches blowing up" made their way to public print. Enough was enough. The matter had to be resolved, and it was resolved in the only manner it could be.

In human terms, I had some sympathy for what Frank Mazzei had to endure. I visited with him briefly after the vote and expressed my regret about the turn of events that had brought him down. He thanked me for my concern. That was the last time we spoke.

One postscript worth noting: The Reference Bureau opinion officially formalized the precedent for when a legislative chamber may act against a member who has run afoul of the law. It was important to the orderly resolution of such cases in the future. It was the only good to come out of the Affair Mazzei.

Case Two: William Duffield

The disbarment of Sen. William Duffield of Fayette County was another matter. Frankly, I could have cared less what happened to him. Crude and obnoxious—William Duffield was the personification of the terms. He was the most unpleasant a man as I had met in my entire career in and around public service. I avoided him as often as I could. And I had no sympathy whatsoever for him or the situation in which he found himself.

The Supreme Court had suspended Duffield's right to practice law because he was found to have misappropriated a client's funds. While technically not a criminal conviction, it was a case where professional conduct reflected adversely on a member of the Senate and, by association, demeaned the body as a whole. Duffield had been sanctioned in the private sector. The question, then, was whether the Senate was going to take disciplinary action of its own.

Senator Gene Scanlon, a lawyer himself, was named chairman of a special committee created to review the Duffield case and recommend a course of action to the Senate. He asked me to serve on the committee staff to deal with press issues. The committee held at least one hearing at which Duffield personally testified in his own behalf. Other testimony was received from independent authorities on what disciplinary action might be appropriate from a public body such as the Senate for the transgressions of a member in a private capacity. Then the committee issued its report. It was very much a senators' report because members like Gene Scanlon, Craig Lewis, and John Stauffer, the senior Republican, were the actual authors. Whatever assistance I provided came in the editing of the document.

The report called for Duffield's committee chairmanship and vice-chairmanship to be suspended for the balance of his elected term. He wasn't happy with the penalty since it deprived him of access to committee funds and staff. He was censured accordingly and didn't fight the Senate action. But he did fight in other ways.

Duffield in the best of circumstances was an erratic personality given to sudden but explosive bouts of temper. His outbursts after he was disciplined became more frequent and more threatening. He seemed to be drinking more, martinis being his drink of choice. As the alcohol mixed with medication he was taking, Duffield became more volatile. He frequently confronted members of the Senate staff, most often in public settings after dinner but sometimes at caucus social events. In one instance that I witnessed, Gene Scanlon gently and supportively led Duffield away after he had confronted an innocent member of the press office staff at a cocktail reception. "Bill, you don't want to do this," Scanlon told him as he walked Duffield to a doorway at the Hotel Hershey and stayed with him until he had calmed down.

Duffield came after me twice, once in the lobby of a hotel in Philadelphia where Franklin Kury had taken a delegation of senators on an inspection of the Philadelphia ports, and the other in a bar at a favorite Harrisburg hangout across the Susquehanna River where legislators, staff, and lobbyists gathered for their nightcaps. In both instances, senators intervened quickly—the first without incident, the second not so.

I was seated at the bar at Catalano's Restaurant talking to another staff person. Duffield was a couple of stools away. Senator Jim Romanelli of Allegheny County sat between Duffield and the staff person with whom I was talking. Suddenly Duffield exploded and made a move to challenge me. Romanelli immediately moved in to keep Duffield back. It was meant to be a friendly intervention on Romanelli's part, but Duffield threw a punch at him instead. Romanelli, instinctively, responded with a couple of quick punches of his own. In seconds, Duffield was on the floor. The brawl was over before it started.

"Good punch, Jim," Duffield said to Romanelli as Romanelli picked him off the floor and dusted him off. I thought so, too. But I stayed quiet. It was one of my rare moments of wise personal discretion.

Fortunately for Duffield, the bar was virtually empty at the time of the after-hours incident. The encounter never made the newspapers. Vince Catalano, the owner, called a cab and Romanelli helped Duffield into the taxi and sent him on his way to his apartment. Vince Catalano, Romanelli, the staffer, and I each had another drink to settle down after the fracas. Romanelli even called Duffield's apartment before we left the bar to be certain he arrived safely. I thought that was a pretty generous thing to do given what had transpired. I don't know why he rose to my defense the way he did—probably to prevent a public incident that would embarrass Duffield and, by association, the Senate again. Whatever the reason, I was grateful.

As fate would have it, years later I came to meet and work with one of Duffield's daughters, Jane, the director of communications at the University of Pittsburgh Medical Center. This was when Governor Robert P. Casey underwent his life-saving heart and liver transplant surgery at UPMC. She could not have been more pleasant a person, and more able a professional. She and her staff were of immense help in working through the governor's surgery and recovery while he was confined at the hospital. Understandably, I never discussed her father that much with her.

Case Three: Tom Nolan

Transgressions . . . it's strange how often the most serious ones have the most innocent of beginnings. This is the tale of a transgression that began innocently enough. Before the final chapter of this particular saga was finished, however, it had a very high political cost indeed.

For me, it all started with a telephone call to my office in the Capitol shortly before Christmas 1975. The caller was Senate Majority Leader Tom Nolan's secretary. She told me he wanted to see me immediately. That in itself was somewhat unusual. Once he was elected to replace Tom Lamb, I had paid Nolan the proper deference he was due as a senator and as leader of the caucus. But I also had maintained some distance from him and his inner circle. Their approach to governing was not mine. Mine was not theirs. I thought seriously about exploring other positions within the staff structure. The Senate president pro tempore, the aforementioned Martin L. Murray, advised me to stay where I was. "He's going to need you," Murray said. So I stayed put.

When Nolan called on me for my services as press secretary to the Senate Democratic caucus, I responded. After all, I was a member of the majority leader's payroll. But that essentially was it. I spent most of my time trying to serve the press relations needs of other members of the Senate.

This particular day I walked the short distance to the majority leader's office. "He's waiting for you," the secretary told me as I made my way to his office suite. Pete Coleman, his chief of staff, and Jack Weinrauch, the caucus legal counsel, were with Nolan in his private office when I entered.

"We're going to lunch and we want you to join us," Nolan said by way of greeting.

"Sure," I replied. "Be glad to."

Minutes later we were on our way to the Maverick Restaurant, a favorite eating place of the politicos, just a short drive from the Capitol. The holidays were not a good time for Nolan this year. His wife of many years had died a few weeks earlier after a long bout with cancer. He clearly was hurting, spending more time in the Capitol since her death. That undoubtedly accounted for his presence that December day.

Except for Nolan, this would not have been an unusual pairing for lunch. Coleman and I went way back. We had been reporters together. We had talked about my serving on the campaign staff of an Ernie Kline run for U.S. senator. And Pete was the one, after all, who first approached me about taking the Senate press job with Tom Lamb after the Democrats won the majority in the 1970 election. When Pete had a falling out with Kline after Kline's election in 1970 as lieutenant governor, he returned to the Senate payroll, where our day-to-day association picked up again. So we had a good history. But at this point in time, he was a Tom Nolan guy and I had no desire to be. Under Nolan's stewardship, we basically kept our space.

Weinrauch, on the other hand, was a newer introduction for me. He left the Legislative Reference Bureau to sign on as Democratic counsel in the latter part of Lamb's tenure. That's when I first came to know him. I came to think of him as an able lawyer. We sometimes socialized together. Coleman and he had one important trait in common in the post–Lamb era. They were both Nolan loyalists. So again, we kept our space.

I interpreted the invitation to lunch as an attempt by the three to assess whether I might be drawn closer to the circle, on the one hand, and whether they wanted me there, on the other. Lunch was pleasant enough, mostly small talk. But it was clear Nolan was hurting.

"You ought to get away, take a trip," either Weinrauch or Coleman suggested. I believe it was Weinrauch because I remember Coleman asking, "Have you ever been to San Francisco?"

Nolan may have or may not. That was immaterial. The conversation turned quickly to how delightful a city it was to visit. It would be good therapy. What's more, Coleman reminded him, there was even an official reason for Nolan to make the trip. A proposed mass-transit system dubbed "Sky Bus" was a major source of controversy in Pittsburgh and Allegheny County at the time. Nolan had been rather outspoken in his opposition to the project, largely, as I recall, on cost-benefit grounds. That would have been consistent with his "spend less" political position on government in general. It did, however, put him at serious odds with other Allegheny County elected officials and his colleagues in organized labor, who were strongly attracted to the job potential of the project.

Nolan should go to San Francisco, Coleman suggested, to inspect the mass-transit system that ran in the Bay Area between the city and Oakland. It was called the Bay Area Rapid Transit (BART) system. Who knows, Coleman opined? After looking the BART system over, Nolan might even come back with a different view on SkyBus.

Nolan was receptive on the idea. But on one condition: The three of us—Coleman, Weinrauch, and myself—had to accompany him. We agreed. A date in February or March was picked for the trip. Coleman would set up the BART visits.

As travel day approached, however, I began to have some serious concerns. I was learning in bits and pieces that the size of the travel party was growing almost daily. Nolan had invited a number of his Senate supporters to accompany him. The political calculation behind the invitations was transparent from the get-go. Nolan would never win unanimous support of the Democratic caucus; his personality and his political style were too contentious, combative, and divisive. He had been elected leader by only a narrow margin in the first place. He needed to keep that majority in place. Inviting his Senate allies (some but not all) along for the California trip was a good step in cementing his support.

The more I learned about the growing size of the travel party, the more my reluctance to participate grew. In truth, there were a couple of reasons for my hesitation. Some were personal, some professional. Principal among them was the fact that the senators who were traveling with Nolan were not the senators I most closely associated with. (Joe Smith and Bill Duffield may have been among them.) Spending four or five days in that company on the West Coast was not high on my priority list.

Second, it bothered me that the trip had turned quickly from a legitimate inspection visit to just another junket. It was the kind of trip I used to write prominently about when I was a reporter. Now I was going to be a junketeer. I wasn't comfortable with that contradiction. I don't presume to suggest I was more honorably motivated than the other people invited on the trip, but I decided to cancel out.

The question was how do I do that delicately? Ultimately, though indirectly, my wife, Toni, came to my rescue. Just months earlier, as a member of the East Pennsboro Township school board, she had had an opportunity to attend the National School Board Association's summer convention in San Francisco. She declined because we had four small children at home and there was no way I could manage them and my work at the same time. She passed for all the right reasons.

I went to Coleman and bowed out, using Toni's situation as my excuse. If it was wrong for her to leave me alone with the children for three or four days to travel to the West Coast, it was wrong for me to do that to her. I couldn't go. In hindsight, it was the right decision in the context of my family obligations. But at the time, I must admit, I considered it primarily a convenient excuse to absent myself from the trip.

Coleman invited one of my press office assistants to replace me on the trip. He had family in San Francisco and was more than eager to accept. I didn't object, though if he had asked I would have counseled him against it. What little I learned about the trip after the fact, I learned from him.

Though the delegation approached double-digit numbers, the visitors, did, in fact, spend considerable time investigating the BART system. The size of the delegation and the bills the group incurred in its spare time may have been debatable. But the official purpose of the visit had been fulfilled. Still, I was glad that I stayed home.

San Francisco Revisited

What is it they say? One good trip deserves another?

It just so happened that a few months after the BART trip, the National Conference of State Legislatures (NCSL) held its annual summer convention in, of all places, San Francisco. Nolan decided to attend. There was nothing wrong with that since he was not only a member but also a leader of the Pennsylvania Senate. Where things started to unravel was when he asked another delegation of his caucus supporters to go along. This time, Nolan and those who counseled him played it too cute by half, and the subterfuge came back to bite them.

The size and identity of any Pennsylvania bloc attending NCSL or any similar legislative conference, and the expenses legislators and staff incurred, were always ready-made news for Capitol Hill reporters. Sort of an annual ritual, you might say. The difficulty the press had in securing the identities of the Pennsylvania attendees and reviewing the expense vouchers they filed were without fail a big part of the stories that ultimately made their way to print. (In the interest of full disclosure, I must acknowledge that as a member of the Senate staff I had attended an NCSL meeting in Seattle, Washington, a year or two previous. Toni accompanied me. The way the Senate calculated traveling expenses in those days—cumulative mileage at eighteen or twenty cents a mile—more than covered our plane fare and many of our incidental expenses. I don't know that my expense records ever were accessible to the press. So as I write about this, I must admit my prior involvement in the reimbursement process.)

But back to the point. Somehow, somewhere, someone made a decision that those traveling in the Nolan party were not going to be listed as attendees at the NCSL conference. Instead, they were going to be classified as a second fact-finding BART inspection team, in hopes of throwing the press off in its pursuit of NCSL attendees.

My memory is fuzzy how all of this ultimately came to light. I do remember that the *Philadelphia Inquirer,* as a prelude to its "Legislature Out of Control" series, sent a couple of undercover reporters to San Francisco to shadow Pennsylvania attendees. The *Inquirer* had done this at least once before with great success. The target the first time was Philadelphia district attorney Emmett Fitzpatrick, and the event was a national conference of district attorneys in Montreal, Canada. The thrust of the *Inquirer* story was that Fitzpatrick spent much more time on the public dime in personal and social activities versus the time he actually participated in the business of the convention. Rest assured, the story was prominently displayed on the

Inquirer news pages. Fitzpatrick lost his reelection bid to a fella who later would become a two-term mayor of Philadelphia and, in the year 2003, governor of Pennsylvania, Ed Rendell. The *Inquirer* story was not the sole reason for the Fitzpatrick loss, but it certainly was a major contributing factor.

You might say the Pennsylvania delegation suffered the same fate at the hands of the *Inquirer*'s undercover investigative team in San Francisco. One report I received from an *Inquirer* Capitol Hill reporter after the NCSL story made the paper was particularly interesting, if not humorous. As it was told to me, the chief clerk of the Senate came down to the lobby of the hotel in which the delegation was staying. He went to a telephone in the lobby to make dinner reservations. Apparently, he forgot his reading glasses. So he approached a young man standing nearby asking him to locate a telephone number for him from the San Francisco directory. The young man could not have been more helpful. The number the chief clerk needed was for a very fashionable and expensive restaurant, the Blue Fox, I believe.

Need I mention that the young man who was so accommodating was a member of the *Inquirer* investigative team. You can guess the rest of the story. He stood close by as the chief clerk made the dinner reservation, a party of twelve to fifteen people, I was told. Most assuredly, you know who also showed up at the Blue Fox that night to confirm the attendance of the Pennsylvania diners. The *Inquirer*, of course. The paper had the time, date, and location. All it had to do in further researching the story was to request and review that specific voucher when the legislative travelers returned to Pennsylvania. The dinner cost in excess of $2,000, as I recall. It was a major piece in the series the paper published, and it all was made possible by an unwitting request for assistance in locating a telephone number.

The publication of the *Inquirer* report set off a clamor within the rest of the capital press corps demanding further access to and accountability for how the legislature—the Senate, in particular—was spending tax dollars. Whether it was a case of the cart before the horse, or the horse before the cart, I'm not certain. But as the press pursued the *Inquirer* story on the extravagance of Senate expenditures, it somehow came to light that a delegation of Pennsylvania senators went to San Francisco ostensibly on a "mass-transit" inspection visit and never in the several days they were there did they bother to actually visit BART.

Of course they hadn't. They were there for the NCSL. "Mass transit" was merely a convenient cover so that the full extent of Pennsylvania Senate delegation at the conference would not stand out. Now the Nolan group was in a quandary. Either it had to acknowledge that no visit was made to

BART or it had to admit that NCSL was the true purpose of the travel. In politics, they call that lose-lose.

The pressure on Nolan, the antispending, antitax majority leader of the Senate, to come clean was intense and irresistible. He directed Coleman to pull together what materials he had on BART and prepare a formal report for the record to share with the zealous press. Since I was press secretary to the caucus, most of the press calls about San Francisco were funneled through me. I had no immediate answers, obviously. When I learned that Coleman was preparing a report of sorts, I volunteered to release it to the press. My thinking was, first, that that was what press secretaries were paid to do, and I wanted to do what I could to minimize the damage to the reputation of the Senate. (Years later, White House Press Secretary Mike McCurry had to speak for Bill Clinton during the Monica Lewinsky scandal for essentially the same reason, though I by no means elevate the Nolan mess to that level of notoriety.) Second, I thought this could be a case where a lawyer who represented himself had a fool for a client. Since I had not participated in either trip, I suspected I could dance around many of the questions that were likely to arise. Nolan, Coleman, and anyone else who participated did not have that escape hatch.

Coleman and his staff worked overnight to put a product to paper. I scheduled a meeting with the press corps for my office the next day. Nolan already had answered the question of why the delegation had not met personally with BART officials. He explained that the meetings with BART had occurred on the first trip. This time, the members wanted to experience the system as any everyday traveler would. It might have been a little lame, but it was plausible. Besides, it was the best answer he had available. The other members of the traveling party deferred (most willingly, I assume) to Nolan as the organizer of the trip.

On schedule the next day, Coleman gave me the copies of the "report" I needed to share with the press contingent. The document clearly was superficial, but it was the best that could be produced on short notice. The reporters, smelling some political blood to let, were quick to seize on how shallow and generalized the report was. They pressed the point with me.

"It reads like it was pulled from some BART promotional brochure," Ed Jensen of the *Pittsburgh Post Gazette* said to me. "Is that where it came from?" he demanded.

"I don't know," I replied. "You asked for the report that was prepared and here it is."

"Do you think this is really a good report?" Charlie Madigan of United Press International asked. "Doesn't seem very deep or substantive to me," he added. "What about that?"

"I'm not going to characterize the quality of anyone else's work," I responded. "I'm sure there are any number of people in this room who might be inclined to pass a value judgment on anything that goes on in this building. I'm not one of them."

Finally the question that came home most directly to me. "Vince," Madigan wanted to know, "were you on either trip yourself?"

"No," I answered, "I was not."

That wasn't meant to exonerate me in any way. It simply meant that I could not answer from personal experience to anything that occurred on either San Francisco visit. That was important because it closed a lot of dangerous or potentially damning doors to further inquiry. It also, in a personal way, kept my professional credibility intact. Any press secretary found to indulge in wrongdoing will have no audience whatsoever with the press corps that he or she must deal with on a daily basis.

In hindsight, I couldn't have been more relieved from a career standpoint that I had jumped ship on the first San Francisco trip several months earlier. I could continue to function on behalf of the Senate Democratic Caucus without a San Francisco taint to my press relations position. More important, a door that would open to me a decade later in my career—press secretary to a Pennsylvania governor—most certainly would have been closed if I had been entrapped personally in the furor over Senate junkets.

The curious chain of events in this particular case, and the damage it ultimately rained on the Senate Democratic Caucus, remain strong in my memory today. I am still amazed at how a proposal so innocently framed and advanced—that Christmas lunch with Nolan et al. seven months previous—had blown into such a political crisis because it was so improperly managed and implemented. It was a classic case of where lack of public accountability can shelter public officials from their good senses.

If it had been understood from the very beginning that the records of Senate trips would be open and subject to a public review and accounting of the funds expended, I doubt the traveling parties would have been put together as they were. Nolan and those who accompanied him believed they would be protected from public scrutiny in the press and other forums. Because they did, they fell susceptible to the mistakes in judgment made repeatedly in these cases. There is a traditional standard to decision-making in the political arena. "How would it look if it appeared on the front page of the *New York Times*?" is the test. If that question was asked and evaluated in that framework, the problems that ultimately arose as likely as not would have been avoided.

I expected the issue would slowly simmer itself out, particularly after the Senate adopted a rule that liberalized the procedures for reviewing Senate expenses in the aftermath of the negative publicity the Nolan trips incurred. I was wrong. The press thirsted for more political blood, disclosing ill-advised expenditures of public dollars by the Pennsylvania General Assembly. This was not going to be a once-and-done case. What's more, it aroused the curiosity of other, more important quarters—the federal government and the U.S. Attorney's office in Philadelphia. There was more to be heard from on this front, and I was to be asked more questions.

Grand Juries—Avoid Them If You Can

I'm not certain what it was exactly that motivated the federal government's investigation of Senate expenditures. I suspect it was a combination of events. The Mazzei case, the Cianfrani case, the *Inquirer* series, and the Nolan-led San Francisco trips sure made the Senate an inviting target.

We learned of the federal activity shortly after Nolan resigned in 1977 as majority leader in his second tax dispute with the Shapp administration. Henry Messinger had replaced him, and I remained on Messinger's staff. Not too far into Messinger's term the FBI issued subpoenas for payroll and other financial records from the senate majority leader's office. Messinger called me over to inform me. He had decided immediately that he would comply and cooperate completely. Not only that, he also decided to put out a public statement about receiving the subpoena in the first place. His theory, and it was correct, was that the news would become public anyway. We had learned from prior experience that U.S. Attorneys' offices were not exactly sieve-proof. Messinger, wisely, wanted to be proactive in the disclosure.

Messinger called Senator Murray to inform him. As a courtesy, I was dispatched to tell Nolan in advance about what was to happen. Nolan was not a happy camper when I told him. But the issue was not open to debate.

Two years later, when I was serving on Craig Lewis's staff, I received my subpoena from the U.S. Attorney's office to testify before a federal grand jury sitting in Philadelphia. The subpoena didn't state what I was going to be asked about, nor did I have any idea of exactly what information I had that might be relevant to the investigation. But when one is subpoenaed, one responds. All I knew going in is that I would *not* be taking the Fifth Amendment on any line of questioning.

Subpoenas to testify in a federal criminal investigation, by their very nature, are the kind of things that tend stay embedded in your memory through the years. My experience was memorable on a number of counts. My first recollection is that grand juries don't run on time. I made no less than three trips to Philadelphia to testify. My first trip, I cooled my heels in a waiting room all day without ever being called. An assistant U.S. Attorney appeared late in the day to advise me that the proceedings had taken longer than anticipated. I would have to come back the next day. I wasn't thrilled because I was anxious to get this behind me.

Having no choice in the matter, however, I returned by train to Philadelphia the next morning. This time I did testify. But before I was escorted into the grand jury room I met with the prosecutors privately. They informed me they were going to pursue two lines of questioning: One related to the majority leader's payroll and payroll procedures; the other related to the San Francisco trips. They concluded with an admonition that reminded me, as though I needed reminding, that this was serious business indeed.

"Mr. Carocci," the lead inquisitor said. "You, of course, will be under oath. Anything less than truthful testimony will be grounds for perjury. You understand that, don't you?"

I assured them I did.

I suppose they had good reason to caution me. They didn't know me from Adam, and they didn't know where I'd be coming from in matters related directly to Tom Nolan, the senator who paid my salary. I wasn't offended.

I was ushered in the grand jury room. I had heard many times the legal saw that a prosecutor who could not get an indictment out of a grand jury proceeding was not worthy of the job or the title. I immediately understood why. The grand jury room itself was very nondescript, a typical government-issue conference room you would find in any federal building. The prosecutors had a metal table in the front of the room and a basic metal chair for the witness. I don't remember who presided, but I do remember that the grand jurors themselves were seated off to the side, also on standard-issue, very basic, metal chairs. Some of the women on the jury were knitting as I entered the room. I noticed they continued knitting as I testified. One or two of the men were reading newspapers. They, at least, put the papers down while I was being interrogated. That was somewhat comforting, but only somewhat. I was not impressed with the jurors' attention span.

The prosecutors walked me through my testimony. It was clear in the payroll portion of the probe that I was a simply a link in a chain of evidence beginning with an exchange I had had with Nolan's payroll clerk. In the wake of Cianfrani's resignation and guilty plea, and coupled with prior Senate missteps, pressure grew on Nolan and the Senate to make the payroll complement of the majority leader's office public. Given the intensity of the media coverage, Nolan had no option but to comply. He directed his payroll secretary to put the list together and get it to me to release to the capital press corps. The morning I was to make the report public, I went over to ask the payroll secretary when it would be ready. She said about noon. She also said that Nolan had reviewed the list and that she was told to drop two names before it was made public. (The two names, it later was learned, were the names of the Cianfrani friend and her sister whose presence on the payroll led to his ultimate imprisonment.) They meant nothing to me at the time, however, not even their connection to Cianfrani.

But I was concerned. "Tell me we're not hiding them," I asked of the payroll secretary.

"No," she responded. "They've been terminated. What you get will be the actual payroll as of this date."

I could have pressed the point, I suppose, by asking when the terminations occurred. But I must confess, I didn't. Once I was assured the list would be complete and accurate as of the date of release, I let the point drop. I didn't want to know more.

The prosecutors asked me at length about that conversation. I assumed it went to the heart of the payroll-padding case they apparently were attempting to build against Nolan. Undoubtedly my testimony was corroboration of the fact that the women were on the payroll and they were dropped on short notice at Nolan's instruction before any public disclosure was made. There was little more I could offer on the subject.

The queries on San Francisco probed my personal knowledge about the events leading up to the first trip and events in the aftermath of the second. I could not speak personally to what occurred on either excursion because I was not there. I assumed the prosecutors were looking to establish that neither trip had an official purpose to it, and thus represented a misuse of public dollars. My testimony in this regard was very limited.

Something troubled me about the line of inquiry. I couldn't quite nail down why I felt so uneasy about the questioning. It wasn't until I was riding the train back to Harrisburg as I reflected on the day's events that it suddenly dawned on me. In their line of questioning the prosecutors had the trips reversed. They had asked me about the second trip as though it had been the first, and vice versa. I knew I had answered all questions forthrightly. But I didn't correct the sequence of events at the time because they had occurred more than two years previously. San Francisco was a very distant memory to me; I hadn't spent a lot of time in the interim thinking about my association with Senator Nolan. I had moved on, so to speak, and gladly.

When I realized that the prosecutors had reversed the sequence of the trips, I knew I had to correct the record immediately. The prosecutors' admonition about perjury was very much in my mind. As soon as I returned to Lewis's Senate office in the Capitol, I promptly placed a call to the U.S. Attorney's office in Philadelphia. I asked Vicki Kirk, Senator Lewis's very able secretary, to transcribe my comments as I spoke to the government lawyers. Surprisingly, I was put through almost immediately to the assistant U.S. Attorney who had conducted my interrogation. Vicki noted the time the conversation began.

My conversation was very short. I told the prosecutor the essential facts of his interrogation were correct as I remembered them. But the order of the trips was reversed. He told me I'd have to return to Philadelphia the next day to correct the record for the grand jury. I wasn't thrilled. But what choice did I have? Vicki, meanwhile, recorded my portion of the conversation and typed a transcript. I probably should have had the document notarized, but I didn't. Fortunately, that never became an issue.

The next day, I was back in the federal building in Philadelphia. The prosecutor was quick to emphasize for the grand jury that I had returned voluntarily and at my own initiative to correct the order of events I had testified to the day before. My appearance was over in a matter of minutes.

I came away from the experience with two fundamental impressions: First, I didn't particularly care to get involved in criminal investigations of this sort again. Second, I pondered just how skilled these prosecutors really were when they couldn't get something as elementary as the sequence of events correct before they pursued them.

One More Time . . . Without Feeling

I had one more train ride to make to Philly in this case.

Tom Nolan, Pete Camiel (the chairman of the Democratic Party in Philadelphia), and Vincent Fumo (Camiel's trusted lieutenant who had a very large hand in the city committee's patronage affairs before his election to the Senate) had been indicted by the federal grand jury on charges related to payroll fraud. Not without reason, I thought. The Philadelphia City Democratic Committee appeared to have easy if not unlimited access to the majority leader's payroll after its support of Nolan in his reorganization contest against Joe Ammerman in 1974.

The San Francisco trips, curiously, were not part of the charges against Nolan. The prosecutors may have found them to be an inappropriate or a waste of taxpayer dollars, but there apparently was no federal criminality involved.

I was called as a witness in the trial to testify once again about my conversation with Nolan's payroll secretary prior to release of the payroll complement. The prosecutors started to press me for more information about Nolan's payroll practices. I couldn't provide any because I had no first-hand knowledge about them. The prosecutors seemed a little upset with me. But I certainly wasn't going to speculate about things I didn't know.

My cross-examination was very brief. Nolan's attorney attempted to challenge the accuracy of my recollection concerning the conversation with the payroll secretary. It was to no avail, since I remembered pretty clearly what had transpired. I also suspected the secretary herself would be called to corroborate as well as identify the women in question.

For a brief moment, the defense counsel started down a different track. "You didn't particularly like Senator Nolan, did you, Mr. Carocci?" he asked.

"I don't understand the question," I replied. Truth was I didn't particularly like Tom Nolan as a Senate majority leader. And I wasn't close to him personally. But none of that colored or influenced my appearance in this case. And I wasn't going to open that door on the witness stand if I could avoid it.

The attorney paused for a moment as he looked at me and reflected. "I withdraw the question," he announced. "No more questions for this witness, your honor."

Camiel's attorney had no question for me. Fumo's attorney asked only one: "Mr. Carocci," he inquired, "none of what you've testified to here today has anything to do with Vincent Fumo, does it?"

"Not to my knowledge," I replied.

"Thank you," the lawyer concluded. "No further questions."

I was dismissed. The trial lasted a bit longer. The jury found all three defendants guilty.

Much to most people's surprise, however, the verdict was overturned about the time of sentencing by the presiding judge, who ruled the federal prosecutors had failed to prove beyond a reasonable doubt that a premeditated conspiracy existed between Nolan-Camiel-Fumo. The judge, Harold Green, was an appointee of President Richard Nixon, so it was hard to suggest a partisan connection or affinity for these three prominent Democrats. Most telling, I suppose, was that the federal prosecuting team did not take an appeal of the judge's ruling. The case was closed.

I'm sure the judge's action must have been great relief for the three defendants who narrowly avoided imprisonment. As for me, it was my first and only up-close and personal introduction to federal criminal investigations and prosecutions. I thought at the time, once was enough. I still think so today.

Three points are worth making.

The first is the sequence of events in this trial reinforced the legal validity of the Legislative Reference Bureau's standard rendered years earlier in the Mazzei case. A conviction is not a final, formal conviction until the presiding judge hands down a sentence. Judge Green's reversal of the Nolan-Camiel-Fumo jury verdict was exhibit one in support of that principle.

The second is that almost twenty-five years later, full and complete access to legislative expense records remained an issue of public debate. As late as January of 2002, the Pennsylvania House of Representatives approved another policy related to public inspection of expenditures by leaders and members of the chamber. Change in the Pennsylvania General Assembly comes very slowly in some instances. Access to the legislature's financial records has certainly been one of them.

Finally, each case I recited here was offensive if not illegal in its own right. But taken collectively, they reflected an error of judgment and conduct that was indefensible. A price had to be paid for such a string of misdeeds. As noted much earlier in this narrative, the Senate Democrats paid for it by the loss of their majority. Perhaps that would have happened inevitably in the normal cycle of electioneering. But clearly, the transgressions of the Senate Democrats advanced the calendar considerably. A quarter-century later, Senate Democrats are still trying to recoup their lost power with no success. That's a steep price to pay for the exigencies of the moment. Political leaders would be well advised to take note and learn.

Chapter 10

★★★★★★★

The Vince

What's there to say that has not been said already in other ways, at other times, by other people about "The Vince" . . . aka "Vince the Prince." Still, let's give it a try.

Vincent J. Fumo of Philadelphia: Lawyer, banker, entrepreneur, public servant, but to his core, a politician par excellence and extraordinaire; a man with a most impressive and expansive résumé: St. Joseph's Prep School; Villanova University; Temple University School of Law; University of Pennsylvania Wharton School; licensed motor-boat operator; charter-boat captain; advance pilot, U.S. Power Squadrons; president of Pennsylvania Savings Bank; director of Independence Blue Cross; and member of Moore Street Civic Association, Philadelphia Justinian Society, American Civil Liberties Union, Americans for Democratic Action, Knights of Columbus (4th Degree), National Sheriff's Association, Order of Sons of Italy, American Mensa Society, National Italian-American Foundation, National Rifle Association, Historical Ship Preservation Guild . . . well, you get the idea. Brash as he is brilliant, tenacious, eloquent and engaging in one moment, inflammatory and indignant in another, outspoken, persistent and perseverant, driven yet divisive. He is all of this and more, sometimes at the same time.

My friend John Baer of the *Philadelphia Daily News* sat down with Fumo one year to conduct what he labeled the "Vince Fumo Political Rorschach Test." It was a very simple exercise. Baer would throw out a name and Fumo would react. For example (as recorded in February 2002):

Baer: Mayor John Street of Philadelphia?
Fumo: . . . an adept ward leader . . . very short term agenda. It's called reelection and after that retirement. And the City by damned!
Baer: The director of Homeland Security [former Pennsylvania Governor Tom Ridge]?
Fumo: [first, laughter; then] . . . a buffoon . . . an empty suit, a good-looking empty suit . . .

Baer called Fumo in this piece "the most candid, over-the-top pol of actual influence in public life." Then he added, "Granted, Fumo can afford to be thus. His South Philly Senate seat's his as long as he wants . . . and he sits at the center of a well-connected, self-protected political web of power."

In my almost half-century association with the Pennsylvania General Assembly, there were but a handful of individuals who I thought left an indelible imprint on the legislative process. Senate President Pro Tempore Martin L. Murray of Luzerne County and the legendary Harvey Taylor of Dauphin certainly were two. Senate majority leader and, subsequently, the longest serving pro tem in the history of the chamber Bob Jubelirer of Blair County was another. In the state House, there were Democrats like Herb Fineman of Philadelphia; K. Leroy Irvis of Allegheny County, and big Jim Manderino of Monessen in Westmoreland County (the most skilled House floor leader of my era), each a former majority leader destined to be Speaker. Among the GOP, there were former floor leaders and, later, speakers like Ken Lee of tiny Sullivan County in the northeast tier of the state; the late Matt Ryan of Delaware County, probably the most statesmanlike Speaker of the House in my time; and, finally, John Perzel of Philadelphia, Ryan's successor and as close to a Jim Manderino in terms of his ability to move the legislative process and agenda along as I saw.

But no list would be complete without the name of Vincent J. Fumo. If not at the top, certainly among the top ten . . . more likely, the top five. Fumo was a player from the day he set foot into the halls of the Pennsylvania General Assembly. He talks the talk, he walks the walk. He is tireless in his efforts to secure more—more of anything . . . money, jobs, whatever—for his city. He is very helpful to his friends; and he constantly bedevils his rivals.

His reach knows no limits. His political tentacles extend virtually everywhere: The Pennsylvania Senate *and* the Pennsylvania House of Representatives; the courts of the city and the courts of the Commonwealth, most notably the Pennsylvania Supreme Court; the Port of Philadelphia; Philadelphia City Council; the Southeastern Pennsylvania Transportation Authority (SEPTA), the Delaware River Port Authority . . . again, you get the idea. For better or for worse, his influence extends to everything he touched—and there is very little of consequence he does not reach out to.

In Fumo's high-wire world, I wasn't even a blip on his radar screen. Nor should I have been. He traveled in much higher power circles so our direct contact was very limited. Yet, on those rare occasions when we happened to become engaged, I, for some reason, was usually on the other side of Fumo's interest.

My first personal glimpse of him wasn't even what you would describe as an encounter or an introduction. It was more of an observation. I had been working as press officer for the Democratic Senate caucus for just a few weeks. I was seated in a staff chair behind Tom Lamb's podium on the Senate floor when this young, high-energy, cherubic-looking lad walked confidently into the chamber from one of the rear portals. I didn't know who he was, but he approached Lamb and said something to the effect of "I'm here, chief."

Lamb replied, "Good, we'll talk later. I have some assignments I want to go over with you." The conversation was that brief.

After Fumo left the floor, Lamb turned to me and asked, "Do you know who that was?"

"No," I replied. "Never met him."

"That's Vince Fumo," Lamb explained. "He's Pete Camiel's guy. He's on my payroll as an assistant legal counsel. I told him he had to be in Harrisburg whenever the Senate was in session. You should know that in case you're ever asked by the press. He's pretty visible in Philadelphia political circles, and the question may come up."

"Thanks," I replied. "I'll remember that." But I never was asked what Fumo did to earn his keep on the Senate payroll. And our paths never crossed during Lamb's tenure.

Impulsive Tom Nolan Makes an Impulsive Decision

The first direct conversation I would have with Vince Fumo would come after Tom Nolan was elected majority leader, something that would not have been possible without the support of Fumo's political patron, Philadelphia City Chairman Pete Camiel.

Nolan was having dinner with Marty Murray's party one evening at a favorite Harrisburg eatery of the era, Lombardo's Gaslight Restaurant, just minutes drive from the Capitol. If it was not the evening of his election as majority leader, it was shortly thereafter. I was among the attendees, but I was seated at a different table than Murray and Nolan. So what I am about to describe was reported to me by those who personally overheard and witnessed the events.

Nolan's group included a reporter named Pat Boyle, the legendary Lindy Lindgren's successor as the Harrisburg correspondent for the *Pittsburgh Press*. Boyle had become a good friend with Nolan after Nolan's election to the Senate. Their Irish heritage and their western Pennsylvania roots made for a natural kinship, I suppose. More important from Boyle's perspective, Nolan made for good copy. Unpredictable as he was, Nolan did not require a lot of prompting to make news with his mouth. Sometimes, however, Boyle had to egg him on. This, apparently, was one of those occasions.

Nolan and Boyle were reported to have been needling each other (as they often did) over dinner, when Boyle teased that very little about the Senate would change under Nolan's leadership; that the system would co-opt him and his free spirit.

Nolan was said to have denied that, insisting that a lot of things were going to change.

Like what? Boyle challenged. "What can you do?"

"What would you say if I told you I was going to fire Vince Fumo?" Nolan was said to have responded.

"You're what?" Boyle asked incredulously. "You're going to fire Vince Fumo? You are not!"

"You bet I am," Nolan assured him. "We're going to cut down on that damn payroll," he asserted.

"Can I print that story?" Boyle asked. Nolan told him to go ahead.

It appeared on the surface to be a win-win for both. Boyle had a good story, Nolan would get good press back home. I don't know for a fact whether Nolan already had plans to dismiss Fumo from the staff, or whether it just sort of spilled out in his spontaneous dinner exchange with Boyle. What I do know is that the decision to cut Fumo was cemented in that conversation, and once Boyle printed it in the next day's edition of the *Pittsburgh Press,* there was no room for reconsideration. That was just one problem. The other was that no one had bothered to inform either Camiel or Fumo of Nolan's intention.

I didn't learn about Fumo's sudden dismissal until the next day when Dick Gerber, a peer of Fumo's and another Camiel protégé working in the Senate, came into my office to tell me that Nolan wanted to see me. I accompanied Gerber to Nolan's office where I was told of the decision to drop Fumo from the majority leader's payroll. But, Nolan added, he needed a letter to Vince. Boyle's press report implied that Fumo was being dismissed because he did very little to earn his keep.

"I need something to make it clear that Fumo was being terminated only because I have different needs on how the majority leader's office should be staffed, and that I regretted if the press misinterpreted that point," Nolan told me. "Clear the letter with Camiel. If it's okay with him, it's okay with me. Here's the number to call when you have something on paper."

I returned to my office and immediately penned a letter to Fumo from Nolan explaining the reasons for the terminations, assuring him it was in no way a reflection on his professional abilities and expressing regret if the abrupt announcement was misinterpreted. I called Camiel and was put right through (incidentally, the first and only time in my life we talked directly). I read Camiel the letter. He said it was fine. I believe he also said he would talk to Fumo. I told Nolan Camiel was okay with the language. He signed the letter and said I could release it. As the release was being finalized, my office phone rang.

It was Fumo. He said he understood a letter was about to be released. He asked me to read it to him. I did. He didn't like it. I can't recall exactly why; perhaps, from his point of view, it didn't make a strong enough case about the value of his service to the Senate.

I could see myself getting middled, and I wasn't interested in that. Besides, I worked for the Senate, not for Fumo. "If you have a problem, you need to talk to Nolan and Camiel," I suggested. "They cleared it, and I'm getting it ready to go. If you want it changed, I need to hear from them." I said I'd wait an hour or so before releasing it to the press. I never heard anything. I double-checked with Nolan about two hours later and was told to put the letter out. I did.

Nolan's letter made for only a short story in most publications. Even the *Philadelphia Inquirer* and the *Philadelphia Bulletin* gave it just passing play. But the sequence of events forever fascinated me. Here was a player of some note in Philadelphia politics, being abruptly dismissed by a Senate majority leader (who could not have been elected without Philadelphia's support) as a result of an idle conversation over dinner with a Pittsburgh newspaper reporter. It only served to reinforce my impression that with Tom Nolan anything was possible. It also marked the first time I was positioned at odds with Vince Fumo. There was more to come.

The Trial and the Senate Ethics Committee

Two years later, while Nolan, Fumo, and Camiel were on trial in federal criminal court, I had a second encounter with this political dynamo. I was now on Craig Lewis's staff and Craig, chairman of the Senate Local Government Committee, also was chairman of the bipartisan Senate Ethics Committee. It fell to the Ethics Committee to decide how to dispose of an issue involving Fumo's status within the Senate.

Even though he was on trial, Fumo had been elected that November to fill Buddy Cianfrani's seat in the chamber. (South Philadelphians were very forgiving of one of their own.) He was scheduled to take his oath when the new biennial session of the Senate convened in January. The problem was that the federal trial had not been concluded. The Ethics Committee was charged by the Senate to make a recommendation on what to do with Fumo when the Senate opened for business.

The issue really didn't require much deliberation on the committee's part. The legal precedent in the Mazzei case had been established that a jury conviction was not final under law until the presiding judge rendered his sentence. Guided by that principle, the committee ultimately would recommend a tradeoff to the full Senate: If Fumo would refrain from taking his oath of office until the trial proceedings were finished, the Senate would refrain from disciplinary action of any sort until the result was known and formalized.

Once again, I had another brief telephone conversation with Fumo on the subject. For some reason, he called me at home one evening demanding to know what was going on with the committee. He wasn't happy with what he was hearing.

There wasn't much I could tell him. The committee was reviewing the case at the direction of the Senate. Where it would take them, I didn't know. If he had some problem with that, he should more appropriately take it up with the Senate and not some staff intermediary. That was the essence of the exchange. Once again, I made the point as discreetly as I could that I worked for the Senate, not for him.

A few days later, I was with Lewis in his Capitol office when a call came from Fumo's attorney, M. Berle Schiller. (This is M. Berle Schiller, a nephew of Governor Milton Shapp who hired Fumo after Nolan dismissed him from the staff of the Senate; the M. Berle Schiller who Fumo later would have appointed to the Pennsylvania Superior Court; the same M. Berle Schiller who would twice run unsuccessfully with Fumo's backing for the Pennsylvania Supreme Court. Tentacles, remember?) Lewis's conversation with Schiller was about as brief as mine with Fumo, but it had a little more heat to it.

Lewis told Schiller what he expected the committee to recommend and he advised him to tell his client not to challenge the recommendation in any way. If he did, Lewis warned, there would be a move to expel Fumo inauguration day and, Lewis added, he would be leading the parade. (Come to think of it, there may have been more to Fumo's challenge to Lewis for the Appropriations Committee position than merely reclaiming the job for Philadelphia.)

As noted earlier here, the jury rendered a guilty verdict; the presiding judge overturned the verdict, and Fumo—an exonerated senator-elect—subsequently was sworn into the Senate. Now I did, in a way, work for him.

Nonetheless, our paths still seldom crossed on a day-to-day basis. Around budget time each year, Lewis would hear reports that Fumo was attempting to undercut his negotiating position in joint Senate-House conference committee negotiations. That may have been so, but his efforts never amounted to much within the caucus.

There were, of course, the two Fumo challenges that I've already recounted to take Lewis out as minority Appropriations chair. That he succeeded was not surprising. That it took him two attempts to do so was.

Why recount my fleeting experiences with Fumo here? Well, the man must be given his due. He's had a tremendous influence and impact on the legislative and political processes of his city and his state since he first was elected to public office. His political and legislative skills were enormous. He wasn't a member of Mensa by virtue of his acquired wealth or political power alone. He could and did play political hardball with the best of them. In the 2003 Pennsylvania municipal elections, Fumo's daughter from an earlier marriage ran as a Republican candidate for township commissioner in Whitemarsh Township. The Pennsylvania Senate Democratic Campaign Committee made a $1,000 contribution to the Whitemarsh Township Democratic campaign effort. There was a message in there somewhere. The Democrats, incidentally, won a political majority on the township board of commissioners. Senate Democratic aides denied Fumo had anything to do with this most unusual contribution. But that's too hard a line to swallow whole. Nothing that campaign committee did happened without "The Vince's" foreknowledge and consent.

Most forces in the political process would want Vince Fumo as an ally. Yet, in all his endless political missions, there always seemed to be an underlying question: What's in this for Vince? What's he really want? Motive undoubtedly was one of the principal reasons Fumo lost to Lewis in his first Appropriations challenge—that, the good work of the committee staff Lewis had assembled, and, of course, the presence and political conviction of Jim Lloyd.

For his part, Fumo seemed to relish his ability to keep folks always on guard. "I often say I'm most dangerous when I wear a white hat," he said in a 2004 interview.

If he is anything, Fumo is testimony to the essence of persistence and perseverance in the political and legislative process. Any setback he suffered was only temporary. He lost to Lewis the first time; he immediately began plotting his successful challenge for two years hence. His first effort to have Philadelphia ally Russell Nigro elected to the Pennsylvania Supreme Court failed. Nigro was back the very next election and won. Fumo failed twice in his efforts to get his friend Berle Schiller elected to the Supreme Court; Schiller ended up each time with a seat on the Superior Court, not a bad landing place for a loser. That's the point about Vince Fumo; set him back one way and he immediately begins planning a different course to essentially the same end.

As a personality, he could be charming or combative—depending on where you stood on his issues. But there is one thing he never was, nor ever will be, which is disengaged on matters he considered important. And, as noted, there was very little he didn't consider important. His worst enemy was political peace. He was most effective when the political pot was boiling; and if it wasn't, he was not at all averse to stirring issues to a boil for his own ends.

In 2003, when Governor Rendell and a majority of the House and Senate were aligned (fragilely, but still aligned) behind the proposal to expand gambling by legalizing slot machine parlors in the state, Fumo was the proverbial fly in the ointment. No surprise there. Fumo was insisting one or two of the slot parlors in the plan be reserved for American Indian interests. Rendell and the other pro-gaming advocates were opposed. But Fumo's clout in the Democratic caucus in the Senate was sufficient enough to withhold the votes necessary for passage since only a maximum of five Senate Republicans were prepared to vote in favor of the gambling expansion.

The proceeds from the gambling initiative were to be dedicated to property tax relief. House Republican Majority Leader Sam Smith of Jefferson County charged Fumo of "single-handedly" delaying if not denying "property tax relief for millions of Pennsylvanians" with his insistence on Indian gaming rights. Still Fumo was unmoved.

When John Baer asked Fumo what he was doing, he replied: "I'm not doing anything."

"Uh-huh," Baer concluded in his *Daily News* account. Expanded gambling ultimately did pass with Fumo's support. The Indian allocation was dropped. What concessions Vince may have gotten in the process, I don't pretend to know, since I had been long separated from state service.

As the year 2003 was winding down, Fumo became the center of another storm, this time involving a non-profit Citizens Alliance for Better Neighborhoods he set up and staffed and directed by aides from his vast political army. It turns out the largest contributor to this organization was Philadelphia Electric Company (PECO) to the tune of a $17 million contribution.

The contribution came after Fumo filed a lawsuit (subsequently settled) challenging PECO's right to bill its electric customers for its debt. Extortion? Probably not because Fumo's too smart to do something so transparent, although the FBI was reported by the press to be looking into the matter. Fumo, himself, was nonplussed by the attention. "I am a creative, entrepreneurial politician," he told Philadelphia radio station WHYY in an interview. "I don't sit in the back row and vote when my name is called. I do what I do for my district and that's my job." There's no disputing that. And, in fairness, the funds contributed to his Better Neighborhoods alliance did go to improvement projects in his Philadelphia Senate district.

One who rallied to his defense was Governor Ed Rendell, saying Fumo was "not the first legislator or government official to squeeze [a company] when he thought it would benefit the public." Of course, Rendell at the time still needed to win Fumo over on his gambling expansion plan if he was to generate the revenues he needed to make local property tax reductions possible throughout the Commonwealth. Common Cause, the good government, nonpartisan watchdog, however, had another take on Fumo's entrepreneurial bent. His method, said Barry Kauffman, Pennsylvania executive director, didn't "pass the smell test," adding, "We certainly expect Senator Fumo to bring resources to his community, but there are right ways and wrong ways of doing that."

With Vince Fumo, you can love him or leave him, but you can't ignore him. One veteran insider told John Baer, "Vince not only wants to be in the game, he wants to be the center of it."

Baer had another view. "Fact is, he did what he did because he can. He can because he is to the legislative process what Beethoven was to piano concertos—genius," he concluded in print. Baer and his source both were more right than they were wrong.

Vince Fumo is very, very good at what he does. Still, from a public policy perspective, with Vince there was always a question of motive. Others more involved with him and the process are better positioned to offer more informed conclusions than I on what drives him, whether it's on gambling, PECO or the many other matters on which he made his presence felt. I do know in my case, for whatever reason, Vince Fumo and Vince Carocci, in their limited contact, usually were in opposite corners. Not that it matters to anyone but myself, but, in some ways, it was a small, personal, private badge of honor I carried quietly with me when I left public service.

Part 3
★★★★★
The Governors

Chapter 11

★★★★★★★

Chief Executive Officer

Governor . . . the chief executive office of the Commonwealth . . . the pinnacle of state political power, prestige, and public policymaking in Pennsylvania. Only a select few of the many who aspire to it actually succeed in getting there.

Six different men served in that high office in the time that I walked the corridors of the Capitol, laboring daily in and around the affairs of state government, from the mid-term of David L. Lawrence of Pittsburgh in the early 1960s through the two terms of Robert P. Casey of Scranton in the mid-1990s. Some I saw up close, very close. Others I saw more from a distance. Three happened to be Democrats; three were Republicans. But whatever their political affiliation, each had his own particular set of public policy priorities and his own distinctive style of governing to achieve them.

Three of the six were encumbered by the one-term limitation that the state Constitution imposed at the time on their tenure—Governors Lawrence (1959–63), William W. Scranton (1963–67), and Raymond P. Shafer (1967–71). One-term governors had a very short political life span. If the political power of the office didn't make them lame ducks from virtually the moment they took their oath of office, their political influence certainly diminished considerably midway through their term two years later when all political focus would shift to the question of who would succeed them. For one-term governors, the window to press their executive agendas was very narrow indeed.

That all changed in 1967 under Governor Shafer when a constitutional amendment was advanced to permit the chief executives to serve a second consecutive term. It had Shafer's support, even though he would not be eligible for a second term himself, and it was adopted overwhelmingly by the voters in a statewide referendum.

With its adoption, the rules of executive governance changed dramatically and, I believe, decidedly for the better. Now, governors had not only the political clout of the office to advance an agenda, but they also had the political life and staying power (assuming the probability of reelection) to make their case over the long term with the state legislature, where the wheels of government turned much more slowly and often, depending on the political alignment, much more grudgingly.

Former Senate Minority Leader Ernest P. Kline, Milton Shapp's lieutenant governor and one who aspired himself to the governorship only to be denied by the electorate, had a take on governing in the state capital which could be applied to the ages. To paraphrase: "Things don't happen in Pennsylvania just because they're right," he said on more than one occasion. "It takes a lot of persuading, a lot of persistence and a lot of time and patience to get things done the way you would want them done."

That's because Pennsylvania is such a diverse state. "A vest pocket of America," as Governor Shafer used to call it on his executive flyovers across the Commonwealth. Pennsylvania is a state in which the culture, the economies, the mores, the values, the needs of a region like northeast Pennsylvania are so distinctly different than metropolitan Philadelphia and its suburbs; where Philadelphians and their suburban neighbors clearly have a different view of life in Pennsylvania than their city and suburban brothers and sisters in and around Pittsburgh; and where none of them is quite the same as life in the southern boundaries of Central Pennsylvania through the rugged northern tier of the Commonwealth. In Erie and Crawford counties to the great Northwest, the way of life, not to mention the geography and climate, are more akin to neighboring Ohio than they are to much of Pennsylvania. (An airline attendant with the former Allegheny Airlines concluded a late flight to Erie one cold winter night with the cavalier comment, "Welcome to Erie, the Mistake by the Lake." It clearly was intended as a light ending to a long day, but, one of her passengers, Erie mayor Louis Tullio, took strong exception. Not long after the attendant found herself a *former* employee of Allegheny Airlines. Apparently, attempts at humor, in vain or not, get lost in Erie in the winter.)

Because of this stark regional diversity, governing in Pennsylvania can be challenging, to say the least. It requires a chief executive to seek out a common ground with the General Assembly, to bring the disparate views of these disparate regions to a common agreement on the public interest of a common objective without settling in the process for the lowest common denominator. That's why Kline understood as a former legislative leader that it took a lot of patience, persistence, and persuasion to achieve a desired end. In that context, for Pennsylvania governors, eight years was much better than four to get done the things they consider important.

Milton Shapp of Merion, Montgomery County, became the first of the two-term Pennsylvania governors with his election in 1970 and reelection in 1974. Richard L. Thornburgh of Pittsburgh (elected in 1978, reelected in

1982), the aforementioned Casey (1986, 1990) and Tom Ridge of Erie (1994, 1998) (the latter whom I did not know and will not presume to write about) continued the electoral precedent started by Shapp.

Something happening about the time of Milton Shapp's arrival in Harrisburg would have profound and lasting effect on governing in Pennsylvania. The General Assembly was emerging as a political and policymaking force of its own, a coequal branch of government in Pennsylvania, if you will, whose members most often had a political lifespan in the Capitol longer than a governor's. Prior to, and into the first half of David Lawrence's tenure, the General Assembly was considered a part-time instrument of government, manned by part-time public servants who essentially volunteered their time and services to the Commonwealth at low pay and short hours. The legislature, in fact, convened for business only once every two years prior to the Lawrence tenure.

That began to change in the Lawrence era when the General Assembly started to meet every year, though the sessions in even-numbered years were limited at first only to consideration of the governor's annual budget. The even-numbered-year session soon morphed into annual, open sessions. Today, the General Assembly functions in the continuing biennial format followed by the U.S. Congress, and state legislators are every bit as full-time as their congressional counterparts.

It might fairly be said that through the Lawrence, Scranton, and Shafer years legislators largely were beholden to their political leadership at both the state and local level for their continued tenure in office. It was that climate that leaders like Congressman William Green of Philadelphia and then-mayor of Pittsburgh Lawrence could dictate to their party caucuses who their elected leaders would be for the forthcoming legislative session, and what agendas they would pursue. By the time Shapp arrived, however, that landscape was changing . . . slowly, perhaps, but changing nonetheless. Legislative staffing and funding were increased steadily through the years, coincidentally, as the absolute power of the political parties began their steady decline. Legislators began to become political entities in their own right with their own political identities in their districts back home. By the end of the Shapp reign, political leaders still had a voice in the legislative process, but it was diminished to such a degree that by the turn of the decade to the 1980s, a Craig Lewis from Bucks County could defeat a Joe Smith of Philadelphia in a contested caucus election for the position as Democrat chair of the Senate Appropriations Committee. Such a revolt of the rank-and-file would have been unheard of twenty years earlier.

Now governors and the political leadership of their parties could no longer simply dictate almost by political fiat to members of the General Assembly on when and how the roll should be called in the Senate or House of Representatives. Now they had to lead; they had to build consensus; they had to, on occasion, bargain for their legislative support (remember Frank Kury and the Sunbury bridge). It was a new game with new rules for the Capitol. The legislature was quick to welcome—even relish—the newfound powers it possessed. The learning curve took somewhat longer for the governors.

What follows are subjective reflections on the tenures and the records of the governors who toiled as I traveled the Capitol in my professional pursuits, along with some comments and insights into their personalities and styles of governance gleaned by personal observations and/or upfront and personal experiences. Let's take them in their order.

Chapter 12

★★★★★★★

David L. Lawrence (1959–1963)

Pittsburgh's David L. Lawrence was "Mr. Democrat" to many in Pennsylvania for more than a quarter of a century. He was elected governor in 1958 after a very successful, four-term run as the "Renaissance Mayor" of western Pennsylvania's most metropolitan city.

Lawrence long had been a major figure in Democratic state party politics. But he fashioned his enviable reputation as a public chief executive by the mayoral alliances he forged with business and civic leaders in the mid-1940s and early 1950s to revitalize Pittsburgh in dramatic ways. The project was one of the most ambitious urban renewal efforts of any major city in the country at the time. Under Lawrence's stewardship, Pittsburgh was transformed from a decaying, blighted, smog-laden urban center linked primarily to the declining steel industry for its economic base into a modern, alive metropolitan enclave with a much more diversified economic foundation and future. The "Pittsburgh Renaissance," it was called, and David Lawrence was its principal public architect.

According to my press colleagues, Lawrence had been a reluctant Democratic candidate for governor. According to conventional press wisdom, the party endorsement, so powerful a political force at the time, would have gone to Philadelphia reform mayor Richardson Dilworth if he had made a bid for it. Dilworth, however, had already lost one race for governor eight years earlier in 1950 and reportedly was doubtful that the conservative state of Pennsylvania was ready to elect a big-city mayor, and a second consecutive Democrat no less, to succeed Democrat George Leader of York County. So it was, as the story went, that Lawrence, content with his position as mayor of Pittsburgh and with really no ambitions to move on, was persuaded to make the race instead. He defeated the Republican nominee, Reading pretzelmaker Arthur McGonigle, by a mere 76,000 votes out of some four million cast to win the governorship. Richardson Dilworth, for all his considerable attributes and accomplishments in public service, never got to be governor of Pennsylvania, though he would try once more.

Lawrence not only became the first Pennsylvania Democrat of the twentieth century to succeed a member of his party in the governor's office, he also became the Commonwealth's first Roman Catholic chief executive. His Catholicism was one of the reasons he reportedly was reluctant to run for governor in the first place. Catholics, he was said to have believed, would not run well in a conservative state like Pennsylvania with its Bible-belted T running through the central part of the state up to and across most of the northern tier.

The "Catholic factor" was also a principal reason Lawrence was initially reluctant to back the presidential candidacy of Massachusetts senator John F. Kennedy in 1960. Lawrence was an Adlai Stevenson supporter. Despite his own success in Pennsylvania, Lawrence reportedly had reservations about the electoral impact Kennedy's Catholicism would have in the Midwest and the Deep South. Kennedy was not very happy with him.

"Off the record," Kennedy asked a Pennsylvania reporter riding with him during a delegate sweep through the Commonwealth, "who does your governor think he is that he's the only Catholic who can win in a state like Pennsylvania?"

Kennedy would, of course, move steadily toward the nomination. Still, Lawrence was very slow to join the Kennedy parade. In fact, it wasn't until just about the time he arrived for the Democratic nominating convention in Los Angeles as chair of the Pennsylvania delegation that he formally turned in for Kennedy. One story that circulated through the press corps (though it might be apocryphal) was that the governor called Kennedy headquarters en route from the airport to declare his support. If that was true, he was just a bit late. U.S. Congressman William Green Sr. of Philadelphia, who shared the political leadership of the Democratic Party in Pennsylvania with Lawrence, had announced his support of Kennedy much before the national convention. The future president never forgot that. While Lawrence appeared to maintain a cordial political relationship with the Kennedy White House, it was clearly understood in the important, inside political circles that Philadelphia's Bill Green was the Kennedy man in Pennsylvania.

Governor Lawrence was midway through his term when I arrived in Harrisburg in the spring of 1961, so my impressions of him were formed from a distance. But they were very positive. As a person, he struck me as a cordial, pleasant sort, the kind you'd love to sit around a table with and listen while he traded political stories with his peers. He had an easy manner with people and often a ready smile on his face. Yet he also was very businesslike in his public demeanor and dress, even in the most social of settings.

When I arrived in Harrisburg, there was a long-established tradition for the governor to entertain the capital press corps and their families each summer at a pool party at the Indiantown Gap Military Reservation, where the chief executive lived at the time. I went to my first one that summer of

1961. The press corps, their wives, their kids, and the gubernatorial staff were dressed casually as befitted the occasion. Governor Lawrence, however, was wearing his ever-present business suit, white shirt, and tie.

About mid-afternoon a group of senior reporters started playing Hearts—Hearts and poker were the journalists' card games of choice—over a picnic table in a shaded area off the pool pavilion. Lawrence shed his suit jacket and sat in. That in itself—the governor of Pennsylvania playing cards with a group of crusty reporters—was fascinating to me. But it was nothing compared to what was to come.

One of the players was a Harrisburg radio and civic personality, Pete Wambach Sr. When I first met him, he was a speechwriter in the office of Lawrence's lieutenant governor, John Morgan Davis. He also doubled as a disc jockey and announcer in the early evenings on one of the local radio stations, broadcasting from a studio at a suburban Harrisburg restaurant and bar, which made the place one of the Capitol crowd's favorite evening gathering places. If someone notable happened to walk by while he was on the air, Pete would mention it to his audience: "There's Jack Lynch of the Associated Press and Gene Harris of United Press International. Good to see you fellas. Do your wives know you're out? Well, they sure do now," he'd chuckle.

Wambach, the gregarious semi-celebrity that he was, certainly wasn't in awe of the political figures or other capital personalities with whom he regularly came in contact. That included the governor of Pennsylvania. Midway through the game, Wambach dropped the dreaded queen of spades on the governor. "Take that, you old sunuvabitch," he exclaimed with a broad smile on his face.

I was kibitzing near by and I was stunned at what I had just heard. My God, I remember reacting. He just called the governor of Pennsylvania a "sunuvabitch"! I can't believe it.

Lawrence was nonplussed. He calmly collected his cards with a touch of a smile on his face. He looked at Pete and said very quietly, "You will pay, Peter my boy, you will pay."

One reporter, I forget exactly who, quipped very quickly: "Don't open any official looking envelopes tomorrow, Pete. You never know what just might be in it."

David L. Lawrence of Pittsburgh was the last of the old-time pols to reach the governor's mansion in Pennsylvania. He rose through the ranks of his party (U.S. Collector of Internal Revenue for the Western District of Pennsylvania, Secretary of the Commonwealth in 1934, Democratic State Chairman that same year, Democratic National Committeeman). He had a

Harry Truman sense of public policy priorities and governing about him, and an old-school premium on party principles, party loyalty, and, above all, the bond of one's word to another in the political process.

Two public policies of his administration stood out in my brief observation of his term: the high priority he placed on highway traffic safety (Lawrence and his wife had lost two sons in a traffic accident fifteen years before his election as governor) and the emphasis he placed on the cautious, careful management of the Commonwealth's fiscal affairs.

Lawrence, as I heard the newsroom vets repeatedly conjecture, was determined that the Democratic candidate to succeed him (the aforementioned Richardson Dilworth) was not going to be saddled with Republican accusations of careless or irresponsible spending by the incumbent administration. No spend-and-tax Democrat would he be, even then, but certainly not in an election year. So his last budget submission was very frugal, very penny-tight, certainly by traditional Democratic standards. But it was of no help to Dilworth. Republican William W. Scranton won an easy, 486,000-vote victory in the 1962 gubernatorial election. Lawrence was heard to complain after the election, "Keeping that budget in balance the way we did didn't mean a damn thing to the campaign." Still, his staff confided, he said if he had to do it all over knowing the result in advance, there was probably very little he would have done differently in preparing and proposing the budget that he did.

Lawrence was the last Pennsylvania governor born in the nineteenth century (1889). He also was the first governor of Pennsylvania to whom I posed a question as a rookie member of the capital press corps. Perhaps that's why I remember his years the way I do.

In those days (long before the advent of television as a major news medium) the governor would hold his press conferences in his inner office. Lawrence would sit at the inner ring of his horseshoe-like desk. The press corps regulars were seated around the rim on the other side. The overflow (and as a rookie, I was most definitely a part of the overflow) sat in leather chairs or sofas strategically placed for visitors along the walls of the office.

Lawrence was ruminating in response to questions about the Dilworth-Scranton gubernatorial campaign when the subject of political polls came up. Polling was in its most primitive stage of development at that time. But one sampling by a Republican pollster out of Philadelphia made its way to print which, if accurate, was none too encouraging for Dilworth and Pennsylvania Democrats.

"Governor, what do you think of polls, and how important are they to a campaign?" I queried from my seat along the wall.

He looked a bit quizzically before responding. It was one of those "You're new around here, aren't you?" looks.

"It depends," he finally answered. "Who took it and how much you can trust it." He added that he thought polls could help determine what issues were most important to people, but he didn't think campaigns should frame their strategies around poll results.

That exchange, in many ways, marked my beginning as a Capitol Hill journalist. It was not an auspicious beginning, to be sure. But it was, for me, a beginning.

Chapter 13

★★★★★★★

William Warren Scranton II (1963–1967)

I was, you might say, an accidental observer to the entry of William Warren Scranton II into elective politics and public service in Pennsylvania and the nation.

In the spring of 1960 I was serving as a second lieutenant in the U.S. Army Intelligence Corps. My duty station was Washington, D.C. My hometown congressman from the Scranton area at the time was a Democrat named Stanley Prokop. Congressman Prokop was a likable fellow from one of the bedroom communities outside the city, but was never regarded as a political power in his own right.

Still, my father encouraged me to pay him a courtesy visit. While serving on Scranton City Council he had come to know Prokop through their mutual travels in Lackawanna County Democratic Party politics. "He's a nice guy, you'll like him," my dad told me. "Stop in and say hello." So I did. In fact, that's exactly what I was doing when our conversation was interrupted by a telephone call from his Lackawanna County district office.

"No kidding," I heard the congressman say. "Well, that'll certainly make things interesting this year."

As he cradled the telephone into its receiver, he looked up at me and smiled. "I've just learned who my opponent will be this fall," he said.

"Who might that be?" I asked.

"William Scranton of the Scranton Scrantons," he replied.

Instinctively, I thought to myself, now that's going to be trouble. But I tried to be supportive. "How 'bout that!" I offered. "Well, he's new to politics. That should work in your favor." I think we both knew we were whistling past the graveyard, in a manner of speaking.

The Scrantons of Scranton were one of the region's most established, most prominent families, not to mention one of the wealthiest. The fact that the city bore the family name was testimony, indeed, to the standing of the Scrantons in the community and the region. Marion Margery Warren Scranton, the family matriarch and the prospective candidate's mother, was particularly active in Republican Party state politics. In northeast Pennsylvania she was universally regarded as a GOP powerbroker.

Bill Scranton's debut as an active political candidate might have been surprising to some, but it really shouldn't have been. He regularly accompanied his mother to Republican presidential conventions where he met and mingled with state and national political leaders of his party. Personally, he could have stepped right out of candidate central casting—in his mid-forties, a graduate of Yale Law School, national public service as a deputy secretary of state during the Eisenhower administration, reputable family, business, and civic ties, and a photogenic young family of his own. It doesn't get much better than that.

Still, his declaration of his candidacy for Congress, formidable though it was, was not so formidable to immediately send tremors of fear through the ranks of the Lackawanna County Democrats. The party, after all, was a very successful and powerful political force in its own right. Democrats outnumbered Republicans by about 50,000 voters in the district, and the seat had been Democratic for a number of years. In that context, and understanding full well the stress, anxiety, and infighting in virtually every campaign for public office, even his mother was reported to have discouraged him initially from making the race. The ultimate question was how well this young blueblood would take to the rigors of a political campaign, how well this "Yaley" would relate to the largely blue-collar, working-class folks who were the core of this particular congressional district.

Candidate Scranton put the question to rest quite early and quite emphatically. Truth was, he took to political campaigning with the best of them. He exhibited an easy and genuine personal touch that won people over in very short order. His family name, resources, and influence may have given him his political entrée. But it was his warmth and his people skills that ultimately carried him to victory by 17,000 votes over Congressman Prokop in November, a character trait he nurtured naturally and to even greater heights throughout his public career. Sadly, his mother died earlier that same year without ever seeing her son elected. But, clearly and without a lot of people outside inner state Republican circles necessarily noting, a new political presence had arrived on the Pennsylvania political scene.

My next encounter with the political fortunes of William W. Scranton II occurred about a year later, again as much by accident as anything. By now I was working the night desk in the Harrisburg bureau of United Press International. Pennsylvania Republicans were beginning to position themselves for the 1962 gubernatorial campaign to succeed Democrat David Lawrence in the governor's residence. Scranton's name always was on any list of prospective GOP candidates. The freshman congressman himself had little to say publicly about the subject. Little to say, that is, until I and other reporters found ourselves on the other end of a late-afternoon conference call from Scranton's chief congressional aide, Bill Keisling. Keisling read a statement on the congressman's behalf that unequivocally disavowed any interest or intent to seek the Republican nomination for governor in 1962. Sherman could not have been more Sherman-like in taking his name out of consideration.

Meanwhile, state Superior Court Judge Robert E. Woodside of Dauphin County and Scranton's congressional colleague, James Van Zandt of Blair County, were among those who had declared their designs on the GOP gubernatorial nomination. Ultimately, and with at least some political backing, they paired up (or were paired up by party leaders)—Woodside for governor, Van Zandt for U.S. Senate. Initial reaction from the press and the pundits was that the Republican race essentially was over. "Woodside–Van Zandt—Who Can Stop Them?" *Harrisburg Evening News* chief political reporter John Scotzin asked rhetorically in a bylined story as the 1962 election year approached.

The conventional wisdom of the moment was wrong. Somebody, if not in fact a collection of powerful Republican somebodies, apparently had some second thoughts about this prospective ticket. As the endorsement process moved closer, the press began to pick up on a growing unease among Republican powerbrokers. The uncertainty seemed to focus largely on Judge Woodside, clearly a well-respected jurist, but untested in the rigors and theater of high-visibility political campaigning. The aforementioned Richardson Dilworth, with his combative personality and political style, was back in gubernatorial harness. He almost was certain to be the Democratic nominee. The closer the calendar moved to the '62 election cycle, the greater the anxiety among GOP insiders over the ability of the judicially tempered Woodside to face off toe to toe with Dilworth in the bare-knuckles campaign most everyone expected this to be.

Democrats had occupied the governor's office since George Leader's election in 1954. Enough was enough. The Republican Party wanted badly to end that run. But Republican financial contributors had little interest in investing in a third consecutive losing campaign for the executive mansion. As questions whether Judge Woodside was the horse to back in this race began to mount, a behind-the-scenes search to find a more formidable and battle-tested candidate began to intensify. Scranton became alternative number one. He told party leaders that he would run only if all sixty-seven Republican county chairmen endorsed him. Sixty-six did. That was good enough. Woodside was encouraged to withdraw. Scranton's race was on.

From the sidelines, there was more than enough political logic to having this engaging young congressman carry the Republican gubernatorial banner. He was a proven winner, a winner no less than in a congressional district that had long belonged to the other party. His service in the State Department and the Congress, though brief, had established his bona fides as a public servant. He had the upbringing and education to legitimize his candidacy. His political pedigree was impeccable. Most important, Scranton had the smell of a winner, and that's what the party wanted most—a winner. Congressman Van Zandt remained on the ticket as Scranton's running mate for the U.S. Senate against Democratic incumbent Joseph Clark. John Scotzin had been at least half-right in his earlier prognostication.

The campaign proved to be as combative as its billing, in a fascinating sort of way. Here were these two patrician bluebloods doing battle in the rough-and-tumble world of elective politics with no holds barred. Dilworth was blunt, outspoken, and in-your-face as advertised. A former Marine, he never flinched from the hand-to-hand kind of warfare political campaigns often demanded. As a successful reform mayor of Philadelphia, he had already established he had the inner toughness to carry the Democratic fight to the largely untested Scranton.

Scranton, on the other hand, was playing on a large political stage for the first time. He had been challenged for the Republican nomination by J. Collins McSparran, the president of the Pennsylvania Grange, a statewide farm organization. The challenge, though credible, was beaten back rather handily. Now the real test was to come. In both the primary and the general election campaigns, Scranton put on display very quickly the considerable and easy personal touches that made him a winner back home. He and his wife, Mary, could work a room like no other political couple that I observed in my years in and around Pennsylvania politics. They'd walk into a reception, he'd head in one direction, she the other. Before they met up again, usually somewhere around the center of the room, virtually every person in the place had shaken the hand and spoken to either the candidate or his wife, sometimes both. Most folks left the event feeling good about the brief one-on-one encounter they had that evening with the prospective governor or his first lady.

Scranton also proved he had more than enough inner mettle to parry Dilworth's frontal assaults. One face-to-face encounter in the city of Scranton was particularly memorable. The *Philadelphia Bulletin*'s Duke Kaminski described the event in this way for those of us in the Capitol newsroom who were not there to witness it for ourselves.

Dilworth's campaign seemed to be faltering as the election drew near. He decided to take the fight directly to Scranton and to take the stand in his opponent's hometown. He challenged Scranton to a televised debate on one of the city's major television stations. He even offered to pay for the time. The Scranton campaign politely declined (probably offering the customary excuse that they, not the opposition, will set their own schedule, thank you.) That was fine with Dilworth. He bought time for a Saturday evening debate on Scranton television, anyway. There was an empty chair set on the stage to dramatize Scranton's absence. Democrats billed the event as the "Empty Chair" debate. The tactic had worked with some success for Dilworth once before in a 1947 Philadelphia mayoralty race. Dilworth strategists hoped it would work as well again. It didn't.

Just minutes before airtime, who should pop into the studio but William Scranton. He was carrying a whitewash bucket, a prop to reinforce his campaign charge that Dilworth was whitewashing some of the transgressions (alleged or otherwise) of the incumbent Democratic Lawrence administration. (Scranton apparently liked props in his political campaigning. Four years later, when the record of his administration was under constant attack from Democratic gubernatorial Milton Shapp, a self-made multimillionaire who spent over $1 million of his personal wealth to win the nomination, the then-governor threw a pile of play money into a Republican rally, declaring: "This is how he [Shapp] hopes to win this election!")

But back to the debate. More accurately, the debate—or was it a confrontation?—after the debate. According to Kaminski, Dilworth, an excitable personality to begin with, was visibly unnerved, angry, and clearly thrown off message by Scranton's eleventh-hour appearance. Whatever advantage the Democratic nominee hoped to gain from the event was lost. Scranton's drop-in was the storyline for the night. And not only did he gain great press for his campaign, but he achieved it at Democratic expense since the Dilworth campaign had paid for the airtime. In politics, that's about as win-win a situation as one could imagine. Dilworth was incensed when the two candidates encountered each other in a corridor outside the studio after the show had ended. It made for great political theatre and the press was there to record it.

As Kaminski told it, with perhaps in a bit of hyperbole, Dilworth got right in Scranton's face, boiling mad. Scranton pointed a finger at him in rebuke.

"Don't you point your bony, effeminate finger at me!" Dilworth shouted at his opponent. According to Kaminski, he appeared just inches away from getting physical.

But Scranton refused to be baited. "You, sir, are a desperate man," Scranton responded coolly as he turned and walked away. Kaminski said he had a smile on his face when he did.

The incident was certainly the most memorable of the campaign. But it was not the decisive factor in the outcome. Scranton defeated Dilworth by 438,000 votes. In the process, his victory established a pattern for Pennsylvania gubernatorial politics that would hold into the twenty-first century. Beginning with the Leader-Lawrence Democratic wins in 1954 and 1958, voters of Pennsylvania elected their governors from the same political party in eight-year cycles. Forty-eight years later, in 2002, the pattern was still holding when Democrat Edward Rendell ended an eight-year Republican reign in the governor's office.

What the 1962 election really established, however, was that the Republican powerbrokers who were so nervous about Judge Woodside's ability to take on the brawling political style of Philadelphia's Richardson Dilworth were so right in their assessment of William Warren Scranton II. "Born of the manor," as Republican House Speaker Matt Ryan would call him years later, or not, Scranton proved to be one tough political campaigner. Now he had to prove that he could govern.

The team Scranton assembled around him was remarkable by Harrisburg standards for its comparative youth and its undisputed familiarity with the ways of the state Capitol. The "Whiz Kids," they were called. The brain trust was headed by Chief of Staff Bill Keisling, Scranton's ranking congressional aide and speechwriter extraordinaire, a former reporter for the *Scranton Tribune*. Jack Conmy, a friend and peer of Keisling's from their days together at the *Tribune*, was recruited from the Dupont Company in Wilmington, Delaware to serve as press secretary. Jim Reichley, whose political roots were in New York state, was the resident thinker and intellectual. He was appointed legislative secretary, but also doubled up as a speechwriter and policy advisor. The only "veteran" on the staff, so to speak, was Bill Murphy, a trusted confidant to Republican U.S. Senator Hugh Scott, who was appointed secretary to the governor. Word had it that Scott insisted he have his man on the inside of the new and still-to-be tested state administration. Murphy was pegged as that guy.

Scranton and his team brought a high sense of energy, what seemed to be perpetual motion and a new operating style to Harrisburg. They were to the Capitol at the time much like the Kennedy crowd was to Washington in the same era. They certainly were eager; they were bright; they also were smart enough to recognize there was much they didn't know about the state capital and its ways. To that end, they forged effective alliances with their veteran

Republican leadership in the legislature. Meanwhile, newly elected Republican legislators like Matt Ryan of Delaware County, a future Speaker of the House, and Bob Butera of Montgomery County, a future House Republican floor leader, rallied to the administration's agenda with their compatible political views and objectives. It was a fun time to be a Republican in the state capital.

There was one Republican elder, however, who the Scranton crowd seemed to shunt aside in the early stages of the new administration. The venerable George I. Bloom, the party state chairman, was to the Pennsylvania Republican Party ("Mr. Republican") what David Lawrence was to Pennsylvania Democrats, one of its wisest operatives and statesman. It did appear at first that Bloom had been relegated to a relatively obscure cabinet post, secretary of the Commonwealth, so that the administration could put a new face on the voice and image of the party. Craig Truax, a young Bloom aide and protégé who was more in keeping with the youthful political style of the new governor and his team, was named to replace him.

The fact that Bloom had trouble meeting with the vacationing governor-elect at Scranton's Hobe Sound, Florida, postelection retreat where the administration was taking shape (reportedly there was a problem with some restrictive covenants barring people of Jewish faith like Bloom access) only compounded the perception. It didn't take the press and the conventional corridor crowd long to conclude that Bloom was largely a non-persona who, if not totally ignored, had little hand in the selection of a new governing team and the planning of the political and policy agenda. The Scranton team quickly came to learn, however, what an asset an old pro like George Bloom could be.

Scranton's first challenge as governor, as with all his predecessors, was to enact a state budget. To balance it, he had to propose an increase in the state sales tax. Raising taxes is always a difficult swallow for the General Assembly, but it is particularly difficult for a General Assembly controlled by a Republican Party, even with a dashing new governor of their own at the helm. Scranton's modest request to increase the state sales tax by one-half cent, later enacted at a full penny, proved to be no different.

The inside story had it that it was George I. Bloom (with or without Scranton's blessing, I don't know) who came to the governor's rescue. He had a back-channel meeting with a rural Democratic member of the House, Erwin "Erg" Murray from tiny Cameron County. Murray agreed to cast a critical vote for the Scranton sales-tax increase. In return, he wanted a commitment from the administration to locate a state highway shed in his county, a very, very big deal for tiny Cameron County. Scranton got Murray's vote.

Cameron County got a commitment for a highway shed. The budget passed and George Bloom's reputation as a very important political counsel to the governor and his inner circle was reestablished . . . as it should have been.

With the sales tax out of the way and a Republican-controlled legislature in hand, Scranton had a very smooth ride his first two years in office. So smooth, in fact, that he caught the attention of the national media and the national political community. With the 1964 presidential election just two years away, it was not unusual in those days for national political reporters like David Broder (then of the *New York Times,* later the dean of the Beltway correspondents with the *Washington Post*) to come to Harrisburg to meet the governor and take their mark of the man and the future he might have in national politics.

I encountered Broder one day in the food line of the Capitol cafeteria. "What is it about Bill Scranton," I asked, "that seems to fascinate the national press corps? He doesn't seem all that special to us here."

"You're probably too close to it," Broder replied diplomatically. He could have said something like, "You guys don't know what you have here." He would have been right, too. Instead, he continued: "From where we sit, he has all the attributes a party might look for in a potential presidential candidate. He's young, articulate, a winner in a Democratic state who runs by all measures a very successful state administration. He has access to money; in fact, he has money of his own. His political bloodlines are first rate. For starters, that's not bad at all." Broder was on target in his assessment of Governor Scranton. The capital press corps did tend to be parochial and often oblivious to the potential of the Pennsylvania politicians they knew best.

Ironically, it was this national exposure that, perhaps, tarnished Scranton's reputation as much as any other event on his public record. In 1964 Arizona U.S. Senator Barry Goldwater, the father of modern-day political conservatism, was heading full speed toward capturing the Republican presidential nomination and control of the national Republican Party, its political machinery, and its political voice.

That prospect struck total fear in the hearts and minds of the so-called eastern liberal wing of the GOP. The so-labeled moderates like Pennsylvania's Hugh Scott and New York governor Nelson Rockefeller turned to Scranton as their Goldwater alternative. True to form when pressed to pursue higher public office, Scranton resisted their persistent entreaties at first. But at some point he had a change of heart. His initial performance on the national political stage proved shaky at best, however.

The National Governor's Association was meeting in Cleveland. Scranton, as one of the Republican Party's brighter lights, was booked for an appearance on the Sunday news show *Meet the Press*. It was a high-profile appearance before a national audience. Word leaked in Cleveland and quickly circulated across the country that Scranton would announce on the program that he would contest Senator Goldwater for the Republican presidential nomination. The national press corps, which just loves a good political fight, waited in eager anticipation.

The announcement never came, however. Scranton hemmed and hawed his way through the program, dancing around both the political impact of a Goldwater candidacy on the Republican Party nationally and his own presidential intentions. Fred Astaire couldn't have tiptoed around the question any better. In political terms, his performance was disastrous. It certainly was embarrassing to the Republican moderates who were pushing him into the race. It had to be embarrassing to him personally. The supposed moderate alternative to Barry Goldwater looked unsure of himself on national television, anything but resolute. He came back to Pennsylvania a paper tiger, an emperor with no clothes who had been exposed as such before a national audience.

As pieced together in later press accounts, there was a simple explanation for what had derailed Scranton's anticipated announcement. It involved former president Dwight D. Eisenhower, a high lord in Republican politics who settled on a farm in Gettysburg after his tenure in the White House ended. No Republican with any national political aspirations dared advance them publicly without first consulting with Ike. Pilgrimages to Gettysburg—to seek if not Eisenhower's blessing or tacit consent, then at least his neutrality—became standard fare in Republican national politics at the time.

The fact that Scranton would consult at length with Eisenhower in advance of any presidential announcement was mandatory. When Scranton had that discussion, according to his staff, he apparently went away with the impression the former president was not opposed to his entry into the presidential derby. In fact, some Scranton aides later suggested, Ike gave every impression he would not at all be adverse to a challenge to Goldwater. Eisenhower's position was critical. He would certainly be among the first whose reaction to a Scranton candidacy would be sought, and if he expressed opposition or even the slightest reservation, Scranton's bid, for all intents and purposes, would be doomed almost from the moment it was launched. Scranton went to Cleveland thinking he had the Ike base covered.

Not so, as the story was pieced together by the press. Eisenhower called Scranton in Cleveland shortly before the *Meet the Press* broadcast. It could have been minutes before the show was to go on the air, or it could have been the night before. I don't really know but my suspicion was it was more the former than the latter. Whenever he called, the message from the former president was indisputable. According to Scranton aides, Eisenhower told the governor he wanted to be absolutely clear. While he might understand the reasons Scranton contemplated a presidential bid, Eisenhower would be no part of a "cabal" to deny Goldwater the Republican nomination. *Webster's* defines cabal as "a group of conspiratorial advisors" intent on carrying out some "secret design." Ike, not particularly known for his eloquent syntax, had added a new word to the national political lexicon of the era. But Scranton understood immediately. Eisenhower would not support his challenge to Goldwater publicly.

What apparently happened as word of Scranton's intentions circulated through Republican political circles was that former Eisenhower secretary of the Treasury George Humphrey called Ike. Humphrey, from Utah, was a conservative backer of Goldwater's. He somehow persuaded Eisenhower that an intraparty fight over Goldwater's nomination would be more harmful to the Republican Party than would a Goldwater candidacy itself. By whatever line of reasoning, Ike must have concurred, hence the call to Scranton in Cleveland. When Eisenhower pulled the rug out from under the governor, Scranton was left to fend for himself on national television. It was not pretty, but there probably was no other way it could play out ... unsteady and uncertain at best, weak and vacillating at worst. The national press corps, which does not like to be misled in such matters after having touted the pending challenge to Senator Goldwater, dubbed the governor the "Hamlet of Harrisburg." (Years later, national Democrats would have a "Hamlet" of their own, New York governor Mario Cuomo who danced around so many presidential bids of his own in the late '80s and early '90s that he came to be called the "Hamlet of Albany." Shakespeare, anyone?)

The ignominy of the *Meet the Press* performance must have gnawed at Scranton more than we in the press could have realized. A few weeks later, and just weeks before the Republican nominating convention was to convene in San Francisco, Scranton had a change of heart. He flew to Baltimore, Maryland, to declare himself formally a candidate for the Republican nomination and launch a belated but furious bid for delegate support.

Jack Lynch, my colleague at the Associated Press, was assigned to cover the Scranton announcement in Baltimore. That morning, as he was walking through the chambers of the state House of Representatives to the governor's office in the state Capitol to make a last check on the governor's itinerary, who did he happen to encounter but Scranton himself.

"Good luck," Jack offered as a courtesy.

"Thanks, boss" (Scranton was famous for greeting most everyone as "boss"), the governor replied. "It looks like I'm going to need it."

Scranton's candidacy probably was doomed from the start. It was very, very late in the process; Senator Goldwater had been mining the core of the Republican Party nationally for far too long and with far too much success for Scranton to deny him the nomination. The Scranton campaign was a kamikaze mission politically. The candidate said his concern over the civil-rights direction of the Goldwater campaign was what most compelled him to make the belated bid. But, I suspect, there also was a personal and perhaps more important purpose to the mission. The political purpose was to give voice to the centrist forces in the Republican Party nationally as its rank-and-file moved in tidal force to the right. The personal? Well, there was a reputation to salvage.

Scranton, by most measures, was successful on both fronts. He campaigned very creditably across the country. In the process, he reintroduced himself to the American public as a thoughtful and articulate public figure. (This would prove important when he was nominated some years later by President Ford to be U.S. ambassador to the United Nations.) But there was no denying Goldwater at the convention, not even in a liberal bastion like San Francisco. It was in his San Francisco acceptance speech that Goldwater uttered a phrase that remains in our political-speak still today. "Extremism in the defense of liberty is no vice; moderation in the pursuit of justice is no virtue," Goldwater declared. Goldwater won a resounding first-ballot victory. Ike's brother Milton, incidentally, made the Scranton nominating speech, but to no avail. The so-called Republican moderates left San Francisco in dismay and disarray.

There was one incident at the convention which, accidentally, gave me a fleeting (very fleeting) moment of national press exposure. A day or two before the roll of the states was to be called to affirm the senator from Arizona as the Republican candidate for president, the Scranton staff desperately sought a move that somehow, some way, might prevent the inevitable. Ultimately, they wrote an open letter to the convention delegates intended to appeal to their common sense and urge them to reflect seriously on where they were taking the Republican Party politically by turning it over to the Goldwater wing.

The letter, unfortunately, contained a number of particularly inflammatory statements. "Goldwaterism has come to stand for nuclear irresponsibility" was one; a "whole crazy-quilt collection of absurd and dangerous positions" was another. There was also a reference to the delegates walking around the convention like "chickens" with their necks "wrung." The Goldwater forces were infuriated, and the letter became a major item of national news from the convention. The matter might have lasted no more than a day, as the focus was about to shift to the nomination roll call itself, if it were not for an interview Scranton gave that very evening to Walter Cronkite on CBS News. In that interview, Scranton took full responsibility for the letter, but (foolishly, it would seem) either offered or acknowledged that it had been sent over his signature without him having read it in advance.

Now the story compounded itself. Here was a presidential candidate telling a national television audience in an interview with the nation's most watched and respected television anchor that such an inflammatory letter had gone out without his explicit personal approval. How in the world could that have happened? That very question kept the story alive for another day.

As the event was explained by Scranton's people on their return to Harrisburg, Scranton's staff had been strategizing late into the night searching for a bold step that might turn the convention around. Time was running short; something dramatic and immediate was required. For whatever reason, Scranton was not accessible at that moment; either his staff had already briefed him on the nature of the communication and felt comfortable in proceeding, or they chose not to run the letter by him at all. Bill Keisling and Walter Alessandroni, two trusted Scranton confidants who in most instances could make decisions in the governor's name, were fingered as the strategists of the letter decision. Keisling put the words to paper, and Scranton's secretary, Gretchen Zeidler (she was very good at duplicating his handwriting), signed the governor's name to it. The letter was delivered and the ensuing uproar broke out in the national press.

The Cronkite interview was to prove especially troublesome for my Harrisburg colleague Dick Graves, who was covering Scranton at the convention for the Associated Press. Graves had duly reported on the letter and the angry reaction it received from the Goldwater delegates. Once that was done, he broke for dinner, apparently unaware that Scranton had agreed to the interview with Cronkite. While Scranton was telling the nation he had neither seen nor personally signed the letter before it was delivered, Dick was having dinner. The AP convention desk reached out furiously for Graves to file an immediate story on the Scranton admission. It took some time for the desk to track him down, and the AP was late getting it on the wire. Dick was a very able reporter and an excellent writer. This was, however, not one of his better moments.

In Harrisburg, meanwhile, the revelation that the Scranton letter went out over his signature without his ever having read it was the talk of the Capitol. In the newspaper business at the time we had a technique we called a "streetcar," where reporters would pick up on a major storyline and put a local angle on it (hence, the "streetcar"). Well, the Scranton letter was my "streetcar."

Everywhere in the building that day, I asked every political type I encountered about his or her reaction to the events in San Francisco. Republican and Democrat alike, they were aghast that a communication of this magnitude on such a national stage would ever have been transmitted without the principal's prior review and explicit authorization. And if it did, they'd be damned that they would admit to such a fact on a national news show. That was the storyline from the Harrisburg Associated Press Bureau that day: "Pennsylvania State Capitol Dumfounded by Scranton Admission."

The AP New York bureau played the story nationally with my byline. I received clips from San Francisco, Denver, and other assorted places. Alas, my moment of national journalistic exposure was forgotten minutes after it occurred. The Goldwater nomination and the frustration it caused the centrist wing of the Republican Party returned the convention proceedings to its natural storyline. But I must admit, I was pleased with my fifteen minutes of national exposure.

This, I hope, does not come under the heading of gratuitous. But it does, I think, come under the heading of interesting. If Bill Scranton Sr. had one trait that never seemed to fail him in any public setting that I observed, it was his genial way with people. It was a trait that, if not inherited, certainly was learnable among his offspring. But that apparently was not the case.

Twenty years after the Goldwater convention in San Francisco, some Scranton loyalists convened a reunion at a farm outside Harrisburg. They billed the event "Veterans of Knob Hill," Knob Hill being the location of the Scranton presidential hotel in the city. My wife, Toni, who had a peripheral role in preconvention activities but did not make the trip to San Francisco, was invited. I went along as her guest. Scranton and his wife, Mary, were their masterful selves in greeting and mingling with the visitors. "Hi, boss, good to see you again," was the usual refrain from the former governor. Everyone seemed to be enjoying the opportunity to reminisce about days gone by.

What struck me most about the occasion, however, was how isolated Scranton's son, Young Bill, seemed from the crowd. All logic suggested it shouldn't have been that way. Young Scranton was Richard Thornburgh's lieutenant governor at the time. His office, his service, his family background, and political connections made him the preeminent favorite to be the Republican Party nominee for governor two years hence in 1986. If ever a crowd was ripe to be worked and enlisted for that effort, this was the one for him.

Yet, while his mother and father mingled with the folks from one end of the pavilion where we had gathered to the other in vintage Scranton style, Bill the son remained essentially off to the side with his wife, Coral, seated for the most part at a table to the rear. I was fascinated at what I was observing. This is really strange, I thought. Why isn't he stroking this crowd like his father and mother?

Throughout the dinner, the younger Scranton and Coral, now joined by their two young children, remained removed from the crowd at their distant table. Perhaps the lieutenant governor believed he already had mingled sufficiently with the group. Perhaps he felt this was not an appropriate occasion for him to politic. I just don't know. I do know he seemed distant and remote from a gathering of people who surely could be—in all likelihood, would be—helpful in his race for governor. I may have missed something that day. But I remember thinking that his father would never have let this opportunity pass this way.

Two years later, I got an entirely different picture of young Scranton. It was my one and only "up close and personal" contact with the son. I had moved on to become the director of government relations for the State System of Higher Education, the administrative umbrella for Pennsylvania's thirteen state-owned universities. The System was only two years old at the time. At my suggestion, we invited both the Democratic and Republican nominees for governor in for a private briefing on this new, important organization and structure in Pennsylvania higher education—85,000 students, most of them from Pennsylvania working-class families. Our purpose was to be certain they knew what we were attempting to do for these kids, and why it was important to them and to the future of our state. Democrat Bob Casey's campaign essentially brushed us off, asking us instead to forward materials to their education policy specialist. Republican Scranton accepted almost immediately.

He came to our offices a block and one-half from the Capitol. He was alone. He sat through an hour-plus briefing from Chancellor Jim McCormick on the System universities, its governance, and the opportunities it offered thousands of Pennsylvania high school graduates to advance their education and enhance their career opportunities. He was cordial, sincere, and inquisitive, fully engaged and genuinely interested in what he was hearing. It was quite a contradiction from the Young Bill Scranton I had seen two years earlier at the Dininni Farm in suburban Harrisburg. Not so, said those who knew or worked with him. He was a young man of contrasting personalities, they said. Friendly one day, distant the next, you just never knew from day to day. It was a contrast one would never associate with his father. Do apples fall far from the tree? In some cases, at some times, apparently they do. Bill Scranton Jr. did make his run for governor in 1986. He lost a very tough and closely contested campaign to Bob Casey by 87,000 votes.

In my mind, there's no question that Bill Scranton Sr. would have been reelected by a substantial margin if Pennsylvania governors had been allowed to succeed themselves at the time he served. He was a man of considerable intellectual and political skills. One on one, he was the best governor I ever saw in interacting with people, no matter their station in life. "I don't know if he can do anything for me," legislators who had issues with the administration would invariably say after meeting personally with the governor. "But he heard me out and he understood." They usually walked away satisfied.

Inevitably, I suppose, one's most lasting impression of public officials such as the governor of Pennsylvania is framed by memories of experiences or personal contacts they had with a particular chief executive. I had three such experiences with Governor Scranton that reinforced for me his extraordinary ability to relate to people. He had Bill Clinton charm without the smarm.

The first (and most lasting) occurred at a press conference Governor Scranton held about midterm to announce the appointment of Dr. J. Ralph Rackley of Pennsylvania State University as the state's superintendent of public instruction (now called secretary of education). The post had been vacant for a period of months. The longer the vacancy lingered, the more of a political embarrassment it was becoming for the governor and his administration. The storyline took hold in the press that the governor was having great difficulty finding someone who would take the job. The question was why? I tried to press the governor on the point at the press conference he called to introduce Rackley.

"Governor," I demanded in my most penetrating reportorial voice, "how many times did you have to talk to Dr. Rackley before you finally persuaded him to accept the position?"

Scranton refused to take the bait. He appeared to bristle just a bit. "Let's see," he replied, pausing a moment for effect. "Oh yes, we talked last night. I believe it was at 8:15. Or it could have been at 8:23. I'm not quite sure." Moving in for the kill, he went on: "And then we talked again this morning over breakfast. I think it was 7:22. It could have been 7:28. I could tell you what we ate if you're really interested, but what's the point? We got the man we wanted for the position. And if it took a bit longer than some might have preferred, the wait was well worth it. Does that answer your question?"

It did more than that. The governor's knockout rebuttal certainly put me in my place. And my press corps colleagues immediately recognized the put-down for what it was—a classic.

Audible guffaws were heard from the press row. "Nice question, kid!" Duke Kaminski of the *Philadelphia Bulletin* barked at me from his seat across the press table. "Got any more like it?"

Marty Sikora of United Press International whispered as he leaned over from across the table, "Welcome to the club."

That was the *coup de grâce,* the ultimate blow to my solar plexus. Sikora, for some reason, rubbed Scranton the wrong way in these press conferences, and the governor frequently made no effort to shield his disdain. Now I found myself in the same company. I didn't like the feeling.

About an hour after the press conference had ended and I had filed my story, the phone rang at my Capitol newsroom desk. It was Jack Conmy, the governor's press secretary. "How you doing?" Jack wanted to know in what I, to this day, still consider the best display of one-on-one press relations I encountered in a decade and a half of either reporting for or working directly with the capital press corps.

"I'm fine," I replied. "I don't know that the putdown was in order, but I'm a big boy. I can handle it."

We chatted some more on the incident when I confessed: "I must tell you, Jack. My worst moment was when Marty leaned over and said, 'Welcome to the club.' That really frosted me. That's one club I don't want to belong to when I'm talking to the governor."

"I know, I know," Jack concurred. "We don't know what it is. But Marty always seems to get to the governor. We tell him about it, and he agrees. But Marty asks a question, and it's the same old thing all over again. Don't worry about it. This, too, will pass." Our conversation ended on that note.

The next morning I walked into the newsroom about 9:30 after my morning stop in the AP bureau downtown. There on my desk I found a folded newspaper. It was the *Scranton Tribune,* my hometown morning paper. My story on the Rackley appointment, with my byline, was the lead story in the paper. I knew my father would be pleased with the prominent exposure I received back home.

Jack had sent it down for me, a peace offering of sorts, I suppose, though none was needed. But there was more. Inside the folded paper was an autographed picture of Governor Scranton with this inscription: "To Vince. Welcome to the club! [*signed*] Bill Scranton."

Later that morning, Jack called to ask if I got the paper. I thanked him for the gesture. But there was something I had to ask for my own gratification. "Did Gretchen sign the picture?"

He assured me it was the governor's signature. I didn't press the point.

The second incident occurred when Governor Scranton was leaving office. He sent notes to all the Capitol Hill press corps thanking them for their courtesies during his tenure in office. Mine contained a handwritten inscription, "Keep up the good work." The note itself was a nice touch on his part. I later learned the inscription was not something he penned with every note he sent to the correspondents. That made it even more personal and appreciated.

Finally, in 1976, a decade after he had left the governor's residence, Scranton was appointed by President Ford (his Yale Law School classmate) to be U.S. ambassador to the United Nations. I was working as press secretary to the Senate Democratic caucus at the time. I sent him a note congratulating him on the appointment and wishing him well in this very high-visibility position. Scranton was kind enough to respond, thanking me for my best wishes. It was an appointment he hadn't sought, he wrote in his note. But when the president asks you to serve, he continued, you don't say no.

Bill Scranton Sr. was one of the two best governors I observed at close hand from the early 1960s to the mid-1990s. (David Lawrence would be a solid third.) What distinguished him most was the class he brought to public service. He was a class act from start to finish. He was a class act when he entered public life. He was a class act during his tenure in public office. And he was a class act when he returned to the private sector. Most important, he served his Commonwealth and his nation when called upon with great skill and distinction. As public careers go, your legacies don't come much better than that.

Chapter 14

★★★★★★★

Raymond Philip Shafer (1967–1971)

Say what you will about Raymond P. Shafer of Meadville, Pennsylvania, but the man did make his mark in Pennsylvania political lore.

No less than eight lieutenant governors just in my frame of reference through the last half of the twentieth century attempted to ascend directly from that office to the governorship. Only Ray Shafer made it. That feat alone guarantees him his place in the state's political history books. (For the record, John Fine's Republican lieutenant governor, Lloyd Wood, lost to Democrat George Leader in 1954; Roy Furman, Leader's lieutenant governor, and John Morgan Davis, David Lawrence's lieutenant governor, had designs on the office in 1958 and 1962, respectively, but failed to gain the support of their party leadership to contest for the nomination. Ray Broderick was the Republican nominee to succeed Shafer in 1970, but lost. Lieutenant Governor Ernest P. Kline also lost in a 1978 primary bid to replace Milton Shapp; and Republican William Scranton III in 1986 and Democrat Mark Singel in 1994 won their party's nominations but lost in the general election.)

It was Ray Shafer's good political fortune to be selected as Bill Scranton's running mate for lieutenant governor in 1962. That gave him his political base to run for governor four years later. It was, however, his political misfortune to have to succeed the highly popular Bill Scranton in the executive office in 1967. Scranton was an icon of sorts to Pennsylvania Republicans and, intentionally or not, he cast a very large shadow over Shafer and his new administration. Succeeding Scranton was akin to succeeding Joe Paterno as coach at Penn State, or Michael Jordan with the Chicago Bulls, or Ronald Reagan in the White House. Very, very difficult to measure up indeed.

Not that Shafer was without the impressive personal and political credentials to take on the challenge: Class valedictorian and star athlete in high school; Phi Beta Kappa at Allegheny College, nine varsity letters in basketball, soccer, and track; college class president each of his four years; student body president his senior year; Yale Law School and a member of a fraternity that included, coincidentally, not only one future president of the

United States (Gerald Ford), but also two future Justices of the U.S. Supreme Court (Potter Stewart and Byron "Whizzer" White), a future U.S. senator (Peter Dominick of Colorado), a future governor of Pennsylvania (Bill Scranton), and a future author of some renown (Walter S. Lord).

There was still more: A PT boat naval commander in World War II (this one didn't get his boat sunk by a Japanese cruiser), more than eighty combat missions, and skipper of the vessel that returned Gen. Douglas MacArthur to Corregidor to fulfill the vow, "I shall return," which he had made so memorably as he evacuated the Philippines under Japanese assault. Commander Shafer earned a Purple Heart and Bronze Star for his wartime service.

After the war, Shafer and his wife, Jane, returned to Meadville, where he entered the private practice of law and taught law at his alma mater. He entered elective politics in 1947 when he was elected to the first of his two terms as Crawford County district attorney. In 1958 he was elected to the Pennsylvania Senate. In 1962 he was tabbed to be Scranton's running mate for lieutenant governor, bringing his impressive personal background, his successful political record, and geographic balance to the Republican ticket. By any standard, his steady rise in Pennsylvania politics was both rapid and admirable. He capped that crest with his election as governor in 1966 by a margin approaching a quarter of a million votes.

Publicly and privately, Ray Shafer was a personable fella. The problem was (and he had little or no control over this), he simply suffered in contrast with Scranton. House Speaker Matt Ryan put the distinction this way in a conversation I had with him in 2002 about the governors under whom he had served. Scranton, in Ryan's words, was "born of the manor," a patrician, of pedigree upbringing. He brought a luster, an aura, a star quality, if you will, to the governor's office. Shafer, on the other hand, was in Ryan's words, "one of us," just a first-term senator from rather rural Crawford County in northwestern Pennsylvania. If not for the fact that he had been tapped as Scranton's running mate, in the minds of many Republicans he had no greater political skills or call on the office than they. In fact, at least three Scranton cabinet members—Attorney General Walter Alessandroni, Secretary of Public Welfare Arlin Adams and Secretary of Internal Affairs John Tabor—were bent on challenging Shafer for the Republican gubernatorial nomination until political realities persuaded them otherwise.

It struck many of us in the press corps that Shafer and his team were as much aware of those perceptions as anyone when the new governor moved almost immediately to distinguish himself from his predecessor. The target of his first public policy objective was major organizational and structural reforms of state government, headlined by the convening of the state's first constitutional convention in almost a century. Scranton toyed publicly with the idea of rewriting the state Constitution of 1874 toward the end of his term, but for lack of time (remember the limitations of one-term governors), lack of political will, or a combination of both, the notion went no further than the discussion stage.

So Shafer set out to succeed in an initiative that Scranton didn't see through. But the move was not welcomed universally among his Republican allies. His GOP leadership in the General Assembly, most notably House Speaker Ken Lee, demurred publicly and strongly. They counseled against making a constitutional convention the first priority of the new administration. Their reasoning, and they were not at all reluctant to share it with the press, was that 1) it would be a hard sell for many Republican members of the General Assembly; 2) it would require the expenditure of vast political capital by the new governor, and in a short four years, most governors had precious political capital to spend on something as chancy as a convention; and 3) while a constitutional convention would be an academic exercise that editorial writers might applaud, the public policy and political gains from an undertaking would be minimal at best. Pick another target as your flagship, they advised their new governor, a target with more tangible political measures like economic development, investment in education, or highways.

Shafer insisted, however. I wrote a column for the Associated Press reciting the differences between the governor and his legislative leadership on the issue. I concluded that the legislative leadership was probably right, that for Shafer to set out on this risky course and fail would cripple the new administration almost before it got started, quite possibly for the remainder of his term. It could be more than a just cold winter for the administration, it could be a very cold three and a half years. Was the political risk and the public gain associated with a call for a constitutional convention worth it? Probably not, I opined.

It was (and still is) rare for Republicans to air their internal differences, political or policy, in public. When Shafer pressed ahead, the GOP majorities in the House and Senate supported their governor, albeit most reluctantly. The convention was convened in 1967. Its powers were limited to specific articles of the Constitution: the legislature; the judiciary; and taxation and finance. One component of the taxation article, however, was ruled off the table in the statute authorizing the convention. The uniformity clause of the Constitution was the provision that precluded enactment of a graduated income tax in Pennsylvania. The income tax long had been the "third rail" of Pennsylvania politics—those who dared reach out to touch it did so at their own great political peril. Few did. That's why the uniformity clause was specifically excluded from Convention deliberations. To have done otherwise would have doomed Shafer's call from the get-go. (Shafer's successor would have a serious run-in of his own with the uniformity clause four years later, but that's a subject for subsequent discussion.)

The convention drew a star-studded cast of delegates. Bill Scranton (there's that shadow again) and former Democratic gubernatorial hopeful Robert P. Casey were elected delegates from Lackawanna County. To emphasize the nonpartisan nature of the gathering, Casey was named vice-chairman of the convention; Scranton was named chair of the Judiciary Committee. World-famous author James Michener was a prominent delegate from his native Bucks County. And lest we forget, so was another future governor of Pennsylvania, Richard L. Thornburgh, then just at the infant stages of his ambitious political aspirations.

But, as events played out, the most important delegates to the convention were the dozen or so members of the Republican and Democratic leadership of the General Assembly who served by virtue of their legislative positions. The elected delegates were largely an amalgamation of civic leaders, academics, and political activists—a very mixed bag, most well intentioned but almost all with very little understanding of the political process and how issues are resolved in a legislative setting. Originally, it was thought the principal reason legislative leadership insisted on a role in the convention proceedings was to protect their own political interests from this "do-good" assembly. And there, undoubtedly, was valid justification to that notion. However, from the larger perspective, the leaders had a very unforeseen but major contribution to make to the proceedings: to give shape and definition to the convention and its recommendations, to lead the delegates to consensus, and conclude the deliberations with a unified and nonpartisan document to submit to the people in a referendum. Without their understanding of the process, and their political skills to reconcile opposing views, the convention either could have ended in stalemate or concluded with a divided front.

The convention, by any civic lesson standards, had to be rated a success. But, frankly, its long-term consequences were hardly extraordinary. The principal recommendations to come from the proceedings were to fix the size of the General Assembly at 203 in the House of Representatives (it had fluctuated according to population spurts prior to that) and 50 members of the Senate; it created a unified judicial system under the Pennsylvania Supreme Court; and it replaced the corrupted justice of the peace system

Lt. Gov. Ray Shafer, a three-sport athlete in high school and college, and yours truly let one slip through our hands in a fall 1965 flag football game between the Capitol newsroom and representatives of the Scranton administration. Joe Bye of the Republican State Committee is to the right, and Paul Zdinak, a new addition to the AP Harrisburg Bureau, is in the center. Shafer's number, "66," was no accident. He was serving notice to the Press Corps that he fully intended to pursue the governorship the next year in a crowded Republican field. I don't exactly recall how the game ended, but I believe it was a scoreless tie, so inept were both teams.

with a district magistrate lower judiciary that required of its members a modicum of legal education and training. Nothing of note stands out in my memory on the taxation article.

Former governors Scranton and George M. Leader were recruited by Shafer to head a "Vote Yes" campaign to win electorate approval of the convention's recommendations. The voters responded favorably in the April primary election of 1968. Shafer, with his convention, had scored the major achievement he had pursued to give his administration its own early identity. I wrote a "mea culpa" column along this line: "They said it couldn't be done; they said it shouldn't be done; but Ray Shafer, to his credit, did it nonetheless." I asked that my plate of crow be seasoned with a touch of salt, pepper, and oregano. The convention—not the column—was to be the high-water mark for the Shafer administration. It was pretty much downhill, politically and policy-wise, for the governor and his administration from that point forward.

With good reason, Ray Shafer and his inner circle had begun covert planning of the 1966 campaign for governor almost immediately after he took his oath of office as lieutenant governor in 1963. In a one-term gubernatorial climate, election cycles had a way of creeping up very quickly on candidates. In political terms, the 1966 gubernatorial election was not that far off. Additionally, Shafer was not the preeminent favorite in the Republican field. The aforementioned Messrs. Tabor of Pittsburgh, Adams of Philadelphia, and Alessandroni, also of Philadelphia, were in the early mix. Alessandroni, in fact, was rumored to be Governor Scranton's personal preference.

But Shafer's political acumen was not to be undervalued. He cleverly and steadfastly worked the vineyards of the Republican Party for three solid years, making friends, building networks, accumulating committed allies, and putting his fundraising base in place. His closest associates established a clandestine political headquarters utilizing space made available to them by Harrisburg businessman, Shafer friend, and philanthropist Stanley Miller. My wife, Toni, serving as the lieutenant governor's scheduling secretary, opened the post-office box that became the secret communication center for the Shafer forces. (More on that later.) By the time the party elders started to weigh the 1966 ticket in earnest, Shafer's political claim on the nomination was virtually irreversible. The considerable political goodwill and support he had built for himself in the intervening three years within the GOP across the state made it impossible to deny him without a bitter and potentially divisive primary fight. Republicans generally avoid high-visibility primary fights like the plague, so Shafer was left with a clear field to the nomination.

Still, the conventional political and punditry wisdom held that there was some internal unease within the Republican Party hierarchy about his candidacy. So, the storyline went, pressure was applied on Alessandroni to join the Shafer ticket as his running mate for lieutenant governor. Alessandroni would add considerable political weight and geographical balance to the campaign. Once elected, he also could serve as a stabilizing force if the Shafer administration stumbled along the way. Reportedly, it was not an easy sell, because Alessandroni was not a number 2 kind of guy. Ultimately, however, he did agree. It was a decision that, tragically, would cost him his life. While on a campaign trip in the spring of 1966, Alessandroni, State

Liquor Board Chairman James Staudinger of Montgomery County, and the pilot of their small plane were killed in a in the fog-shrouded mountains of western Pennsylvania near Fayette County.

Alessandroni's death, coming as it did shortly before the May primary election, was a severe shock to the party and a severe jolt to the spirit of the campaign. The grief was genuine because Alessandroni was one of the party's more respected figures as a person and a politician. Just as Shafer was beginning to establish himself as a candidate of gubernatorial timber, he now had to find an acceptable replacement for his running mate. But first there was a legal hurdle to leap. For the Republican establishment to select a new candidate for lieutenant governor, Alessandroni had to win the spring primary election posthumously as the Republican nominee. Thanks to the strength of the Republican Party organization, he did, by 260,000 votes.

Another Philadelphia attorney, Raymond J. Broderick, was chosen to replace him. Broderick also brought an impressive personal resume to the ticket: Magna cum laude from Notre Dame, Class of 1935; University of Pennsylvania Law School, 1938; retired U.S. naval officer with the rank of lieutenant commander. Credible credentials to be sure. Still he was not Walter Alessandroni, and he had none of Alessandroni's political identity and reputation. His only prior link to elective office was that of township commissioner in Plymouth Township in southeastern Montgomery County. So unknown was he when he was selected, the popular refrain among the capital political talking classes was to ask, "Ray Who?" Broderick, an outgoing and likable Irishman, was somewhat of a surprising find. He took to campaigning with a real zest, a definite plus given the condition that put him on the ticket. Most important, he did the campaign no harm. As second fiddles go in politics, that's as much as the top of the ticket expects or needs from running mates.

Shortly after the Primary Election, the Shafer campaign found itself with another problem on the table, one that was self-inflicted. Democratic Philadelphia millionaire Milton Shapp had defeated the Democratic Party's endorsed candidate for governor, state senator Robert P. Casey, in a very costly and contentious primary campaign. Whispers about serious Shapp campaign election irregularities ran rampant in the aftermath of the balloting, rampant enough that the Republicans thought they had sufficient evidence to file suit, which they did.

Their primary purpose was to damage the credibility of the Democratic nominee by giving a public airing to the charges. But Shapp's forces fought back. They filed a countersuit charging the Shafer campaign with irregularities of its own, much of it related to the clandestine operation in Stanley Miller's warehouse.

The case was heard by Judge Carl Shelly in Dauphin County Court, the court of record in these types of cases at the time before the statewide Commonwealth Court was created. I was covering much of the proceedings for the Associated Press until a potential personal conflict arose. My wife, Toni, who had left the lieutenant governor's office long before the primary campaign and was a stay-at-home wife at this point, called me at the AP office in the Capitol newsroom one day during a luncheon recess of the proceedings.

"I've just been subpoenaed by the sheriff of Dauphin County to testify in the case," she told me. "I'm supposed to be there this afternoon."

"What possibly for?" I asked, puzzled.

"Well, they can't find Bill Greenlee," she explained. "I'm being called to testify that I opened the post office box on his instructions."

"Well," I responded. "You really don't have much choice in the matter. You're going to have to go. I'll have to let Harry know. I can't cover the case if you're going to be on the witness stand."

Bill Greenlee was Shafer's first chief-of-staff in the lieutenant governor's office. He was a member of the Shafer inner circle, someone who was intimately familiar with the strategy and covert planning of the lieutenant governor's campaign. When the Shapp countersuit was filed, Shapp's attorneys were looking to subpoena him but couldn't locate him. That's why Toni was called. They would build their evidence brick by brick, if necessary.

I immediately advised AP Bureau Chief Harry Ball of the dilemma. We both agreed instantly that someone had to the replace me at the courthouse, at least until Toni's appearance was concluded. After that, we'd make a final determination whether the conflict would preclude my covering the trial any further.

It never came to that. Greenlee presented himself at the courthouse that afternoon. "I hear someone's been looking for me," he is reputed to have commented. Since he could be asked the questions about the secret political operations that may have violated existing Pennsylvania election law, including when the post-office box was opened, Toni was excused without having to take the stand. Neither she nor I was very happy with Greenlee at that point.

Since Toni was not a material witness, I returned to my coverage duties. The case dragged on for another few weeks. Both campaigns suffered minor public embarrassments, but no major revelations were uncovered on either side. Shafer's secret political operation became a matter of public record. It may have pushed to the edge of Pennsylvania election law, but it did not break it. Shapp's campaign, on the other hand, was exposed for paying for the endorsement of some prominent professional athletes. Philadelphia Eagles running back Tim Brown was one who still comes to mind.

Judge Shelly, a former district attorney, met with a group of reporters when the trial had concluded to share on a background basis what was likely to come next. He suggested both sides had taken liberties with Pennsylvania election law, but neither established sufficiently that the other side had explicitly crossed it. If either expected a major political coup, Shelly advised, both would most likely be sorely disappointed with his ruling. The electorate, not his ruling in the case, would have to decide the winner of the November general election. And that's, essentially, the way it worked out. Neither campaign that I recall relied on much, if anything, from the suit-countersuit. In retrospect, in terms of time, cost, and political gain or loss, it was a wash. Once concluded, it was almost a nonevent with no measurable influence on the election results.

One other troubling incident once again drew Toni and me indirectly into the Shafer campaign. While some other reporters and I were reviewing one of the campaign's periodic finance reports in the state elections bureau, what should pop out at me but this: a $1,000 contribution recorded in the name of Antoinette Carocci.

Now I knew that was not the case. On my small salary, neither she nor I had a $1,000 to spare for any election campaign. I immediately pondered whether one or more of my reportorial colleagues would see the recorded contribution, as well. More important, what I would say if they asked me about it? Fortunately, the question never came up.

But I was more than slightly agitated. I confronted a Shafer campaign operative (Fred Speaker, a close Greenlee associate whom Shafer would appoint as his attorney general late in his term) that very day. The conversation went something like this:

Me: "Fred, one of your reports lists my wife as making a $1,000 contribution. I know she didn't. How did it happen, and what are you going to do about it?

Speaker: "I don't know anything about it. I don't know how it happened. I don't know what can be done, but I'll check into it for you."

Me: "Somebody better. And it better not happen again."

I felt between a rock and a hard place. I knew someone had misrepresented that contribution in an official election report to the state. I suppose I could have (maybe should have) written something about it. But I didn't. In my day, reporters reported the news, they didn't make it. Truth is, if it weren't for my wife, I would never have known a contribution such as that was misreported. So I just let the matter pass. But I went to great lengths to check out subsequent Shafer reports, first to ensure the deception wasn't repeated, and second to determine if I could find any other questionable contributions. (I couldn't.)

Speaker, meanwhile, got back to me the next day. He confessed it was impossible to determine how Toni's name came to be listed in the report, nor who might have been involved. He assured me it wouldn't happen again. It didn't.

In spite of the disruption created by Walter Alessandroni's untimely death and the minor embarrassments emanating from the election irregularity lawsuits, the Shafer campaign and the Republican Party headed confidently into the fall election cycle. William Scranton's popularity among the electorate was solid. Shafer had established his credentials as a political candidate without any serious setbacks. And, most important, the Democrats were a seriously divided party, despite their best efforts to portray it otherwise. The maverick Shapp had defeated Casey by attacking the party establishment and its leaders as out of touch and out of date. Now he had to rally those same Democrats he had attacked in the spring to his campaign in the fall. It would not be easy.

Nothing much of the campaign really stands out as pivotal. The Shafer/Broderick ticket essentially pledged to build on the good work and good standing of the Scranton administration. The Shapp campaign, though it tried mightily, failed to find a theme or a cause that resonated with the electorate. One incident just days before the November balloting probably best typifies the hurdles Shapp had to leap for most of the campaign.

I was traveling with the Shapp party for the Associated Press that day. He was campaigning in the Lehigh Valley with the election just days away when he learned Shafer was going to be in town that very morning for an editorial board interview with the Allentown newspaper. Whether or not the newspaper called Shapp to invite him over for a joint appearance, I'm not certain. It is a possibility, although it would have been a serious lapse in journalistic etiquette, in my view. But the source aside, as soon as Shapp heard about Shafer's whereabouts, he immediately broke off his campaign schedule and raced by car over to the paper.

Shapp had been trying mightily but without any success to engage Shafer in as many joint appearances as possible. The Republican standard bearer was playing to protect his frontrunner position as the election drew near and he simply wasn't going to give his underdog opponent any opportunity to share a platform with him. Shapp saw this encounter in Allentown as perhaps his last, best chance to share a public forum with his opponent, ideally, put him on the defensive on some of the issues that separated them and, in the process, gain some needed momentum for his faltering bid.

Shapp arrived at the newspaper building before Shafer did and immediately advised the editors and staff of his presence and his eagerness to participate in a joint discussion. He, in fact, stood in the lobby by the newsroom elevators waiting for Shafer to arrive. Shafer was clearly stunned to emerge from the elevator only to be greeted by Shapp. The exchange went something like this, as I recall:

Shapp: "The editors want us to do a joint interview, Ray. How 'about it?"

Shafer: "I'm here to do mine. You can do yours anytime I'm finished. That's between you and them."

Shafer immediately walked by Shapp, entered the newsroom, and began greeting the assembled reporters who were watching events transpire with some fascination. "Hi," he smiled as he extended his hand confidently to each staff member within in reach. "I'm Ray Shafer. Good to see you."

Shapp pursued him doggedly throughout the newsroom. "Come on, Ray," he chided. "Let's do a joint interview. The paper wants it, let's do it."

Shafer refused to take the bait. "Milton, the paper asked me to come in and talk to them. That's why I'm here. Once that's done, they're free to talk to you all they want about anything they want. That's between you and them, but that's the way it's going to be." That ended the encounter. Shapp never did get his joint appearance. The best he could do was to needle Shafer about his reluctance to take him on before he returned to the rest of his schedule.

The paper's photographers had been recording the exchange as it unfolded in the newsroom that day. That weekend, just seventy-two hours before the Tuesday balloting, the Allentown pictures were relayed across the state by the Associated Press and played in most of the major newspapers. Shapp actually had Shafer on his heels, but you would not have known it unless you were there to witness it personally. The picture that ran that weekend portrayed a tall, smiling, jut-jawed Ray Shafer, very much in charge, while forlornly to the side stood a diminutive, sloop-shouldered Milton Shapp. The image the photo presented was very damaging to Shapp. If there were still undecided voters out there, the picture hardly beckoned them to his cause.

In all my years in and around the political process, I saw only one other encounter that came anywhere close to what I witnessed that day between Shapp and Shafer. Almost a quarter of a century later, in 1990, in Philadelphia I was serving as press secretary to Democratic governor Robert P. Casey at the time. Casey was an overwhelming favorite for reelection, never mind renomination at the time. But still, he was being challenged in the Democratic primary election by a Montgomery County political gadfly named Phil Berg. The cutting issue to the Berg campaign was abortion. Casey, of course, was adamantly pro-life. That put him at distinct odds, certainly, with his party nationally, and, probably, with many if not most of its Pennsylvania activists as well. Berg's ostensible purpose in his challenge was to give voice to the pro-choice wing of the Democratic Party in Pennsylvania. It was really to get Phil Berg another fifteen minutes in the sun.

In any event, Berg, like Shapp, had learned of Casey's presence in the city that day. Like Shapp, in search of a breakthrough moment, Berg came over to the event site to sandbag the governor. The state police security detail alerted me that Berg was in the hall outside the event room waiting for the governor to leave. Television cameras were present in great abundance.

I advised the governor. He had no immediate reaction and went about his business with his luncheon address. At the conclusion of the talk, the governor took his leave. "Let's go," he said as our small traveling party moved out of the ballroom with him. He went directly to the corridor where Berg approached him.

"Hello, Phil," Casey acknowledged as he kept right on walking to the waiting elevator.

"When are we going to debate, Governor?" Berg demanded from the rear. "When are we going to debate?"

Casey turned slowly as he entered the elevator, looked Berg straight in the eye and said in that deliberate, penetrating way of his: "There's going to be no debates, Phil." End of conversation. As if on cue, the elevator doors closed leaving an ignored and speechless Phil Berg behind. In Casey circles, the incident became known as the great confrontation that never was.

But back to the subject at hand. Shafer won the election by 241,600 votes.

If I might be permitted another personal aside, the Shafer campaign was good to me in more ways than one. It certainly gave me my first professional opportunity to cover a high-profile election as a journalist. It was financially rewarding as well, though in a very legitimate way. Shafer's campaign staff had started a $10 pool, open to virtually all comers including the press corps. The winner would be the person who picked the victorious candidate and the victory margin that most closely matched the statewide results posted by the Associated Press at 8 A.M. the morning after the election.

I was traveling with Shafer two weeks out from the election when I entered the pool. I remembered the advice I had heard from John Scotzin of the *Harrisburg Evening News* years earlier in connection with another newsroom election pool. John counseled to always submit a specific number to avoid the possibility that someone else might settle on the same rounded figure. So I picked Shafer by a margin of 212,235. And then I forgot about it.

Toni and I were having dinner at home the evening after the election when the telephone rang. It was Manny Stampler, a member of Shafer's state police executive detail. He called to tell me I had won the pool. I was surprised but not overwhelmed. "That's nice," I said casually.

Stampler understood immediately that I had no idea how much I had won. "Vince, do you know how much money was in the pool?" he asked.

"Not really," I replied. "$200, $300, I guess."

"Vince," he informed me, "there was $750 in the pool. I have it with me. I can drop it off if it's convenient."

"Convenient?" I said. "You come right over. We have dinner ready if you haven't eaten." Seven hundred and fifty dollars in those days, on a reporter's salary, was a substantial chunk of change.

A couple of other points about the pool are worth recalling. The first was that Scotzin's advice was well taken. It turned out my 235 votes were critical because Don McDonough of the *Philadelphia Inquirer* had picked Shafer by 212,000 even. The AP's number at 8 A.M. was something like 212,833. The next time I saw McDonough, he greeted me warmly. "Carocci, you sonofabitch," he exclaimed. "What made you pick such a crazy number?"

I told him of Scotzin's advice. "It was meant for occasions just such as this, " I said. He had to agree.

The second point was how surprised I was to learn of some of the other entries in the pool, and how close they thought the election would be. Governor Scranton, for example, was reputed to have picked Shafer, but only by a margin of 75,000 votes or so. U.S. Senator Hugh Scott had Shafer by slightly more than 100,000 votes. Hardly a great vote of confidence in either case, I thought. Either Shapp's money had them worried, or their presumed misgivings about the lieutenant governor had not completely evaporated over the course of the campaign.

Toni and I bought our first color television set with the winnings. It was a Zenith console, thirty-six-inch, I believe. We bought it from Stanley Miller, the same Stanley Miller who lent his warehouse to the covert Shafer operation four years earlier. Stanley signed on with the Shafer administration as a $1-a-year consultant to the governor. It gave him entrée to the governor's office, a small but important symbolic reward for his efforts on Shafer's behalf. Later, Shafer appointed Miller secretary of public welfare. Incidentally, we enjoyed that Zenith for better than fifteen years before we had to finally retire it.

One other incident to the Shafer campaign is worth recounting. At the time, it seemed like nothing. Shafer was in Pittsburgh, I believe, where he was to be joined by the Republican governor from Illinois for an event. The morning of the event, the press was informed the governor had to return to Springfield to attend to some state business. We thought little of it.

It was only after the election that I learned, and reported, exactly what had happened. The governor of Illinois was en route by state plane to Pittsburgh. Someone on the Shafer staff, however, suddenly remembered the governor had just signed a state income tax into law in Illinois. The income tax still was anathema in Pennsylvania. The Shafer folks determined it might not be a good connection for the electorate to make.

So the campaign contacted the governor in midair and asked him to scratch the visit. He apparently took it in good graces. I was told he had the plane rerouted back to Springfield. But he did have some advice for Shafer. "You tell your governor the first thing he needs to do after he's inaugurated is to enact a state income tax," he was said to have counseled as his plane was rerouted. "State governments can't live without it these days." His words, as future events would have it, proved to be somewhat prophetic.

A word about the team Ray Shafer assembled around him.

Bill Sennett, an Erie attorney, and Art Sampson, an executive with General Electric in Erie, two of Shafer's closest supporters and advisors and members of the original covert group, signed on as attorney general and budget secretary/secretary of administration, respectively. They were joined by Bob Bloom of Meadville, a longtime Shafer friend and confidante, as secretary to the governor. (Bloom, incidentally, was appointed to the Public Utility Commission shortly before Shafer's term ended. The story had it that the price for his confirmation by the Republican-controlled Senate was for the executive branch to vacate the Senate wing of the Capitol to provide additional office space for the senators. Bloom stayed on in Harrisburg long after the Shafer administration came to an end. He served succeeding Republican governors in a variety of capacities, including secretary of revenue and two additional appointments to the Public Utility Commission.)

Sennett, Sampson, and Bloom were considered the closest triumvirate to the governor. Hugh Flaherty of the *Philadelphia Bulletin* came aboard in a policy and speechwriting capacity. And Jack Conmy stayed on as press secretary. Curiously, Bill Greenlee never joined the Shafer staff. He and the prospective governor had a falling out. The reasons are unknown to me to this day. But no damage to either. Shafer was governor; Greenlee became one of the state capital's most successful and richly rewarded lobbyists and, politically, he was an important fundraising ally for many a candidate, Democrat and Republican alike, though more for the latter than the former.

The Shafer-Conmy marriage never quite worked. Conmy served Scranton skillfully as press secretary. One got the impression, however, that the same enthusiasm and chemistry Conmy clearly enjoyed with Scranton never quite developed with Shafer. He ultimately left before the administration ended, to be replaced by Bob McCormick, a veteran of government public relations work under a number of Republican governors. The Conmy experience registered a lasting point with me. He was a brilliant press secretary under Bill Scranton, the man who brought him to Harrisburg. He was just slightly adequate under Ray Shafer. It suggested to me that for one to be truly effective in public service in a high place like the governor's office, one had to have a strong, strong sense of allegiance and compatibility with the person under whom he or she served, and, equally important, had to share the goals to which the governor aspired. Without that sympatico and commitment, whatever role a person played in the governor's office, it would be just a job. And if it was just a job, one simply went through the motions as Conmy did under Ray Shafer.

I know when I shifted from journalism to public service in 1971 I had that political, personal, and philosophical compatibility with Marty Murray and Tom Lamb in the Senate. I surely didn't with Tom Nolan. When Milton Shapp succeeded Shafer in the governor's office, he went through a series of three or four press secretaries over the ensuing eight years. I was never asked to serve, though the position had been a silent ambition of mine since I arrived in Harrisburg. I knew, however, that if I had been approached, I would have turned the position down. I was not compatible at all with Governor Shapp, his style of governance, his agenda, or his people. I must acknowledge, conversely, he and his staff never missed me, either.

The Shafer team, collectively and individually, was a good, solid group, but undervalued by most people. In many journalistic and legislative comparisons, they never quite matched up to the reputation and performance of their Scranton predecessors. I believe it was because their governor simply lacked the star power and aura of his predecessor.

The Shafer tenure could be labeled earnest, but unspectacular. He convened the constitutional convention; he successfully advocated a constitutional amendment permitting governors to serve a second consecutive term (though he himself was not eligible); he signed legislation into law eliminating the Department of Internal Affairs as an elective statewide office (replaced by the appointive Department of Community Affairs, later to morph under the Ridge reign into the Department of Community and Economic Development); he signed the bill creating the Department of Environmental Resources; and, though reluctantly, he also signed the Public Employees Collective Bargaining Act. The convention, clearly, was his greatest success, but even there he had to live with his legislative critics (most of them Republican) that it was the wrong objective at the wrong time for his new administration.

Shafer's one moment of significant national exposure occurred at the 1968 Republican convention in Miami when he was asked to deliver the nominating speech for New York Governor Nelson Rockefeller. He did it creditably. But, again, unspectacularly. This was the convention that gave the nation the Republican ticket of former vice-president Richard Nixon and Spiro Agnew, then a little-known governor of Maryland. To demonstrate the potential for irony in politics, both Nixon and Agnew, of course, ultimately resigned in disgrace from office—the only president and vice-president in the history of the country to do so. When Agnew resigned because he was found to have accepted kickbacks from transportation contractors when he was governor of Maryland, Nixon replaced him with U.S. House Minority Leader Gerald Ford of Michigan. When Nixon resigned because of the Watergate scandals, Ford was elevated to the presidency, of course, and picked Rockefeller to serve as his vice-president. No one, not even the most perceptive seer of political events and rising personalities, could have predicted that bizarre turn of events the night some six years earlier when Raymond P. Shafer of Meadville appeared before the Republican National Convention in Miami to nominate Nelson Rockefeller of New York for the presidency.

After the Republican convention and his fifteen minutes in the national spotlight, Governor Shafer returned to the state capital, essentially to finish the remaining year and a half on his term. It was not a productive time for him or the Commonwealth. The rift that was created with his Republican legislative leadership over his call for a constitutional convention two years earlier never quite healed. The tension compounded as he entered lame-duck status. That denied him the political muscle he needed to keep his legislative troops in the fold because he certainly could not expect any help from his loyal opposition in the Democrat Party.

The strain between the Republican governor and his Republican legislature reached its breaking point in the struggle to pass a new budget in 1970. Revenues were very tight and it would be a very difficult budget to balance without some additional tax revenues. Asking for increased taxes is a difficult political chore for a governor at any time. Proposing a tax increase in a governor's last year in office would be doubly difficult, if not impossible. But Shafer had no choice; he had to ask for something.

The governor attempted to finesse the issue by proposing a stand-by income tax. The tax would trigger in only if state revenues fell below a certain level. It was, in its way, a clever political approach to the problem. The legislature, if it approved, would not be levying the tax; the governor would actually do the dastardly deed. If state revenue collections failed to match the spending levels contained in the budget, Shafer was asking for the authority to invoke the tax at a rate necessary to keep the budget in balance. In a way, it was a bold move on his part. But it was doomed from the start.

The very thought of a state income tax was a nonstarter to most legislators, certainly Republican legislators. It certainly had little or no public support among the electorate. Even Lieutenant Governor Broderick, now the Republican standard bearer for governor in the 1970 campaign against Milton Shapp, broke publicly with Shafer on the proposal. The opposition Democrats were in no mood, political or otherwise, to be of help. They took a hands-off position, essentially letting the Republicans stir in their own stew. The budget stalemate went nowhere. Senate Minority Leader Ernie Kline, who also happened to be Shapp's Democratic running mate for lieutenant governor, predicted it would take a new state administration to pass this budget.

That is fundamentally what happened. Prior to the 1970 November election, the legislature approved an eight-month budget that could be balanced by existing state revenues. That would carry the Commonwealth into the term of the next governor. It would be left to the new administration to pass a budget for the balance of the current fiscal year, as well as for the ensuing fiscal year to begin next July 1. It was an unprecedented situation for Pennsylvania state government, certainly in modern times. And it further detracted from Shafer's command of the governance structure and the legacy his administration would leave for historians. But he was virtually powerless to do anything about it.

One last note to the legacy of the Shafer administration. In the governor's final year Fred Speaker, a Harrisburg attorney of some renown and a Shafer loyalist, replaced Bill Sennett as attorney general when Sennett returned to Erie and his law practice. The appointment was made primarily to build Speaker's legal resume and reputation. Speaker apparently had ideas of his own.

Shortly before noon on Inauguration Day when Shapp was to take his oath, Speaker ordered the electric chair dismantled. As state attorney general, he was empowered to do that. It was a stunning act. It almost transcended Shapp's inauguration in the news coverage. Speaker, for the first time acknowledging his strong opposition to the death penalty, said he never told Shafer about it beforehand. Shafer never took issue with that.

The act could have been overturned by the governor, of course. But Shafer was powerless to do so, even if he would have wanted to. He was a *former* governor by the time Speaker's directive became known. Shapp, it so happened, was as anti–death penalty as Speaker. He never reversed the order.

So it was that the death penalty was put on hold in Pennsylvania in 1970 by the unilateral action of one exiting state official. As the constitutionality of the death penalty was argued out for what seemed to be interminably in the courts, no convicted murder was executed in the Commonwealth until the administration of Governor Tom Ridge in the late 1990s, trice removed from the Shafer administration. By this time, lethal injection had replaced the electric chair as the method of implementing a death sentence for a heinous crime in Pennsylvania. The "chair" that Speaker unilaterally ordered dismantled remained ever so. It is in the possession of the Pennsylvania Historical and Museum Commission. There have been private discussions within the commission about the possibility of exhibiting the chair as part of Pennsylvania history. The idea always has been rejected.

So where does all this leave Raymond P. Shafer's place in history? Up for discussion, I suppose, for people who care to indulge themselves in such conversation.

Shafer was a good man with a solid political reputation and an even stronger personal resume. He obviously possessed considerable professional, personal, and political skills or he would never have risen as high as he did in Pennsylvania public life. Regrettably, he lived in the shadow of William Warren Scranton from the first day he took office. He never quite emerged in his own right. It is not dissimilar to the situation in which George H. W. Bush found himself when he succeeded Ronald Reagan in the presidency. Both Scranton at the state political level and Reagan at the national were regarded as icons by their party. Both had a star quality about them. Shafer and Bush were decent, honorable men. Their greatest failing was they lacked the political luster of their predecessors. It was a shortcoming neither was able to quite fully overcome during his term in office.

Shafer, surely, struggled mightily to make his own imprint on state government. But it seemed the more he struggled, the more pronounced his difficulties became. The budget stalemate that marred his last year in office was probably as representative of his command on the machinery of state government as any other event. To many, he was a forgotten man.

When House Speaker Ryan submitted to an in-depth personal political profile and interview on the Pennsylvania Cable Network in 2002, capping a distinguished forty-year career in the Pennsylvania House of Representatives, he was asked to reflect on each of the governors with whom he served. He rattled off recollections of each one of them, Scranton through Casey. He forgot completely to mention Ray Shafer.

I happened to cross paths with Speaker Ryan about a week after the interview was telecast. Since we both arrived in town at about the same time, we indulged ourselves with other reminisces about earlier political life in Harrisburg. I mentioned I was particularly taken with his reflections on the governors. I never mentioned his omission of Shafer. But Ryan did. "You know," he said. "I missed Shafer totally. I feel bad about that, I really do."

I'm sure he did. Unfortunately, the oversight probably was representative of the general view of the Shafer administration. Raymond Shafer was the only man in modern Pennsylvania history to be elected governor directly from the office of lieutenant governor. That fact, more than any other, will be his most distinguishing note in the history books of Pennsylvania. He served with a high degree of commitment. He probably deserves better than history likely will afford him. But that's just the reality of his tenure.

Chapter 15

★★★★★★★

Milton J. Shapp (1971–1979)

When you stop to reflect on the tenure of Milton Jerrold Shapp as governor of Pennsylvania, a number of recollections come immediately to mind. He was, after all,

The first of Pennsylvania's two-term, modern-era governors;
The governor who removed coin boxes from the toilets at the Howard Johnson rest stops along the Pennsylvania Turnpike;
The governor whom the state police executive detail literally carried from the grounds of the three-year-old Governor's Residence across the street from the Susquehanna River to escape the raging waters rising in the wrath of Tropical Storm Agnes;
The governor who signed a landmark state lottery into law to provide Pennsylvania senior citizens with a modicum on property tax relief;
And the governor who finished behind no-preference in the 1976 Florida presidential primary election.

The list could go on, I suppose. But in the end, the inevitable conclusion you reach after eight years of Milton Shapp in the executive office is that he will most be remembered in Pennsylvania political annals for two principal reasons:

He was the first candidate for governor in the state—the first for any statewide office, for that matter—to retain high profile out-of-state political consultants who introduced the mighty power of saturation television advertising to Pennsylvania political campaigning.

And, if not the national trendsetter, he certainly was years ahead of what now has become a common pattern in American politics for individuals of substantial wealth to fund their bids for high public office from their considerable cache of personal millions (a pattern candidates like Mayor Michael Bloomberg of New York and U.S. Senator Jon Corzine of New Jersey would take to a high art form at the end of the twentieth century).

Milton Shapp was an outsider in state Democratic politics from the day he began his pursuit of public office in Pennsylvania. A native of Cleveland,

Ohio, a graduate of Case Institute of Technology (now Case Western Reserve University) with a bachelor's degree in electrical engineering, Shapp migrated to Pennsylvania after his World War II service in the U.S. Army Signal Corps. He was a pioneer in the fledgling cable television industry, a technology few understood at the time, and made his entrepreneurial mark in business by promising to bring television to "mountain-locked communities" across the nation. He started his company, Jerrod Electronics Corporation, with five hundred dollars and two employees. Twenty years later, when he sold it to enter elective politics, it was valued at $50 million and employed 2,100 people.

Shapp's first bid as a political candidate was as brief as it was noncompetitive. He announced in 1964 that he would enter the Pennsylvania primary to challenge for the Democratic Party's nomination to the U.S. Senate. The nomination held a lot of promise for the Democratic nominee. Lyndon Johnson had replaced the assassinated John Kennedy in the White House and the political landscape looked ripe for Democrats across the country, particularly with conservative Arizona senator Barry Goldwater heading the Republican ticket. Republican U.S. Senator Hugh Scott looked particularly vulnerable in that scenario, and rightly so.

Shapp went so far as to begin assembling his own campaign staff and organization. Fred Walters, a senior member of the Associated Press Harrisburg Bureau and one of my early mentors in journalism, signed on as Shapp's press secretary. But in the face of widespread opposition from the established leadership of the party, almost as suddenly as he announced his candidacy, he announced his withdrawal. Poor Fred Walters read about his candidate's decision in the morning newspaper.

Two years later, Shapp was back on the Pennsylvania political landscape, this time as a candidate for the Democratic nomination for governor. And this time he was not to be deterred, Democratic leadership opposition or not. In fact, his 1964 experience with that party leadership may have convinced him that the Democratic establishment would never support his political aspirations. So, at age fifty-four, he was *in,* and he was in to stay. His party-endorsed opponent was a freshman state senator from Scranton by the name of Robert P. Casey.

The two candidates could not have been more different in the image they presented Democratic voters. Casey was a handsome man with an attractive wife and an equally handsome young family. The Caseys were as photogenic as they come, a campaign's dream team in many ways. Shapp was exactly the opposite. Stoop-shouldered, of diminutive size, always seen in a nondescript but customary blue suit, blue shirt, and maroon tie, Milton

Shapp would never have been mistaken for Robert Redford in that classic political film, *The Candidate*. Photos often were his own worst enemy. Advantage Casey, and decisively so.

But if Milton Shapp wasn't an 8 × 10 glossy photo, he certainly was something else. Once committed, he was as determined as they come; tenacious as a bulldog, and, in spite of what appeared to be a very subdued personality, he never flinched from a tough fight. This little man had a lot of steel to him.

Shapp hired a political consultant from Massachusetts by the name of Joe Napolitan to come to Pennsylvania and direct his outsider campaign against his party and its endorsed nominee. Napolitan was the first hired gun to come into the state and assume a high-visibility political role that I can recall. His success in managing the Shapp primary campaign earned him considerable national publicity. In retrospect, it may have been, in fact, the one political campaign that more than any other of the era that gave birth to political consulting as a cottage industry across the country.

The theme of Shapp's Napolitan-directed campaign was "Man Against the Machine." Its heart and soul was a devastating thirty-minute film of the same name which virtually saturated, at great personal expense to Milton Shapp, Pennsylvania television in the last days leading up to the primary balloting. Its producer was Joseph Guggenheim, a filmmaker of some renown. The film was part biographical, for Shapp was a virtual unknown to most Pennsylvanians. It introduced him as growing up in a working-class family; his father ran a hardware store; he worked his way through college in the depths of the Depression; he secured his first job driving a coal truck; he served his country in the U.S. Army before returning to civilian life; and he converted a $500 investment into a $55-million business enterprise.

But the biggest impact of the film was political. It attacked the Democratic Party establishment as a closed corporation whose leadership was out of touch and unconcerned about the needs of real Pennsylvanians. The closing visual was particularly graphic. The Democrats had a party functionary (Larry Rooney was his name, I believe) who performed a variety of mundane chores at party events. The day the Democratic State Committee met in private session to endorse Bob Casey for governor, Larry Rooney was the doorkeeper. Shapp's television cameras were there to record the scene. They were not allowed in the proceedings themselves. So the film captured Larry Rooney closing the doors of the meeting room to Shapp's cameras, and, by extension, the Pennsylvania electorate. Rooney may even had his hand up to the camera as the scene closed. The visual effect was devastating.

This shot, in just thirty seconds or so, captured in a very, very visual way the essence of the maverick campaign: One man, Milton Shapp, fighting to open the doors of the Democratic Party in Pennsylvania against the rigid, old-school opposition of the party machine and its established leadership. It hardly required any accompanying narrative to reinforce the point. I can't remember whether the film attacked Casey or simply dismissed his credentials as minimal. Actually, Casey was not the target. Shapp's fight was against the leaders of the state Democratic Party, and in this portrayal, Casey was merely a puppet of the party bosses.

The film aired with considerable fanfare on television stations across the state every night for the last ten days or so of the primary campaign. Nothing of its sort had been seen before in Pennsylvania. It was an expensive undertaking, but money was of no concern to millionaire Shapp. Besides, because Pennsylvania voters had never seen anything like this before—this unprecedented reliance on television advertising with a half-hour political documentary as its keystone—the tactic earned Shapp, Napolitan, and their outsider campaign a lot of free press in the process. In politics, to borrow a phrase, that's priceless.

Casey, meanwhile, had no personal fortune or established political reputation of his own to drive his campaign. He was totally dependent on the traditional powers of the Democratic state organization to turn out its vote across the state. The party couldn't deliver. Its organizational ability to do that had been dwindling noticeably. With Republicans in control of the executive branch since 1962, the traditional spoils—jobs, entrée, access—that go to political victors and their rank-and-file were denied to the Democratic Party. Additionally, one of the party's traditional sources of grass roots support—organized labor—actually looked favorably on the Shapp candidacy. In fact, the Pennsylvania AFL-CIO had named Shapp in 1963 its "Man of the Year" primarily for his hiring and promotion policies related to women and minorities. He was the first businessman to be so selected. He may have been the last, though I don't know that for a fact.

Shapp upset Casey by 49,000 votes in the Democratic primary election. It was ranked as a major political upset from the conventional perspective because, at the time, the organized political parties seldom lost their endorsed candidates to a primary challenge by mavericks from outside their ranks, even self-financed mavericks like Milton Shapp. If proof was needed, this was at the very least a sign that, in Pennsylvania, the power of the established Democratic Party was in a state of serious decline. It also sent a message to other politically ambitious Democrats that, with well-financed campaigns and well-organized political strategies, they could take on their party organizations and win. (Bob Casey, incidentally, in reflecting years later on this, his first of three failed bids for the governorship, concluded that this was the one political decision in his career that he would have reversed if he had it to do over again. In hindsight, he recognized that he simply wasn't ready politically to reach so high at that point and may have been a victim of his own hubris.)

Shapp, now having slain one dragon, set out to do the same to his Republican opposition. But first he had to somehow bring back into the fold for the fall those very same Democratic regulars he had attacked so ferociously in the spring. It didn't quite work out as well as he would have hoped.

Joe Napolitan stood in the wings of a raucous Democratic State Committee meeting, the first after the primary election, as the candidate attempted to put his stamp on the party structure by designating York County attorney Robert Kane as its state chairman. He succeeded, but not without a lot of shouting, dissent and contention. Lieutenant governor nominee Leonard Staisey attempted to put the best face on the situation by declaring to no one in particular as the meeting was adjourning, "We leave here united!"

Napolitan knew otherwise. "These people don't know just how badly discredited they are," he said of the Democratic State Committee members in a brief exchange with the press after the meeting. It was as much a comment uttered in disbelief as disdain. Now, for better or for worse, it was on to the fall campaign against Lieutenant Governor Ray Shafer and the opposition Republicans.

The campaign was memorable on at least two counts that had nothing to do with the issues that divided the candidates. Most curious was the fact that though Shapp was the first Jewish candidate for governor in the history (certainly modern history) of the Commonwealth, the Jewish community was badly divided over his candidacy. Some were outspoken in their opposition to him. When I asked a member of the Jewish faith whom I came to know during the campaign about it, he responded, "He's not the Jew that most of us want as the standard of our faith representing us in the governor's office." I never did come to quite understand this Jewish split over one of their own. Perhaps it had to do with the fact that early in his adult life Shapp had changed his name from Shapiro because of his concerns about the prejudice members of the Jewish faith might encounter in their professional pursuits. Perhaps he didn't adhere strictly enough to tenets of the faith. (I remember meeting him for breakfast when I joined up with him on his second campaign for governor four years later and him ordering "crispy bacon, really crispy bacon" with his eggs.) Perhaps it had something to do with the way he conducted his business. Perhaps he was just an outsider with them as well. I just don't know. I do know the split within the Jewish community over the Shapp candidacy was real and it was fairly public.

The second element of the campaign was more compelling and certainly more far-reaching. In the mid-1960s Pennsylvania suffered from a serious political anomaly. Even though the candidates for governor and lieutenant governor were paired politically on their respective party tickets, they were elected separately in the general election balloting. Theoretically, the voters could choose a governor of one party and a lieutenant governor of another. It had happened before in other states, most notably California. But it had never happened in Pennsylvania.

The year 1966 was a distinct possibility, however. Leonard Staisey, a well-regarded state senator from Allegheny County, had been endorsed by the state party as Bob Casey's running mate for lieutenant governor. Casey/Staisey was the party ticket. Shapp responded by pairing with Westmoreland County commissioner Jim Kelly, son of a former congressman later to become a state senator and, ultimately, a judge on the Pennsylvania Commonwealth Court. Shapp beat Casey, but Staisey beat Kelly.

I don't believe Shapp really cared. Staisey, who was 90 percent blind from childhood, was well regarded politically among Democratic Party regulars; more important, he was extremely popular in his heavily Democratic region of southwestern Pennsylvania. His presence gave the ticket standing in that important area with its Democratic voting patterns. In fact, it may have done more to heal the bitterness of the party regulars—if any healing was truly possible—than anything else the nominee might have done himself. In short, Staisey was a very large plus for this maverick nominee who could use as many pluses as he could find in a divided Democratic Party.

The Republicans, meanwhile, had suffered a serious jolt by Walter Alessandroni's death in that tragic airplane crash in the mountains of southwest Pennsylvania. Shafer's selection of an unknown and untested Ray Broderick as Alessandroni's replacement on the ticket added little if any political stature or presence to the GOP campaign. A move to elect Republican Shafer governor and Democrat Staisey as lieutenant governor became a subject of open, fairly widespread, serious talk within the political community of both parties. It was probably the most interesting storyline to the entire campaign.

Shafer's campaign was pretty much standard fare—build on the progress of the Scranton administration with seasoned leadership. Shapp, meanwhile, was a candidate full of ideas, but some of them didn't play well with the electorate. His proposal to put "free college" within the reach of every young Pennsylvanian was greeted with great skepticism. It simply didn't fly and, in the final analysis, may have put every initiative he had to offer in serious doubt with the electorate.

The candidate also shot himself in the foot in the closing days of the campaign. In a television interview Shapp charged, spontaneously it appeared, that he had been offered a bribe—a major political contribution in return for the right to name some ranking officials in his administration, the Public Utility Commission and the State Insurance Commissioner primary among them. The Republicans immediately jumped on the issue by demanding that Shapp reveal publicly the source or sources of the reputed offer. He declined, saying it was not a crime to make the offer; the crime would have been in accepting it. Candidate Shafer, Governor Scranton, and U.S. Senator Hugh Scott remained hard on the case, pressing Shapp daily to come clean. "No one's offered me a contribution in exchange for the right to name officials in my administration," Shafer argued to some great effect at virtually every stop he made before campaign's end.

Taken cumulatively—"free college," the bribe, the split in the Democratic Party that never closed, and, oh yes, dare we forget that photo of Shapp chasing Shafer around the *Allentown Morning Call* newsroom—Shapp's campaign probably was doomed. He continued to play his outsider role as a successful businessman who would bring tested business practices and experience and a populist political agenda targeted to consumers and the elderly to the state Capitol. His fall campaign also relied heavily on another half-hour television documentary that saturated the airways again in the days leading to the election. The TV strategy that had proven so pivotal in his primary win over Casey because of the ground it broke in Pennsylvania political campaigning had very little impact in the general election. Pennsylvania voters had come to know a good bit about Milton Shapp by the time November rolled around. They didn't need television to introduce him any longer as a candidate for governor. They were content to make up their own minds this time around without the external influences attempting to sway them.

Shafer defeated Shapp by 241,581 votes. Broderick's margin over Staisey was much less, only 61,000 votes. The Shafer/Staisey movement had steam behind it, but just not enough. It did give the press something to write about. And it was of sufficient political concern that Pennsylvania election law was changed soon thereafter to require that the governor and lieutenant governor be elected jointly, similar to the way we elect our president and vice-president.

At the end of the 1966 campaign, few outside of Shapp's inner circle gave much thought to where Milton Shapp would be politically in four years. The real instant winner was Joe Napolitan. He became a political celebrity virtually overnight by the force of Shapp's primary victory over his party. Napolitan, like so many others suddenly thrust in that spotlight, could not resist the temptations of national exposure. He gave a number of interviews to the national media. Most of them suggested Napolitan's strategy to rely on the television documentary had more to do with Shapp's primary victory than the candidate or his political message. In fact, in one interview he made some crack about having to package Shapp like soap flakes to sell him to the electorate. It didn't sit well with Shapp and his inner circle.

One other element of the 1966 gubernatorial campaign needs to be addressed before moving on: the treatment Milton Shapp received at the hands of the *Philadelphia Inquirer* under the ownership of Walter Annenberg. It was embarrassing at the least, and professionally disreputable at the worst.

Walter Annenberg, for reasons still explicitly unknown to me, had a death-wish feud with Milton Shapp. The most conventional line was that Shapp had insulted Mrs. Annenberg in someway in a Philadelphia elevator in the presence of her husband. Whatever the reason, the *Inquirer* simply hounded Milton Shapp when he sought the governorship in 1966.

I wrote earlier of the *Inquirer*'s pursuit of the storyline that Shapp had been treated for a mental health disorder a year before. Shapp was forced to publicly deny he had psychiatric treatment in 1965, or that he had been a mental patient in a Philadelphia hospital. (He said he had been hospitalized on doctor's orders in August and September of that year suffering from exhaustion "with the possibility of a heart condition.") Hit man Joe Miller wrote the denial story two weeks out from the election. Editorial page political columnist John M. Cummings refused to permit the denial to die a natural and quiet death. Three days after publication of the Miller story, his column was headlined, "A Political Rumor and Its Denial." Cummings wrote, "Milton Shapp denies he was ever in need of psychiatric treatment [concerning reports that] for a period of time in 1965 he was in Graduate Hospital of the University of Pennsylvania for mental treatment. Shapp says he was institutionalized suffering from exhaustion and possibly a heart condition." Cummings concluded his commentary this way: "Let's return to Milt's statement that he wasn't in the hospital for psychiatric treatment. He had a physical breakdown and needed a long rest. This should put an end to all the amateur speculation on the mental condition of the Democratic candidate for Governor." No candidate for high public office in Pennsylvania had been damned with fainter praise.

The *Inquirer*'s coverage of Milton Shapp (and others) was noted prominently in the paper's obituary of Walter Annenberg in October of 2002. Now under new ownership (the Knight-Ridder chain with the Miami Herald and the Detroit Free Press as two of its flagship papers), the Inky's Andy Wallace and Rusty Pray wrote of Annenberg, media magnate, U.S. ambassador to the Court of St. James, and philanthropist to countless educational and charitable causes:

> Though he spent most of his working hours in his 12th floor office at the Inquirer Building . . . he visited the newsroom once a week. When he did, he usually communicated only with city editor Morris Litman and political writer Joseph Miller.
>
> Gaeton Fonzi reported in *Philadelphia Magazine* in 1969 that Mr. Annenberg often called the newspaper after receiving an early edition to kill or downplay stories that he did not like or that were on topics of which he did not approve.
>
> There were certain people whose names were not to be mentioned in the *Inquirer:* Among them—for a time, as the list changed a lot—were former University of Pennsylvania President Gaylord P. Harnwell; singer Dinah Shore; perennial presidential candidate Harold Stassen; comedian Imogene Coca; a former head of the Philadelphia Stock Exchange, Elkins Weatherill; consumer advocate Ralph Nader and the entire Philadelphia 76ers team.
>
> Mr. Annenberg was said to have ordered the *Inquirer* staff to write negative articles at times, such as one critical of Curtis Publishing Co. after *Holiday,* a Curtis magazine, reported that he had been snubbed by Main Line society.
>
> During the 1960s, the *Inquirer*'s reputation was further damaged by two embarrassing incidents. One was the conviction of Harry Karafin, the newspaper's top investigative reporter, for blackmailing city firms to keep unflattering stories out of the paper.
>
> The other was a smear campaign the *Inquirer* conducted against Milton Shapp during the 1966 Pennsylvania gubernatorial campaign. A negative slant was put on every Shapp activity, even his decision to change his name from Shapiro to Shapp when he was young One notorious piece of mudslinging that year was done by political reporter Miller. He got the candidate to deny that he had ever been in a mental hospital, then dutifully reported the denial.

In the case of Walter Annenberg's *Philadelphia Inquirer,* the prosecution rests.

Milton Shapp, if he was anything, was as persistent as any man in his pursuit of high political office in Pennsylvania. His failed bids for the U.S. Senate and governor not withstanding, in 1970 he was back again, this time for a second run at the Democratic nomination for governor. Not so coincidentally, Joe Napolitan was among the missing. Another apparent character trait of Mr. Shapp was that he also had a long memory.

The political climate in Pennsylvania was entirely different this time around. Where as in 1966, the Commonwealth was in stable and steady condition with William Scranton at the helm, Pennsylvania in 1970 was on the brink of fiscal and political disarray. Political science professors G. Terry Madonna, then of Millersville University of Pennsylvania, and Michael Young of Penn State–Harrisburg portrayed the situation this way:

> In 1970, the economy of Pennsylvania was in shambles, as the state wrestled with its perennial problem—a large state budget deficit and high unemployment. The outgoing Republican governor, Ray Shafer, proposed an income tax, but the Republican candidate in 1970, incumbent Lieutenant Governor Ray Broderick, opposed it. Milton Shapp . . . used his success in business to argue persuasively that it would take a businessman to get the state out of debt, its leadership problems solved, and the economy jump started.

Drs. Madonna and Young had it exactly right. Pennsylvania was facing a serious revenue problem once again; Governor Shafer proposed his standby income tax as the means to balance the state budget as a last resort; Republicans in the legislature revolted; and Broderick broke with Shafer as he waged his own campaign for governor. The political cards certainly were aligned in Milton Shapp's favor.

But first there was the matter of Robert P. Casey to be disposed of once again. Casey was now the state auditor general, elected two years after his primary loss to Shapp in 1966. Casey again was endorsed by the Democratic Party state organization to be its candidate for governor. Shapp was running once more as an outsider. For Democratic voters, it was Casey-Shapp II. Not quite the "Thrilla in Manila," but as heavyweight political confrontations come and go, it certainly would do.

This time around the track, Shapp toned down his "Man Against the Machine" rhetoric. One of the lessons he apparently learned from 1966 was that there was no profit in winning the battle of the primary in the spring only to lose the war of the general in November. Shapp had not been idle in the four years since his loss to Shafer; he had spent considerable time cultivating as many political allies as he could muster throughout the state.

Though many of them, if not most, still were party irregulars, they gave him an organization of loyalists to set in motion in both the 1970 primary and the general elections. The spoils would be theirs to reap if Shapp was successful in November.

I had moved on to the public information office at Penn State at the time. Shortly before the primary, the *Inquirer*, now under Knight-Ridder ownership, called with an offer for me to return to Harrisburg and join up with Bill Ecenbarger in the paper's newly constituted capital bureau. I accepted. My assignment the day I reported to the job was to hook up with the Casey campaign and stay with him for the final two weeks of the primary election.

No sooner did I arrive than a political crisis erupted for the Casey camp. Philadelphia mayor James Tate, volatile as always, ostensibly was backing Casey again for governor. He made some remark to the effect that Casey would be an able governor if he kept his nose clean and was a good boy. The press asked Casey for his reaction. He retorted something to the effect that he was nobody's "boy," and somebody should tell that to the mayor for him. The mayor reacted no less angrily and threatened to withdraw his support. This was a case of two tempers clashing in a very public way. Casey was urged to break from his campaign schedule and rush to Philadelphia to make his peace with Tate. He declined.

Casey relied, instead, largely on the persuasive powers of Philadelphia Democratic City Chair (and a former Senate colleague) Joe Scanlon to, if not patch things up with the mayor, at least keep the city organization working in his corner. Senator Scanlon, unfortunately, was hospitalized at the time with an ailment that eventually claimed his life. His ability to broker a peace offering with Tate from a hospital bed was limited. The city of Philadelphia went for Shapp in the primary. While Casey was winning forty-plus of the sixty-seven counties in the state, the most populous Democratic counties went heavily for Milton Shapp. Once again, he vanquished Bob Casey in a Democratic faceoff for governor, this time by the margin of about 240,000 votes.

Now the two-time Democratic nominee once again turned his sights on the Republican opposition in the fall. Broderick had selected a relatively unknown Beaver County Common Pleas Judge by the name of Ralph Scalera to be his running mate. (One of the Broderick campaign's earliest commercials attempted to give some identity to the Republican ticket by triggering voter curiosity in asking, "What's a Broderick/Scalera?" It was cute but not very effective.) Ralph Scalera was undoubtedly a good man. He had proven his bipartisan electoral appeal in a strong Democratic county like Beaver. But he brought absolutely nothing politically to the ticket.

Broderick's campaign, meanwhile, was contained essentially on five three-by-five index cards that he always carried with him and referred to in virtually every appearance he made. The issue cards were his battle call. For the press covering the campaign, the only question was in what order he would rearrange the cards at any particular stump stop. Broderick's premise was that the state's fiscal house could be put in good order once again without an income tax, standby or otherwise, through solid, tight fiscal management, and he was the candidate to bring that to the table. The aforementioned Jack Conmy, incidentally, signed on to manage the Broderick campaign. It probably was not one of his better career decisions.

Shapp, meanwhile, had less difficulty this time in making his peace with the party regulars he had defeated once again. Like love, the Democrats found political peacemaking was easier the second time around. Senate Minority Leader Ernie Kline had been Casey's endorsed running mate for lieutenant governor in the 1970 primary and was nominated to run with Shapp on the general election ticket. While Kline proved an effective link to the disgruntled Democrats, the fact was the Democratic rank-and-file were hungry for a political victory. It really didn't matter whether it was Casey or Shapp at the top of the ticket; what mattered most politically was that after eight years of Republican rule, a Democrat would now be governor.

In 1970 the issues and political momentum were all with Shapp and the Democrats. The inability of the General Assembly and the Shafer administration to enact a state budget and what role taxes, income or otherwise, would play in the ultimate resolution were the primary issues. This theme reconciled very nicely with Shapp's background as a successful businessman who pledged to bring proven business techniques to Harrisburg.

There was one other notable difference between 1970 and 1966 from my seat in the press gallery of the gubernatorial arena. That was the treatment the Democratic candidate received from the new management at the *Philadelphia Inquirer*. As the campaign unfolded, the *Inquirer* editors assigned Bill Ecenbarger and me to write two complementary articles: Bill's piece was to lay out the true state of Commonwealth fiscal affairs as he could most comprehensively piece it together; my contribution was to explain how the fiscal mess was playing into the gubernatorial campaigns of the two candidates. Bill's piece was a very detailed and analytical assessment of the unsettled fiscal situation and its consequences for state services and programs. I wrote that in many respects the election came down to whom the voters believed: Ray Broderick, who insisted that there was another turn to the no-new-tax political wheel; or Milton Shapp, who said the only solution rested with the difficult decisions the next administration had to make on taxes.

The articles appeared in the Sunday *Inquirer* two weeks out from the general election. As it happened, I joined up with the Shapp campaign the next day to cover the election homestretch. In an obvious attempt to stroke me and, perhaps, determine what biases if any I brought to my campaign coverage, I was invited to meet Shapp for breakfast (the "crispy bacon" breakfast) that morning in the hotel where the candidate and his entourage were staying. After the usual small talk, Shapp turned the conversation to the pieces in the Sunday *Inquirer* the previous day. He said he thought the *Inquirer* had done a real public service to lay out the case in the way it did. That wasn't surprising because the story line blended well into the theme of the Shapp campaign. The articles weren't written to do that; that's simply where the facts took them.

Shapp and his campaign staff were very much aware of the treatment his campaign was getting this time around from the *Inquirer*. So much so, in fact, that the candidate was moved to comment on it publicly at a campaign rally in Delaware County a few days before the balloting. I was in the press row off to the side while Shapp recounted how different his experiences were this year versus four years prior. To my surprise, he injected the *Inquirer* into his musings. He told the audience how scrupulously objective and balanced the *Inquirer* had been in this campaign and looked over to me and said, "Vince, you tell your editors for me your newspaper has been more than fair, and how much I appreciate that." The Democratic faithful applauded.

I was somewhat embarrassed. It made me think of Ray Shafer's unpleasant encounter with Duke Kaminski of the *Philadelphia Bulletin* four years earlier. For a moment, I had to ask myself if I had been doing my job the way it was supposed to be done. I quickly concluded I did it the only way I knew how to do it. A newspaper's primary purpose—the same should be said for all forms of media—was to inform its readers as accurately, fairly, and completely as it was in its power to do. The *Inquirer* and I simply were doing what we were supposed to be doing in our coverage. Neither the paper nor I should have been praised for that.

Shapp was an easy victor over Ray Broderick in 1970 with an impressive margin of 500,200 votes. With no state budget in place and state revenues running short of projections, Broderick's claim of solving the problem without resorting to taxes simply was not credible.

There's one other story about the 1970 election campaign which should be told if only for the enjoyment (all mine, to be sure) in the telling of it. On general election night I was in Philadelphia reporting on the results of the legislative races for the Pennsylvania House and Senate. The Democratic sweep was so commanding and definitive, it didn't take very long for the *Inquirer*'s election stories to be written for the next morning's editions. In fact, we were done well before 11 P.M. Now it was time for a drink.

Gene Harris, the paper's chief political writer, some other *Inquirer* staffers, and I headed over to Shapp's hotel headquarters. We figured this was the place to find the celebration and join in. We figured wrong. The place was shut down tighter than a drum. Shapp had issued an early victory statement and headed home with his wife, Muriel. The Shapps and their staff were not a partying bunch, apparently. Not even in victory.

Now our options were sorely limited, and the stakes were high. Either we found an election party or, God forbid, we'd end up buying our own drinks. For journalists of my generation, there could be no worse fate. So we made our way, more in desperation than anything else, to the Broderick hotel. And what did we find? We found a party. And what a party! I remember wondering, "Don't these people know they lost?" In the best tradition of the Irish in a time of sorrow, the Broderick team decided that night, consciously or subconsciously, that having been beaten so soundly, they might as well drink away the hurt. And they proved themselves very good at it.

As I was wandering around the campaign suite, someone, I can't remember whom, introduced me to a woman (attractive, as I recall) who said she was from Harrisburg. We chatted. At some point, she asked me if I was a lawyer. I told her, no, I was a reporter for the *Philadelphia Inquirer*. She wasn't impressed. Our conversation ended seconds later. I went on my way and she on hers. After my second drink, I called it a night. I remember passing by the lady as I was leaving. She was in the clutches of some young man. I assumed he was a lawyer.

The next morning, about 7 A.M, I called the *Inquirer* desk to get my assignment for an election-day follow-up. I next called Toni to check how things were at home with her and the kids. Then I hit the shower. By 7:30–7:45, I was at the elevator of the Philadelphia Sheraton (which also happened to be Broderick's hotel). The elevator door opened, I entered. There to my right was the aforementioned young lady. She was wearing a purple jumpsuit (jumpsuits were in vogue at the time) and she had on a large pair of round sunglasses. She looked like she had had a very difficult night.

She spoke first: "Do you remember me?" she asked.

"Should I?" I responded?

"Weren't you at the Broderick suite last night? That's where we met." she reminded me.

I played dumb. "Oh, okay," I said. "Nice to see you again. How are you?" I asked—like I didn't know.

"Not so good," she explained. "I lost my purse last night. I'm in desperate need of a cup of coffee. If you're going to the coffeeshop, would you buy me a cup of coffee?"

What could I say? "Sure," I agreed. "I'll buy you a cup of coffee." One cup wasn't going to do it. She needed at least a large pot for any hope to get her sea legs back. But I was too much of a gentleman to suggest that.

We walked to the coffee shop and entered together. I no sooner opened the door than I saw at least twenty people who knew Toni and me. Oh, oh, this is trouble, I thought. But the reaction I received was interesting. The men seemed to be chuckling. Some were discreetly giving me the thumbs-up sign. Way to go, Vince, they seemed to be suggesting. Their wives, however, had a different slant. *Quite* different. You could see it in their eyes. If looks could speak, I would have heard them say, "Shame on you! You, with a perfectly delightful wife and two beautiful children at home. How could you, you cad?" Understandably, no one came over to exchange pleasantries. How could they? What were we going to say to each other, "How was your night?"

Well, I stewed over this for most of the day. I thought about nothing else on the train ride back to Harrisburg. I had a decision to make. Do I tell Toni or not? I still was undecided when I arrived home. I was going to let instinct and the natural course of events make the decision for me.

We had dinner, I bathed the kids and read the usual bedtime stories, Finally, Toni and I were in the kitchen finishing up the dishes (a dishwasher was not yet a part of our household budget). I decided then to tell her. I assume I concluded it was better for her to hear it from me than from one of the people who saw me that morning in the coffeeshop.

So I told her the story essentially as I related it here. I had no idea how she was going to react. Initially, there was no reaction to speak of. The silence seemed like an eternity.

Finally, she responded. But there was a distinct threatening tone to her voice as she spoke. It warned me there'd be hell to pay if I weren't telling her the truth. "I guess I'm going to believe you," she said. "But only because you're not clever enough to make up something like that." She was right. I wasn't.

But back to more important musings. It was fortunate for Shapp that in winning the governorship, he also had a Democratically controlled General Assembly to assist him. There was no time for rejoicing over their ballot collective successes the previous November. No sooner had Shapp taken his oath in January 1971 than he and the legislature had to balance the unfinished budget of fiscal 1970–71 within thirty days, and almost immediately thereafter, the new governor had to submit a new budget for fiscal 1971–72. Without a Democratic legislature—more specifically the first

Democratic-controlled state Senate in thirty-four years—it is doubtful Shapp could have navigated the budget and tax mess as expeditiously as he did. And he had to do it not once, but twice.

Shapp's Democratic leadership in the General Assembly—Senators Murray and Lamb and House Speaker Fineman, Majority Leader Irvis, and Majority Whip Manderino—responded brilliantly to the challenge. It was no small feat, believe me, majority status in both chambers or not. Taxes are never easy to enact, and the dreaded income tax made the challenge even more imposing, particularly in the Senate where the Democrats had no votes to spare and the Republicans were solid in their opposition to the first Shapp income tax proposal. And once Shapp signed his 3.5 percent income tax proposal into law, the GOP led by attorney Perrin Hamilton, a former member of Ray Shafer's cabinet, filed a class-action suit challenging the constitutionality of the levy. The first income tax contained at Shapp's insistence a poverty exemption for low-income Pennsylvanians. Hamilton's suit argued that the exemption violated the uniformity clause—the very same uniformity clause that was taken off the table in the deliberations of Ray Shafer's constitutional convention four years earlier. The state Supreme Court decided in Hamilton's favor. So it was back to the drawing board for Shapp and his legislative majority. The response was a flat tax of 2.3 percent enacted in August.

The income-tax votes were particularly difficult and politically dangerous for a number of newly elected Democratic state senators, Joe Ammerman of Clearfield and Centre counties, Henry Messinger in Lehigh County, and Pat Stapleton of Indiana County primary among them. All three had won in Senate districts that traditionally voted Republican. Without them, the Democrats would never have achieved a political majority in the Senate in the first place. Now they were being asked as almost their first order of business to vote for not one but two state income taxes. Politically, that's as perilous as it could get for freshmen lawmakers, especially freshman lawmakers from districts that traditionally voted with the other party.

Ammerman and Messinger never wavered. They had some idea of what was in store in Harrisburg if they were elected. Their attitude once inaugurated was that if it had to be done, then let's do it. We'll deal with the political consequences as they arise. (Both went on to reelection and distinguished service in the Pennsylvania Senate.)

Pat Stapleton was another matter, and for good reason. His district was solidly Republican. He was a surprise winner in May of 1970 in a special election to fill an unexpired term created by the death of his entrenched Republican predecessor, the notable Albert Pechan, a Kittanning dentist in

Armstrong County. In fact, Stapleton, a minority Indiana County commissioner at the time, went to bed election night thinking he had lost. The late returns from neighboring counties carried him to a narrow victory. But he had to stand for election to a full four-year term in just two short years. The income tax could cripple his prospects. He voted for the first income tax because of the urgency to get the state's fiscal House in order. But a second, just months later? That took some doing, particularly since two of his freshman colleagues—Bill Duffield and Tom Nolan—were off the ship this time around. Stapleton had to be kept in the fold.

By the time of the second tax vote in August, I had left the *Inquirer* to become press secretary to the Senate Democratic caucus. I sat in on a session Ernie Kline had with Stapleton before the roll was called in the Senate. Kline was there to shore up Stapleton's political courage. I was there to assure the senator he would receive all the press relations help we could provide to minimize any political fallout back home. Poor Pat had no easy choice: Either the fiscal situation of the Commonwealth was thrown into turmoil once again, or a second state income tax had to be enacted with his vote. Pat had to decide which alternative was worse.

He voted ultimately in support of the second income tax. We immediately gave Stapleton all the public relations protection we could. He issued a statement the night of the vote. He said throwing the fiscal affairs of the Commonwealth into chaos once again would have been more damaging to the public interest than adopting a budget that required a new income tax to balance it. Stapleton's 41st Senatorial District at the time was home to not one but two state-owned colleges—Indiana and Clarion, both economic engines in their communities. His statement emphasized in particular detail the funds that would flow to these two institutions; also, the funds every school district in his four-county region would receive from the budget as adopted, and the other state assistance the budget would channel into the district. He concluded by saying he was elected to make hard choices when necessary. This was, admittedly, as hard a choice as a legislator could be asked to make, but it was unavoidable. If there were a political price to pay for preserving fiscal stability for the Commonwealth, Stapleton went on, he was prepared to pay it. The statement didn't rise to the level of a profile in courage, but it certainly played on the theme.

Stapleton survived both income-tax votes with no great difficulty. I know because I was assigned to coordinate his campaign for a full four-year term in 1972. His reelection was testament to his own great standing back home. Pat Stapleton was popular in his district because he was a regular guy before he got elected; he stayed a regular guy after his election. He was accessible to his constituents; he was attentive to their needs, individually and collectively. And he was attentive to his Senate responsibilities—a 99 percent–plus voting record throughout his thirty years of service in the chamber. For his first reelection, we devised a campaign plan that played to these strengths, and it worked.

Pat's opponent was a former House Republican member from Indiana County. Stapleton also sought reelection in this conservative farm and coal-mining district on a ballot that featured Richard Nixon against George McGovern for president. Republicans outnumbered Democrats by 10,000 registered voters. Pat Stapleton clearly was in the Republican campaign crosshairs. This was not going to be a walk in the park. But Pat Stapleton's standing with his constituency was so strong that he not only won reelection; he beat Richard Nixon's victory margin in the district. The income-tax votes were never a factor when the voters went to the polls. In fact, it seldom came up. Stapleton had more trouble with his constituents over the Senate's slow disposition of the Frank Mazzei case than he did with the income tax. "You gotta do something about that Mazzei," they told him quite directly and frequently. We heard it virtually every day we walked the streets of his district together. Once the Senate expelled Senator Mazzei, that disappeared as an issue and Stapleton's campaign was waged and won on his terms.

As a footnote to the income-tax deliberations, it should also be noted for the record that the issue of a "bribe" came back to torment Shapp once more. Tom Nolan, the anti-tax/anti-spend maverick Democrat from Allegheny County, charged publicly on the Senate floor in the first income-tax debate that his brother was offered a $25,000 job with the state if the senator could be persuaded to support the governor on the tax. Shapp acknowledged the alleged offer came from a campaign supporter, but said the man in question "was not in a position to offer anything" on the administration's behalf. The governor immediately referred the matter to his attorney general for investigation. The culprit later was identified in the attorney general's report as a labor liaison to the Shapp campaign. Nothing really ever came of the matter because no hard evidence existed of a direct "quid-pro-quo" offer, and no offer was made directly to Nolan. The incident did, however, say something about the type of supporters who were drawn to Shapp's candidacy throughout the state.

Governor Shapp, by any objective measure, had a very successful first term in office, due largely to the loyalty and persuasive powers of his Democratic legislative leaders. Frankly, the support he drew in the General Assembly from his party's leadership and rank-and-file, in my view, had less to do with an allegiance to him personally, and more to do with their broader commitment to the principle of loyalty to a governor as the elected leader of their party. Party loyalty . . . now that's an old-fashioned concept you don't see much of today where modern politics is driven more by personality and celebrity and individual survival than by party structure and party philosophy. I don't know that the political process is any better for it, either, but that's a discussion for another day.

The Shapp agenda was very much in keeping with what one would expect from a Democratic state administration. As characterized in his official state biography on record with the Pennsylvania Historical and Museum Commission, Shapp's policy objectives were driven by a "strong sensitivity to the plight of the disadvantaged and the 'little guy,' and an overriding conviction that government must serve as an advocate of all the people." In addition, unusual for most Democrats of the era, Shapp also liked to boast that his "business-like approach" to government had saved taxpayers $225 million. It was difficult to quantify, but it also was difficult to disprove, sort of a, "you have your numbers, I have mine" exchange. Whatever, the Shapp agenda proved to be a very acceptable formula for Pennsylvania from 1971 to 1975.

That agenda featured aggressive but creative use of the Pennsylvania Industrial Development Authority (PIDA, established years earlier in the Democratic administration of George M. Leader) as the chief job creation engine of state government. The administration claimed 454 business loans valued at $214 million. PIDA had a strong environmental-protection thrust in the area of strip-mine control and land reclamation. The administration also generated a serious legislative debate on the high cost of auto insurance, a debate that ultimately resulted in Pennsylvania becoming one of the first major states in the nation to enact a "no-fault" auto insurance law.

That no-fault debate in the Senate was one of the most substantive that I witnessed in thirteen years on the staff of the chamber. It also involved a little-known episode that spoke volumes to the premium elected officials of the era paid to the notion of party loyalty. Tom Lamb was the majority leader of the Pennsylvania Senate. He was also an attorney in private life. Lamb sincerely believed the concept of no-fault auto insurance was constitutionally defective. He was opposed to it for that reason. Marty Murray, the Senate president pro tempore, an insurance businessman in what limited private life he had at the time, was a strong supporter of the governor's no-fault proposal. A serious split on the issue by the Senate's two leading Democrats certainly could have proven fatal to passage of the bill. Lamb would have none of it and fashioned a reasonable solution. He told Murray he could not support the legislation and that he would speak against it on the floor of the Senate. However, recognizing his obligation as the floor leader of a Democratic caucus most of whom supported the "no-fault concept," Lamb also said he would not try to sway any other senator (Democrat or Republican) to his position. Lamb kept his word. The bill passed the Senate and was signed into law. If Lamb had chosen to make a serious fight over the issue, the fate of the bill would have been very much in question. Yet he found a position that was consistent with his individual view, but in no way undermined the policy objective of a Democratic governor and the majority of the Democratic members in his caucus. We don't see much of that these days, either.

Shapp also approved legislation creating the state Department of Aging. But the signature achievement of the Shapp administration over its entire tenure was, without question, enactment of the Pennsylvania state lottery, largely the legislative handiwork of the aforementioned Frank Mazzei. Shapp and Mazzei were pictured together on the front pages of most newspapers in the state when the lottery bill was signed into law in 1971. Proceeds were dedicated to programs for the elderly—property tax relief at the start. A state-run lottery to assist the elderly was a forerunner for the nation at the time and became an instant financial success for the Commonwealth. The revenues it generated soon permitted the program to expand to provide free mass transit and, in the succeeding term of Richard Thornburgh, prescription drug coverage through PACE. A landmark innovation among the fifty states, PACE remains a national flagship for state programs providing prescription drug assistance to its low-income elderly population.

Shapp also gained national attention when he intervened not once but twice in 1974 to avert strikes by independent truckers and a shutdown of gasoline service stations across the country. He was a risk taker, and the fear of failure did not deter him in pursuit of his objectives. That was one of his greatest pluses as a governor. His greatest shortcoming, in my view, was with some of the people he brought into state government with him who would later come back to cause him political harm.

Shapp's governor's office staff was largely first-rate, however. His principal aides were Dick Doran and Norval Reese, both of Philadelphia and both able in their own right. Doran was a product of Philadelphia city politics and a close associate of former Philadelphia congressman and mayor William Green, the son of Congressman William Green of John F. Kennedy fame. Doran was a pragmatist in his view of politics and politicians. Reese, on the other hand, was an unabashed liberal, a do-gooder who paid little heed to the niceties or protocols of the profession.

Inevitably, there had to be tensions between the two as they rivaled for the ear of the governor. Shapp had a reputation as someone who usually listened to the last person he talked to on a given subject. The inside joke was that Doran and Reese struggled daily to be the last one to leave the building with the governor. In the newsroom, each time the governor would unveil a new policy initiative, the capital press corps would speculate whose stamp was on the program—Doran's or Reese's. That told us who won the jousting the night before.

Ron Lench, a former state representative from Beaver County and a close ally of Lieutenant Governor Kline, was Shapp's first legislative secretary. He also proved to be a versatile troubleshooter for the administration moving from position to position whenever trouble broke out. Charlie McIntosh, highly admired for his fiscal expertise and universally respected for the integrity of his word, was Shapp's budget secretary.

Shapp's brother-in-law, Julian Rothman, served as secretary to the governor. He had no particular credentials or background. But he was the brother of the governor's wife, and that was all the credential he needed. He knew the governor and his habits and he had the governor's trust. Most important, he had Mrs. Shapp's trust. Rothman proved to be congenial enough, but, so far as anyone could tell, he neither added to nor detracted from what the administration proposed to accomplish. The general view was that Rothman's principal role was to serve as Mrs. Shapp's surrogate in protecting the governor each day from those who sought an audience with him.

The most troublesome questions surrounding Shapp's staffing operation centered around his personnel (read that, patronage) office. It was headed by Sam Begler of Pittsburgh and Dennis (Harvey) Thiemann of Erie, two of his staunchest political allies. Begler and Thiemann ran this operation with an iron hand and, so far as could be determined, their will and whim. They played the patronage game with such a fervor that Andrew Jackson would have been proud. To the victors went the spoils, and Begler and Thiemann dispensed the considerable spoils as they chose. Some critics speculated how much say, if any, even the governor had in the patronage process.

Rewarding one's supporters is as old as the political system itself. The problem for this governor, however, was that so many of the hires were Democratic irregulars. They owed their positions not to a party, but to Begler and Thiemann. The rules they had to follow to be hired were Begler and Thiemann's. An aura of "anything goes" seemed to permeate throughout the Commonwealth. By Drs. Madonna and Young's count, almost four hundred Pennsylvania politicians were indicted, convicted, or pleaded no contest to a variety of criminal and civil charges between 1970 and 1978, the years Milton Shapp was governor. Not all, obviously, had a connection, direct or indirect, with Shapp. But the climate was foul with misconduct, it was truly pervasive, and it did serious and lasting damage to the reputation of the governor and his administration, not to mention the Democratic Party itself.

One other note of interest on the personnel side. Shapp went through five press secretaries in eight years: Tony May (my former associate at the Associated Press); Roy Nassau, a former Philadelphia television personality; Ed Mitchell, a young man from Wilkes-Barre; Jim Dorris, fresh out of college at Penn State who earned himself an appointment as a deputy press secretary under May; and finally, Mike McLaughlin, the son of a Philadelphia public relations stalwart with political ties to the Philadelphia Democratic Party. Apparently, it must have been heavy-duty work.

Milton Shapp was reelected to a second term, the first governor of the modern era permitted to succeed himself, defeating Republican businessman (and, later, a Reagan federal cabinet member) Drew Lewis by a margin of over 300,000. Things started to unravel quickly soon thereafter.

Some of the very same irregulars who Shapp brought into government got his administration into trouble by their conduct. Most notable was Frank Hilton, Shapp's secretary of property and supplies (forerunner to the existing Department of General Services). Hilton was an active Republican from northwest Pennsylvania; however, he was never able to crack the GOP inner circle. So he signed on to the Shapp campaigns of 1966 and 1970 and was rewarded with a cabinet post for his effort. Hilton had to resign after he was indicted (and later convicted) in federal court of a kickback scheme related to state contracting. Ron Lench was named to replace him and turn that department around.

A number of Democratic county chairmen, meanwhile, came under prosecutorial fire for their patronage activities, particularly in regard to employment in the county highway sheds the state operated through the Commonwealth. "Jobs for sale" was the thrust of the scam. If someone wanted a job with the state, well, contributions to the Democratic county organization were a requisite. At least one county chairman, from Indiana County, went to jail because of the practice. The investigative trail never made it back directly to Shapp's personnel managers, but the practice appeared to be too common and too widespread to be unique. More notably, no one of any standing within the administration made an overt move to halt it or condemn it.

The atmosphere of corruption grew to such proportions that Shapp, himself, was called to testify before a Republican House investigative committee.

Shapp met the challenge full square by agreeing to appear personally. He concluded, correctly so, that he was not going to ignore this transparent assault by his political opposition. It was the only time in my memory that a governor testified personally before a legislative investigating committee. The fact that, in this instance, the governor appeared to testify about allegations of wrongdoing in his administration made the three-day episode all the more newsworthy. The hearings from the House Majority Caucus Room were televised on public television across the state. To accommodate the standing-room-only crowds that were expected to gather, television monitors were set up in the Rotunda for those who could not gain access to the hearing room.

It was high political drama of a sort seldom seen to play out so publicly in the Capitol. Republicans smelled blood and political gain in these hearings. They hired two professional investigators to chart the probe and lead in the questioning of witnesses, Michael Willman, a former investigative reporter for the *Philadelphia Inquirer,* and Steve Freind, a former FBI agent from Delaware County who later was elected to eight terms in the state House Representatives and would become one of Gov. Robert P. Casey's staunchest allies on the subjects of auto insurance reform and abortion controls. Freind and his colleague's charge at that moment, however, was to be the Republican hit team to make the case against the Democratic governor and his administration in the court of public opinion.

Despite the questionable activities surrounding some elements of the administration, Shapp himself was no easy target. He more than held his own against the thrusts and parries of his inquisitors. One exchange in the proceedings stood out.

Shapp was in his second (or it might have been his third) day of testimony when under the direction of Stephen Freind a subpoena for his personal income tax statements was handed to him. Shapp was enraged and justifiably so. Here he was, testifying before the House Committee without condition, and he was slapped with a subpoena like a witness in hiding. He had been answering their questions, face to face, without exception, he charged. Yet they had the audacity to serve him with a subpoena for his income tax statements solely to make him look bad in the eyes of the public, he continued. That was outrageous, he declared. All they had to do was ask and they would have had what they had requested.

The inquisitors had overplayed their hand. The exchange resulted in an apology of sorts from Steven Freind. But the incident, brief though it was, worked to Shapp's advantage. It made it appear that the governor was being victimized unfairly by a partisan legislative committee in what had all the trappings of a political witchhunt. That was not lost on many of those who took the proceedings in by television, and Shapp came out of the hearings stronger politically than when he went in. But the suspicion of wrongdoing within his administration never completely faded. Moreover, the transgressions that gripped the Pennsylvania Senate in the late 1970s under the control of his political party only compounded the perceptions that things were terribly wrong in Harrisburg.

A number of other factors contributed to the second-term doldrums. One key element was that the outspoken and unpredictable Tom Nolan had replaced the conciliatory Tom Lamb as Senate majority leader. Where Lamb kept his differences with the governor private, Nolan welcomed the opportunity to make his differences (and there were many, particularly in fiscal policy) known publicly at virtually every opportunity. Also, as noted, the Republicans for a time won back control of the House of Representatives. This gave them a platform from which to attack the administration and its alleged misconduct virtually at will.

Finally, Shapp himself contributed mightily to his sagging political fortunes when he made an ill-fated bid for the Democratic presidential nomination in 1976. At least one cabinet member, Education Secretary John Pittenger, resigned reportedly in protest. Shapp was embarrassed nationally when he finished behind no-preference in the Florida presidential primary, despite his active presence in the state and his aggressive campaign to woo the heavy Florida Jewish population to his cause. He was, if not a joke on the national political landscape, certainly a caricature. He returned to the Capitol to find his stature diminishing almost daily. For most of the remainder of in his term, he was virtually a nonplayer politically.

For what it's worth, my impression of Milton Shapp is that he was a well-intentioned, well-motivated man who had a genuine special affection for the plight of consumers, the underprivileged, and the elderly. That, more than ego gratification, seemed to drive his pursuit of elective office. Milton Shapp struck me as a Franklin Delano Roosevelt Democrat, a New Deal Democrat who, like Roosevelt, believed in an activist government committed to helping people who couldn't help themselves. There is no denying the conviction of his populist roots.

But he was a poor judge of character and he was loyal to some of the characters who found their way into his administration to a fault. In the end, the Frank Hiltons, Sam Beglers, and Harvey Thiemanns came to symbolize the administration at the highest levels. His state police commissioner, Rocco Urella, had to resign in the wake of a serious law enforcement dispute with his attorney general, J. Shane Creamer. That didn't play well with the public, either. When Milton Shapp's term wound down, his administration, if not under a cloud of outright corruption, certainly had a strong aura of something amiss about it. When he left town, he departed as he came in—still very much the outsider. Few that I knew lamented his leaving.

Chapter 16

★★★★★★★

Richard L. Thornburgh (1979–1987)

Of all the governors I write about, this will be the most difficult chapter to put to paper.

Why? Because Richard L. Thornburgh was a paradox: a man with impressive, yea impeccable public service credentials, yet a man whose private actions often belied the public image he presented. The late House Speaker, Matt Ryan, put it to me this way in that conversation we had about governors under whom he served. "Thornburgh was one tough sunuvabitch when he wanted to be," Ryan said. "I really liked him for that. He had steel in his character." Ryan might call it "steel." Others thought of it more as meanness. The bond that Matt Ryan formed with Richard Thornburgh through the years was very tight, tighter than many might have suspected. The governor delivered the eulogy at Ryan's funeral in 2003.

Now let's be absolutely clear: I did not know—do not know—Richard Thornburgh personally. He did not and does not know me. Then and now, if we passed on the street, he would have no idea who I was. So the perceptions I have to share are, admittedly, entirely subjective on my part, framed primarily from contacts I had with his administration from my vantage point on the minority staff of the Senate of Pennsylvania. But the truth is, I saw contradictions in Richard Thornburgh that I unable to shake to this day. He reminded me in many ways of Richard Nixon. The principal difference was that Nixon was transparently insecure. Richard Thornburgh, on the other hand, had the gravitas and the persona to keep his inner instincts largely hidden from public view.

Publicly, Thornburgh postured himself as a person of the highest integrity, someone far above the traditional give and take—some might call it the "scratch-my-back, I'll-scratch-yours" approach—to politics and governing. Lofty, to be sure. The trouble was, in many ways, Richard Thornburgh was as calculating, combative and cunning (in some ways much more so) than many of the very same politicians for whom he professed such disdain. In the rough-and-tumble world of politics, that may not be a fault. But in this case, it is a contradiction in style worth noting.

Thornburgh brought a prosecutor's no-nonsense approach to state politics, honed from his six years (1969–75) as a U.S. attorney in western Pennsylvania and from two years (1975–77) as assistant U.S. Attorney general in charge of the Justice Department Criminal Division in Washington, D.C. Thornburgh was a prosecutor to his core. When he campaigned as the Republican nominee for governor in 1978, he essentially asked the voters to send him to Harrisburg so he could clean the place up. The Shapp administration's reputation for bad conduct if not actual misfeasance made it an ideal target for Thornburgh's political pitch. This is the way Professors Madonna and Young characterized the political environment in Pennsylvania in one of their regular commentary columns at the time:

> No single issue . . . dominated a governor's campaign the way in which political corruption did in 1978. And never did the background of a candidate fit the issues of the moment better. The Republican nominee in 1978 was Dick Thornburgh, who as U.S. Attorney in Western Pennsylvania, had won 40 convictions of politicians in both parties. His campaign against corruption in state government was unrelenting . . . few could deny that political corruption was the dominant issue in 1978, and that Thornburgh's credentials were impeccably suited to take advantage of the issue.

Thornburgh actually got his start in Pennsylvania politics in a very modest way when he was elected a delegate to the constitutional convention convened by Ray Shafer in 1967. It was the only electoral contest he won before his successful bid for the governorship eleven years later. There was, however, in between, one losing bid for a congressional seat from Western Pennsylvania.

Thornburgh gained his political standing as someone to watch in Pennsylvania Republican politics by his corruption-fighting service as the Western District U.S attorney. Veteran GOP congressman J. Irving Whalley of Somerset County was one his first notable convictions on a charge of payroll padding. The Whalley case was important to Thornburgh's long-term political future because it established his bona fides as a federal prosecutor who paid heed neither to party affiliation nor years of public service. That conviction cleared the way for him to go after Democrats like Frank Mazzei, Congressman Frank Clark, and State Representative Max Homer without a taint of partisanship or unchecked political ambitions to his motives. The formula worked very well for him.

Once his prosecutorial reputation spread across the state, Thornburgh vaulted high on the list of potential candidates for the Republican gubernatorial nomination in 1978. The GOP entered the election cycle in a position so strong it drew a large field to the spring primary. Thornburgh had some very influential political backing in his bid, most visibly from the grand dame of Republican politics, Mrs. Elsie Hillman of Pittsburgh. But he had no free ride to the nomination. Among the other challengers were House Majority Leader Bob Butera of populous Republican Montgomery County in the southeast, and Senate Majority Leader Henry Hager of Williamsport in Lycoming County, a haven of Central Pennsylvania–style Republicanism.

Topping the field for lieutenant governor was William Scranton III, the former governor's son and a young political comer who would make an ideal running mate for whoever was the eventual winner of the GOP gubernatorial nomination. But not even young Bill with the Scranton name, reputation, and good standing within the party could avoid a primary contest. He was challenged by a Republican county official and former state legislator from Delaware County, Faith Ryan Whittlesey, who in her campaign constantly dismissed young Scranton as "The Son." Her point was that Scranton III was in the race by virtue of his family credentials and nothing more. It might have had a ring of truth, but it didn't sell. Thornburgh and Scranton were nominated fairly handily. (Ms. Whittlesey, incidentally, later was appointed U. S. ambassador to Switzerland by former president George H. W. Bush in the late 1980s.)

Thornburgh and Scranton made a formidable team with the just right mix of political standing and geographic balance. As they set their sights on the fall campaign, their Democratic opposition, already weakened politically, was about to make the Thornburgh-Scranton ticket all that much more attractive to the Pennsylvania electorate.

The Democrats had to endure another testy primary nomination contest for governor. This one was a three-way race between former Pittsburgh Mayor Pete Flaherty, former auditor general and two-time Democratic gubernatorial hopeful Bob Casey of Scranton, and Shapp's lieutenant governor, Ernest P. Kline, who just happened to be Casey's endorsed running mate in a Pennsylvania primary election eight years earlier. The lineup certainly did make for strange bedfellows on the Democratic ballot in 1978. Flaherty was the eventual winner, thanks largely to his western Pennsylvania voting base and his mayoral reputation for political independence. As testament to the standing of the Shapp administration with the electorate, Kline finished third in the race, a distant third at that.

Flaherty, however, may have gotten too cute by half in his primary election strategy. There was another Robert Casey in the race, most suspected at the urging of the Flaherty forces. This Casey was a schoolteacher and ice-cream salesman from Pittsburgh who filed for the office of lieutenant governor. It was common knowledge that the Flaherty folks were touting the line out west: Flaherty/Casey—you can have them both. The Real Bob Casey finished second to Flaherty in the Democratic gubernatorial vote; the Pittsburgh Casey won the Democratic nomination for lieutenant governor. The Flaherty tactic proved successful in the spring. The ploy came back to haunt the ticket in the fall.

As the Pittsburgh Casey and his background became more exposed across the state, the potential drag he could have on an already troubled Democratic ticket in November became readily troublesome for Flaherty's candidacy. Word had it that Flaherty and others in the party tried mightily to persuade Pittsburgh Casey to step aside and have the party substitute a replacement. (I presume the first person to be approached would have been Scranton Bob Casey, but I doubt if he would have accepted the offer.)

Pittsburgh Casey would have none of it, however. He was enjoying his newfound celebrity too much. He was not about to withdraw. I remember being introduced to him in the press box at a Penn State football game he attended that fall as a guest of the University. It struck me how nervous and unsure he seemed as university officials introduced him to the other press box guests. But this was his fifteen minutes in the sun, and he was going to make the most of it. By the time the fall campaign began in earnest, Pittsburgh Casey's shortcomings and lack of experience or credentials to be lieutenant governor had been sufficiently exposed that they became a serious drag on the ticket. Most Pennsylvania voters came to understand what their choices were in November, and went with the Thornburgh/Scranton ticket by 228,100 votes. There were other reasons why Pete Flaherty lost, the shadow over the Shapp administration certainly prime among them, but the Casey ploy was a major one.

Governor Thornburgh brought a very basic approach to governance with him when he took his oath of office in January 1979. Essentially, his was a three-point plan: 1) manage the fiscal resources of the Commonwealth very conservatively; 2) pass the state budget on time; and, 3) stay out of trouble—political or otherwise—because this administration would brook no misconduct on the part of those who represented it. As principles go, these certainly would do fine. But no one, even the most friendly of observers, could label them visionary or ambitious. The Thornburgh administration was true to itself during its eight-year run. Governor Thornburgh ran a very tight fiscal ship; his state budgets were passed on time (an important flagship achievement for the administration each year); and the administration was relatively scandal free.

The governor's mettle was tested sorely very soon after his inauguration. Governors usually learn very quickly that they had better be prepared for the unexpected because adversity had a way of striking on very short notice in very strange ways. Thornburgh's first crisis certainly did. A reactor malfunctioned at the Three Mile Island nuclear power plant at Middletown, just a few miles away from the state capital. A threat of a nuclear meltdown (coincidentally, as the film *The China Syndrome* was playing to large audiences at movie theatres across the country at the time) was looming dangerously over the entire central Pennsylvania region. Thornburgh advised pregnant women to remain indoors as plant operators grappled unsuccessfully to bring the facility under control. Ultimately, the federal Nuclear Regulatory Commission had to be called in to direct the effort. Dr. Harold Denton took operational control of the plant. Denton's calming presence, his constant visibility, the clarity with which he spoke at his daily media briefings and his confident demeanor had a great soothing effect on the region. (I had occasion to meet him personally years later during a visit he made to the operations center of the Pennsylvania Emergency Management Agency during the Casey administration. I took advantage of the introduction to thank him personally for the air of reassurance he brought to a region where the fear of nuclear disaster was very real, indeed.)

Thornburgh, likewise, remained very visible during the crisis. His demeanor was critical to the preservation of order in a region that was in danger of moving almost daily to the edge of evacuation if not actual panic. Half the families in the area (including the Caroccis with their four young children) left for more distant locales until the crisis had passed. But Governor Thornburgh kept a steady hand throughout. It won him national acclaim when the crisis passed, and rightly so. Actually, the Commonwealth's strategy was essentially to stand by as events played out under the skillful guidance of Dr. Denton and his NRC colleagues. But it was the right strategy for the moment, and the Governor carried his role off with aplomb. It was, in my view, the high-water mark of the Thornburgh administration.

If Richard Thornburgh played his TMI hand with great finesse, he painted a much different picture of himself on other issues and events with which I was personally familiar. There we saw a man who could play inside, hardball politics with the best of them. Take prescription drug assistance to Pennsylvania seniors, as one example.

Senate Democrats headed by Jim Lloyd fought hard and long to enact a prescription drug program to be funded from the abundant proceeds of the very successful state lottery. The Thornburgh administration resisted behind the scenes at absolutely every turn. Yet when the program passed with strong bipartisan support over the governor's quiet objections, he quickly took to the television airwaves with great vigor and wide visibility to tout the program in public service commercials. A viewer would have thought Governor Thornburgh fathered the idea. Nothing wrong with that—just a perk that goes with the office when successful programs are launched. But it did smack just a bit of politics as usual. There was a character of some notoriety from New York City's Tammany Hall, George Washington Carver by name. George Washington Carver printed his name indelibly in the nation's political lore with his reputed political credo that confessed that he saw his opportunities and he made the most of them. In the case of prescription drug assistance for Pennsylvania seniors, so did Richard L. Thornburgh.

The governor also was not reluctant to fight politics with politics to achieve a political end. Early on in his tenure, he found that Senate Democrats were blocking his nominees to the state Liquor Control Board under the two-thirds confirmation requirement (thirty-four votes) in play at the time. No question the Senate Democrats were serving their selfish partisan ends by keeping their appointees in place. The LCB, after all, was a lucrative source of political fundraising for their caucus. So Thornburgh changed tactics. If he couldn't gain political control of the board, he would join forces with those advocating abolition of the liquor control system in Pennsylvania. It was a political decision, pure and simple, warranted certainly by the partisan obstructionism of the Senate Democrats. But would he have pursued privatization with such dedication if his nominees to the LCB were placed in office? That's still an open question.

There are other examples of the political side of Dick Thornburgh that he professed not to possess. He was the only governor in the history of the Commonwealth, certainly modern Pennsylvania history, to hold political fundraising events in the Governor's Residence. There's just something unseemly about people being charged a price of a political ticket to visit and mingle with the governor in the publicly funded Governor's Residence. Other governors, of course, hosted their financial supporters at the residence in a variety of ways during their tenure, but the attendees were not charged the price of a political contribution to be there. The costs of those events were borne by the host's personal or campaign funds. Not so with the Thornburgh fundraisers. Several fundraising events were held at the residence leading up to his re-election effort in 1982, and the governor apparently had no qualms about the practice. Once again a strange contradiction for a man who relished in his political reputation as a nonpolitical straight-shooter. Of course, the Thornburgh practice paled in comparison to the indefensible techniques Democratic President William Jefferson Clinton employed years later with his fundraising White House coffees and teas. Clinton took the use of public perks as a political resource to a high art form. But Dick Thornburgh went down the same path much earlier, just in tinier steps.

There were two other episodes with the governor that demonstrated the contradictions between the public man and the private man. Both involved my boss at the time, Senator Craig Lewis. One occurred during the governor's 1982 reelection campaign. There were plenty of hints that the administration was doling out lucrative state legal contracts to Pennsylvania law firms that happened to be among the governor's largest financial contributors. "White-collar patronage," the practice was labeled by Thornburgh's critics, admittedly most of them among the loyal opposition. Lewis, in his capacity as minority chair of the Senate Appropriations Committee, made a formal request of the administration for a listing of all outside law firms that had received state legal contracts. The administration resisted. Lewis took the administration to court and the administration continued to resist and dragged the proceedings out.

The case went all the way to the Pennsylvania Supreme Court. The court ultimately ruled in Lewis's favor on the ground that he was entitled to the information by virtue of his position with the Appropriations Committee and the budgetary oversight authority inherent therein. The court handed the decision down the afternoon of New Year's Eve day, 1982, about 3 P.M. Even though this was almost two months after Thornburgh's reelection, the administration still continued to delay turning over the information. They didn't take defeat lightly. Lewis was forced to protest to the court. The court subsequently set a deadline, about a week's time, as I recall, for the administration to comply. Consistent with its pattern of resistance, the administration waited until the last minute of the last day to deliver the material. It made it in the door just minutes before the 5 P.M. end-of-business deadline. The Governor's Office under Richard Thornburgh, officer of the court himself, was not quick to respond to court orders that went against them—at least this court order.

I may have been the one who suggested to Lewis that he seek the information in the first place. Truth was, there was as much a political motivation to the suggestion as any other consideration. We thought if we matched the lawyer list to the list of Governor Thornburgh's political contributors, we might verify the practice of "white-collar patronage." If so, it was legitimate fodder to be raised in the ensuing campaign by the Democratic candidate for governor, whomever that might be. The Thornburgh people understood that and that's undoubtedly why they dragged the proceedings out. The records did suggest there was an element of "white-collar patronage" to these legal awards. But they weren't illegal awards. The *Philadelphia Inquirer*'s Wally Roche did a story on the contracts, and it was displayed prominently in the paper the next day. But it was essentially a one-day event with no legs, political or otherwise. Still, once again, this governor and his team who positioned themselves to be so above politics as usual proved they could play the game with the best of them.

Probably the most revealing and most egregious encounter with the Thornburgh administration came over a federally funded weatherization contract awarded through the State Department of Community Affairs to a community-action group affiliated with state senator Milton Street of Philadelphia. A word or two for context is in order. Milton Street was an African American community activist of some renown in the city before his election (as a Democrat in both instances), first to the state House of Representatives and, subsequently, to the state Senate. Most of the workforce in the weatherization organization that received the contract were members of Street's political army.

The weatherization contract was called to Craig Lewis's attention from a number of sources. One primary source was a series of investigative reports broadcast by KYW-TV in Philadelphia. Essentially, KYW cameras caught the employees of the organization spending most of their days lolling around the office doing little if anything to weatherize the homes of low-income Philadelphia residents. Additionally, the series established that what little work had been done had been done defectively. Lewis, by now, had gained some public prominence in Philadelphia and elsewhere by his chairmanship of the Senate Ethics Committee and later his watchdog work with the Senate Appropriations Committee. That's undoubtedly why this matter came to his desk. He was nudged along by the office of Philadelphia congressman William Gray, no friend of Milton Street's, and perhaps a KYW source as well.

Milton Street clearly was a principal actor in this political play. Street had gained his public celebrity with his frequent Philadelphia street demonstrations. He relished his role as first a community activist and then a political maverick, and he played both roles for everything they were worth. The more commotion he caused, the more publicity he gained; the more publicity he gained, the larger his reputation grew.

Early in Thornburgh's first term, now–Senator Milton Street changed his political registration from Democrat to Republican. The move helped to secure Republican control of the chamber more firmly. His conversion should have come as no surprise. Street was just being Street. He and the aforementioned George Washington Carver were political brothers in at least one respect. They saw their opportunities and they took advantage of them as they came along. Milton Street cared little for political labels or affiliations. The question wasn't so much what prompted him to make the switch. The question was what was the price that was paid, and who paid it.

The lucrative weatherization contract certainly would qualify in that regard. The contract was steered to Street's community action group by Secretary of Community Affairs Shirley Dennis, herself a fellow African American-traveler of Street's in Philadelphia community action activities. Shirley Dennis was one of the Thornburgh administration's showcases for gender and racial diversity, so her political standing within the Thornburgh hierarchy and the Philadelphia black community was very strong. She wore that banner proudly, and she was not to be challenged idly. But her imperious management style did little to endear her to her subordinates in the department. A number of them came forward privately during the Lewis probe, and they were very helpful and cooperative throughout.

What Lewis's investigation fundamentally discovered was that Dennis played the most instrumental role in directing the contract to Street's group, and the process she employed at the very least violated established department protocols in moving it along. Her signature on the contract was dated days before the necessary approvals were obtained from her department subordinates. It should have been the other way around because they had the prior responsibility to review the terms for propriety before sending the contract to the secretary for final departmental signoff. By signing the contract before the subordinate reviews were completed, Dennis could not have been more emphatic that she wanted this contract approved, no questions asked. The contract ultimately was passed along to the governor for his signature, which was a mere formality once it had obtained the necessary department approvals. With the governor's signature, Street and his organization foot soldiers had a significant funding source of federal dollars.

The Lewis inquiry obtained enough evidence of rule-bending to blow the whistle publicly and to refer the case to federal and state authorities. The question was how to do it. Lewis settled on a press conference (he was as alert as the next person to political opportunities) at which he would detail the specifics of his findings on the contract award, denounce the process, call for Secretary Dennis's resignation or removal and make the necessary referrals: One to the state attorney general to determine whether the award violated Pennsylvania contracting law; the other to the federal U.S. attorney's office to determine whether the nonexistent or defective work violated federal Housing and Urban Development contracting law. Neither resulted in any criminal litigation, however.

At the same time, Lewis took great pains to distance Governor Thornburgh personally from the case. His public statement made it clear he believed the governor did not have foreknowledge of the process by which the contract came to him for signature. In fact, Lewis and I met with George Seidel, the governor's legislative secretary, and a press aide George brought with him, to share our information and assure them privately that Thornburgh was not our target and that Lewis intended to emphasize publicly that there was no evidence whatsoever of any culpability on the governor's part.

What's most revealing, once again, is how Thornburgh responded. We had gone what we thought the extra mile to be fair with the governor. What we got from him in return was an unleashing of the attack dogs. We had expected the governor would not casually dismiss a member of his cabinet. But what we did not expect was that the administration would send out his deputy general counsel, Richard Glanton, himself an African American, to attack Lewis as both racist and antifeminist for his charges against Shirley Dennis. I was stunned at the intellectual dishonesty of the administration's response. As a prosecutor, Richard Thornburgh would have investigated a case of potential political corruption such as this with all the resources he could command. As governor, however, the administration ignored the message and attacked the messenger.

The Dennis case and the Glanton response, probably with some prompting from Dennis and Glanton themselves, also aroused the black activist community in Philadelphia. One in particular who took up the call was a very vocal though not always informed radio personality by the name of Mary Mason. She also happened to be a Street ally. Not even a week later Mason was leading a delegation to Harrisburg to confront Lewis for his racist, antifeminist attack on poor, defenseless, guiltless Shirley Dennis. I was present for the ranting and raving in Lewis's office. It lasted for about a half hour. Nothing came of it except some sharp words, principally from the visitors. Mason continued to blast away at Lewis, however, on her daily Philadelphia radio show on a black station in the city. Like Street, Mary Mason's celebrity was best ensured when conflict and turmoil prevailed.

The incident confirmed for me once again the contradictory sides of Richard Thornburgh's political personality. Sending Glanton out to brand Lewis a racist not only ignored the facts presented to the administration, it was completely unfounded. Craig Lewis, for better or for worse, might have been many things to many people in his public life. But he was neither biased nor bigoted on the basis of race or gender. To charge him with prejudice against blacks and women was disingenuous in the very least, but that was the way Richard Thornburgh's subordinates responded. And I seriously doubt they could have done it that way without if not the governor's explicit direction, then certainly his consent, tacit or otherwise. Once again, this man who climbed the political ladder by the virtue and righteousness of his reputation revealed a mean streak to his personality that was in conflict with his public persona. What was it Matt Ryan observed about the governor? "Mean sunuvabitch . . . !!" Ryan meant it as a compliment. Here it would be taken as a pejorative.

As the 1982 gubernatorial election approached, the private Thornburgh was known only to a few. The public Thornburgh was a presumptive favorite for reelection, so much so that no Democrat of any stature came from the sidelines to challenge him. The nomination went almost by default to a little-known Democratic congressman from Lycoming County, Allen Ertel. Ertel had two qualities that recommended him above all others: He was a winner in a congressional district that traditionally voted Republican; and he really wanted to make the race. When engaged, he was dogged in his pursuit of public office. His tenacity as a candidate marked his successful race for Congress, and he was no less tenacious in his race for governor. He had two major hurdles to surmount. Politically, no one in the political and pundit community gave him a whisper of a chance to defeat Thornburgh. Personally, he was not the easiest person to embrace.

Yet Thornburgh won reelection by a mere 100,400 votes. Ertel was much more competitive than expected east of the Susquehanna River. As the count moved westward, the race still was very much up for grabs. The irony was that Ertel lost the election in the traditionally Democrat southwest, where his margins were much less than Democratic candidates usually recorded.

Republican Thornburgh won Allegheny County, with a Democratic registration margin of 293,000, by 6,500 votes. That could be explained by Thornburgh's Pittsburgh roots perhaps. What was not so easily explained were the vote totals in other southwestern counties. Cambria County had a 14,000 Democratic registration margin, but Ertel won the county by a mere 6,400 votes. Fayette County had a 10,500 Democratic registration margin, but Thornburgh won the county by 4,400 votes. Washington County, with 44,500 more registered Democrats than Republicans, went for Ertel by only 10,000 votes; and the crown jewel, Westmoreland County with 72,000 more registered Democrats voted Ertel by a paltry 4,800 votes. Lamented one Democratic senator from southwest Pennsylvania, "If we had known he [Ertel] was going to be this close, we probably could have done something about it."

That was probably an oversimplification, but, as I analyzed the results, a couple of factors did come into play in keeping the Thornburgh margin to such minimal dimensions. The first was that the governor was not as popular politically within his own party as conventional wisdom perceived him to be. There was that certain arrogance to his administration and his team, and that may have cost him internally. Another was that the air of inevitability that pervaded the conventional thinking at the time might have prompted some Republican leaders to treat the election too casually. Finally, some western Pennsylvania Democrats, thinking the election result was preordained, may have cut their own deals, which they were prone to do when the occasion demanded. But, margins aside, impressive or not, a win is a win and Thornburgh became the second Pennsylvania governor in modern times to serve a second consecutive term.

Assessing the Thornburgh record as governor, aside from TMI and his tight and timely stewardship of Commonwealth fiscal affairs, there was in this one man's view little of consequence to distinguish him and the course he charted for Pennsylvania and its future. He did support and help push through the General Assembly a welfare reform bill that quickly became dubbed "Thornfare" by its critics. He also endorsed and signed into law legislation that bound the fourteen Pennsylvania state colleges into a single, unified State System of Higher Education. That was good for the institutional structure of the universities, though the individual presidents, each jealous of his own turf and standing, may not necessarily thought it so at the time. But the creation of the State System was not a purely altruistic act on Thornburgh's part. The tradeoff, I was told later when I served on the System's central staff, was a commitment from the governor to sign the legislation in return for his political endorsement for reelection by the Association of Pennsylvania State College and University Faculty (APSCUF), the state system's faculty union.

After completing his two terms as governor, Richard Thornburgh went on to serve first as director of the Institute of Politics at Harvard's Kennedy School of Government (1987–88) before being appointed U.S. attorney general under presidents Reagan and George H. W. Bush. His press clippings from Washington were less than laudatory. He and those of his Harrisburg staff that accompanied him apparently found the political climate and the media scrutiny much more difficult to accommodate than they had in Harrisburg. Dave Runkel, his press secretary in the state capital who went in a similar capacity to the U.S. Justice Department, had to resign over a leak about a criminal investigation into activities involving former Philadelphia congressmen William Gray. Inquiries of this sort are supposed to remain confidential until some formal action is instituted. This one became a matter of public discussion and the resulting furor demanded that someone's head had to roll. It was Runkel's. In retrospect, it may not have been totally coincidental that the Congressman Gray under inquiry was the same Philadelphia official whose office nudged Craig Lewis along in his investigation of the Thornburgh administration's award of the Street weatherization contract.

Thornburgh resigned the office of attorney general in 1991 to return to Pennsylvania and seek the U.S. Senate seat left vacant with the tragic airplane death of incumbent Republican John Heinz. Again, he was a preeminent favorite going into the race.

Democratic Governor Robert P. Casey, after much deliberation and one brief flirtation with former Chrysler president Lee Iococca, had appointed Harris Wofford, his state secretary of labor and industry, to fill the Heinz vacancy until a special election that Fall. Harris Wofford was a right honorable gentleman of the first order, thoughtful and deeply committed to public service. In the era of John F. Kennedy, Harris had earned an admirable record on civil rights with direct links to Martin Luther King. He was an early proponent of the Peace Corps with a personal relationship to Sargent Shriver, the Kennedy brother-in-law who became the first Peace Corps director. He was a college president (Bryn Mawr); served as Democratic state chairman during the Casey run for governor in 1986; and then joined the Casey cabinet. But, for all intents and purposes, he was an unknown political commodity. When compared with the public credentials of Richard Thornburgh, Harris paled. And he had never run for public office before.

Thornburgh returned to Pennsylvania expecting a coronation. Instead, he found an election. Wofford proved much more formidable a candidate than even his most loyal supporters could have anticipated. I remember a conversation Governor Casey had with James Carville, the political consultant who signed on at Casey's insistence to direct the Wofford campaign, in the governor's hotel suite during a National Governors Association meeting in Seattle, Washington. "Harris is just about one of the nicest people I've ever met," Carville told Casey as the campaign was under way. "But he don't know squat about politics and running for office. I don't know if we can make this work." Casey assured Carville he would do all in his power to help the Wofford candidacy, and he did.

Carville and Wofford hooked on to health care as a focal issue for their campaign. Harris appeared in one particularly poignant television commercial filmed in the corridor of a hospital. In the ad, Harris said in America, we accept the fact that every person was entitled to his own lawyer. Well, he added, he wanted to make certain every person also had access to his own doctor. Send him to Washington, he urged, and reform of the national health care delivery system would be his highest priority. It was a very, very powerful visual and a very, very effective political message.

Thornburgh, meanwhile, trumpeted his long and successful career in public service. The principal theme of his campaign was that he was someone seasoned in public affairs, someone who had "walked the corridors of power" in Harrisburg and Washington. It backfired. Harris railed repeatedly against those insiders who had "walked the corridors of power" in the state and nation's capitals, but in the process had lost touch with the needs and concerns of real people. The attack was a nice complement to Harris's populist views on health care and other issues, and it resonated with the electorate.

Still as the election approached, Thornburgh remained the favorite in the eyes of the press and the punditry class. If a Wofford trend had developed, it was not detectable to even the most penetrating of political observers. So what a surprise election night was to most everyone. Early returns, as they arrived in the Wofford election suite, were most promising. Harris Wofford was running particularly strong in the suburban counties around Philadelphia where Democrats seldom did well. Casey took a phone call from Carville shortly after the polls closed and the first returns came in. "Governor," Carville reported, "we're not only going to win; we're going to kick his ass but good." Carville was right on the money. The rout was on. Wofford won by 339,000.

It was one of the grand nights of my fleeting association with elective politics. I had flown with Governor Casey to Philadelphia election night to await the returns. I encountered Harris for a moment as he was making his way from his suite to claim victory. Extending my hand, I said: "Congratulations, Senator. This is one of those rare times in politics when the good guy really did win." It truly was.

Richard Thornburgh went on to serve as Under Secretary General at the United Nations for personnel, budget and finance matters in 1992–93. It was the highest-ranking position any American ever held at the world organization. Then, as an independent examiner for the Bankruptcy Court, he spent fifteen months in 2002–3 dissecting the illegal practices at WorldCom, which culminated in the largest bankruptcy in U.S. history. His public resume continues to build impressively to this day. In 2004, he was appointed co-chair, with former Associated Press chief executive Louis D. Boccardi, to head an investigation into CBS News mishandling of suspect documents purportedly related to President George W. Bush's Air National Guard Service.

Yet, the contradictions between the public Thornburgh and the private Thornburgh are impossible to shake. A professional associate of mine of long standing told me he found Thornburgh to be one of the most easy conversationalists and as cordial and congenial a man as there was to have served in the governor's office. That may be true. I certainly have no reason to doubt him. Still there was a hidden dark side to the Thornburgh character that was troubling—a vindictiveness, if you will, reminiscent of Richard Nixon and his enemies list, an intolerance of political criticism and political opponents, and a penchant, as we saw in the Lewis-Dennis episode, to assassinate the character of his critics if need be.

State Treasurer R. Budd Dwyer, who committed suicide in his state capital office shortly before he was to report for sentencing on a federal conviction involving political contributions, believed to the day he died that it was Richard Thornburgh who put the federal authorities on to him because he (Dwyer) had questioned the legitimacy of travel expense statements involving Mrs. Thornburgh. True or not, I have no way of knowing. I do know it was a suspicion shared by others who walked the corridor of the Capitol during that sad Dwyer episode.

As told to me by another professional associate, Thornburgh himself gave a peek to his personality at an appearance he made before the journalism professional society, Sigma Delta Chi, in Pittsburgh as his tenure was coming to the close. Asked how he handled criticism from the press, Thornburgh was said to have responded that he had no problem with attacks on him. But if anyone attacked members of his family . . . well, he very often had to be restrained physically from responding.

So where does that leave us? Well, those who want the governor's personal view on his political career should read his 2003 autobiography, *Where the Evidence Leads* (he still is very much a prosecutor to his core). To those allies of his out there who, no doubt, hold an entirely different view than I of the governor, I say: Step up and tell your story. As for me, well, this is where I must come down on the man.

Part 4
★★★★★

The Casey Years

Chapter 17

★★★★★★★

The Casey Pursuit

Dogged—there's just no other way to characterize it. Robert P. Casey of Scranton simply was dogged in his pursuit of the Pennsylvania governorship. It's all a matter of record—old history to most folks—but still bears some repeating here. Three times between 1966 and 1978—1966, 1970 and 1978, to be exact—Bob Casey sought the gubernatorial nomination of the Pennsylvania Democratic Party. Three times he was denied.

But as Casey was fond of saying frequently, in private and in public, in paraphrasing legendary Green Bay Packers Coach Vince Lombardi: There was no crime in getting knocked down; the crime was in not getting back up. Casey had been knocked down a couple of times in his public career, not to mention several times in the case of his personal health. But he never, ever failed to get back up.

Let's be clear at the outset. I was privileged to have served on the governor's staff under Bob Casey from 1987 to 1995. He was a man to be admired in so many ways: admired for the commitment and conviction, the vision and passion he brought to public service; his personal integrity; his indomitable strength of spirit; but admired most, in my humble view, for his role as a husband and a father. I was and remain to this day, I confess, an unabashed admirer.

Politically, there's always been something puzzling about Bob Casey's electoral record. While Pennsylvania's Democratic voters rejected him for governor on three occasions, they and the electorate at large embraced him totally in his races for auditor general. He first was elected auditor general in 1968 by a plurality of 444,000 votes, exceeding Vice-President Hubert Humphrey's victory margin over Richard Nixon in the state that year. In 1972 he won reelection by 531,000 votes while Nixon was sweeping George McGovern in Pennsylvania's presidential balloting by 917,000 votes. "The Best Auditor General Pennsylvania Ever Had" was the slogan of his reelection campaign. However, Democrat State Treasurer Grace Sloan, whom Casey succeeded in the office (and his running mate on the ballot), retorted irritably: "I don't know about that!"

Every election is different, of course, and in his races for auditor general he was not confronted with 1) Milton Shapp's money and television assault in his first run for governor in 1966; 2) the shifting political alliances within the Democratic Party in his re-run against Shapp in 1970; and 3) the Pete Flaherty/Pittsburgh Bob Casey gambit in bid number three when he finished second in a three-man field that included Lieutenant Governor Kline (Flaherty 574,889; Casey 445,146; Kline 223,811). That might explain it.

When his second term as auditor general ended in 1976, he returned to the private practice of law (which he interrupted that one time in 1978 to challenge Flaherty and Kline) and by all accounts he was pretty good at it. But he never quite shook the gubernatorial bug. After an eight-year hiatus during the Republican reign of Richard Thornburgh, Casey announced in 1986 that he would seek the Democratic gubernatorial nomination for the fourth time. (In his moving autobiography, *Fighting for Life,* Casey writes in more intimate detail about what motivated him to reenter political life when he did. I recommend it for those interested in pursuing the subject further.)

Casey's announcement was greeted with some restraint within Democratic Party circles. After all, he had been away from the political arena for eight years. What made him think 1986 would be any different than 1966, 1970 or 1978? (I must confess, I wondered that myself.) His skeptics quickly derided him as the "three-time loss from Holy Cross" (his college alma mater). But Casey persevered. First, he dispatched former Philadelphia district attorney Ed Rendell in another contested Democratic primary by 164,000 votes. (Rendell would sixteen years later, in 2002, successfully resurrect his own gubernatorial ambitions by beating none other than Bob Casey's son, Auditor General Robert P. Casey Jr., in a Democratic primary by upwards of 90,000 votes.) Casey Sr. went on to edge Richard Thornburgh's lieutenant governor, the aforementioned Bill Scranton Jr. by 86,000 votes in the fall. After the scandals of the second Shapp term and eight years of Republican rule in the governor's office, Pennsylvania Democrats were ready to rally around a winner. Bob Casey of Scranton was the guy. He was about to fulfill the longest quest of his adult life.

It was inevitable, I suppose, that if I eventually should make my way to the office of the governor, it would be in an administration led by Scranton Bob Casey. It was, however, by distinctly separate and convoluted paths that we both arrived as and when we did. And, in the process, I learned that in the advancement of one's career, sometimes the best answer is "no." Let me explain, briefly.

Twice in 1966 I was recruited from my position with the Associated Press to join campaigns for governor. Bob Casey was the first to call. I had met Casey almost four years earlier when he came to Harrisburg in 1963 as a freshman senator from Lackawanna County. He knew my family name because of my grandfather and father's involvement in Scranton city politics. I knew about him before he arrived by virtue of his reputation as a political comer with a promising future in Democratic state politics. Our paths crossed frequently in our respective roles, he as a senator, me as a reporter covering the state Senate.

When he decided to run for governor in 1966, I was among those he approached about joining his campaign staff. We met in his room in the old Harrisburger Hotel (now the Fulton Bank Building), across the street from the Capitol. He told me of his gubernatorial aspirations, and that he expected to win the endorsement of the Democratic Party (very important in those days). And he offered me a press relations position with his campaign. I was so intrigued that, after talking with my wife, I called him back a day or so later and accepted.

Then a bad case of cold feet set in. My apprehensions were sparked by two considerations. The first was that wiser, more experienced associates at the Associated Press—Bureau Chief Harry Ball and senior correspondent Jack Lynch, in particular—cautioned me that with Philadelphia multimillionaire Milton Shapp and his deep pockets poised to challenge the party leadership for the nomination, a Casey win was no foregone conclusion, endorsement or not. "Casey could lose and never make it to the general election," Lynch cautioned me. "What would you do then?"

Very good question, one for which I didn't have an answer. It took on even more compelling weight because Toni was pregnant with what we hoped would be our first child. In that situation, where personal and political conditions appeared to conflict, I had to confront the core question of the moment: If Casey lost, what would I do to support my family? Truth is, I just didn't know. Because I didn't, I wasn't prepared to accept that risk. Back then, journalists didn't hop back and forth between politics and the profession as they do today when celebrity is as important a credential as are training experience, and track record. So a few days after I told Casey I would come aboard his campaign, I had to call him to tell him I had changed my mind. Casey, always the gentleman, accepted my rationale most graciously and wished me well. I did likewise.

A short time later, a second overture came to get into politics. This one took me totally by surprise. State Attorney General Walter Alessandroni was about to be endorsed as the Republican candidate for lieutenant governor. He called me out of the blue and asked me to meet with him. I did, and he offered me a position as his campaign press secretary.

I was very flattered. Alessandroni was one of the most well-respected and highly regarded political figures in Harrisburg at the time. He was tough, and he was smart. He appeared not to tolerate fools very easily. He certainly wouldn't ask a fool to serve on his campaign staff. His offer, in my view, was a high personal compliment. But I understood immediately I couldn't accept after having turned Casey down. As a matter of courtesy, I told the attorney general I would consider the offer. I called him back within a matter of days and told him, I'm sorry, but no.

In the course of a few weeks, I had made two fateful decisions. Little did I know just how fateful they were at the time. Milton Shapp did go on to beat Bob Casey in that 1966 Democratic primary election, as we all know. Forty years later, I still don't know what I would have done professionally in the wake of that loss. As events played out, Toni's pregnancy ended in a miscarriage. It was a great disappointment for both of us. With the benefit of hindsight, to not have compounded the deep personal loss we both felt at the moment with other anxieties over my professional livelihood was, indeed, a blessing in disguise. Truth was, professionally, I probably wasn't ready myself for that kind of career transition.

The Alessandroni saga had a more tragic end to it. That summer, Alessandroni was flying with the chairman of the Pennsylvania Liquor Control Board, James Staudinger, in a chartered private plane to Somerset County, where Alessandroni was to address a liquor industry convention. The flight ran into some bad weather and the plane lacked the necessary instrumentation to navigate in the clouds. The plane went down in the fog, mist shrouded mountains of Fayette County. Alessandroni, Staudinger, and the pilot were killed on impact. I found myself riding for the Associated Press to the crash scene with Jack Conmy, Governor William Scranton's press secretary, who was dispatched to the site by the governor to coordinate recovery efforts. There is no doubt in my mind that I would have been on that plane with Alessandroni if I had accepted his offer. Fate, once again, had been kind to me . . . very, very kind.

There's one footnote that should be added. As I was leaving the Casey interview, he asked if I could suggest anyone else he might approach to join in his campaign. I gave him the name of Jack Lynch, my AP colleague. "I don't know if he'd be interested," I remember saying. "But if he were, I'd definitely try to get him." When I talked with Jack about the offer I received, I made no mention that I had suggested his name to Casey. Casey did eventually approach Jack, and, to my surprise, Jack, in spite of his counsel to me, accepted.

On reflection, however, I came to understand his professional situation was considerably different than mine. Though he had a young family at the time, he had been with the AP for more than twenty years dating back to his days as a part-time copy boy in Philadelphia. He had been reporting on the Hill for a dozen years. His reputation and his network were well established. He was ready for a career change. If Casey lost, prospects were very good someone in or out of politics or government would pick him up very quickly. The same didn't apply to me. I had neither Jack's considerable experience nor good reputation on Capitol Hill.

After Casey lost to Shapp in the first go-around, Jack (with Casey's help) was hired as the executive director of the Democratic State Committee. When Casey was elected auditor general in 1968, Jack was named his executive deputy, a position he held until his untimely death at the too young an age of fifty from Hodgkin's disease. Casey remained close to the Lynch family. When he was elected governor, he brought Jack's wife, Dee, into the office as the governor's office receptionist. Frank, Jack's oldest son, worked for a time as a reporter with the *Harrisburg Patriot-News*. He joined the Casey administration as press secretary in the Department of Labor and Industry. When I became press secretary, I brought Frank over to work with me in the governor's office as a deputy press secretary. Make that one circle closed in the strange world of politics.

Probably the most direct connection I had with Casey's three unsuccessful bids for governor came in 1970 when I was assigned by the *Philadelphia Inquirer* to cover the final two weeks of the Democratic primary, the first on the road with Casey, the second with Shapp. Primary election night I was assigned to Casey's hotel headquarters where I covered his concession speech. It was not a happy occasion, obviously. The next morning, my city desk assigned me to do a post-election interview with Casey. I drove to his modest Scranton home, just minutes away from the city's downtown. Casey greeted me at the door in his pajamas and bathrobe. He could have held me at bay at the door. Instead, he invited me in.

The Caseys were having cereal for breakfast, and being the gracious people they were in victory or defeat, they asked me if I'd like some cereal or eggs. I declined. I wanted to get my quotes and get out of there. I felt like an intruder. Casey was a gentleman. He answered every question I had about the race and the results. I remember the last question I asked him that morning before I left his home. "What are you going to do today?" I inquired.

"Probably take a drive," he responded. That, I thought, was as good a way to end the interview. I did.

When Bob Casey finally achieved his political dream of being elected governor, I had nothing to do with the campaign. I was the director of government relations for the State System of Higher Education (SSHE) at the time. I voted for Casey. But I was not active in a political sense. In fact, our paths had not crossed since he left Harrisburg except for one brief greeting at a SSHE event at which he spoke during the gubernatorial campaign. At that, I believe once the pleasantries were exchanged, my only other contribution was to point him in the direction of the men's room at the Hotel Hershey. Once Casey was elected, I suppose I may have permitted myself an idle thought or two about being invited to join the administration. But I really had no reason to expect to be. Then a strange sequence of events occurred which made me think a position with the new administration was not out of the question.

It was about 11:30 P.M. on a Sunday night in November shortly after Casey's election when the telephone in our bedroom rang. Toni and I had retired for the evening and were more than slightly startled by a call at that hour. It was State Senator H. Craig Lewis, my employer on my last stint on the staff of the Pennsylvania Senate before I moved on to the State System of Higher Education. Craig explained that he had been in the company of the governor-elect that very night at a Bucks County Democratic dinner. For some reason, my name came up in their conversation as a possible candidate for secretary of legislative affairs. As Craig relayed it to me, it went something like this:

"Do you think he'd be interested?" Casey asked.

"I don't know," Lewis replied. "But I sure can ask to find out."

That was the purpose of the call, Lewis explained. Casey had given Craig his office telephone number for me to call if I were interested. "If you are, I'd call him tomorrow," Craig said.

"I am, and I will, " I replied. And I did.

I was traveling with Chancellor Jim McCormick in Philadelphia the next day. But I managed to break away discreetly for a moment and place the call to Scranton. Casey was tied up but his secretary said she would give him the message. Where could I be reached? I told her I couldn't because I was on the road. "I'll call him tomorrow morning," I said. I placed the call Tuesday morning from the privacy of my office. Casey was busy again—which, I suppose, was to be expected from a governor-elect who was just beginning to assemble the team for his new administration. I left my office number and waited for a return call. It didn't come for a week.

I was attending the chancellor's regular Monday morning senior staff meeting when my secretary, most apologetically, interrupted to announce

Governor-elect Casey was on the telephone for me. I remember Chancellor McCormick saying to me, "You had better take that call."

I was instantly out of my seat and heading toward my office. What I did not know was that the chancellor was following close behind. I closed the door to my office as soon as I broke the entryway, essentially shutting the door in the chancellor's face. My secretary later told me he had a stunned look on his face as he turned sheepishly and walked back to his conference room. I was embarrassed by that, but to the chancellor's credit, we never discussed the incident.

My conversation with the governor-elect was fairly brief and to the point. I congratulated him on his election. I told him I was calling at the suggestion of Craig Lewis, and that if Casey was interested in considering me for legislative secretary, I was interested in being considered. But in fairness, I told him that while I certainly voted for him, I did nothing in the way of actively campaigning for him.

"Well, if you read the paper this morning," he responded, "you'll know that wasn't necessary."

I had read the paper and was surprised—as was most of the Harrisburg political establishment—to learn Casey had designated Bill Keisling as his chief of staff. It stunned Democratic insiders for a number of reasons. First, Keisling was a Republican. Second, he had served as a chief of staff without portfolio in the administration of former governor William W. Scranton from 1963 to 1967, what seemed in the Capitol to have been ages ago. Third, he had not been particularly visible on the Harrisburg political scene for almost fifteen years. The appointment did not sit well, particularly in the Democratic legislative circles that Casey would have to woo and win to his agenda. But Casey was never one to follow conventional political protocols, particularly in personnel matters. That also may help to explain why he had so much difficulty in his first three attempts to win the Democratic nomination. Democratic politicos always felt unsure they do could business—translated, patronage—with Casey and his strong independent streak.

I told Casey I had read about the Keisling appointment, so I understood what he was saying. Casey told me they were reviewing a number of personnel appointments, and that they (he may have said Keisling by name) would get back to me. End of conversation. I told no one, except Toni, of course. But the word of my pending appointment apparently began to make the round of Harrisburg insiders. Cliff Jones, a preeminent figure in Pennsylvania state politics, bumped into me after the annual December dinner of the Pennsylvania Society in New York City and said he understood congratulations were in order. I demurred, because nothing had been sealed at that point. But I took it as a good sign.

Shortly thereafter, I received a call from George Seidel, former governor Thornburgh's legislative secretary. He offered to meet with me for breakfast and talk through informally the rigors of the position. I told George that while I thought I was under active consideration, I had not been offered the job. Still, if he wanted to meet, I'd certainly appreciate it. We did, in fact, meet.

The clincher concerning my pending appointment came with a sudden telephone call from my sister, Marie Antoinette, in Scranton. "What's going on?" she wanted to know. "Are you going to work for Casey?" I asked her what she meant. She told me about a chance encounter my mother and she had with Morey Myers (Casey's close friend, confidant, and his first general counsel) at a funeral in the city (Scrantonians are very religious about paying their respects to the dead). Marie Antoinette explained that Myers told my mother, "Congratulations, Mrs. Carocci. We're delighted to have Vince with us." So, my sister wanted to know, what's the deal? I told her where I had left it with Casey and was waiting for a call back.

The call never came. I learned much later that Keisling, once appointed chief of staff, had been delegated the primary responsibility for assembling the governor's inner office staff. Keisling, looking for the unconventional approach as a signal there would be a new way of doing business in Harrisburg, is said to have persuaded the governor-elect to consider appointing the first woman legislative secretary in state history. The question was who?

The answer came just days before the inauguration. The new legislative secretary was to be Helen Wise of State College, a one-term member of the House of Representatives who was working at the time in New Mexico for that state's teacher organization. I heard the news in a call from Mike McLaughlin, who had also been interested in the position. He had served as Milton Shapp's press secretary. He then moved during the Thornburgh years, at my recommendation, to serve as chief of staff to Senate Minority Leader Ed Zemprelli. I thanked him for the call. I didn't have much else to say. How could I? It wasn't my appointment to make.

Truth was Helen had as many credentials if not more than I to lay claim to the position. She had served as statewide president of the Pennsylvania State Education Association, a powerful, powerful political organization in the Commonwealth. She also had served that one term in the State House of Representatives before losing her bid for reelection. Her only major negative was that she had moved to New Mexico after her defeat and had lost contact with the legislative process and the legislative personalities. But, all things considered, that was a problem that could be easily remedied. Me? Well I was, after all, still the director of government affairs for the State System of Higher Education. I was ready to move on in that role.

One of my first tasks after Helen's appointment was to write her a letter of congratulations. I had two objectives in mind. The first was to request a meeting at some convenient time to introduce myself and the new system to her. Though she herself was a teacher and certainly familiar with the system universities as the state's primary academic spawning ground for teachers, Helen was a proud alumnus of Penn State. She was devout in her devotion to the university. In fact, she was an elected alumni member of the Board of Trustees. Since Penn State was SSHE's prime competitor for state appropriations, I wanted to be certain the system had a fair airing and an open ear in the administration hierarchy. My secondary motive was to let her know without saying as much that there were no hard feelings about her appointment. I assumed she would somehow have learned I was a primary competitor for the position. Not that it mattered to her (she got the job, after all), but I didn't want that to interfere with my future relations with her or the administration. I left it that I would call in a few weeks to find a convenient time for me to visit.

The call came, instead, from old friend George Seidel. I'm sure he was calling on Helen's behalf since they had a long professional relationship dating years back to their service together at the Pennsylvania State Education Association (PSEA). George asked if I was bothered by being passed over, and would I at all be open to the possibility of working for and with Helen as her chief legislative deputy? I told George I was over whatever disappointment I might have felt, and that the prospect of working in the governor's office even as a deputy secretary still had some appeal to me, but that I needed to come to a firm understanding on some issues—responsibilities and compensation prime among them. If the governor's office (meaning Helen) wanted to discuss a position under those conditions, I'd certainly sit down with them.

Two days later, Helen's secretary called. She said Helen appreciated my kind congratulatory letter, but she was calling on another matter. Would I be available to meet with Helen the next day? I knew exactly what the purpose of the meeting was to be. We met and Helen outlined her plans for the office, saying she desperately needed a strong assistant. Would I be interested and available? I told her I would, but my salary requirements were higher than what they were paying deputies at that time. I wasn't going to take a salary cut just for the privilege of working in the governor's office. Helen told me she had flexibility on salary, even if it meant doing without a second deputy. We left it that she would get back to me.

Once again, I waited for a call back. Once again, it seemed an eternity in coming. I decided to force the issue when I happened by coincidence to encounter Bill Keisling in a Capitol corridor. "Bill," I said. "I'm sure you know of my discussion with Helen Wise. That was almost two weeks ago. I'm not about to sit, twisting in the wind. I'd like to do it. But you folks have got to make up your mind. If you or the governor isn't interested in my services, just say so, and we can all move on. I went through this uncertainty once over the legislative secretary's appointment. I certainly wasn't going to go through it again over the deputy's appointment. Please have someone tell me, yes or no, so we can get on with it either way."

Keisling was apologetic. He said Helen and he were most interested in bringing me on staff, but as hectic as activities were in the first days and weeks of a new administration, they just had not had the opportunity to sit down with the governor and confirm the appointment. I told Bill I appreciated that. But it was not fair to me or the system for this to be unsettled much longer. He assured me it would go to the top of his priority list, and I could expect to hear shortly.

This time, the call did come. It was from Helen. She wanted me as her deputy. The governor approved the offer. When could I start? She was overwhelmed with work, and without help. We settled on a start date—two weeks, I believe, with the condition that I could assist the system in the search for my successor. Twenty years after I was first approached, I finally was going to work for Scranton Bob Casey in the governor's office.

Chapter 18

★★★★★★★

Reforming the Liquor Control System

To control or not to control? Okay, that's a lame and shameless paraphrase of the Bard from Stratford-upon-Avon. But (aside, perhaps from the submission of his first state budget), that really *was* the most immediate question confronting Governor Robert P. Casey and his new administration when it took hold of the reins of state government in January of 1987. Not so much *whether* to control the sales of alcoholic beverages in Pennsylvania, but *how*.

State control of liquor sales had been a way of life under the mandate of Pennsylvania law since national Prohibition was repealed in 1933. Lawmakers of that era apparently believed the most responsible public policy in the aftermath of Prohibition was to at least contain the availability of spirits by restricting sales to a network of state-established liquor stores. The state Liquor Control Board, in fact, was organized for business only four days before liquor sales in the Commonwealth became legal once again in December 1933. Thus it has been ever since.

Since then liquor control in Pennsylvania has grown into a very substantial enterprise for state government. Almost seven hundred state stores are located strategically across the Commonwealth. Some three thousand people are employed by the enterprise in its administrative, compliance, and sales functions. Most important, the multimillion-dollar sales generated at state liquor stores each year return millions of dollars in tax revenue annually to the state General Fund coffers. The fate of the system is now and long has been a very consequential public policy decision for the Commonwealth.

Democrat Milton Shapp was the first governor in my memory to broach publicly the notion of privatizing the system, which he did in the mid-1970s, about the same time he was removing token boxes from toilets on the Pennsylvania Turnpike. But the idea never went very far beyond the discussion stage until Dick Thornburgh succeeded Shapp in the executive office.

Governor Thornburgh, of course, launched the most serious assault on liquor control when Senate Democrats—for their selfish political interests related largely to political fund-raising and jobs—obstructed the confirmation of his nominees to the state Liquor Control Board. He aggressively joined forces with the privatization folks, largely liquor industry interests whose profit motives made them more than disinterested stakeholders. The privatization movement found an important ally in the media, newspaper editorial editors in particular, who added considerable voice to the chorus of so-called free-enterprise advocates. Of course, the potential revenues the media could reap from liquor advertising under a free enterprise system—advertising that was banned under the control system—was not inconsequential, either.

Arrayed against privatization was a substantial bloc of legislative and social interest opposition. Legislative Democrats were almost unanimous in their opposition. It was largely a jobs issue with them; the LCB's three-thousand-plus employees enjoyed some form of job protection either through unionized collective bargaining or by civil service status. There were no job protection guarantees for this workforce in a decontrolled environment. A considerable number of legislative Republicans also were opposed, though for entirely different reasons, having largely to do with unfettered access to the purchase and consumption of booze. Church groups and other social interest organizations such as Mothers Against Drunk Drivers (MADD) shared their concern. Together, their collective opposition was powerful enough to turn back the Thornburgh initiative. But the mere power of his office gave the issue a high-profile political visibility that would not diminish easily or quickly.

What was driving the debate in January of 1987 when Governor Casey assumed office was the so-called Sunset concept of legislating, a reform theory to lawmaking very much in vogue at the time. The theory held that every program or agency funded by the state should be reviewed for its performance and cost effectiveness every three, four, five years or so. Those not expressly reauthorized in law by a date certain simply would fade out of existence and into the sunset (thus the term "sunsetted"). The date certain for liquor control was June 30, 1987. And the stakes were high because without any statutory authority, the state store system would be out of business, and, unless it was replaced (which was not likely in such a short time frame), no one would have the legal right to sell liquor anywhere, anytime, in any way throughout the Commonwealth.

What compounded the political situation for the antiprivatization forces was the fact that the LCB was an agency very much discredited at the time in the arena of public opinion. Two of its members were active Democrats; the third was an active Republican whose primary role was to press the Thornburgh privatization agenda in any way he could. The board's repeated squabbles in public sessions only put a stronger focus on the issue. The Democratic majority on the board was its own worst enemy. Their posture was so arrogant, so insensitive to legitimate consumer concerns, so tone deaf to the groundswell of opposition growing about them that the privatization forces had no better target than the board itself, and their managers of the liquor control system. The Democratic majority members also were naïve. They thought all they needed to survive was a friendly governor. They were wrong.

Casey had committed to continued liquor control as the most responsible public policy in his campaign for election. But his support was conditioned very squarely on the institution of major, demonstrable, and measurable reforms in the system and its management. So virtually from day 1, the mission was to pull together a major, demonstrable, measurable reform package that would be acceptable within a short five-month time frame to a General Assembly with some sharp divisions on the subject of liquor control. It was the first assignment given to me that February of 1987 when I joined the administration as deputy secretary for legislative affairs.

My role was principally that of a facilitator. Working with administration lawyers, and our allies in the General Assembly on both sides of the political aisle (of which there were considerable numbers), we shaped a proposal that both removed enforcement of the liquor laws from the LCB and placed that responsibility in the state police and took the power to hold hearings and render judgments on violations of state liquor law out of the LCB and established a quasi-judicial, independent cadre of administrative law judges. More important in terms of customer concerns, the proposal

1. empowered the LCB to exercise its volume purchasing power—the largest single purchaser of spirits in the world—to secure better prices for its customers;
2. authorized sales, discounts, rebate coupons, and credit cards in the liquor store;
3. permitted variable operating hours consistent with the shopping patterns of particular regions of the state;
4. retained the ban on liquor advertising; and
5. established a Bureau of Consumer Affairs as a standing arm of the LCB.

As a gesture to privatization legislators largely from southeastern Pennsylvania (the wine and cheese crowd), the legislation called for the establishment of at least four wine specialty shops throughout the Commonwealth, each of which ultimately proved unable to sustain itself financially and eventually had to be discarded after a reasonable pilot test.

Most important, once the bill was enacted, Casey nominated three very credible appointees to replace the incumbent board, including the Democratic chairman who endeared himself to the Senate Democratic leadership by his political fundraising prowess. The chairman was more than surprised and upset with his removal; outraged would be more like it. But whatever he felt, he was gone. The Casey nominees were confirmed, in fairly short order by Senate confirmation standards. The Democratic appointees were former State Representative James Goodman of Schuylkill County and Oliver Slinker, a Dauphin County businessman. The Republican was former Allegheny County GOP chairman Bob Fohl, whom Casey came to know when they both served as delegates to the 1967 constitutional convention. (One of the concessions the administration made during the legislative process was to add a requirement that no more than two members of the board could be of the same political party as the appointing governor. Senate Republicans demanded that, and it was an easy tradeoff to make.)

The governor was very explicit in his charge to the new board: Make the system work in a professional, consumer-sensitive way. And they did. The first two major hires were a professional director of operations with a background in commercial retailing and a professional director of administration with an academic degree in administrative procedures. With the new professionals in charge and the cronies either gone, demoted, or neutralized, a new order set in. The liquor stores were redesigned, prices were stabilized, sales were introduced, and hours improved. Variety brands were made available in adequate supply, and point-of-sale referrals on customer request were instituted. One technique I found particularly compelling was that those distillers offering customers a break on prices were given prominent display space in the stores; those that did not were not. Leveraging, I think they call it. Made good marketing sense, too.

Reauthorization of the liquor control system was, without question, my most demanding and, once accomplished, my most professionally gratifying experience in the year I spent in the governor's legislative office. It was also very revealing—regrettably, in a disillusioning way. I thought from my thirteen years on the staff of the Pennsylvania Senate I had come to know the legislative personality. And I came to regard most of the members of the Senate and House with whom I came into contact to be essentially decent, intelligent, well-motivated, and fairly modest people. I was proud to have been in their employ and associated with them in the legislative process. But when I moved to the executive side of state government, I came to see another side of the legislative personality, a side that was not pretty. I found not all, certainly, but too many legislators—to my great dismay, more so on the Democratic side of the aisle than on the Republican (though Republicans say the converse was true when they held the governor's office)—to be often petulant, frequently petty, almost always demanding of their governor, and seldom satisfied, even at attempts to meet them more than half way. I would have thought they would want to serve causes greater than their own self-interest and political survival. Too many of them, in my view, did not. That was disappointing.

Before we move on, let's reflect just a bit about prices and quality-of-life issues. First, prices. Let there be no mistake: Liquor prices in Pennsylvania are not driven by the fact the system is a control system. They are driven by the taxes that are levied on each bottle of spirits sold in the Commonwealth. There's the state's sales tax; there's federal excise taxes; and there's an emergency liquor tax enacted in the mid-1930s to provide relief from the Johnstown flood. The latter was supposed to be temporary, but it has yet to be repealed. The point is this. Customers will never see major relief in liquor prices, whether in a control or privatized environment, until something is done about the taxes imposed on each sale of spirits. It hasn't happened to this point. It's not likely to happen any time soon, if at all.

As for quality of life issues, in my view, they should not be casually dismissed or undervalued. When, for example, was the last time you saw crowds congregating or loitering, or traffic congesting for that matter, around state liquor stores? Particularly state liquor stores located in metropolitan neighborhoods where the potential for civil unrest on hot summer days or nights is always a matter of concern to authorities. When was the last liquor store you visited surrounded by litter or garbage? Or when was the last time you read about an underage drinker buying his or her spirits from a state liquor store? Seldom, if ever, because the much maligned (though unfairly so) state store clerks have the responsibility to guard against that. Are we comfortable the same care would apply in a profit-making system? I'm certainly not. And we cannot ignore societal problems surrounding driving under the influence. Tragic as DUI always is, it is doubly so when it involves teenagers. I know of no case where teenage victims of DUI purchased their alcoholic beverages from a state liquor store.

Will life as we know it go on if the state control system is converted some day to private enterprise? Probably so. But given my druthers, I'd stay with control primarily for the quality of life reasons above all others. Prices are not at all out of line with surrounding states; access is not at all inconvenient; and the shopping experience is not all unpleasant. What's to complain about? Pennsylvania may have been only one of eighteen states with a liquor control system in force at the time of the Casey reauthorization. Today, it may be one of only two or three. So what? In the course of the debate over great human events, where you purchase you liquor is not even a burp in the discussion. Like I said, life goes on.

In point of fact, the Casey plan to modernize and reform the Pennsylvania liquor control system worked so well that almost twenty years later liquor control as a major consumer and/or political issue is essentially nonexistent, though it certainly hasn't disappeared. It surfaced slightly in the 2002 campaign for governor. Republican nominee Attorney General Mike Fisher, a long-time privatization advocate, and one of Governor Thornburgh's principal Senate managers in his failed drive to end liquor control, pressed the issue once again in his campaign against Democratic nominee, former Philadelphia mayor Ed Rendell. Rendell was, basically, new to the issue and said he supported some unspecified tinkering around the edges. But liquor control had no legs in the campaign and certainly was not a major factor in the outcome. Meanwhile, the LCB in 2002 and 2003, on its own initiative, took steps to make the system more price sensitive and consumer accessible. The board launched a pilot plan to permit discount state stores to operate in selected locations on Pennsylvania's state borders and later unveiled a plan to open liquor stores adjacent to grocery stores for more customer convenience. A few stores also were permitted to operate on Sunday, also on a pilot basis. Strikes me, that's three ways to privatize the system without actually privatizing it. There are probably more in the pipeline.

Some twenty years later, I remain very gratified by what we did with liquor control in 1987. A lot people deserve the credit for restoring credibility and confidence to the control system. With control advocates like the late senator John Shoemaker, a Dauphin County Republican and the chair of the Senate Law and Justice Committee, the reform that was outlined for the governor's consideration was truly bipartisan. Once the governor endorsed the approach without reservation, the lawyers crafted the legislative language. Legislators from both sides of the aisle and social interest groups such as the Council of Churches and MADD, perhaps for different rationales, rallied to support it. Big Jim Manderino's support as House majority leader was absolutely critical to our success. Tony Barbush and Marc Volavka, his principal aides, were invaluable in assisting the administration (and me) as we worked through the labyrinth that can often be the legislative process. Once the reform was enacted, the new board made certain it worked as intended. The governor signed House Bill 1000, "An Act Relating to Alcoholic Liquor," into law just days before the June 30 deadline. I was never one to accumulate a lot of personal testimonials for any minor successes I might have had in any of my career endeavors. But I was proud of this one. To commemorate the event, I have hanging on the wall of my office at home a framed copy of the first page of House Bill 1000. It is inscribed: "To Vince Carocci, With Thanks for Helping to Make This a Reality." It was signed, "Bob Casey."

Chapter 19

★★★★★★★

Bouncing Around the Governor's Office on the Way to a Dream

John Denver may have had his country road to take him home, but Pennsylvania governors always seem have their rocky roads to navigate. It just seems to go with the territory, particularly in the first year in office. The administration of Robert P. Casey was no exception. By any measure, 1987 was a rather bumpy one for the new governor and his staff. Harrisburg and the way state government worked had changed immensely from the time Governor Casey had served in the Pennsylvania Senate and as Pennsylvania auditor general. The most notable change, perhaps, was the emergence of the General Assembly as a full and coequal partner in the processes of state government and one that wasn't at all hesitant about asserting its territorial prerogatives. So there was a considerable learning curve for both the new governor and his staff, and it took some time to catch on.

To Casey's credit, he recognized the governor's office wasn't functioning as crisply as it should, and that his personal staff wasn't serving him quite as well as was needed—more so, I think, from inexperience or unfamiliarity than from ineptitude. As the first year of the administration drew to a close, Casey did what he frequently did when he thought he had a problem. He consulted with his most trusted political confidant, James Carville. Carville, true to his character, didn't waste time on a lot of niceties or protocols. He recommended a major reshuffling of the governor's staff.

Bill Keisling (after an appropriate grace period) resigned as chief of staff. He was replaced by Secretary of General Services Jim Brown, a Casey loyalist from Scranton and a key player in the governor's successful 1986 campaign. Two deputy chiefs of staff, also veterans of the Casey campaign, were appointed: Jack Tighe for administration and David Stone for communications. Helen Wise was moved from legislative secretary to secretary of the Cabinet, a position much better suited to her considerable people skills and high energy. My old boss in the Senate, Tom Lamb, was named legislative secretary. Tony May, Governor Shapp's first press secretary and a former AP colleague of mine, came on board as a new secretary of public information, charged with coordinating the administration's public information and press release functions. A lot of changes, to be sure, but in sum, changes decidedly for the better.

Me? I was told the administration wanted to take better advantage of my long and diversified experience in and around state government. I was moved to another newly created position, that of secretary for government operations. My principal function was to assume administrative control of the processing, nomination, and confirmation of some three thousand gubernatorial appointments, including judicial vacancies. I would also serve as the principal administration liaison with the state Senate on confirmation of gubernatorial nominees. And I was to be available for trouble-shooting projects like the liquor-control fight if and when they arose. It was a promotion of sorts. The pay was a little bit more (which my family appreciated) and the title "Secretary" was of higher rank in the pecking order of state government than "Deputy Secretary" (which I appreciated). I remained secretary of government operations for the better part of a year and a half until another sequence of totally unexpected events began to unfold.

There are a few things in life that I could honestly claim to know as fact in advance of their happening. I knew from the first moment I set foot on the Penn State campus and saw my first edition of the *Daily Collegian* that I wanted to be sports editor of the paper some day. I knew I wanted to marry and raise a family. And I knew that if the opportunity to serve as press secretary to a Pennsylvania governor ever presented itself, I would jump at it. Of course, for that to happen there had to be a governor who wanted me to serve in that capacity. And that just didn't seem in the cards.

By the time I joined the Casey administration, I had been out of the news business for almost seventeen years, since 1971, to be exact, when I joined Tom Lamb's staff with the Pennsylvania Senate. A lot about the profession had changed in the interim, not the least of which was the decline of newspapers, the rise of television as the dominant force in journalism, and all the technological advances that accompanied that transition. I was a print journalist, not a broadcast journalist . . . still am, I suppose. In that context, it was no coincidence that when I was asked to join the Casey administration, it was in a legislative rather than a press capacity. But even more important, Governor Casey already had a press secretary. He also had a deputy chief of staff for communications and a secretary of public information, to boot. There was nothing to suggest the lineup of this triumvirate was going to change in the ensuing months.

Except for something called an election—more specifically, Governor's Casey's bid for reelection in 1990. As the governor was gearing up in the fall of 1989 for his reelection bid, one of his first orders of business was to gain some control over and some political comfort with the daily operations of the Democratic State Committee. Casey had learned a hard lesson about Pennsylvania Democratic politics through the years. The Democratic State Committee, even when it ostensibly was supporting a candidate, could not guarantee that candidate electoral success. But it certainly could cause a lot of unnecessary problems—particularly in the areas of jobs and political fundraising. So it was understandable that he wanted someone he could trust running the daily operations at State Committee. He turned to Tony May and asked him to move over to party headquarters across the street from the state Capitol as the State Committee's executive director. Tony agreed. That raised the question of who, if anyone, would replace him.

Tony confided to me that he had recommended me for the public information position. (There's a twist of fate for you. When I left the AP in 1968 to go to Penn State, Tony took my place in the Harrisburg bureau.) I wasn't surprised to learn Tony was going over to State Committee because the word had been circulating quietly through the corridors of the governor's office for a couple of weeks at least. But I was surprised to learn that I was under consideration to replace him in the public information function. A couple of days later, I received a call from Jim Brown, now firmly in installed as chief of staff. He said he wanted to talk to me. I told him to come down whenever it was convenient (my office was a floor below the main complex of the governor's office.) He said he'd be right down, and he was.

When he closed the door to my office, I suspected he was here to talk to me about replacing Tony. But there was more. The conversation, as I recall, went something like this.

"Tony's going over to State Committee for the election campaign," Jim said.

"I suspected as much," I responded. "The word was making the rounds around here."

"We're not going to fill the position, per se," Jim went on. (Well, why are you here?, I wondered to myself.) "We'd like you to move into that slot and have you serve as press secretary as well."

"What?" I was absolutely stunned. I tried to contain myself. "What's happening with Bob?" I asked, referring to the governor's incumbent and able press secretary, Bob Grotevant, himself a former Capitol reporter with United Press International and the *Philadelphia Daily News*.

"We're going to assign him to Special Projects," Jim replied.

"Does he know that?" I continued.

"He will," Jim assured me. He said he was going to talk to Bob next. "Are you okay with this?"

Gov. Robert P. Casey of Scranton inscribes his signature in the cement base of the Philadelphia Convention Center as Philadelphia mayor Wilson Goode looks on. The convention center was to be a cornerstone of downtown economic development in the city, and it was constructed with a substantial contribution from the Commonwealth. Yet, as much as the governor did for the city throughout his tenure, it seldom seemed enough to Philadelphia leaders and the media. As press secretary to the governor, I came to travel with him on many, many occasions such as this.

I wasn't okay with the notion of pushing Bob out of his job, I thought. But that was not of my doing. "I am, if you and the governor are," I replied.

"We are," Jim said.

There was, however, one question I had to raise before the deal was sealed. One of the problems, at least as I saw it, with the press secretary/

public information secretary/communications deputy chief of staff arrangement was that on any given day anyone of the three could be found speaking for the governor, sometimes two in the same day, depending on the number of reporters reaching out to them. So many voices representing a single administration could be confusing if not contradictory.

"Who's going to speak for the governor?" I asked.

"The press secretary will," Jim said.

"Does David [Stone, communications deputy chief of staff] know that?" I asked.

"He will," Jim responded.

I had heard enough. I was ready to go. But there was one other personal matter that had to be resolved as well. When I raised it, I thought for an instant I had pushed the envelope too far. Toni and I were scheduled to leave within the week for a trip to Italy. It was to be our first trip out of the country, we were looking forward to it, we had been planning for it for over a year, and it was important to me as a Carocci. (My grandfather had told me many times as I was growing up how much he wanted to return to visit the native land that he had left as but a young lad of three. He died before he could make the trip. I pledged to myself that I would do it for him.)

I told Jim Toni and I were off to Italy, to return in twelve days. If that was a problem for the governor and him, I would have to pass. Jim seemed taken aback momentarily. But, after a pause that seemed like an eternity to me, he said two weeks shouldn't make any difference. We had a deal. We shook hands, and he left. The appointment would be announced in a matter of days, he said, once the other folks involved were informed. (The appointment was announced publicly before Toni and I left. We had a marvelous, memorable trip. Italy was as exciting to tour as we had anticipated. But I also was eager to return to assume the duties of press secretary to the governor. When the time came to come back, I was ready.)

I never learned what prompted the governor and Jim to move me into the press secretary's position. I never asked because, frankly, I didn't spend a lot of time wondering about it. It was a life's ambition that I had, in rare moments, mused about through the years. Now it was to be fulfilled and I was about to learn if I was up to it.

If there were learning curves for new governors and their staff (and there certainly were) there also was a learning curve for new press secretaries. And the rapid pace of the news business being what it is by contemporary standards, that learning curve could be so short as to be almost nonexistent. Events gripped me immediately in my new role. One involved abortion; the other state prison riots. What better way to break in, I suppose.

For me, the abortion issue was more a matter of press logistics than public policymaking. (It will always be "press" rather than media with me.) The governor's adamant pro-life opposition to abortion was well known in Pennsylvania. He supported whatever restraints the state could apply on abortion that pass constitutional muster under *Roe vs. Wade*. In an act that took some political courage on his part, he vetoed the first abortion control legislation to reach his desk because in his view it failed that test. It disappointed Pennsylvania pro-life advocates and surprised his foes on the other side of the question. Immediately, however, he set out to form a bipartisan legislative alliance that could craft and enact a bill that would stand the constitutional challenge that would inevitably come. (This one would, incidentally). The issue facing me that Friday, just days after I was on the job as press secretary, was to coordinate the release of information surrounding the governor's signature on the state Abortion Control Act. In the process, I quickly was introduced to press ire when announcements that had been anticipated all day were not delivered to the Capitol newsroom until late in the day.

I had hoped to have the statement in the newsroom by mid-afternoon that Friday. But the governor worked late into the day on the exact phrasing of his statement. No one dared rush him when he wasn't ready to be rushed. Governor Casey had a well-earned reputation as a very deliberate decisionmaker. (He was once introduced to a banquet audience by his friend and former counsel at the auditor general's office, the impish Bill Smith (now deceased, unfortunately), this way: "The governor is the only man I know who takes an hour and one-half every Sunday night to watch *60 Minutes*." The governor roared, I'm told.)

The governor also was a man who placed great premium on his choice of words and their exact meaning. I assumed that was a trait he developed during his student days under Jesuit educators at Scranton Prep and the College of Holy Cross. He knew what he wanted to say on most subjects. Truth was, he was his own best wordsmith, and he wasn't ever satisfied until he felt comfortable that the words he used were the words he wanted. So no statement from this governor was ready until he said it was. This one, of such personal and policy import to him, took him the better part of the day to edit and complete. The press corps couldn't do much but sit around, call me for a status report and wait; I couldn't do much more but to take their calls, try to calm them down, and promise the statement would be down to the newsroom as soon as it was ready. Neither party, I must confess, was too happy with the state of affairs. But neither the press nor I could do much about it either. The statement finally reached the newsroom about 6 P.M. that evening. They threw a caustic "Thanks a lot, Vince" at me. I don't think they meant it, and I can't say their agitation wasn't at all warranted. Not only did this mean that the capital news corps had to work overtime to file their Friday night stories. Most of them also had to spend a portion of their weekend reaching out to sources and writing a Sunday piece amplifying on the reaction to and consequences of the governor's action. So much for the weekend care and feeding of the capital press corps in my first significant encounter with them in my new role.

One other aside about Bill Smith, before I move on. Bill and Jack Lynch were the governor's most valued and trusted aides in the auditor general's office. They were not only his top aides; they were among his best friends. And Bill, with that irreverent humor of his, could make the governor laugh like no other I knew. I particularly remember an incident that occurred when the staff golfed with the governor on primary election day, 1990. We played our round at the Scranton Country Club before we were to convene at a downtown hotel that night to welcome what we all anticipated would be an easy renomination victory over a nondescript challenge from the aforementioned Phil Berg of Montgomery County. Bill, understandably, was paired in the same foursome with the governor. As he told the story, Governor Casey hit his tee shot on the first hole, a converted par 3, into a sandtrap to the right of the green. Not a good start. Bill told me the governor grumbled all the way to his ball about having to hit out of a trap on the very first hole and on only his second swing of the day. When the moment of reckoning was confronted, Casey not only got the ball out of the trap, he put the damn thing in the hole for an impressive birdie 2!! "Phil Berg is in deep, deep shit today!" Bill deadpanned as the ball rolled into the cup. Smith told me Casey had a good laugh at that as well.

My second on-the-job indoctrination came just days later when a riot broke out at Camp Hill State Prison across the Susquehanna River from the Capitol. It was a Monday afternoon, I recall, when the disturbance occurred. Prison officials, however, reported the insurrection quelled within a matter of hours and the prisoners were returned to their cells. We thought we had dodged a very nasty, perhaps dangerous situation.

The governor had on his staff at the time a speechwriter named Emerson Moran, who as a New York reporter covered the Attica prison riot in New York State. That riot ended tragically with a number of deaths in a violent shootout after days of irreconcilable stalemate. Emerson recalled that a special study commission reviewed the uprising and had concluded that one of the most grievous mistakes in that episode was the decision of New York governor Nelson Rockefeller to inject himself personally into the negotiations with the rioting prisoners before the uprising was put down.

"Keep the governor distanced from the riot until the prison is back under control," Emerson counseled Chief of Staff Brown and me in a brief conversation late that day as news of the insurrection circulated through the Capitol. It was good advice.

With the prison ostensibly back under control, Casey met the next day with Corrections Commissioner David Owens and institution officials to thank them publicly for the skill and professionalism they exhibited in returning order so quickly. Or so we thought. Hours later, Casey and Brown soon were off to Scranton for a Lackawanna County Democratic dinner that night. I was home about 6:30 P.M. or so when my telephone rang. It was my deputy, John Taylor, calling. "Vince, they've started another riot at Camp Hill," he told me.

"John, you've got to be kidding," I said more in hope than in earnest.

"Sorry, I'm not. They've taken over the prison again," John repeated.

"Oh, shit," I muttered to myself as I headed immediately back to the Capitol.

The situation this time was much worse than the uprising of a mere forty-eight hours ago. Not only had the inmates taken control of much more of the institution, they were burning down as much of the place as they could. And they held six prison guards hostage. It was serious. We could only pray this did not turn deadly.

General Counsel Jim Haggerty and I met up in the governor's office. We received a report from the prison. This riot was not going to be so easily put down. The inmates' control of the institution was much stronger than the day before, and the flames from the grounds were getting stronger and higher by the moment. State police were assembling and the Pennsylvania National Guard had to be called to secure the perimeter. Jim called Scranton to alert Brown and the governor.

"We'd better tell the governor he should leave that dinner immediately and return to Harrisburg," I suggested to Jim.

It was not the easiest recommendation for Jim to pass on. After all, the governor was home with his friends and a lot of Scranton pride was on display that night. But we both knew there really was no alternative. Most important, the responsibility of the office demanded that the governor return immediately (nor did he demur once informed of what was transpiring). Equally important were the potential repercussions of any delay. The last thing the governor needed on his watch was a second prison riot within twenty-four hours. News footage of him sitting at some political dinner

120 miles away while a prison across the river from the Capitol was burning would have been devastating to his capacity to govern for the remainder of his first term, and probably just as devastating if not more so to his prospects for reelection just about a year away.

"We'd better get the governor out of there now, and on his way back immediately," Haggerty told Brown. Within minutes the governor was on his car phone confirming his departure and asking for a full assessment of the situation.

The governor came immediately to the Capitol where he and we remained until after midnight. Jack Tighe and David Stone were dispatched to Correction Department offices on the perimeter of the prison to give the governor his personal eyes and ears to events. I spent most of the night fending off reporters asking for the governor's comments, reactions, plans, any straw of information they could grasp at in their 24/7 news cycles. I remembered Emerson Moran's admonition. I strived mightily (and successfully, I might add) to keep the governor publicly on top on the situation but disengaged from direct involvement in negotiations and discussions with the inmates. It was a difficult balance because we knew the inmates were monitoring events over the radio. The more the news report raised the governor's presence, the greater our concerns grew that the inmates might attempt to leverage the guards they were holding in custody to demand the governor's personal involvement. Fortunately, the situation never came to that.

After midnight, we moved our monitoring station to the governor's residence. We encouraged the governor to get a few hours sleep. Jim Haggerty, Jim Brown, and I would take shifts during the night hours keeping abreast of developments; and we intended to wake him immediately if it were necessary. He went to bed about 2 A.M., as I recall. Developments at the prison pretty much went into limbo until the early morning hours. A state police assault team was assembling outside the prison walls, at the ready to enter when the order was given. Jack Tighe called the governor about 6 A.M. The state police command requested authority to enter the prison and retake the institution. The officers were armed, but their ammunition were pellets designed to stun, not kill any inmate who resisted. The assault force was prepared to take back the institution section by section, if necessary. But the commanding officer did not want to give the inmates any more time than they already had to prepare for the assault that they had to know was coming.

The governor came to the telephone immediately. He reviewed the situation with Tighe and gave the go-ahead. Within two hours, the prison was back under control of the authorities. No lives were lost; no prisoner escaped from the grounds. The only damage that was suffered was damage to prison property itself, a small consequence to pay considering the potential harm that could have occurred to human life and the surrounding community.

In the aftermath of the riots, important questions had to be asked and the administration had to answer. Principal among the questions, of course, was how it came to pass that a second riot could break out within twenty-four hours after the first disruption had been declared contained. That was the ultimate question. Casey ordered Corrections Commissioner Owens to conduct a full investigation and pledged to make public *all* details in the report Owens would submit. David Owens was a solid professional and a good man. But this inquiry would cost him his job. The first report released by Commissioner Owens had either altered or omitted information damaging to Camp Hill prison officials. The credibility of the report, the commissioner, and by implication, the governor, was called into immediate question. Casey would have none of it; he ordered that everything be disclosed fully.

But there was a price to pay for withholding some of the information in the first place. It was in this context that Jim Haggerty called David Owens to discuss the chain of events. I was with Haggerty in his office at the time of the call. David told Jim at the conclusion of the conversation that he was prepared to offer his resignation if that were necessary. "If you offer it, David, the governor will accept it," I heard Haggerty say. Owens did; and so did the governor.

Shortly thereafter, I was dispatched to the newsroom to release the missing information and announce that Governor Casey had accepted Commissioner Owens's resignation. I was immediately surrounded by reporters, television cameras, and television lights and peppered with questions about the investigation, the governor, Commissioner Owens, and whether the resignation was forced or not. It was the typical media mob scene you see on evening news shows time and time again. Only this time, I was the fella in the middle of it all, the fella who had the explaining to do. I remember watching the 11 o'clock news that night and thinking, "So that's what that looked like. Wow, what a circus!!"

The next day I was traveling with the governor in Philadelphia. He was on the car phone with James Carville. Before Carville earned his national reputation as a political consultant par excellence by getting Bill Clinton elected president in 1992, he first earned his reputation as a political consultant even worth looking at by getting Casey elected governor in 1986. Casey and he were very tight. When Casey had political or governmental problems, Carville was inevitably the one he turned to for counsel and strategy. When

Carville spoke, Casey usually listened. There were very few (not even a Bill Smith) in whose judgment Casey trusted almost without reservation. As we were riding to the governor's destination, I heard him conclude his conversation with Carville by saying, "He's right here." With that, he handed the car phone to me, saying, "James wants to talk to you."

Since I was not active in the 1986 campaign, I only knew Carville by reputation. And his reputation was that of a brutal, hard-driving, confrontational, in-your-face political strategist who spared nothing, certainly one's feelings or dignity, least of all, to achieve his political ends. "The Ragin' Cajun," he was called, and with good reason. So when I took the phone in hand, I didn't quite know what to expect.

"Yes," I said. It was the first time we spoke directly. There would be another significant conversation we would have about a year and a half later. But for the moment, I hoped my apprehension would not be transparently obvious.

"Hey, you're good," Carville told me. "Damned good. You really handled yourself well last night." He had watched the newscasts of my encounter with the newsroom crew the night before. He thought I commended myself very well under the pressure of the moment. It was, I must admit, good to hear. Personally, I was gratified. More important, in terms of my ability to represent him and his administration in public forums, I knew it was an important expression of confidence for the governor to hear. The significance of that at such an early stage of my tenure was not to be underestimated.

"Thank you," I said to James, as I handed the car phone back to the governor.

Chapter 20

★★★★★★★

The Budget from Hell

I don't know if 1991 was a good year for wine, but I do know it wasn't a good year for governors across the country, Pennsylvania's Robert P. Casey included. Call it a case of a failing national economy. That's exactly what it was—and for governors in most states across the country, it posed a host of fiscal problems so serious that it made their public lives just simply terrible. In Pennsylvania, the problem was compounded by the fact Governor Casey had just been reelected to a second term by over a million votes, the largest margin of victory ever bestowed on a successful gubernatorial candidate in state history, and the principal theme of his reelection campaign was that things had never been better in Pennsylvania. The premise, obviously, was that there was more of the same to come in a second Casey term.

Between 1987 and mid-1990, the economic climate and fiscal strength of Pennsylvania state government had seldom been better, so much so that Casey was able to fulfill his 1986 election campaign pledge not to raise taxes in his first term with no difficulty at all. But now, entering the second term in January of 1991, with the national economy in a virtual free-fall since late October–early November of 1990, the administration was looking at a very unsettling fiscal predicament. Revenues were down, entitlement expenditures were up, and a large deficit loomed. The combination of circumstances made a tax increase for fiscal 1991–92 all but inevitable. The only question was exactly how substantial the increase was going to be.

The governor knew from June of 1990 that the Commonwealth's condition in the new fiscal year beginning July 1 would be very precarious, at best. With a stable national economy, things were going to be very, very tight. If the economy spiraled downward as the national economic indicators suggested it would . . . well, that spelled disaster. The governor went to great lengths when he signed the 1990–91 budget to warn the public that hard times may be coming. The state of the economy heading into 1991 was just too fragile, he said. He was very straightforward in acknowledging that he could not repeat for his second term the pledge he made for his first, that taxes would not be increased. We would just have to see how the economy played out over the next year, he said in his budget-signing remarks. Casey

Governor Casey delivers his second inaugural address on a cold Tuesday in January 1991. He was re-elected by the largest margin ever afforded a candidate for the office in the history of the Commonwealth. There was little time to rejoice, however. Pennsylvania was in dire fiscal straits brought on by the national recession of 1990–91, and recovery efforts would consume the administration for the next eight months. Courtesy of the Pennsylvania State Archives, Harrisburg.

would repeat this warning throughout his fall campaign. The problem was that no one seemed to hear it because the admonition was drowned out by the "Beautiful Day in Pennsylvania" storyline of his reelection campaign.

And the economy did, in fact, turn for the worse. The downturn began in October, a month before the 1990 election. By the time the full impact of the decline had manifested itself in November and December, the election was over and landslide Bob Casey—no longer the "three-time loss from Holy Cross"—was preparing to be inaugurated to a second term.

A word about the reelection campaign. My role in it was nil, for good reason. The governor, prudently and judiciously, took great pains to separate his governmental staff and his political team. One worked for the taxpayers, he reasoned. Their efforts shouldn't be diluted by campaign considerations. The other worked for his reelection. They should not be mixing public policy functions with political decisions. Sometimes the lines became blurred, but we all worked very steadfastly to maintain that distinction and, for the most part, we succeeded.

The unspoken rule was that I answered only questions the media raised concerning government and policy. The campaign press secretary, Karen Chandler, a Carville protégé, answered questions about politics. I made it a point at the beginning of each day to talk with Karen to be certain she knew what I expected to occur from my perch. She, in turn, would keep me abreast of what the day was expected to bring from hers. In that way, we not only succeeded in keeping our functions separate, we also usually avoided being blindsided from the other direction. The arrangement worked. Not one question of conflict was raised throughout the campaign.

At one point, however, Chandler was criticized in the press by anonymous Casey aides, who were quoted as saying she was much too aggressive and irritating in her style and approach to the job. Carville had recruited her to serve as press liaison and spokesperson for the governor's local tax-reform initiative, so it wasn't surprising that Carville came immediately to her defense. "That's just some people in the press office who are worried about protecting their jobs once this campaign was over," he told the reporter who wrote the anti-Chandler critique in the first place.

Carville's quote irritated me. I knew none of my deputies were involved in the campaign to even speculate on the job Chandler was doing for the governor. I also knew I was not the source of the quote. What I didn't know was if Jim Brown and/or the governor harbored the same suspicion as Carville. I immediately went down to Jim's office in the governor's suite.

"Jim, I read Carville's quote, and I want you to know if there's the slightest notion on the part of the governor, or anyone close to him, that I was the source of those quotes criticizing Karen, well you can have my resignation immediately," I said flat out. "I understand loyalty; and I don't backstab colleagues anonymously. But if there's any suspicion that I or anyone in my office was the source, then I should go. You just tell me."

Jim said not to worry. He suspected he knew who the real source might be (as did I); that neither he nor the governor thought it was me or the press office. "Why do people do these things?" he wondered aloud.

I could only answer, "Insecurity, I suppose." Nothing more was said, at least to me, about the matter.

But during the second Casey term, I had reason to think of the incident often. By and large, the Casey staff was free of the backstabbing and undercutting that frequently went on in a political environment where people tend too often to advance their own ambitions at the expense of one or more of their colleagues. It was good to be a part of such a loyal and relatively ego-free team, frankly. However, word frequently reached me from the second floor, inner confines of the governor's office that Karen was a constant and vocal critic, often directly to the governor himself, of how the press office was functioning. Why people do that, I still don't know. "Insecurity, I suppose."

Heading into Bob Casey's second term, the 1990 reelection campaign proved to be the easiest part of the equation. Now came the hard part, the part that Adlai Stevenson, so prescient forty years earlier, called "Governing!" Robert P. Casey's governing skills were about to be tested as they had not been tested before.

The exact dimensions of the fiscal problems confronting the Commonwealth started to define themselves almost immediately after the governor's reelection. What started out in October as a bottoming out of the economy became a plummet by November, with no end in sight. Governor Casey huddled with his fiscal staff and senior advisors in late November. I sat in primarily to be educated for my press functions. A deficit of major, perhaps massive proportions appeared inevitable, stretching to the neighborhood of $1 billion, and that was after the governor cut current spending by a quarter of a million dollars and reduced new departmental budget requests by another $750 million. (The governor also ordered that top executives in his administration, including himself and his senior staff, go without pay for one biweekly pay period.) The dimensions of the problem were becoming clearer with each passing week. How to break the news to the people of Pennsylvania who had just been told things were never better was another matter. But try we had to.

We took our first crack by having the secretary of public welfare write a memorandum to the secretary of the budget early in November officially advising him that the state's medical assistance program for the poor was running a serious shortfall that could not be reversed. We made the memorandum public. A few weeks later, the budget secretary sent the governor a communication that the worsening economy had thrown projected revenue collections totally out of kilter. We made that public as well. It was not the best of timing, however, because few people were paying attention to matters of state during the Thanksgiving/Christmas holiday season.

The rubber hit the road in January with the governor's second inaugural. The sober reality of a multimillion-dollar deficit and a massive tax increase was beginning to set in. The situation was compounded by the fact the governor decided a salary increase for his office and his cabinet, enacted by the General Assembly in 1987 to take effect in 1991 with the inauguration of a new or reelected state administration, whoever that might be, would be implemented on schedule. It was not the best confluence of events. It didn't help that Mark Singel, Casey's lieutenant governor, was quoted publicly as saying the governor would have been better advised to defer on the salary increase.

Meanwhile, the Republican opposition was piling on and enjoying it. After all, they had just been whipped by one million votes. If payback was their aim, they didn't ignore their opportunity to take their best shot. The firestorm had started. It reached a peak when the governor presented his budget to a joint session of the General Assembly calling for about $1-billion-plus in new taxes, House Republicans hooted him. "If you have a better idea, let's hear it," the governor snapped back in an off-the-cuff reaction. It was going to be a long, hard summer in Harrisburg.

Casey, who valued his integrity as much as he loved his family, was having his veracity questioned—by his political opponents, by editorial pages across the state, and by citizens in their everyday conversations. It did not sit well with him. I remember one particular lecture I received from him as the flames were blazing around us. The press clippings and the public criticism were wearing on him. He and I had just finished a brief conversation in the governor's office when he admonished: "We need to fight back hard on this. We're not going to take this with equanimity!"

I recognized it immediately for what it was—a direction for me to abandon my relatively low-key, detached approach to relations with the press corps and fight back aggressively on his behalf. He wanted me out there punching for him, and he wanted to be certain I understood. I did. But a confrontational style did not fit me well. So I doubt I ever satisfied him sufficiently on that score.

On more than one occasion early in the budget ordeal, I began to wonder if I were going to survive in my job. It was not out of the question, given the intensity of the moment, that I could be removed or replaced. Sure enough, with no advance notice, one day in February a call came that made me think I was on my way out the door, if not out of the administration entirely, certainly the press secretary's office. The governor had just submitted his annual budget to the General Assembly. The direct line to my phone from the governor's suite one floor below rang. It was the governor's personal secretary, Bonnie Seaman.

"James wants to meet with you here in a hour," she said. She was, as always, very polite. But she was also very direct. "Bring the clips with you!"

She meant, of course, James Carville, and she was referring to the special set of press coverage clips we had been compiling since the fiscal difficulties became apparent to all. "I'll be there," I responded. It would be my first direct conversation with Carville since we talked briefly on the phone of the governor's automobile in the aftermath of the Camp Hill prison riots. Here it comes, I thought. I'm probably out of here. I remembered all too well the role Carville played in the staff reorganization three years earlier. But the more I pondered the prospect of that meeting, the feistier I became. To hell with it, I said to myself. I can't be what I'm not. If that's what they want, they can have this job. I don't want it if the governor doesn't want me in it.

I trekked down the one flight of stairs to the governor's inner office at the appointed hour. James hadn't arrived yet. I waited for him at the conference table in the governor's private office.

"What's going on?" he asked as he entered. "The governor's calling me, the family's calling me.

"What's going on?" I responded: "They're calling me, too!" as I gave him my summary and assessment of the situation from my perspective. "They're having a hard time with it," I said.

James asked to see the clips, which he thumbed through. When he finished, he looked at me and said, "Don't they understand that you can't raise taxes and stay popular?" Then the clincher: "You're doing a good job. Keep it up. This will pass."

Our meeting was over. I had not been axed. Why I don't know. I do know that if James had said I should go, I would have been gone. No more discussion. I doubt if James, who went on to much greater fame and fortune in national politics, would remember our lonely encounter over the governor's conference table that day in 1991. I never forgot it. And, as he suggested, I kept "it" up the only way I knew how.

The budget took eight months to settle. They were the most difficult eight months of my five years on the job. Taxes were raised about $3 billion. Democratic legislators took the view that if they were going to have to raise taxes, they were going to raise them enough to take something home with them—like more aid to education, more aid to colleges and universities, more programs that benefited their constituencies. Once the budget passed, time began to take its healing course. Casey regained his standing with the public. His integrity was on the road to recovery. The economy started to build again, sufficiently so that he reduced taxes twice before his term ended. One time around the tax track was enough for him. (I second the motion.) And when he left office, he turned a $500 million surplus and another $500 million in savings to his successor. I'd call that vindication.

Chapter 21

★★★★★★★

The Longest Week

If the tax and budget fight of 1991 were the longest, most contentious, and most demanding eight months of Robert P. Casey's tenure as governor—and in the context of his public endeavors, I believe they were—the five days he spent in New York City for the Democratic National Convention in 1992 would probably rank as a very close second. In retrospect, that shouldn't have been surprising.

Political tensions between Governor Casey and the presumptive Democratic nominee, Arkansas governor William Jefferson Clinton, had been building long before the Democrats gathered in New York City. It broke in the public arena with a crack Casey made to J. W. Apple, the *New York Times* chief political reporter, in a telephone interview before the April 1992 Pennsylvania presidential primary election. Apple had called to ask Casey how Clinton would fare in Pennsylvania. Casey, never a big Clinton fan, called him "a blip" on the political radar screen with no pockets of organized or deep support in the Commonwealth. The *Times* played the story page 1. The Clinton people read it. They didn't forget it.

I never asked the governor directly why he was so wary of Clinton. Bob Grotevant, my predecessor, told me he believed it had something to do with the impression Casey developed of the man during meetings of the National Governors Association. Grotevant told me he thought Casey found Clinton too smooth, too cute, and too slippery for his taste. Maybe too much of a party animal for his taste, as well, Grotevant suggested. For whatever reason, give the governor credit—he had the measure of the man's character early on.

By the time of the 1992 Democratic national convention, however, "Slick Willie" (as he was dubbed by the Arkansas press corps) had the nomination in hand, and after eight years of Ronald Reagan and four years of George Herbert Walker Bush, winning the White House—not character—was paramount to national Democratic leaders. That may say as much about them as it does about Clinton.

Casey had been at odds with those very same leaders for some time now over the issue of abortion on demand. His steadfast opposition to abortion had been aired any number of times in any number of public forums. The proposition was fundamental for Casey. He believed that abortion was wrong morally, wrong as public policy, and for the Democratic Party it was wrong politically because it was a direct contradiction with the rich tradition of the Democratic Party in speaking out forcefully in defense of the underprivileged, the oppressed, and the defenseless. And who, he reasoned, was more defenseless than the unborn child. It wasn't a question the National Democratic Party wanted to be asked; and it wasn't a question that it wanted to have to answer—certainly not at the coronation of its next presidential nominee.

Casey had asked repeatedly, both publicly and privately, for an opportunity to speak to the convention on the subject of abortion prior to his arrival in New York. Democratic Party leaders were having none of it. They simply refused to acknowledge the requests. Once he hit the Big Apple, Casey was determined to fix it so that they couldn't ignore him any longer. The governor gathered his staff in his hotel suite shortly after his arrival the Sunday night of convention week. He was going to send a letter to Convention Chair Ann Richards, the governor of Texas and a strong pro-choice voice in the party, asking again, this time in a public way, for an opportunity to address the delegates. He scheduled a press conference for the first thing Monday morning to make the letter public. A Democratic governor from a major state warring with his party at its national convention on the emotional issue of abortion was *news* by any definition. Tony May and I worked into the wee hours faxing notices of the news conference to the national and state press corps scattered at hotels throughout the city.

Casey's insistence in pressing the abortion issue didn't sit well with the Pennsylvania delegates. His rupture with the Clinton people and the national party leadership already had a price to it. The hotel accommodations at the New York Sheraton where the delegation was assigned were modest at best. In addition, the delegation was seated in a balcony position in Madison Square Garden, the convention hall, far removed from the floor and center of activity. And now the governor was going to rub even more salt into the wound by pressing ahead with his anti-abortion rhetoric. When the governor appeared to greet the delegates Monday morning at a welcoming breakfast, he was received politely but coolly. Icily might have been more like it. His appearance and his remarks were short and to the point. The delegates didn't complain that he was so brief.

By contrast, U.S. Senator Harris Wofford was embraced warmly and enthusiastically when he appeared before those very same delegates. Harris went to the U.S. Senate in 1991 by virtue of an appointment from Governor

Casey after the airplane crash that tragically claimed the life of incumbent Republican John Heinz. In November 1991 he defeated Pennsylvania's Republican superstar, former governor and U.S Attorney General Dick Thornburgh, to fill out the remaining three years of the Heinz term.

Senator Wofford had Governor Casey—as much as any single person, probably more so—to thank for that, although most of the convention delegates really had no way of knowing just how true that was. Casey committed a very large part of his personal prestige, time, and energy to raise the money Wofford needed to be competitive in the race against Thornburgh. I remember sitting in a suite in Seattle, Washington, during the National Governors Conference earlier in 1991 and listening to James Carville (who was directing the Wofford campaign at the governor's insistence) tell Casey that he had never met a nicer man than Harris Wofford, but that he was going to get annihilated in the Thornburgh election because he just didn't understand the nitty-gritty of politics and wasn't going to have the resources necessary for a creditable campaign.

"He will," Casey assured Carville. "I'll see to it." And he did. He pitched the National Democratic Governors Association—"Thornburgh has a glass jaw," Casey told them. "He can't take a punch. But we're going to raise the money to hit him, and Wofford is going to win." He was greeted with polite skepticism. But he kept plugging. He pitched the National Democratic Senate Campaign Committee, which also was less than convinced, and he tapped his private preserve of contributors (always from a campaign office and telephone a few blocks away from the state Capitol). Thanks largely to Casey's efforts, Wofford raised the money to get on television. Thornburgh and the national Republicans may have expected a coronation of their own; instead, what they got was a campaign and Wofford delivered a knockout.

To his credit, Wofford always acknowledged publicly and privately the great debt he owed the governor for his effort. But having beaten Thornburgh, Wofford became a darling of the Pennsylvania Democratic Party in his own right. He also was on very good terms with Bill Clinton, so much so that he had at one point been on Clinton's short list of potential vice-presidential nominees. So when he appeared after Casey at the delegation breakfast meeting, he was welcomed emotionally and physically by the delegates. It was duly reported back home. So all the signs were there from the very beginning that this was going to be a very, very long week for Casey and those associated with him. It was … it certainly was.

Casey held his first press conference of the week at the appointed hour Monday morning. It was packed. The governor publicly repeated his request to the convention leadership for an opportunity to speak and chided the alleged party of inclusion for shutting out the chief executive of a major political state. The press conference made some first-day news. Some national correspondents called for interviews. The governor was booked on C-Span for later that week. National Public Radio scheduled him for a live interview after the opening evening speeches. (Unfortunately, he never made it on the air until well after 1 A.M. because the opening keynote speeches by U.S. Senator Bill Bradley—of basketball fame—and former U.S. Representative Barbara Jordan—of Nixon impeachment fame—ran on interminably.)

His difference persisted with the Democratic Party leadership as well. The convention parliamentarian wrote him a perfunctory letter denying him for the first time on the record the opportunity to speak. The stated reason: Convention rules stipulated that only those who were pledged to support the nominee of the party could address the assembled delegates. Casey was clearly at odds with the presumptive nominee and party platform plank on abortion. Request denied. The next morning, Tuesday, before the adoption of the platform that night, the pot boiled over, and before the day was done, I thought there was a good chance Casey was going to send me home.

The governor held still another press conference repeating his request to speak on the abortion issue before the platform vote. Whether the reporters were tired of this same song from the governor, or whether their true philosophical leanings on abortion were coming to the fore, I can't say. But I do know the session soon deteriorated into a literal shouting match between Casey and the press corps. He reprimanded them for showing their biases on the subject; they, in the way they posed their questions, chastised him for being so intransigent and single-issue. It wasn't a press conference; it was almost hand-to-hand combat. I looked for the most discreet but quickest way to bring this confrontation to a halt and did in the most tactful way I could.

When the proceedings concluded, Casey walked off the stage in that determined, purposeful way of his. His back clearly was up. Jack Tighe and I and one of his sons-in-law (Bill McGrath, as I recall) followed him back to his hotel suite. "All right," he demanded. "Let's hear it. What'd you think? Sometimes you just have to let them have it back."

I suspected by virtue of the fact that he even asked the question, he was not pleased with his demeanor at the press conference. I know I was the first to respond. "Governor," I remember saying. "You may send me home for this. But that didn't go well for you out there. Not at all." I continued: "No one articulates the pro-life case more eloquently or more persuasively than you. But that's when you speak calmly, thoughtfully on the subject.

You do that and people listen. Today, you were angry and your anger doesn't play well on television because television is a hot medium. You're going to come off on national television tonight as an angry man. And you and your message will suffer as a consequence. This is not going to be a good day for you." (When you think of television as a "hot" medium, think Vermont governor Howard Dean and his political implosion before the cameras after the Iowa Democratic caucuses in 2004.) Neither Jack nor Bill McGrath disputed directly what I had to say. But they didn't exactly reinforce my view, either. Essentially, their assessment was that any negatives from the morning press conference were likely to pass by nightfall.

They were right, but for the wrong reason. Later that day, Ross Perot announced he was dropping his independent race for president. Casey and abortion instantly were old news in New York. Perot was a hot political commodity; his third-party candidacy had been getting a lot of attention from the punditry. His withdrawal put a new dynamic on the 1992 presidential contest against incumbent Republican George H. W. Bush. (Perot eventually reversed himself, reentered the race and may, in fact, have cost President Bush his reelection that year, but that interpretation still is subject to dispute.) But for that day, Perot's greatest value was to wipe Casey and his anger off the evening news that night. It was, in my view, a blessing.

Two events later that day reinforced for me the wisdom of my counsel to the governor on the damage he could suffer in losing his temper. The first was when I was approached by KDKA-Pittsburgh radio talk-show host Fred Honsberger while the Casey press conference was under way, but before the hostilities had escalated. "I don't agree with the governor on his position," Honsberger told me. "But I do agree he should be allowed to speak to the convention." He asked me for an opportunity to do a one-on-one, face-to-face interview with the governor for broadcast to his afternoon audience back home.

I pitched the interview to Casey after our conversation in his hotel suite. The interview was not without risk, I acknowledged. Honsberger was a frequent critic of the governor on a host of state issues—most particularly the tax and budget battle of 1991. But, I reasoned, I believed he'd play this issue straight and the governor would have an opportunity to make his case again. Casey agreed. He was as calm with Honsberger as I'd seen him and as eloquent as usual. The interview went off without a hitch. It was one of the better ones he gave that week.

Later that day, Mary McGrory, a national icon in political journalism, came into the suite to interview him for her *Washington Post* column. Mary was decidedly pro-choice, but I believe her sense of fair play was offended by the autocratic hand of the convention leadership in dealing with Casey. I suspected she also found the governor's Irish spunk reminiscent in many ways of her own Irish upbringing. It was clear as they conversed the two had a connection. Casey was his usual persuasive self. His tone and approach were very much under control for the most part.

At one point, however, his voice started to rise and his agitation level with the treatment he had received began to well up again. McGrory and Casey were seated at the dining room table in the governor's hotel room across from each other. I was against the wall, facing McGrory. Casey's youngest son, Matt, was against the other wall, behind McGrory but facing the governor. As the governor's tone began to get a little testy, I looked over and saw Matt. He was gesturing to his father, pumping his palms down. The message was clear: Cool it, Dad, Matt was signaling. Stay cool. Don't lose your temper. Casey caught Matt's signal. He regained his composure and the moment passed. This interview also went well.

What follows is admittedly editorial. The opinions expressed herein are mine and mine alone. But they accurately reflect the impressions I formed in observing firsthand the proceedings of the Democratic National Convention in New York City in 1992. They did not leave a good taste in my mouth about my chosen political party, the direction it was taking and the people who were leading it.

For Robert P. Casey, governor of Pennsylvania, this was not a convention; it was more like a siege. It was for Mrs. Casey, too, since she invariably accompanied her husband to his press conferences and his public appearances in the convention center. Every time the governor appeared in public to press his case on the abortion issue and for the opportunity to speak to the delegates, activists from the Pennsylvania delegation were there to register their displeasure and disdain, not so much in words, but by the contorted expressions on their faces and their body language.

These women were self-proclaimed defenders of free speech, inclusion, and compassion. But their definition of free speech and inclusion applied only to those who agreed with them. It was my first personal and up-close encounter with their philosophical hypocrisy. A number of them had a hand in a serious affront to the governor and Roman Catholic Democrats in advance of the convention. They had manufactured campaign-button-size pins with a head shot of Casey imposed on the body and religious garb of Pope John Paul II. The buttons were to sell at five dollars each, supposedly to defer convention expenses they might incur. The buttons were beyond the pale of proprietary, political or otherwise. Yet when the organizers came under the justifiable criticism they did from Pennsylvania clergy across a wide range of religious affiliations, their response was, "Lighten up, everybody. It was just meant in jest." I never saw the buttons in New York. But the bad manners of this group of "ladies," using the term generously, should not be forgotten and should be condemned once more. Consider it done.

Convention organizers went out of their way to embarrass the governor as well. The night the platform with its abortion-on-demand plank was adopted—the plank Casey wanted to oppose in his request to address the convention—Casey was surrounded in his convention seat by placard-waving women and their "We're pro-choice" signs. It was a scene ready made for pictures, and the news photographers and television cameramen flocked like lemmings to record it. To his credit, Casey smiled that dignified smile of his throughout. He wasn't about to give these zealots the satisfaction of showing any discomfort by their presence around him. Another outrageous example of bad manners and total intolerance from the abortion-on-demand crowd. The governor had to be seething inside, but he was not about to sink to their level. Score one for him on the dignity meter.

The ultimate indignity came in the speeches leading up to the adoption of the platform with its abortion plank. Among the speakers was Kathy Taylor of Hershey, Pennsylvania, both pro-choice and Republican. She, in fact, was a principal surrogate for Republican gubernatorial candidate Barbara Hafer in Casey's 1990 reelection campaign. Nothing epitomized the rigid, lockstep approach of the Democratic Party leadership and their complete sellout on the abortion issue than the appearance of Kathy Taylor before the Democratic National Convention. In their world, national Democratic party leaders would not allow the Democratic governor of Pennsylvania to address the presidential nominating convention of his party because he differed with them on the issue of abortion. But a Republican woman from Hershey could because she did not. Nothing was so premeditatedly designed by convention organizers to publicly slap Casey and other pro-life Democrats from Pennsylvania in a national forum than the Kathy Taylor appearance.

I could understand the slights convention organizers rained down on Casey—the second-rate hotel for the Pennsylvania delegation, the seating in Madison Square Garden far removed from the convention podium and the television cameras, the affronts on his repeated requests to speak. As the governor was fond of saying, "Politics is a contact sport. It's not a place for the faint of heart." He challenged the party and its presumptive nominee. There was going to be a price to pay for that. But what I could not accept then, and cannot accept now, is the rank hypocrisy of the Democratic leadership and the interest groups that drove them. This convention and this party were run by a bunch of brownshirts who would have been right at home in Hitler's Germany. I grew up in a Democratic Party framed in the rich and noble tradition of Franklin Roosevelt, Harry Truman, and John F. Kennedy. This was not the party I knew. I saw the direction it was taking, and the people who were leading it there. I didn't like what I saw. Our son Tom had it right when he told me one day far removed from the convention: "Dad, as long as you're working for the governor, I'll stay a registered Democrat. But once you're done, I'm gone. These people and the politics they practice are an embarrassment." I couldn't disagree. If this was how the Democratic Party was going to conduct itself under the stewardship of Bill Clinton and his running mate, Al Gore, I wanted no part of it. A decade-plus later, I still feel the same way. I still resent the influence of so-called Clinton Democrats on the national Democratic Party and the style of deceptive, disingenuous politics they practice. I am puzzled that so few others are as well. Me, and my solitary voice and vote, well . . . I'll still take Harry Truman any day.

With the Clinton/Gore nomination secured and with their message on hardball politics delivered in a variety of aforementioned ways, the Clinton folks suddenly shifted gears. They tried to calm the waters with the governor. They had given him a taste of how they handled dissent and dissenters. Now, I'm certain, their aim was to bring him back to the fold if they could. Harris Wofford stopped by Casey's suite the day after the platform vote to visit his friend, the governor. "Tell him to take Al Gore's telephone call," Wofford said to me as he walked by.

"I will," I responded. "But you might want to suggest it to him yourself since you're on your way in to talk to him." Wofford nodded.

Sure enough, as Casey later related it, Gore did call. He wanted to assure Casey that neither Clinton nor he had any hand or foreknowledge in the Taylor appearance, the governor said. Casey said he told Gore: "I can accept that. But somebody did. Who might that have been?" Gore said he didn't know, but would get back to the governor on that. If that call ever came, I never heard about it. The best intelligence I could gather was Kathy Taylor's name was given to convention organizers by Kate Michelman, president of the National Abortion Rights Action League (NARAL).

As for Gore . . . well, none of us had reason to know it then, but as hindsight and subsequent events eventually established, it was our first introduction to Clinton/Gorespeak. Clinton/Gore Democrats were masters at avoiding or bending the truth when it suited their personal or political objectives. It was a technique they employed in their drive to the White House; it was a technique they employed while in the White House; and it was a technique Gore employed as he raced frenetically to succeed Clinton in the Oval Office. Gore did invite two of Casey's sons—Bob, the incumbent auditor general seeking reelection, and Pat, making his second race for Congress in northeast Pennsylvania—to speak to the 2000 Democratic Convention about their father. They did, for three minutes in nonprime time. I can't help but think Gore was just four years late in his gesture, and I can't help but wonder if the invitation would have been extended at all if Pennsylvania were not so critical a state to his election bid. I must also admit I was a little disappointed that the Casey sons accepted the offer, but I understand it wasn't my call.

I had one brief discussion with the governor while in New York on the subject of who knew in advance about Kathy Taylor. "James had to know," I said, referring to Carville. Casey rejected the notion immediately, saying he didn't think so. Personally, I believe the governor just couldn't bring himself to accept the idea that this close political advisor and personal friend would have permitted that to happen. My view was and remains that there was no way, given Carville's role in the Clinton campaign, that he could not have known. To have known about Kathy Taylor and not stopped it as unnecessary speaks volumes about Carville and the win-at-any-cost mentality he and his kind bring to politics. At the very least, a call from him to the governor directly that week to apologize, if not for Clinton, then for himself, certainly was in order given the history between the two men. I believe if he had called, I would have heard about it eventually. I didn't. So I can only conclude the call never came, though they may have talked about it privately in later conversations that I may be totally unaware of. After his political celebrity grew, Carville wrote a book of some national prominence called, *Stickin'* . . . *The Case for Loyalty*. Looking back on New York in 1992, I can't help but conclude that this was one case where he failed miserably in holding himself up to that standard of conduct.

As confrontational as the week was, Casey had his moments of good exposure. A national C-Span interview went well. On his way out of the studio, he was greeted by former California governor Jerry Brown, himself an outcast of the Clintonites for the aggressive campaign he waged against the nominee in several presidential primaries across the country. "They should let you speak," Brown told Casey as they passed each other.

"You, too," Casey replied. The newspaper *Newsday* invited Casey to write a piece for its op-ed page entitled, "What I Would Have Told the Democratic Convention If I Were Permitted to Speak." He took them up on their invitation. The article essentially reiterated the governor's compelling proposition that by adopting a position of abortion on demand, the Democratic Party was turning its back on its long and ennobling history as defender of the downtrodden, the underprivileged, and the defenseless. Publication of the Casey piece led to other requests for interviews convention week, and other requests for similar pieces in other national newspapers across the country.

Casey may have been shunned, insulted, harassed, and ignored by his party. But he may, in fact, have received more exposure by its refusal to let him speak than he would have received by allotting him some time. Ten minutes in non-prime time, before what undoubtedly would have been virtually an empty hall, would have settled the issue of fairness. The governor's admonition would have gone unheard and unnoticed. In fact, the media reports probably would have focused on the fact that the governor insisted on being heard, yet when he spoke no one came to listen. He might have been embarrassed. As it was, he left New York with his dignity intact and his reputation enhanced.

Twelve Minnesota delegates wearing Casey for President buttons over the slogan, "We want our party back," cast their ballots for him during the presidential nominating vote. Those votes will remain forever on the record as a part of the Democratic National Convention of 1992. I suspect the support of the Minnesota delegates also was of great comfort and solace to the governor for the very difficult week he had endured. As for me, well, I just left town on the first train out of New York the morning after the presidential and vice-presidential acceptance speeches. I dropped my materials off at the office in the Capitol and headed home. That afternoon, I played a solo round of golf. The next morning, Toni, the kids, and I headed for a week's vacation at the Delaware shore. I can't recall ever needing or appreciating time to decompress more.

The tensions between Clinton and Casey remained very much in play though fairly under the surface during the subsequent general election campaign. The governor never worked actively for Clinton, though he never publicly opposed him, either. He did studiously avoid an appearance at the Lackawanna County fall dinner in 1992 because Mrs. Clinton was going to be there. He did not want his presence to be misconstrued as a tacit endorsement or acceptance of the Clinton candidacy. His absence was duly noted in the media and, I should add, by the Clintons who still had their own set of issues to settle with the governor. They did, one way in particular.

The day before the presidential inaugural, Clinton held a luncheon for the nation's governors as part of a unity celebration. Casey was invited and, of course, he accepted. Clinton was going to be president in twenty-four hours and Casey believed he owed it to the dignity of the office to be there. The lunch was held at the Library of Congress. Casey was seated at a back table as far removed from the president-elect as one could be and still be in the same room. In sports, you'd call it the cheap seats. His luncheon companions were the governors of such heavyweight states as Idaho, South and North Dakota, and similar environs. Another Democrat at the table was outgoing Maryland governor William Donald Schafer. Schafer had endorsed President George Bush for reelection just days before the balloting. He, too, had a price to pay for his disloyalty. Casey, who had turned down an invitation to speak on abortion to the Republican National Convention, also was approached about an endorsement by former New Hampshire governor and former Bush White House chief of staff John Sununu. He respectfully declined. He was at odds with his national party leadership, but he was not about to desert his party and the principles it once espoused.

Leaving the lunch, Casey chuckled to himself as he reflected on his distinguished group of luncheon companions. The Clintons certainly have long memories, even when they win, he observed. "Course," he mumbled with a smile on his face, "I did call him a 'blip on the screen' on the front page of the *New York Times*. I may not have forgotten that, either." As the governor was fond of saying, "Politics ain't beanbags."

My own contacts with Clinton were almost nonexistent, I admit, and what follows is subjective on my part. I was introduced to him once at the staff party of the Democratic Governors Association the night before the 1990 NGA summer meeting in Selma, Alabama, adjourned. It was more than coincidental, I believe, that Clinton and former Ohio governor Richard Celeste were usually the only two Democratic governors to party regularly with the staff at these affairs every year. Their friends said they were simply being sociable. Their not-so friends said they were simply party animals. Not so coincidentally, both had to confess publicly to marital infidelities during their terms in office. I was introduced briefly to Clinton in Selma by Bob Walters, an old friend and Harrisburg colleague who had gone on to write first for United Press International and then the Scripps/Howard chain out of Washington. We met by chance at the NGA and used the occasion to renew acquaintances over dinner.

Bob was the first to tell me of Clinton's reputation for womanizing. The subsequent public record seemed to bear Walters out. Bob took me over to Clinton at the staff party and said, "Bill, I want you to meet Vince Carocci, an old friend and Bob Casey's press secretary."

Clinton smiled in that disarming way of his and said, "Bob, it's good to see you again. Vince, it's nice to meet you," He was gripping my outstretched hand at the time with his other hand on my shoulder as if we were about to become close friends and confidants. "You work for one of the really good governors," he said. Of course that was before Casey talked to Johnny Apple of the *New York Times*. I didn't realize it then, but for about four minutes that night in Selma, Alabama, I was on the receiving end of the famous Clinton charm offensive. It was, on first encounter, rather hypnotic. But the more I watched it from a distance, the more it struck me as transparent.

There's no denying the Clinton presence on the American political scene, but I don't have to embrace it. In my lifetime, only Richard Nixon made more of a blot on the office of the presidency than William Jefferson Clinton. Oh, for Harry Truman! The national Democratic Party today needs more of his kind more than ever before.

Chapter 22

★★★★★★★

Health: The Issue That Just Wouldn't Go Away

Considering his athletic abilities, it's surprising that Bob Casey would be haunted by his health throughout his two terms as governor. He was a stellar high school athlete, skilled enough to make the Holy Cross basketball team in college in the early 1950s when "The Cross" (with the likes of Tommy Heinsohn and Togo Palazzi) was very competitive on the national scene. He was also, I'm told, more than a pretty fair baseball player. If he had serious problems with his health prior to his inauguration in January 1987, it was a fact known to very few people. But once he became governor, Casey was bedeviled with a variety of ailments that would trouble him throughout his tenure.

The first was quadruple heart-bypass surgery his first year in office. He recovered nicely, however, and missed but a few weeks from his desk. The most striking aspect of that event was the weight loss he experienced after his surgery. Most people didn't consider him heavy or overweight when he took his first oath of office in 1987. But his much thinner frame following the bypass surgery was a rather dramatic contrast when set alongside the girth he carried in his inaugural pictures. This was the only visible side effect to the bypass surgery. When he returned to the Capitol, he went back full steam.

The surgery, however, set the stage for persistent rumors about the state of his health. It was no accident the rumors seemed to intensify every time the governor faced a political crisis. I can't remember how many times during the '91 budget fight that I had to deny rumors he was going to resign for health reasons.

I remember one exchange with Pat LaForge of the *York Daily Record*, which went something like this:

"I hear the governor is really sick and is on the verge of resigning," LaForge inquired.

"Not true," I responded. "Just not true."

"Are you saying the governor is not having serious health problems?" the reporter pressed on. "I'm told he is."

"Not that I'm aware of," I said. "Who told you, and what did he tell you?"

"I can't say, but have you asked him about it?"

"No, I haven't. And I don't intend to. I see him every day and he's working very hard at getting this budget settled."

"Why won't you ask him?" the reporter pressed on. "You must be aware of the reports making the rounds about his health. Is he?"

"He may be," I said. "But I'm not going to ask him to dignify this rumor mongering by anonymous sources. Let these heroes who are spreading this garbage come forward and publicly make their claims. Then I might respond. But until they have the courage to put their claims about his health on the public record, and identify themselves in the process, we're not going address the subject. He's on the job every day."

There were any number of variations to that conversation after the governor's bypass surgery. Joe Serwach of the *Harrisburg Patriot-News* asked me directly if the governor had cancer because his frame seemed to be getting slighter, and his color was not as good as it might have been. "I don't know that. I'm not going to ask him for you, and this conversation is off the record," I responded angrily. "If you have some medical evidence or authority to raise the subject, then you can raise it. But until you do, you should be ashamed to even speculate on something like that."

I advised Casey about the conversation. I alerted him that if Serwach ever got the chance, he probably was going to ask him about it. Sure enough, he did. The governor had just completed a public event at the Residence when Serwach saddled up to him nervously. "Governor," he said, "I'm sorry but I have to ask you this question: Do you have cancer?"

Casey never blinked. "No, I do not," he responded. "And frankly, I don't see why I should even be asked the question. How do you deny a negative? Just to answer the question gives it some validity. But the answer is no—emphatically, no."

It was no surprise the next morning to pick up the *Patriot-News* and read a headline across the top of the page: "Casey Denies He Has Cancer." The denial was enough of a basis to print a story reporting on the rumors circulating about the state of the governor's health. His gaunt physical appearance only reinforced the buzz.

Those of us who worked with him on a daily basis realized he didn't look as healthy as he might have. But we also saw him every day working long, long hours at being governor. He never missed a beat. The fact is that he wore many of us out with the stamina and endurance he applied to being chief executive. There would be many an evening when he convened members of his staff around his desk in the governor's office discussing an item of state business long after normal working hours had passed. Most times, the sessions would end when Mrs. Casey called on the private line to tell him to get back to the Residence and let the rest of us go home. Thank heavens for Mrs. Casey. It was always a delight to be in her presence. But we never appreciated her more than when she made one of those calls, or else we would have been there hours more than we were.

Amyloidosis. Until I went to work for Governor Robert P. Casey, I had never heard of the word, much less the disease. But it was an affliction that took the life of Pittsburgh mayor Richard Caliguiri much earlier than his time on this earth should have been. It also claimed the life of Erie's legendary mayor Lou Tullio a short time later. Both were good friends, personally and politically, of Bob Casey.

So it was curiously coincidental that Governor Casey should become the third member of this amyloid trifecta. In November of 1990, after his reelection, heading into his second-term inaugural, three years removed from quadruple-bypass surgery, the governor was diagnosed with a form of this genetic disease for which there was no known cure. Given its long-term prognosis, amyloidosis made the governor's bypass look like a walk in the park. His condition was detected in tests taken during a routine physical examination at the Hershey Medical Center. Mrs. Casey and he deliberated when to share the news with their children—not an easy task to be sure because of the hereditary nature of the affliction. Once that bridge was crossed in April 1991, the governor had to decide whether (and how) to share the news with the people of Pennsylvania.

It all came about on very short order the following June. I was called into Jim Brown's office and informed there would be a press conference the next day in the governor's reception room. I was told about the ailment and directed to announce the next morning, close to the given hour, that the governor would be holding an important press conference that afternoon. The Cabinet and the senior staff were to be briefed at 11 A.M.—two hours before the news conference. The governor and his Hershey doctors were to be present in the reception room. A third specialist from Sloan/Kettering Clinic in Minnesota was to participate by telephone hook-up. Until then, the lid was to be on. That, it proved later, was to be somewhat of a mistake.

The next morning the press office put out an alert of a major press announcement by Governor Casey. Immediately, and understandably, the retirement talk fired up again. I did, as I recall, tell every reporter who called that I could not speak to the subject of the press conference before the appointed hour; but I could say retirement for health or any other reason was not a part of the announcement. That's as far as I would go. But some others, it turned out, had no hesitation to go farther. As Brown briefed the Cabinet and senior staff, I was called from the conference room to take an urgent call from a Philadelphia television station producer/reporter. "Vince," he told me urgently. "I've been told the governor suffers from some rare disease called amylo-something. I can't spell it. I've been told it's serious but not immediately life-threatening. Will you confirm at least that much for me?"

"Al," I said. "I'm sorry, but I can't help you even if I wanted to. You'll just have to wait for the governor's press conference." Some cabinet members were not in town but had been briefed by Brown by phone. One of them, apparently, could simply not honor the request to stay quiet so the governor could make the announcement in his own words, in his own way. I recalled Jim's question when Karen Chandler's work was challenged anonymously in the campaign: "Why do people do that?" I still don't have an answer.

At 1 P.M., the governor and his doctors from Hershey Med made their appearance at the press conference. The specialist was piped in from Minnesota by conference phone. Governor Casey announced that he had been diagnosed with amyloidosis, a disease virtually unknown to most Pennsylvanians before the Caliguiri and Tullio cases. The disease was so little known, so recently identified, in fact, that you couldn't find mention of it in Encyclopedia Brittanica as near back as twenty years. Essentially, it's an abnormal buildup of protein around a critical organ like the heart, liver, kidney, or spleen to such a degree it impairs normal function. In Casey's case it was detected primarily around the liver. The critical card was that the disease always was fatal. There was no known cure.

Casey's staff stood silently throughout the reception room as the governor made his condition public. There were some encouraging elements to the announcement, minor though they were. The governor's affliction was diagnosed as familial amyloidosis, the least aggressive strain. Mayors Caliguiri and Tullio, by contrast, suffered from primary amyloidosis, the most severe strain as the name implies. The doctors all went to great lengths to assure the assembled press contingent that the governor's illness was caught in an early stage and that it was very different from the Caliguiri and Tullio conditions. With proper treatment and diet, he should suffer no physical malfunctions that would impair his ability to function as governor; and yes, they were most confident he would serve out his term with no difficulty.

The press conference went on for some time, naturally. Governor Casey said if it weren't for the persistent rumors about his health, there probably would have been no reason to hold the press conference in the first place. But he acknowledged the reality of the rumor mill and concluded that the people had a right to know about his condition, and that he owed them that explanation personally. "The issue isn't how I feel," he said. "It's how I'm functioning, and I'm functioning just fine!"

We all gathered in the governor's inner suite once the press conference concluded to assess how it had gone. It didn't take but a matter of minutes for us to realize this story and questions about the governor's continued health were going to persist for as long as he held the office. An AP story out of Philadelphia, filed minutes after the main piece out of the Capitol, quoted other doctors from the city in a manner which, if not totally contradictory, certainly raised some skepticism about the prognosis of Casey's doctors. The implication of the Philadelphia piece was that this condition could be more serious than either the governor or his doctors acknowledged. It noted that Caliguiri had said essentially the same thing about his condition, and that he died before his term was finished.

That piece, more than any other item written or broadcast about the Casey news conference, set the backdrop to the story that never quite vanished. And because it was reported throughout the state so soon after the Casey announcement, it was an item that we could never quite correct or modify. Though we tried. Jim Haggerty, as the governor's general counsel, called AP management in Philadelphia almost immediately to advise them their story was off base and thoroughly inconsistent with what was said by Casey's doctors—doctors who had examined and treated him through the years. The Philadelphia doctors had not; how could AP put more credence in what they had to say versus the comments of the physicians who had treated Casey, Haggerty demanded? (There was a reason for Haggerty to make the call as the governor's general counsel. In such matters, a protesting press secretary easily could be dismissed. Lawyers who might be in a position to file suit against an offending party could not.) The AP stood by their story, but agreed to add Haggerty's comments and protest for balance.

Regrettably, the damage had been done. No amount of catching up could change the initial impression. The word on the governor's condition was out, all right. But thanks to the Associated Press, my alma mater, the word was that Casey suffered from this disease for which there was no known cure; that it already had killed two of Pennsylvania's most prominent mayors within years of each other; and that, finally, independent doctors believed the governor's condition could be more serious than he portrayed it. It was not how we would have painted the picture if we had controlled the printing presses. But we learned a valuable lesson about the power of first impressions and the capacity of the Associated Press at the time to shape them by its quick transmission capability. It would hold us in good stead two years later.

The details of Governor Casey's dual heart and liver transplant in 1993 have been chronicled innumerable times. There was no better account, and with no more authority than by the governor himself in his book *Fighting for Life*. The book was perfectly titled. Throughout his public career, Casey waged one fight for life after another: First, there was the fight for his political life in the face of three rather convincing defeats for the gubernatorial nomination of his party; second, the fight for his very own life challenged, initially, by a quadruple bypass, and then, more ominously, a life-threatening affliction requiring a combination heart/liver transplant that had been rarely performed anywhere in the world; and, finally, of course, his eloquent, courageous, and steadfast fight for the right to life for the unborn child. It is worth reading and I'm not about to repeat the details of any of those sagas here. Rather my purpose is to recount the events surrounding the transplant as I lived them then and recall them now.

I was called down to Jim Brown's office one June day in 1993 and told to be at the Governor's Residence that evening. The governor had a major medical announcement to make the next day, and he was meeting with his team of doctors that night. I was to be present for that meeting, and to set in motion the mechanics and logistics of alerting the press for the session the next day.

We gathered in the living room. The governor and Mrs. Casey were there, of course, but none of the children, as I recall. Also present were Jim Haggerty, Jim Brown, Jack Tighe, and me from the staff and Dr. John Fung, one of the two principals from the transplantation team of the University of Pittsburgh Medical Center (UPMC).

I learned for the first time that night that the governor and Mrs. Casey had met privately in Pittsburgh weeks before with Dr. Thomas Starzel, head of the UPMC transplantation staff. The details of how Governor Casey first came into contact with Dr. Starzel are long a matter of public record. Catherine Baker Knoll, the state treasurer at the time, gave the governor Starzel's book on transplantation. Ultimately, he called Dr. Starzel to acknowledge receipt of the book and thank him. Casey asked Starzel whether there was anything that could be done to counter the amyloidosis. Starzel researched the issue and called back a short time later saying a liver transplant might work if Governor Casey could withstand the rigors of the surgery. This exchange led to their clandestine meeting in Pittsburgh, where the decision was made for the governor to undergo testing to determine whether he might qualify for a liver transplant.

That's what the governor was going to announce the next day, a Friday: He was headed to the Pittsburgh University Medical Center the next morning

(Saturday) to undergo two days of testing for a possible transplant. The governor expected to return to Harrisburg on Monday, hopefully with a favorable prognosis.

Our purpose that evening was to review the governor's proposed statement and walk through the logistics of the press conference the next day. One aspect of the discussion will remain with me forever. The governor's proposed statement opened with the declaration that he had some "good news" to report. He then shared the details of how he came upon Dr. Starzel and his team, what was to happen over the weekend, and what the next steps would be assuming the prognosis was favorable. When the content of the statement was opened for discussion, I recall I was the first to comment. "Governor," I said, "I understand where you are coming from. But I wonder if you can call a liver transplant operation, 'good news.' Wouldn't something like 'hopeful' or 'encouraging' be more appropriate to the situation?"

The governor, always the English major that he was, and with that first-class Jesuit education that he had, didn't need to be counseled very often on his choice of words. Besides, this was personal. "If you were in my position," he told me, "believe me, you'd think it was good news!" The discussion continued for a bit more. Mrs. Casey and Jim Haggerty seem to share my notion. From a family perspective, the prospect that a transplant could reverse the governor's amyloidosis certainly was good news. It might even be characterized as great. But to the public, the prospect that their governor was confronted with a major surgery of this sort, and all the questions inherent therein as to his continued fitness to serve, might not seem all the "good." It was agreed "good" would be dropped and "encouraging" would be substituted.

The meeting lasted for a couple of hours, wading through the details of the testing, the press conference, and what the doctors might say. The doctors at Hershey had been brought into the discussion. It was essential that nothing they might say would inadvertently contradict the comments and procedures of the new team of doctors from Pitt. Travel plans to and from Pittsburgh over the weekend were reviewed. We were as ready as we could be to make this announcement public.

The preparations for the press conference were set in motion the first thing Friday morning. Once my notice of the 1 P.M. event was out, I stopped taking telephone calls from reporters. I wasn't about to discuss anything in advance of the governor's own announcement. So I spent most of my day, before and after the press conference, speaking with the public information director and other staff at the Pitt Medical Center, preparing for the governor's arrival the next morning and the brief encounter he would have with the press corps there.

The press conference in the Capitol was the major event you would have expected it to have been. Lots of reporters, lots of cameras, lots of buzz. The governor announced he was to be tested to determine his suitability as a candidate for a liver transplant. Dr. Starzel spoke of how the transplant could reverse the amyloidosis, and what the prognosis for the governor's long-term life might be, particularly his capacity to continue to serve out his term. Dr. Fung, the lead transplant surgeon, spoke to what a liver transplant operation would entail and for how long the recuperation period might be.

Remembering our experiences with the Associated Press and the third-party doctors they interviewed in the amyloidosis announcement, Jim Brown decided to take a gamble Friday morning. He suggested we bring an AP reporter in and share with him on a strictly embargoed basis the outline of what the governor was going to announce. Jim, to his credit, recognized that the AP story would be the first to reach the general public, and that public perception would be determined by the tone and facts contained in the AP report. Jim wanted to be certain the AP got it right the first time around. Good for Jim, shame on me, because it was my job to think of such things. But at least we covered the base. The AP reporter came to Jim's office for the pre-press conference briefing. He was free to file the story as soon as the governor went out to the reception room with his doctors. That's exactly what happened. The AP got it right from the get-go. And we were never trying to catch up with the story the rest of the day, thanks to Jim's quick thinking.

The press conference went on for as long as there were questions to answer. I remember one reporter asking the governor how he felt about all of this. "I think it's good news," he responded. "It's the best news I've had in a long time. From where I sit, believe me, it's good news. Really good news!" We had convinced the governor to substitute the word "encouraging" in his prepared statement. But "good" was the word he wanted to use. And he did. Never argue with an English major from Scranton Prep and the College of the Holy Cross.

We left for Pittsburgh early Saturday morning on the state plane. Mrs. Casey accompanied her husband, of course. Jack Tighe and I were the staff aides on the trip. Jack, a Pitt grad, was a gubernatorial appointment to the University of Pittsburgh Board of Trustees. He was handling the logistics with Pitt Medical center officials. I was along to work on press arrangements and handle their inquiries throughout the weekend. I fully expected to return on Monday. I carried only enough clothes for three days. If the governor and Mrs. Casey had more luggage, I never saw it. So far as I can recall, Jack was similarly packed. There was nothing of which I was aware to suggest foreknowledge on anyone's part that the governor's stay in the hospital was going to be longer than the weekend.

AP photographer Paul Vathis met us at the state terminal to photograph the governor's departure. I remember the governor took Mrs. Casey's arm to steady himself as he climbed the two or three steps to enter the cabin. He paused at the cabin door, turned, and flashed a confident "V for Victory" sign before entering. With those formalities out of the way, the plane taxied to the runway and we were off.

The conversation on the plane was very casual. Most of it, as you might suspect, dealt with the media coverage of the governor's press conference the previous afternoon. The consensus was the coverage was very accurate and very fair. We all felt we had achieved our objective from a media standpoint. Certainly, we weren't dealing with any unsubstantiated rumors or allegations. I know the governor felt encouraged that perhaps some remedy was available to arrest his deteriorating medical condition brought on by the amyloidosis. Mrs. Casey, I suspect, was grateful for the prospect that better days might be ahead for her husband, but certainly apprehensive over the medical challenge he faced in the meantime.

I had spent most of Friday afternoon on the telephone with the medical center information director finalizing media arrangements for the governor's entry into the hospital. I also sat in on a conference call with the Pitt Medical Center president, who for the first time raised the possibility that the test results, particularly tests on the heart that would be critical to his ability to withstand the rigors of a liver transplant, might require the governor to remain in the hospital. Jack Tighe said we would have to deal with that if it happened, but we were not going to speculate about it beforehand. Until that conversation, my antenna was fixed solely on a liver transplant. For the first time, I came to understand that it was the heart tests that would be critical to determining what happened next.

Sometime Friday afternoon, I received a telephone call from Dennis Roddy, political writer for the *Pittsburgh Post-Gazette*. He asked if there were any way he could get a one-on-one interview with the governor before he entered the hospital. I knew the governor liked Dennis. I also was convinced Dennis liked the governor. I suspect their shared Irish heritage . . . there's that kinship, again . . . played no small part in their connection. I also expected Dennis's piece would be fair. Most important, since Pittsburgh was where the governor was going for testing, why not exclusive quotes in the Sunday *Pittsburgh Post-Gazette* where the action was taking place? I raised the prospect with the governor. He agreed. The only question was how could we get Roddy and the governor together without the rest of the awaiting media becoming aware. We concluded the best possibility would be to slip Dennis in the governor's auto at the Pittsburgh airport. He could conduct the interview with Governor and Mrs. Casey on the way to the hospital. The only condition was that Dennis had to be dropped off a couple of blocks before the governor's limousine reached the hospital entrance, where we knew the media would be assembled en masse.

The plan worked. Dennis had exclusive quotes from both Caseys, which the rest of the media picked up the next day. The essence was that the family was optimistic about the governor's prospects for better health. Most important from a political perspective, the governor proclaimed himself extremely determined, with or without the transplant, to serve out his second term, which still had eighteen months to go. Roddy's story played big on the front page of the *Post-Gazette* the next morning. It amplified and personalized the comments the governor made in the hospital foyer before being admitted for the tests, particularly the angle of serving out his term. The governor and Mrs. Casey talked with the press for about ten minutes before going into Admissions. A press center had been set up by the medical center staff at a nearby auditorium. We pledged to give the media ample notice once there was some definitive information to impart. Little did I know how soon that would be.

Jack and I met with the Pitt medical staff over lunch in a conference room off the Pitt Medical Center's presidential suite of offices. Included in the group was Dr. William Follansbee, the lead cardiologist on the test team. The results of the first tests were not very good, he informed us over soup and sandwiches. He said he doubted whether the governor could leave the hospital without jeopardizing his health. The unspoken fears of the day before were now quickly becoming reality. We all immediately grasped the full implication of what we had just heard. This was no longer just a question of transplant testing. The situation now had transformed into a very case of life and death for the governor.

Amid the flow of conversation, I suggested to Jack that we have a briefing that afternoon. The press was aware in general of the testing the governor was to undergo, but the possibility that the governor was not going to leave the hospital was something no one had even speculated about publicly. Before the liver transplant question could be addressed, the condition of the governor's heart suddenly had vaulted into the primary health consideration. My judgment was that we needed to have a public discussion of the criticality of the heart tests almost immediately to brace the public for what we feared might be even worse news to come the next day. Jack agreed; Dr. Follansbee was quite willing and prepared to participate. We scheduled the briefing for mid-afternoon.

The session went as well as could have been expected. Dr. Follansbee did a magnificent job in laying out, almost in laymen terms, the reasons for testing the heart first, and the implications those results would have on the governor's potential as a candidate for the liver transplant. He did so without shading the truth; nor did he minimize the significance of the test results. What he didn't do was engage in any speculation or theorize as to what the initial results might be suggesting. Appropriately so. If the tests had been conclusive, we all would have had to deal with that set of facts at the Follansbee briefing. At that point, however, the results were only partial and suggestive. From the very beginning, we were committed to a course of full disclosure, but only disclosure of information dictated by the facts. We weren't there yet, and we weren't about to engage in an exercise of hypothetical "what ifs?" The Follansbee briefing that Saturday afternoon was consistent with our policy: It established the stakes of the heart test results without triggering any premature speculation about immediate dangers to the governor's life. There the matter rested for the overnight reports, and appropriately so.

Our worst fears were confirmed the next morning. I went to early Mass Sunday morning at the Cathedral in downtown Pittsburgh, which just happened to be near our hotel. I knew if I didn't make Mass before the day started, chances were very good I was not going to get there at all that day. And given the potential of what we were dealing with, this was not a good day to miss Mass.

Jack must have alerted Jim Brown overnight, because Jim and Deputy General Counsel Dick Speigelman flew in on a commercial flight first thing Sunday morning. We all soon learned the tests confirmed that the governor's life was at high risk if he left the hospital. Amyloid deposits had formed around his heart muscles and had virtually shut off blood circulation to the rest of his body. A fatal seizure could come without warning. The doctors recommended that he remain in Pitt Medical Center for safekeeping. A liver transplant was still a possibility; but only if he received a heart transplant first.

We made preparations for the announcement from the medical team. We also made preparations to set up temporary offices in vacant medical center space so the governor could continue to administer to the duties and decisions of his office, even though he was in a hospital room under close medical watch. The doctors explained the medical situation to the press. The governor's capacity to function was not impaired at the moment, they said, but the condition of his heart brought on by the amyloid buildup was too severe to permit him to move too far from the medical center. He would be placed on a list for a heart/liver transplant; meanwhile, he would be monitored from the hospital.

I read a statement that the governor had approved expressing his concurrence in the advice of his medical team, and his confidence that the ultimate outcome would be just fine. He thanked the people of Pennsylvania for their support and now he asked them for their prayers as he confronted this ordeal. How long this arrangement would be acceptable politically was a question to which we had no immediate answer. This much was certain: Short of resignation, which Governor Casey would never contemplate, this was the only arrangement we had available to us. The news of the governor's continued hospitalization was so startling and of such magnitude, the media had no time to explore the governor's fitness to continue to serve. It also would have been a bit crass of them to raise it so quickly. Those questions were going to come, I was certain. For now, we had just bought ourselves another day.

As a measure of protection, however, the governor agreed to talk over the telephone that evening with Russ Eshleman of the *Philadelphia Inquirer*. Russ was the only reporter he would talk to directly that day—or for some time to come, as it turned out. Russ, we knew, would be fair. And the governor needed some vehicle to sound a public expression of his mood, his fitness and his ability to function from the hospital. I slipped the governor's telephone number privately to Russ. I gave him a time to call. The conversation went off as scheduled. The governor was his usual, determined, and upbeat self. He fully intended to carry on, he said. We had bought at least a day before the drumbeat over resignation would start. I was certain it would, but for now, the public needed time to digest the news that their governor was going to be hospitalized for an indefinite period of time. We would deal with those other questions as they arose.

Jim, Jack, and I met with the governor and Mrs. Casey in his hospital room about 5 P.M. to discuss our operational logistics before we called it a day. Jack and I would remain in Pittsburgh on the health watch. Jim from Harrisburg, Jack and the governor in Pittsburgh, would confer daily as often as necessary to deal with the governmental issues. I remember the governor was very explicit in his directions to us. He wanted to be very forthcoming about his situation and developments as they occurred. "This is the public's business," he said. We also determined that while we on staff would continue to represent him on matters of state, details on the medical situation were to be in the sole purview of his team of doctors. We would be kept informed and we would consult with them prior to any announcements, but the information and the medical prognosis were to come from the doctors, and only the doctors. I remember the governor's direction to us as we were leaving his hospital room for the evening. "Forward," he said. "Forward" it was; I just didn't know where "Forward" was going to take us. The answer would come before the day was out.

Jim Brown and Dick Speigelman flew back to Harrisburg that night. Jack and I returned to our rooms at the Holiday Inn, just a few minutes walk from the hospital. Jack ordered a hamburger and fries from room service. I believe I had the same. We reviewed the day's events, planned how we were going to approach business the next day, and then broke for the evening. Or so we thought.

I know I anticipated the governor would be on the telephone the next day conducting matters of state. He just wasn't the kind to pull back, hospital confinement or not. I expected to be fielding calls all day about what he did, with whom he talked, what he decided, and why. Meanwhile, we had other decisions to make about the availability of the doctors and what they might say while everything medical was on hold pending the availability of a donor heart and donor liver. As fate would have it, we never had to confront those issues.

The telephone rang in my room about 10 P.M. It was Jack Tighe. "Showtime," he said. "They think they have a donor. Let's go."

Jack had been called by the medical center staff. A potential donor had been identified. The governor was at the top of the waiting list for a donor heart and a donor liver. Tentatively, the surgery was set for 6:00 the next morning. The governor's children were being flown in to Pittsburgh through the night to be at their father's bedside. Jack and I had to get to work on the proclamation transferring power to Lieutenant Governor Mark Singel when the governor was wheeled into the operating room. The language of the transfer had been finalized earlier that day by Deputy General Counsel Dick Speigelman. We had no idea we would use it so quickly.

Working with the director of the medical center public information staff, it was decided there would be no advance notice of the surgery. Rather we would release a press statement first thing Monday morning announcing that the governor had been taken to surgery after transferring the powers of his office to Lieutenant Governor Singel. Medical briefings would occur throughout the day as developments warranted. Jack and I left the hospital about 2 A.M. for a shower, to return promptly to deal with the public notification.

I've read and I've heard about how the governor and his family spent the night waiting for the surgery to commence. That's really all I know because I did not speak to the governor, Mrs. Casey, or the children that night or the next day as the family waited for the surgery to be concluded. I did speak to Lieutenant Governor Singel at the lieutenant governor's residence at Indiantown Gap to alert him that the press statement was going out as soon as the governor went into the operating room. As I recall, we were apprehensive, but I could tell by the tone of Singel's voice that he was ready to take on the challenge for however long it was necessary. I must confess my mind was not so much on how the lieutenant governor would fare in the days ahead. My immediate concern was what this day would bring.

Sometime about mid-morning, Dr. John Armitage, the heart transplant surgeon, and his team of assistants appeared along with Dr. Starzel to announce the governor's heart had been replaced. Dr. Fung, the liver specialist, was at work replacing the governor's liver as Dr. Armitage spoke. It would be hours before the tedious liver surgery would be complete. But the first hurdle was crossed.

The rest of the day was one of watching and waiting. The press corps milled around the media center. Every movement was closely watched for news of developments. Jack and I walked over to the media center at midafternoon just to get some fresh air and a change of pace from the tedium of waiting. Before we knew it, we were on stage doing a briefing, even though we told the assembled journalists we had nothing, absolutely nothing to report on the governor's condition. Didn't matter. The media was starved for information. We spent most of the session recalling developments from the previous day and the governor's response or reaction to them. I have the tape. I watch it occasionally.

About 8:30 P.M. that night the doctors appeared to announce the liver transplant was completed; the governor, with his new heart, had endured the delicate procedure; he was taken to recovery where he would remain under very close monitoring for a few days. There were the to-be-anticipated questions about the nature and length of recovery and when, if ever, the governor could be expected to resume the powers of his office. The only definitive answer the doctors could give was that they expected the governor should be fully able to serve once his recovery was completed. But no one could predict how long that would take. The two headlines for the day: Governor Casey survived a rare heart/liver transplant; doctors say he will be fit to return to office. Considering the physical and emotional ordeal that Casey and his family had been through the last forty-eight hours, those storylines were very welcome, indeed.

Jack and I went back to our hotel for a good night's sleep. We had to man the temporary offices early the next morning and brace ourselves for the questions that were certain to come. The process we had worked out with the medical staff was for the doctors to conduct at least two detailed briefings each day for the rest of the week, even if there was nothing new about the recovery to report. Often there was not. I remember one early briefing Dr. Fung reported the governor had sipped on a Popsicle for nourishment. The press wanted to know the flavor. (I think it was grape.)

Anyone from the governor's staff was a ripe target for the news-starved media. Anytime Jack, I, or anyone else from the governor's office who happened to be in town appeared at the media center, we were besieged for on-camera or on-air interviews. My voice and face were becoming very familiar to the Pittsburgh population. Often the interviews bordered on the sublime. I remember one female TV reporter asking me Monday afternoon if I would make myself available for a live shot on the 6 o'clock news. I said I would. (After all, it was my job.) I waited for almost a half-hour in the hot evening air to accommodate the station. When her report finally arrived, she recapped the day's developments, turned to me, and asked, "Vince, how is the governor doing?"

I responded, "The doctors say just fine, so we're encouraged."

With that she turned to the camera, thanked me, and said, "Back to you at the studio." The whole episode lasted about fifteen seconds. I had waited around for almost an hour. Oh well, all in a day's work, I suppose.

That same reporter approached me at mid-afternoon the next day. She apologized profusely for the shortness of the previous evening's interview. Would I be good enough to go on camera with her for the 6 o'clock report that night? She promised we'd have more time to discuss the governor's condition. I said okay, not that a guarantee of time mattered. That night I appeared again about 5 P.M., as requested, in case the producers decided to move the report up. They didn't. Sometime into the 6 o'clock hour, they switched to her at the hospital. She gave her recap of the day's briefing, introduced me again, and said, "Vince, you all must be pleased with the news to this point."

"Yes we are," I said.

With that she said, "Thank you very much, Vince," turned to the camera, and declared, "That's it from here." Abraham Lincoln once observed, "Fool me once, your fault. Fool me twice, my fault." This was my fault.

We had a number of issues to deal with over the next couple of days. Prime among them was whether the governor received preferential treatment in securing a donor heart and liver so quickly. The organ transplantation unit in Pittsburgh, which just happened to be headed by a bishop (Episcopal, I believe), vehemently denied he had. And no one was able to produce evidence otherwise because there was none. Governor Casey was the only person in the United States needing both a heart and liver transplant the night a donor was located and, as such, was at the top of the transplantation list for the dual surgery. Those rules, I understand, have since changed. But they were the rules that were followed in the governor's case. He stipulated from the very first meeting he had privately with the doctors in Pittsburgh that he should receive no special treatment, whatsoever. And he wasn't!

The second question was whether the governor's surgery was covered by health insurance? It was, though I suspect it might have been a very close, close call on the insurer's part. A heart transplant was clearly a covered procedure. So, too, a liver transplant. But a dual heart/liver transplant? Those were so rare you could count them on one hand. A case clearly could have been made that this was an experimental procedure. Medically necessary, absolutely. Experimental? Perhaps, because they had been done so infrequently before. And the recipients had relatively short life spans afterward. There may have been only one living survivor in the world at the time. But the call was made that health insurance would pay—and would have paid no matter who the patient might have been. That, for all intents, settled that discussion. I did learn much later on that the operation was not the most expensive claim paid by the Commonwealth health insurance plan. A bone-marrow transplant several years earlier held that distinction. Incidentally, once the insurance bills on the procedure came in months later, the governor's office released the figures to the public.

So it went that first week. We maintained the media center for the full week and held to our daily press-briefing schedule. The medical news was reassuring. But there really wasn't that much to report. I suggested, and Jack agreed, that we invite the media in for a tour of our temporary offices. They were rather sparse with spare metal desks, filing cabinets, chairs, telephones, spare computers from medical center storage. I believed it would be good for the papers and television to carry pictures of the offices so that any misperception of luxurious or special accommodations would be dispelled at once. The Commonwealth was reimbursing the medical center at the region's prevailing floor-space rates so that was not a problem.

The tour achieved its purposes. Our facilities never became an issue. I do recall, however, that our good friend Dennis Roddy showed up for the tour with a tape measure in hand. He measured the square feet in my assigned office versus Jack's and found that mine was slightly bigger by a square foot or so.

"Dennis," I asked, when he pulled his measure out, "what in the hell are you doing?"

"Never you mind, Vince," he responded. "My readers have a right to know you have a bigger office than Tighe." I think he was needling Jack, although I can't be certain. I do know he reported the measurements in the next day's paper.

The governor's recuperation was slow but steady. There were a few bumps in the road. One night he apparently suffered from a severe case of chills, which the medical staff told me required treatment and monitoring but was not life-threatening. Fortunately, it passed in less than twenty-four hours.

Our schedule became fairly routine once the media center was shut down after the first week. Jack and I would man the temporary offices in Pittsburgh waiting to address any eventuality as it might occur. Jim Brown coordinated daily with Acting Governor Singel on matters of state back in Harrisburg. My biggest personal crisis that first week was one of grooming. I had but limited clothing with me, and one can only mix and match two sport coats, two shirts, and slacks in so many ways for so many days. Laundry I had to do myself in my hotel room. Toni solved that problem by sending out a suitcase and suitbag midweek with the state police detail that came to Pittsburgh to relieve the crew that was there.

By Friday, the situation had settled into enough normalcy that I could get home for the weekend. I hitched a ride back to Harrisburg with Mark McManus, our son Tom's roommate who was attending Pitt grad school while Tom was attending Duquesne Law. It was good to get home and clear my head. That was the pattern that held for most of the governor's stay in Pittsburgh. I would leave for Harrisburg Friday afternoons and drive back early Monday mornings. Charlie Lyons, Jim Brown's deputy, would come in to relieve Jack. The system worked pretty well. I was in constant contact with the Pitt public information staff throughout the weekend keeping abreast of the governor's progress and any media calls the medical center might be entertaining.

The word from the medical staff was almost without fail generally encouraging—slow but seemingly steady progress almost every day. We kept the media sufficiently informed, and the news was favorable enough to keep the coverage fair and unalarming. That was a big asset in those first weeks as the doctors reported daily on the governor's condition. We never attempted in any way to spin the condition in a certain direction. Truth is we really never had to.

I had no direct contact with the governor, or with his family for that matter, in the immediate days following the surgery. One situation required attention, however. The identity of the governor's organ donor became public knowledge. The *Pittsburgh Post-Gazette* cleverly matched the Sunday obituaries to the governor's transplant surgery and concluded correctly that the governor had received the heart and liver of a young black man from Monessen named Michael Lucas.

Michael Lucas literally had been beaten to death on the doorstep of his home in, it later developed, a drug case. The Pittsburgh organ-transplant organization had no option in the ensuing press clamor but to schedule a press conference with the donor's family for midweek. The purpose was to reaffirm the integrity of the organ-transplant system in southwestern Pennsylvania and to establish once again that no rules were skirted or preferential treatment given in the decision to assign the victim's organs to the governor.

Like the medical reports, that, too, was the truth. No rules were bent; no preferential treatment was given. I came to learn subsequently that if the victim's lungs had not been damaged so brutally in the beating, Michael Lucas's organs would have gone elsewhere. The doctors and the organ donor staff told me that someone in need of a lung and a liver was ahead of the governor on the transplant list. If the victim's lungs had been suitable for transplantation, they would have gone to the other person, along with the liver the governor so desperately needed.

Normally, there is no immediate contact between a donor family and a recipient family. But given the extraordinary visibility of this case, it became clear to me (and others) that the Caseys needed to express their gratitude to the Lucas family before that press conference. The question, "Have you heard from Governor Casey or his family?" was certain to be asked, I thought. "No" wouldn't have been a very acceptable answer. So I suggested that Mrs. Casey write a very private note from the governor's family for the transplant organization to deliver to the victim's mother. She agreed instantly. She and her children wanted the victim's family to know how much they appreciated their generosity in donating the organs. The only reason they had refrained from doing so was because of the transplantation protocols between families.

The note was passed on to the donor family prior to their press conference. I do not believe the question of contact arose in that environment. I simply wanted to be certain that if the question ever was asked at any time, we had the right answer for the right reasons. We treated the note as confidential. The Lucas family could make it public if they chose. The Casey family would not. We regarded it as a private correspondence between one wife and mother to another. That also was the right thing to do for the right reason, in my judgment.

Chapter 23

★★★★★★

Reflections, Recovery, Reentry

Looking back, a couple of events from our five-week stay in Pittsburgh still stand out in my memory. The morning a few days after the governor's surgery and his release from intensive care I answered the telephone in our temporary office space in the hospital. "Governor's office, Vince Carocci," I answered as I always did.

"What's happening in Harrisburg?" the voice on the other end of the line asked. It was the governor.

I attempted to gather my wits and my thought processes quickly. "Everything's fine, Governor," I said. "How are you doing? You sound pretty good for what you've been through."

He said he thought so, too. But he still wanted to know what was happening in the outside world, particularly the state capital. I thought to myself, the last thing I wanted to be doing at that moment is talking to this man about the goings-on in the state capital. He had just undergone extended, life-saving surgery. I'm not sure worrying about what's in the morning newspapers was part of his recovery regime. But he was just Casey being Casey.

I told him things were going fine in the Capitol. Lieutenant Governor Singel . . . *Acting* Governor Singel, really . . . had just signed a major workers' compensation reform bill, which was a significant legislative accomplishment and priority of the administration. I rattled off a few other news items of interest and then quickly attempted to pass him off to Jack. "I suppose you want to talk to Jack," I said. "He's right here."

"I will," Casey replied. "What else is going on?" His curiosity was still in command. I didn't necessarily have visions of a relapse. But just in case, I didn't want to be on the other end of the line if it happened. Fortunately, my fears were misplaced. He did just fine.

As he progressed through the recovery phase, the next issue we had to address was the matter of how to reestablish contact between the governor and the public. We had been reporting through the doctors on his daily progress. But no one had seen the governor since he entered the hospital weeks before. I fully anticipated the press asking us at some point that if the governor was doing as well as reported, why couldn't they visit with him, if only briefly. I wanted to head that off because while he may have been recovering according to medical measures, I couldn't imagine that his physical appearance in those early days would be reassuring to either the press or the general public. And first impressions were going to be critical, particularly in terms of his capacity or fitness to serve out his term.

So we decided on a mid-course strategy. The governor had begun initial physical therapy and rehabilitation. I suggested a crew from the state's Commonwealth Media unit be brought in to videotape the governor doing some rehab and release that to the media. We also could sit him down with a Commonwealth Media interviewer who would chat briefly with him about his surgery, his recovery, and his intentions.

We filmed the governor walking through the hall of the hospital to his therapy station in a sweat jacket, slacks, and trainer sneakers. It was the first time I had seen him since the evening before his surgery. He looked pretty good to me, all things considered, though his gait was understandably ginger. Commonwealth Media cameras filmed him walking, still very gingerly, to be sure, on a treadmill. They filmed him meeting with his secretary, Bonnie Seaman. And he did a brief interview as planned with a member of the Commonwealth Media staff. We released the videos as soon as Commonwealth Media could process them. The media accounts all mentioned that this was the first glimpse of the governor since his surgery and noted, rightly so, that what was released was released through the governor's office. But the visuals and the interview of the governor helped to establish his physical presence. Yes, he was up, about and breathing as the doctors had said. And, yes, he repeated his intention to return to the governor's office and serve out his term. That was sufficient for the moment.

The recuperation was relatively hurdle free for much of the governor's time in the hospital. Dr. Starzel was an aggressive recuperator. He wanted his patients up and about as soon as possible. So he pushed rather than coddled the governor. The governor responded because he had immense faith in Starzel's judgment. And why not, given the ordeal he had just endured?

Just how aggressive Dr. Starzel could be was impressed upon me midway through the recuperation. I was home for the weekend, as had become my usual practice since the recovery was proceeding nicely. Toni and I were out to dinner Saturday night at a local restaurant when I received a call from the executive detail at the Governor's Residence. They wanted me to know that the governor had left the hospital for a few hours that afternoon. Without any public announcement, he attended a summer picnic the medical center transplantation staff conducted annually at a neighboring park. His attendance was unannounced even to the transplant unit. They didn't know he was coming until . . . well, there he was.

It was a great afternoon to be out in the sunshine. I suspect the governor welcomed the few hours of fresh air, his first since he had entered the hospital in what seemed an eternity earlier. I was told he shook hands for a while, then sat in a chair enjoying the people and his environment. Then I learned the kicker.

Mrs. Starzel, some years younger than her husband, had a convertible she just adored. And she insisted that she drive the governor, top down, back to the hospital, much to the chagrin of his state police escorts. But once the governor and Mrs. Casey agreed . . . well, that's just the way it was going to be. So there was the governor of Pennsylvania, fresh from a double heart/liver transplant, cruising the streets of Pittsburgh one sunny Saturday afternoon in a bright red (or was it yellow?) convertible, top down, breeze blowing gently. A Kodak moment for sure, except for the apoplectic state police security officer riding anxiously in the rear seat and a second trailing in the executive car wanting the whole episode to come to an end quickly and safely!

"Did he [the governor] make it back, okay?" I asked the switchboard.

"Yes he did," I was told.

"How're Ray and Critch holding up?" I inquired, referring to Officers Ray Litzenberger and Ray Critchfield (the former had ridden with and the latter had trailed the governor in the executive auto on the return to the hospital).

"We think they're coming around," the officer at the end of the phone joked.

"Fine," I said. "Thanks for letting me know. Let's let it ride for the time being. If any calls come in tonight or tomorrow, get me at home. If not, I'll deal with it when I get back to Pittsburgh Monday morning."

Word of the governor's excursion didn't reach the media until sometime after my return to Pittsburgh. Thanks to my briefing Saturday night, I was able to confirm for my inquisitors the essential elements of the governor's foray to the picnic. I was asked why we didn't announce the visit. "We didn't want to spoil the picnic," I responded. "If the media had shown up, it would have become a circus. The governor wouldn't have wanted that. What it really means is that his recuperation is coming along just as the doctors would like."

I didn't mention that neither I nor anyone on the governor's staff learned about the picnic drop-in until after the fact. There was no reason for me to do that. It turns out some folks at the picnic took pictures of the event. The Pitt Medical Center public information staff secured some negatives, which we released to the Associated Press and the local newspapers. They showed a smiling, healthy-looking Governor Casey in sport shirt and slacks relaxing outdoors on a Saturday afternoon. One twist. He was wearing a straw hat to protect him from the sun (the kind Chi Chi Rodriquez wore on the golf course) and he rarely wore a hat. The next time I talked to him I told him he looked pretty sporting in that chapeau. He chuckled and said he thought so, too. Not exactly a Bill Smith moment, but it would do

The next outing we did announce. The transplantation unit was sponsoring a Night at the Ballpark at a Pittsburgh Pirates game one night shortly after the picnic. The point was to promote organ donations, and what better messenger than the physical presence of the governor as exhibit one. Dr. Starzel even wanted the governor to throw out the ceremonial first pitch. The governor wasn't quite prepared to do that, but he did agree to attend and be introduced.

That afternoon an officer with the security detail and I went down to the ballpark to stake out the area where the governor could walk by the press as he entered. We planned for him to greet the media and submit to a couple of quick questions. If it came off all right, it would be another boost to the public perception of the governor's recovery. If the governor stumbled or appeared weakened, however, it could have been a problem. There had been no clamor about resignation from the day he entered the hospital. We didn't want to start one now that he was approaching the day of his release. But if the doctors were quite comfortable he was up to the occasion, that was enough for he and Mrs. Casey. The ballgame it was.

We announced the time and place of the governor's arrival at the ballpark. I went to the stadium an hour and a half ahead of schedule to be certain preparations were as we discussed them. The Pirates had a baseball cap for the governor touting Major League Baseball's annual All-Star contest that was to be played next year in Pittsburgh. I gave him the cap as he got out of his car. He put it on and walked over to the press area, pronounced himself doing well, said he was glad to be at a ballgame on a beautiful summer night. As a kicker, he said he planned on returning to Pittsburgh next year for the All-Star game.

The governor shook hands with a few reporters as he made his way by. Our friend Dennis Roddy was one of them. Dennis came up to me afterward and exclaimed, "My God, Vince, his hand was warm! His hand was warm!" Dennis remembered previous handshakes when the governor's hands were stone cold due to poor circulation brought on by the amyloidosis. For him, it was truly a revealing encounter. "I really think he's going to make it," Dennis said to me. "I really think he's going to make it!"

Once again, another press encounter, authentic to its core, that reinforced the perception that the Casey recovery was on schedule. It was now becoming only a matter of time: Time for him to leave the hospital, time for him to return to Harrisburg, time for him to resume the powers of his office.

Governor Casey had one more trip to make from the hospital prior to his release. Dr. Starzel wanted to have an outdoor reception at his home to celebrate the governor's discharge. The governor wanted very much to have the opportunity to thank the Pitt staff for the care they provided him and the comfort they provided his family. We made the decision not to make a public announcement of his appearance because we wanted to avoid the media glare his presence surely would command. One local TV station did learn about the event, however, proving once again that it is virtually impossible to keep the travels of a high-profile public personality private for any length of time. The governor did a brief interview with the reporter as he entered the Starzel home. The next day he was to be discharged.

We spent most of the day preceding the governor's release planning for his public exit. Just as he talked to the press on his way into the hospital five weeks earlier, we knew he had to talk to the press on his way out. The question was where? We tried to balance the governor's endurance level with the intensity and duration of the questions we anticipated the media would want to ask. I believe I suggested we reopen the press center for the day; drive the governor over, and put him on stage with his doctors where they had given their daily briefings that first week.

Jim and Jack vetoed that. They didn't want him in a captive position on a stage where it would be difficult for him to leave. There also were three steps to be navigated to get to the stage, and they didn't want to risk having that on film, either. It was good thinking on their part. Finally, it was decided the governor would walk out the same door he came in, through the main medical center lobby. The media would be cordoned off in the same lobby when he left just as they were when he entered. The preliminaries, including the announcement of the time and his point of departure, were completed. I drove back to Harrisburg to fly back to Pittsburgh the next morning on the state plane that would bring the governor back to the capital.

Departure day, quite a crowd had gathered off to the side of the hospital lobby to observe as we waited for the governor to appear. I remember the sustained applause that grew spontaneously from these visitors once the governor came around the corner into public view for the first time in six weeks. The reception had to make the governor, Mrs. Casey, and son Matt feel very good. It gave me chills, frankly, but then I tend to be sentimental about things like this.

The governor spent about ten minutes responding to questions from the media. He appeared strong and lively. He said he was determined to return to the governor's office. He got his back up one time when a reporter asked how long he thought he could continue to serve. "The people elected me to this job to finish the term, and that's exactly what I intend to do, okay?" he barked back. It was a flash of the old Casey fire. But, he added wisely, he wasn't going to set an artificial or arbitrary timeline to resume the powers of the office. The pace of his recovery would determine that.

With my traditional "Thank you, governor," I concluded the press conference at an appropriate pause in the questioning. I wanted to get the governor on his way without seeming to abruptly shut the press off. I believe we accomplished that. The governor made his way to his car, paused to shake hands with medical center officials, waved the way politicians do to the folks who were watching, and entered the car clearly under his own power. He was on his way home. Unbelievable in a way, given the critical condition of his health and the major surgery he endured just so short a time ago.

A half-hour later, he was in the plane taxiing for takeoff. Mrs. Casey, Matt, and I were the other passengers. The dutiful state police executive detail was seated as usual. The flight was calm, the sky clear blue, and the conversation surprisingly casual given what he and the family had just endured. When the plane touched down, I remember I looked over at him and said simply, "Welcome home, Governor." Mrs. Casey and Matt clapped their welcome. All the Caseys had broad, broad smiles on their face.

A crowd of about one hundred Casey fans and followers, including Acting Governor Singel, was waiting for him at the airport hangar. I was the first off the plane, followed by Matt and Mrs. Casey. Moments later, the governor appeared in the doorway of the plane and the greeters broke out into a sustained applause and shouts of "Welcome back." He waved back just as enthusiastically as they greeted him.

The Harrisburg press corps, which had no contact with the governor since he left for Pittsburgh almost a month and a half before, was cordoned off in front of the hangar door. The governor made his way over to exchange what I hoped would be but very brief pleasantries. The day and the exit had gone well, and I didn't want his endurance stretched unnecessarily. The sooner he was in the car en route to the residence, the better, in

Governor Casey meets with the assembled press corps in December of 1994 moments after reassuming the powers of his office following life-saving heart and liver transplantation surgery at the University of Pittsburgh Medical Center six months earlier. It was a historic moment for the governor and the Commonwealth. Courtesy of the Pennsylvania State Archives, Harrisburg.

my view. The governor, however, had other ideas. He clearly was rejuvenated by his release and the reception he received in both Pittsburgh and now the capital. He wasn't ready to leave as quickly as I would have preferred. But who was I to question him on that score? He was clearly enjoying himself and he wanted to take it all in.

Cameramen and photographers also were awaiting him at the Residence entrance. He opened his window to wave and declared, "It's good to be back." With that, the troopers drove his car into the garage, over the doors of which the staff had placed a banner reading "Welcome Home, Governor." The release from the hospital was complete. Casey was home. Now we had to deal with his outpatient recuperation and his return to office.

In hindsight, it was truly amazing. Less than two months after lifesaving, double-transplant surgery, the governor of Pennsylvania had returned to the Residence. To the obvious question of when he would reassume the reins of office . . . well, neither he nor his doctors had an immediate answer or an immediate timetable.

Matt and Mrs. Casey met with the media the day after the governor's return to Harrisburg. It was an opportunity for them, on behalf of the family, to thank the people of Pennsylvania for their expressions of support. It was also an opportunity to talk a bit about the governor's recuperation schedule. Essentially, recuperation involved some very close monitoring by the Pitt medical staff interspersed with some visits, either by the Pitt staff to Harrisburg, or by the governor to Pittsburgh. Obviously, the objective was for the doctors to keep close tabs on his progress and on his reaction to his medication.

Each time he went to Pittsburgh, we announced the visit in advance. He would fly from the state hangar at the New Cumberland airport. Invariably, there would be a reporter or two present to ask him about his recovery and whether he had set a timeline for a return to office. The answer to the recovery was simple: It was progressing nicely. The answer to the question about resuming the powers of the governorship was not so simple. Usually, he would say he would do it just as soon as he felt up to the task and his doctors concurred. Truth was, Casey being Casey again, was staying in touch on matters of the state almost daily from the residence. And the fact was Lieutenant Governor Singel was functioning very ably as acting governor. There was nothing on the table or on the horizon that might force the issue that we could see.

During the summer, the governor began working with a physical therapist on an exercise regime. To keep his presence and his progress in public view, he and his therapist did at least one television and one newspaper interview from the Residence. At the request of Paul Vathis of the Associated Press, he also took a photo-opportunity walk in Bermuda shorts, sport shirt, and walking sneakers along the Susquehanna River. Paul's picture played prominently in newspapers across the state. I remember a couple of passing motorists happened to notice the governor walking and tooted their horn to let him know they were with him. The governor waved back. He seemed pleased.

On early return visits to Pittsburgh, the governor and Mrs. Casey usually were met by an assembled cast of reporters who would question the governor briefly on his way in for a checkup. But they had such confidence in the routine and the information they were receiving from his doctors that they did not bother to stake the hospital out until he left. The drill was that the Pitt Medical Center would put out an announcement of his departure and a brief summary of the doctors' findings and medical assessment. The doctors—particularly Dr. Follansbee, the able, articulate, cooperative cardiologist who coordinated these checkups—would make themselves available by telephone for reporters who wanted something more direct. The process never failed us once, which was testament to the accessibility of the doctors, the integrity of the system we had established, and the confidence the reporters had in the medical information they were receiving from the doctors. Even when the governor had to be readmitted for a few days (twice, as I recall), the system worked. No alarm bells went off in either instance. I was not always present during the hospitalizations, but I was in constant contact with the Pitt Medical Center information director, and the governor's office was consulted or advised in advance of what the periodic medical statements would contain.

The governor's first formal public appearance was the annual Pennsylvania Gridiron Show, in Harrisburg like in Washington, D.C., a night for the press to lampoon politicians. The governor, traditionally, is given the last word to lash back. In this case, just the governor's presence was word enough. But he was feeling so good he decided he would present his own skit in response, just as he had each of his six previous years in office.

When I first arrived in town in the early 1960s, the governor simply would get up, recite a couple of one-liners that his staff had prepared digging back at the press, and the dinner would be concluded. Former Governor Dick Thornburgh changed all that when he and his staff did an on-stage spoof based on *Ghostbusters*. From that point on, it became a challenge to outdo the previous year's gubernatorial presentation, no matter who the governor happened to be. The dinner had now devolved into an evening where the press spoof was politely tolerated; the feature performance was and remains the governor's office response. Thanks to the advances in television filming and the availability of the Commonwealth Media Center, Governor Casey and his staff raised the gubernatorial response to new and unprecedented heights. It became a very elaborate video production, but the Casey folks were able to pull it off because they had some very creative people on the staff. I contributed very little to the Casey script. My role usually was limited to a bit player in one of the scenes.

In 1993, with the anticipation of the governor's first formal public appearance very much in focus, the Casey staff did a takeoff on the governor's surgery. He played the part of Beldar Conehead (made famous by Dan Akroyd on *Saturday Night Live*). Both he and Mrs. Casey, good sports that they were, donned rubber coneheads for their scenes. The theme was that the governor's cone had collapsed. Scenes were shot at the medical center with the governor's doctors playing their roles, and apparently enjoying it. Actual newspaper headlines from the governor's surgery were interspersed into the video with vivid effect. And the governor carried out his role like an acting veteran.

His sense of humor was an interesting aside to his public character. This very formal, usually very reserved man just loved to let loose for these video productions. One year he donned a leather jacket, jeans, and boots, slicked his hair back, put on a pair of bikers' sunglasses, and took Mrs. Casey for a simulated ride on a Harley. His final year in office, 1994, the theme was the Top Ten questions of what the governor would do when he left office. One scene had him in the worst-looking sports jacket imaginable, chasing ambulances looking for clients. The final segment of that production had him in Austrian shorts and hat as Father Von Trapp leading his staff in a version of "So Long, Farewell, Good Night" from *The Sound of Music*. My line, as I recall, was to sing, "Now I can tell the press to go to Hell."

But to return to the Coneheads. The production brought the house down. The governor was warmly received. He made it through the evening in very good shape and seemed to enjoy himself. Two of his doctors were his guests for the performance and he graciously acknowledged them in his remarks prior to the video. He was another big step closer to finishing out his term, and the night served to further negate any doubts that still might have existed about his physical or mental capacity to do so. The only question was when he would take the step.

Actually, the decision may have been forced on the governor as much as it was calculated on his part. Under state law the governor is required to present a formal midyear budget briefing to the General Assembly and, in so doing, to the public itself. Because Pennsylvania's fiscal year runs from July 1 through June 30 of the succeeding year, the midyear briefing always occurs in early December. Lieutenant Governor Singel, who had served very ably in Casey's stead working closely and cooperatively with Jim Brown who was representing the governor, was prepared to do the briefing. But Singel, now looking to make a run for governor the next year in his own right, wanted to put an even more indelible mark on his service as acting governor.

As I heard it from Jim Brown, in the weeks leading up to the to the midyear briefing, Singel suggested that if Governor Casey was not back in office by then, he intended to put his own priorities forward in presenting the report on the state's fiscal condition. Singel had been faithful to this point to the Casey agenda. But this new turn signaled that he had reached a point where he no longer was content to be a stand-in as governor; he now wanted to put his own imprint on policy prior to his campaign for the position. That didn't set well with Casey. He fully intended to reclaim the duties of his office for the last year of the Casey administration. It was not going to be, by default, the first year of a Singel administration.

The governor took one last trip to Pittsburgh to get the doctor's assurances he was physically up to the task. He was readmitted for a complete evaluation of his condition and recovery before he announced his intentions to return. And he returned to Harrisburg in a day or two with the doctors' okay. He announced he would resume the powers of governor the day after the midyear budget briefing. That cramped the lieutenant governor's plans to a great extent. Rather than putting his signature on policy priorities for 1994, Singel was left with but a forum to discuss his view of the office and the policies he believed important after serving in an "acting" capacity for six months. His comments, frankly, were lost in the crush of understandable interest surrounding the governor's formal and physical return the next day. I can't say there was a grand design to have it all play out that way, but that's the way it did.

Considerable staff time was spent deliberating the best way for the governor to resume the powers and duties of his office. The possibility of an address to a joint session of the General Assembly was contemplated at one point, but quickly discarded. Ultimately, it was decided that the governor would come to the office from the Residence on the designated morning. He then would go out to the reception room before a crowd of invited guests and, with his family behind him, formally reassume the reins of government. That's the way it was scripted; that's the way it happened. And it worked out well.

The morning of his return, the AP's Paul Vathis came to the Residence grounds to photograph the governor leaving the home for the Capitol for the first time in six months. Commonwealth Media was there to provide pool coverage for television. It was a cold, wet day; dampness, wind, and chill filled in the air. Not the best first day out for a man who had survived heart/liver transplant surgery, and whose immune system had to be suspect. Still, as I recall, the governor went coatless for his reappearance. He found a throng of wet and cold reporters awaiting him on the steps to the Capitol. He waved and smiled broadly as he exited his car and walked to the entrance. Security and I moved him along out of the weather. Inside, a crowd of Casey supporters and staff had gathered in the corridor holding a banner proclaiming "Welcome Back, Governor."

The governor greeted his friends and then entered the private elevator to his second floor office. Moments later, he walked into the office suite he had left six months before, to be greeted by another group of delighted staff and family. The invited dignitaries, including the legislative leadership and members of the Cabinet, awaited in the reception room. As soon as he was settled, the governor, Mrs. Casey, and their children walked out of the office, down the outer corridor, and into the reception room. He was greeted once again with sustained applause. His handsome family gathered behind him. Their pleasure this day surely was more personal than political. Their father had survived an excruciating ordeal. His faith, his determination, his fighting spirit, and their constant love and support had carried him from the throes of death to continued life and a promising future with them and their children.

The governor's remarks were superb, as usual. Once again, he proved that his best statements were those statements he had edited. He hit all the right chords. He thanked the lieutenant governor for his able and dedicated stewardship; he thanked the members of the General Assembly for their expressions of support; he talked of the challenges he believed were still confronting the Commonwealth, and how he proposed to address them; and, most of all, he thanked his family for their daily love and comfort through his ordeal. He also expressed his heartfelt gratitude to the people of Pennsylvania for their prayers, their patience, and their well wishes. He concluded by declaring: "It's great to be back!" There was hardly a dry eye in the room when he finished. Matt, who had been his steadfast companion during his recuperation, and the governor exchanged a high-five. Photographers captured the moment for posterity. If ever a picture was worth a thousand words, this was the one.

Chapter 24

★★★★★★

The Final Year

All things considered—particularly in light of the ordeal he endured over the previous six months—Governor Robert P. Casey's final year in office went about as hurdle free as he could have expected. His health and his stamina were improving steadily and he was dealing daily with the problems of governance that every governor encounters in the discharge of his duties. In short, Casey was back and he clearly was in charge. Of that there was never any doubt! What tensions surfaced were largely political—political differences with half the House Democrats over his last budget; and political strains with the Democratic candidates for governor and U.S. senator in the 1994 elections. This is how it all unfolded as I saw it and recall it.

First, the budget. As fate would have it, December traditionally is a time when the governor and his budget secretary closet themselves at the Governor's Residence, meeting with individual cabinet and agency heads to review their budget requests for the new fiscal year. So the fact that Casey was away from his desk at the Capitol more than he was at it the first weeks of his return was standard fare for that time of year. (Just to protect ourselves against some probing reporter, Bonnie Seaman and I kept a daily log of his gubernatorial activities and meetings for the first month or so of his return. If asked, we wanted to have chapter and verse of his schedule readily at hand and not have to reconstruct it days or weeks after the events. Surprisingly, we were never asked.)

The 1994–95 state budget, Casey's eighth and last submission, was problematic almost from the moment it was presented. And the problem was with the House Democrats. Casey was always cautious—"conservative," some Democrats complained—in his spending initiatives. From the first day of his first term, he had been determined to avoid encumbrances in one budget that would add significant spending on to succeeding budgets. His commitment to social programs, particularly those in the area of women and children services, never wavered. But neither did it set spending floors that would cause subsequent budgets to soar. Except for the unforgettable anomaly in 1991, all prior Casey budgets fit that mold and this last one wasn't going to deviate. That did not sit well with the House Democratic leadership and half their caucus. I suspect they thought the governor's spending wasn't "Democratic" enough for the 1994 election cycle. But Casey wasn't moved by their opposition. Instead, he instructed Budget Secretary Mike Hershock to work as cooperatively as necessary with legislative Republicans in both the House and Senate to arrive at a consensus as early as possible, but a consensus that was consistent with the primary thrust of his budget submission, which was to combine controlled spending geared to targeted objectives with one last round of tax cuts to lessen the impact of the levies imposed in 1991.

Pragmatic politics would not have permitted it any other way. There really was no choice but to bring the Republicans into the budget process because they still controlled the Senate and the House, 26–24 in the case of the former, 102–100 (with one vacancy) in the case of the latter. A so-called Democratic budget crafted solely by Democrats might have livened up the legislative proceedings a bit by giving the Democrats something to rave about. But in the backdrop of the 1994 gubernatorial campaign, it could not have passed on its own merits. And politically, a prolonged fight in the legislature over the budget would have been more harmful to Democratic electoral hopes in November than enactment of a budget that could not clearly be labeled "Democratic" in its promises.

Half the Democratic caucus in the House agreed with Governor Casey. With that bloc of Democrats in hand, and the Republican legislative leaders on board, the budget was passed on time and with little fuss. For a chief executive who had been so badly debilitated only six months earlier, that was no small feat. In December of 1994, just a month and a half before his term was to end, Governor Casey's midyear budget could report the administration would leave office with a projected half-billion surplus to hand over to his successor. The recovery from the dark days of 1991 was complete.

When it came to the politics of the last year of the second term . . . well, that was another matter. The governor's relationship with Democratic Party regulars—the state committee and the county chairmen in particular—was always at arms-length at best. He didn't quite trust them and what motivated them. That's why Harris Wofford was asked to serve as Democratic state chairman following Casey's nomination as the party's candidate for governor in 1990, and why Tony May was dispatched to the State Committee as its executive director in 1994. For their part, organization Democrats knew how Casey felt about them, and they didn't quite like it. Peaceful coexistence is the most accurate way to describe the accommodation they had with each other in things political.

So it shouldn't have been surprising that political problems began to surface early in the 1994 election year. What was surprising, perhaps, was with whom the strains occurred: First with his lieutenant governor, Mark Singel, and later with his good friend and U.S. senator, Harris Wofford. Let's stipulate for the record right here: I was not always privy to the governor's innermost political thought processes, nor did I ask him directly about them. Didn't think it was my business, frankly. But I had a fairly up-close-and-personal view of the sequence of events and this is how I saw them play out over the course of the year.

First, the case of Mark Singel. The lieutenant governor had a host of admirable traits to bring to the political process. He was bright, likable, articulate, energetic; he had a relish for public service and he was thoughtful in the way he went about public policymaking. Most important, perhaps, he thought of politics more as a vocation than an avocation; he had a real love for the game and the playing of it. He had been an enterprising state senator from Cambria County before he was tabbed by Casey to be his gubernatorial running mate in 1986. His exuberance for the give and take of the political process was at once his greatest asset and, perhaps, his greatest liability. If Singel had one consistent shortcoming, in the view of those who watched him through the years, it was that he just could not seem to contain himself in his zeal to establish and build his own political identity. In spite of Casey's repeated admonition, "Like it or not, we're joined at the hip," Singel set out early in the second term to move on his political ambitions. In the process, his public pronouncements on more than one occasion put him at odds with the administration and the governor he served. The tensions that began to build never quite dissipated and the result was that Governor Casey never did offer Lieutenant Governor Singel more than tepid support in his 1994 campaign to succeed him.

Early in 1991 after the second Casey/Singel inauguration, I may have contributed inadvertently to the developing split. The lieutenant governor called me over to his office one day for a private conversation. He told me he was thinking of challenging incumbent Republican U.S. Senator Arlen Specter in the 1992 elections, and he asked me what I thought. I told him if that's where his political instincts took him, well, there was a certain logic to the idea. (He had, after all, been an aide to a U.S. congressman and had served as a Pennsylvania state senator over the course of his relatively young career.) So, effectively, I said nothing to discourage him. But what I didn't say, because I thought it was so obvious that it didn't need saying, was that he certainly needed to share his intentions with the governor before he did anything else. I would have thought given their association and the fact that, in Casey's words, politically they truly were "joined at the hip," that would have been a given. Anyone with even a smattering of political smarts certainly should have understood that from the get-go.

But Singel apparently missed the obvious. A few days later, an Associated Press story appeared reporting that Singel was contemplating a race for the U.S. Senate. We later learned it was Singel who invited the reporter to his office for the interview. The story caught the governor by surprise. And with him already immersed in the Commonwealth's troubling fiscal situation, he was none too happy about it. When the press inevitably asked him for his reaction at the first opportunity, the governor's reaction was cool and most unenthusiastic. Pennsylvania had some serious fiscal problems, he said. Furthermore, he and the lieutenant governor had campaigned so hard to earn a second term and, having been just inaugurated to their second terms, this was neither the right time nor the right priority, he thought, for either of them to be thinking of moving on to another elective office.

The governor's point was hard to miss. But whether Singel picked up on it or not, he was undeterred. He did, in fact, seek the Democratic nomination for the U.S. Senate in 1992. The governor stayed neutral. It was not the best of timing. For one, Singel got caught up in the tide of the so-called Year of the Woman. He lost the nomination by 153,000 votes to a virtually unknown woman from the Philadelphia area, Lynn Yeakel. I suspect the Commonwealth's budget problems and the $3-billion tax hike that was enacted to resolve it was not helpful to his campaign, either ("joined at the hip," remember). But his major misjudgment, in my view, was that Singel failed to share his intentions with the governor before proceeding. My guess is that if Singel had approached Casey about the Senate race, Casey would have counseled him against it. My guess is that Singel would have proceeded in either case. But at least he would have known where the governor stood before he encouraged any speculation about his possible candidacy in the press or the political community.

The second rift occurred almost at the same time Singel was making his Senate ambitions known. This one involved the salary increases the General Assembly had enacted in 1987 to take effect for the legislators elected in 1988 and thereafter, and for the governor elected in 1990 and the Cabinet that would assume office with him or her. The leadership of the General Assembly, on both sides of the political aisle, wanted to raise legislative salaries in 1987 when Casey took office. Governor Thornburgh, understandably, wasn't about to sign a pay raise on his way out the door; newly inaugurated Governor Casey was not about to sign a pay raise bill as one of his first acts on the way in. He insisted that any salary increase legislation be prospective for both the legislative and executive branches: 1989 for the new General Assembly and 1991 for the next state administration. That way, if the pay increases were a problem for voters, they'd first have an opportunity to register their protest in both the legislative and gubernatorial elections that would follow before the increased salary levels took effect.

By the 1991 inaugural, Casey was working mightily to contain the looming budget deficit by a combination of spending freezes, substantial cuts in the Cabinet's budget requests, layoffs, and even a payless payday for the state workforce, including the governor, his senior staff, and his Cabinet. It was in that context that Bob Zausner of the *Philadelphia Inquirer* approached Casey in the hallway outside the governor's office and asked if he was going to accept the higher salary. He said he would. I know his primary consideration was not for himself, but for his Cabinet. He said the Cabinet had labored very hard the first four years under the old salary structure. The members were now entitled to continue their labors under the higher salaries approved four years earlier.

The fact the governor was going to accept his pay increase and would allow the higher Cabinet salaries to take effect as well was, understandably, splashed around the Commonwealth by the media. Increased compensation for public officials always is big news in Pennsylvania. It is doubly big when the state is in as poor financial shape as Pennsylvania was at that moment. Lieutenant Governor Singel, when asked about the governor's decision, said he thought he would have been better advised to delay the increases until the Commonwealth was on firmer fiscal footing. Once again, Governor Casey had been blindsided by his lieutenant governor. (As an aside, another to jump into the fray was Republican Auditor General Barbara Hafer, the GOP candidate Casey had defeated for governor just three months before. She said, given the Commonwealth's current fiscal straits, she would not accept the higher salary of her office. There was probably a little "Take that!" to her motives, but like the governor frequently said, politics in Pennsylvania ain't beanbags. She deferred on her raise until the 1991 budget and tax package was passed.)

The final straw in the Casey/Singel political relationship, as I came to understand it, was when word reached Casey that Singel was going to moderate his (Singel's) staunch pro-life views to rally women to his gubernatorial campaign. Apparently, one of the lessons that Singel either learned or was reinforced for him in his failed U.S. Senate bid was just how important the woman vote could be in Democratic politics—Lynn Yeakel, Exhibit Number One. He was said to be determined to do what he had to do not to lose them again, even if it meant a course alteration in his stance on abortion. That was it for Casey. Singel was selected as Casey's running mate in 1986 for a number of reasons: electability, his roots in Democratic-rich Cambria County, his record as a member of the Pennsylvania Senate. But as important as any single other factor was his steadfast opposition to abortion. Just the notion that he might waver on this issue for political gain in his pursuit of higher public office was enough to put Casey off.

Casey never was publicly critical of his lieutenant governor, but neither was he active nor vocal on his behalf. Congressman Tom Ridge, the Republican nominee, and his staff were quick to grasp the electoral value of Casey's idleness. With the exception of one early slip related to job creation in Pennsylvania, which drew a sharp rebuke from the governor, they made certain they said or did nothing directly or indirectly critical of the governor that would energize him on Singel's behalf. Ridge won by some 235,000 votes. Many Democratic loyalists blamed Casey for the defeat. My own view is even Casey's active support would not have turned 235,000 votes around. 35,000 or 40,000? Maybe. But 235,000? No way.

One comment, editorial and subjective, to be sure—perhaps even presumptuous on my part—but I believe Mark Singel still has the potential to serve his Commonwealth in some public capacity, if he wants to do that. What mistakes he made in the second Casey/Singel term largely were mistakes in judgment that all young men are prone to make in the eager pursuit of their careers. Having observed Mark Singel first as a state senator and then as lieutenant governor and acting governor, I remain convinced that young men of his intellect, his instinct, and his commitment to politics and public service should be encouraged to engage in rather than disengage from both. "The only thing necessary for the triumph of evil is for good men to do nothing," wrote Edmund Burke in 1795. Well, Mark Singel is a good man and his promise shouldn't be easily written off or ignored.

The split with U.S. Senator Wofford probably troubled the governor even more than his differences with his lieutenant governor because their long bond was as much personal as it was political. In 1994 Wofford was a candidate for a full six-year term in the Senate. Casey had appointed Wofford three years earlier to fill the vacancy created by John Heinz's death. There's no question Wofford wanted the appointment very badly and informed the governor as much. The governor was reluctant initially because he believed Harris's political philosophy might be too liberal for mainstream Pennsylvania. At one point in the appointment process, the governor flirted with the possibility of naming Chrysler chairman Lee Iacocca (a nationally renowned figure who had family roots in Allentown) to the vacancy.

My information was that Casey was alerted to the possibility of Iacocca's interest by his good friend, U.S. Rep. John Murtha of Johnstown. Murtha, went the story as I heard it, had met Iacocca at a Washington social event and, somehow, the matter of the Heinz vacancy and the pending appointment came up in their discussion. Whether Iacocca raised the subject or Murtha did, I'm not certain. But Iacocca apparently expressed an interest and Murtha relayed the conversation to Casey. Casey, Carville and Jim Brown flew to Detroit to meet secretly with Iacocca. I was not informed (deliberately, I learned later) of the trip so as not to be in a position to respond to press questions if the word of the mission somehow leaked out.

It did. An Associated Press reporter—the same one who first published the story about Mark Singel's interest in running for the U.S. Senate—called a couple of days later asking if the governor had taken a private trip to Michigan, purpose unknown. I went to Jim Brown.

"You don't want to know," Jim told me.

I understood immediately what Jim was saying. He and, I assume, the governor didn't want to discuss in public whatever the trip was about if they could avoid it. And I didn't press the point. I got back to the reporter and told him I was not personally aware of any such trip and had nothing else to share on the subject. It wasn't exactly a denial. But it wasn't confirmation of any trip, either. He didn't have enough to go with a story, and I didn't know any more about a plane ride to Michigan than I did before the question was raised with me.

The story became public a day or two later, and the prospect of an Iacocca appointment became mute when Iacocca announced through his Detroit office that while he was flattered by the governor's discussion with him about the U.S. Senate, he had to respectfully decline. Casey and Carville had emphasized two points to Iacocca: The first was that the appointee would stand for election in November to fill the balance of the Heinz term; second, politics in Pennsylvania was no finishing school. Whoever was named to replace Heinz should not underestimate the depth or the intensity of the electoral process in the state. Iacocca, apparently, concluded he had neither the stomach for nor the desire to subject himself at that stage in his distinguished career to the punches and pulls of Pennsylvania politics. So he took himself out of consideration.

Once Iacocca's disavowal went on the record, Pennsylvania Republican officials were quick to jump on the jaunt to Detroit. In their spin, the Democratic Party in Pennsylvania was so devoid of talent that its governor was forced to go out of state to recruit a suitable appointee to the U.S. Senate. They also attacked Casey for taking so long (a couple of weeks) to fill the Heinz vacancy. My response was very simple and straightforward: For the governor to have known about the interest of a figure of national repute like Lee Iacocca and not pursued it would have been derelict on his part, to say the least. That's why he went to Detroit. As for timing, I said the governor's principal obligation was not to make the quickest appointment to the U.S. Senate, but the best appointment to represent Pennsylvania and its people. The voters, ultimately, would decide, I said, how well he fulfilled that responsibility to them when the balance of the Heinz term was up for election a year and one-half hence. (They certainly did.)

With Iacocca yesterday's news, the governor settled on Wofford's appointment. Casey's conditions were twofold, I was told: First Wofford would bring Carville and crew on to manage his campaign for election; second, when the issue of abortion came up as it inevitably would, Wofford would proclaim his support for the Pennsylvania Abortion Control Act, which already had its constitutionality upheld by the U.S. Supreme Court. With those conditions in hand, Governor Casey personally saw to it that Wofford was in a financial position to be competitive politically when he squared off with former governor and U.S. Attorney General Dick Thornburgh. He personally spent countless hours at a desk away from the state Capitol on the phone raising funds necessary for Wofford to be viable. He probably scratched for money for Wofford harder and longer than he did for himself in his prior gubernatorial campaigns. In the end, he gave Wofford the financial and political wherewithal to wage a viable campaign against Thornburgh.

I accompanied the governor to Wofford's 1991 election night hotel in Philadelphia. Clearly, this race politically was as much about Casey (particularly after the Iacocca flirtation) as it was about Wofford. Wofford was Casey's appointee. A Wofford loss was a Casey loss. I was hoping that whatever the outcome the race would be close enough that Wofford and his appointment would be deemed credible by the chattering classes. Instead, Wofford stunned the state and the country, overwhelming Thornburgh by 340,000 votes.

Wofford's victory in his 1991 race against Thornburgh was the country's first political bellwether that President George H. W. Bush might not be so invincible, after all. And how's this for irony? Bill Clinton of Arkansas had Bob Casey of Pennsylvania . . . no fan of his . . . to thank as much as anyone for setting the foundation of his election to the presidency one year later. Now that really does make for strange bedfellows.

Clinton found a political soulmate in Harris Wofford. Harris, in fact, figured heavily in preconvention speculation as a possible Clinton running mate for vice-president in 1992. He even met with the presumptive Democratic nominee in advance of the New York City convention before Clinton ultimately settled on Tennessee senator Al Gore. By the time Clinton was inaugurated, his political, personal and philosophical connection with Wofford had been wired.

Casey's differences with Wofford, not surprisingly, came over abortion. Despite his commitment to the Pennsylvania Abortion Control Act, Wofford's position seemed to soften after he went to the nation's capital. He seemed to swing closer to the Clinton pro-choice view. An abortion debate was under way in the U.S. Senate. Casey called Wofford personally to request him to support an antiabortion amendment that was to be offered on the Senate floor by Senator Dan Coates, Republican from Indiana. The amendment, as I recall, was a provision similar to Pennsylvania law. It may have dealt with parental notification. The White House and the Senate Democratic hierarchy were opposed to the Coates amendment. Wofford told Casey he was opposed as well.

As I heard the governor replay the conversation to a small group of his staff, he told Senator Wofford—not as a threat, rather as a fact of political life—that if he (Wofford) opposed the amendment, then he (Casey) could not campaign for him in the fall. Wofford held firm. It was an important political vote for Clinton. Wofford, when push came to shove, went with the president who charmed him and against the governor who appointed him. So Casey sat out the Wofford campaign as well. Wofford lost to Republican Congressman Rick Santorum by 87,000 votes. In my mind that Casey's active stumping for Wofford conceivably could have altered the outcome. But Wofford had a choice to make and his decision to support the Clinton position on abortion may have cost him his seat in the U.S. Senate. Casey's critics within the Democratic Party accused him of political treason. I believe it was more a matter of principle to the governor. And I respected him for it.

One footnote on the Casey-Wofford relationship: I learned as this was being written that Wofford paid Governor Casey one last visit before the governor passed away. If breaches between the two needed to be healed, they were, I was told.

With the elections over, the last month and one-half was spent working on the transition from a Casey to a Ridge administration. Casey instructed his team to be as cooperative as possible. We were.

The inside joke in the administration was that given the governor's zest for the job, the Casey administration would not wind down; rather, the clock would simply run out. And the governor proved us right, working right through his last day in office. His one final act, I must admit, was to dispense one last plate of largesse to his native region in northeast Pennsylvania. He went to Scranton to present a development check for the city's new downtown mall. I accompanied him.

When Bob Casey was elected in 1986, he proclaimed to those communities he believed had been largely ignored in the past by state government, "Now, it's our turn." He spent his first day in office in the small town of Monessen in southwestern Pennsylvania. He spent his last day in office in Scranton in northeast Pennsylvania. There was a symmetry to his term as governor, and the visits on his first and last day as chief executive were as consistent as they were symbolic. Bob Casey, if nothing else, was true to his commitment to the forgotten communities of Pennsylvania and the people who called them home.

When we arrived back in Harrisburg, Casey went to the Residence for his last night there. I dropped my state car off at the Capitol Plaza. Our youngest son, Steve, picked me up and drove me home. I had a drink, probably two—rare for me on a Monday. That evening our telephone rang. It was the governor. He told me he wanted to thank me for my service, that he knew he could be demanding, but that I had served him and the Commonwealth well. He appreciated my efforts very much and wanted me to know it. It was a gracious call for him to make.

"Governor," I told him in response. "You made it possible for all of us to serve. What's more, you made it possible for us to walk out of the Capitol when your term ended with our heads held high and our integrity in tact. Thank you for that."

Inaugural morning, I went for a run at 7 A.M. My "fifteen minutes in the sun"—the capstone of my Capitol journey, so to speak—were over.

Postscript

★★★★★★★

Robert Patrick Casey, governor of Pennsylvania, January 1987–January 1995.

He died in June 2000, much before his time. He was sixty-eight. The disease that he had battled so valiantly for almost a decade finally claimed his life. His last year, we're told, was particularly difficult. He was bedridden and hospitalized most of the time. We're also told Mrs. Casey never missed a day at his bedside. That was not surprising given their devotion to each other.

It must be left to others, admittedly more detached than myself, to render a more objective judgment on the stewardship and legacy of Robert Casey as governor of Pennsylvania. Casey himself declined to do so. When asked repeatedly by the media as his term drew to a close how he thought he and his administration would be remembered, invariably, he would respond, "I'm not into self-definition. In the final analysis, whatever the people decide I stood for, that's okay with me."

For my part, I believe the people evaluate their governors on the basis of the answer to three basic questions: (1) What did he say he'd do if he got to be governor? (2) What did he do after he got there? And (3) Was the state in better shape after he left office than when he arrived?

I would not presume to weigh or argue the merits and public policy agenda of one administration, in my time, versus another. Each in its own way, I believe, attempted to be true to itself. I know that certainly was true of Governor Casey and the convictions and commitment he brought to his long and distinguished career in public service.

"What did you do when you had the power?" Casey was fond of asking repeatedly in his public appearances.

My answer, in his case, would be a lot of good in a lot of ways!

Virtually all editorial opinions written on his administration at the end of his tenure reached the same conclusion. Perhaps the *Pittsburgh Post-Gazette* in its January 1, 1995, term-ending editorial most accurately and completely captured the essence of the Casey administration and the Casey stewardship. Under the headline, "Governor Casey: His Stewardship Showed Integrity and Responsibility":

Perhaps no one in Pennsylvania history wanted to be governor more. After witnessing his eight years of service, we would say that few have handled the job as well.

The paper called him a "responsible steward of state revenues" who believed in "limited spending growth and low taxes," yet maintained the Commonwealth's "commitment to education, human services and public infrastructure."

The editorial then went on to tick off a long list of achievements, to include:

Being "bold enough to champion local tax reform in 1989 though it was ultimately rejected by the voters";
Being "tenacious enough to achieve auto insurance reform (despite the heavy stakes of various lobbies)";
Being "gutsy enough to pursue the cleanup of the state's air and water (in the face, recently, of a more reluctant citizenry)";
Beginning "a health care program for children of low-income families";
Expanding and renovating "an antiquated prison system"; and
Forcing "school districts to become more responsible for special education."

The paper called Casey "bullish on job creation and economic development, particularly in the state's rust-belt zones" and concluded:

> The main story is that the Casey administration . . . served the state well. It sought to return Pennsylvania to prosperity at a time when larger economic forces conspired against it. The fact that Governor-elect Tom Ridge will have essentially the same mission is not a poor reflection on Robert Casey's stewardship—only testimony to how enormous the job really is.

I would add to that list,

Doing more than any of his predecessors to empower women in the decisionmaking circles of state government with the appointment of twelve to Cabinet-level positions in his eight years as governor;
Creating the precedent-setting PennVEST clean water infrastructure program, which made possible $1.5 billion in loans to 800 communities across the Commonwealth which were home to three million people;
Helping to alleviate the financial burdens of the working poor by increasing the poverty exemption of the state income tax not once, but four times; and

Transforming the state Liquor Store system to such a successful degree of customer sensitivity that it was eliminated for, all intents and purposes, as a subject of political and public policy debate for more than a decade.

The governor took some blows, to be sure. But the most telling mark of a leader is not how he handles his successes, rather how he responds to his adversities. Robert Casey passed the test with flying colors.

His steadfast opposition to abortion won him few friends among the chatting classes, but he never wavered in his conviction. When his local tax-reform initiative was resoundingly defeated in a voter referendum, he launched the most aggressive antidrug program in the history of the Commonwealth. When the Camp Hill prison riots assaulted his administration, he responded with the most aggressive program of prison expansion of any prior administration in state history. When he was battered at the Democratic National Convention, he emerged with his reputation as a man of principle substantially enhanced. And once he had weathered the turmoil and discontent of the 1991 budget and tax dilemma, he responded by lowering taxes in each of his three remaining years.

Casey left town with a smaller state payroll than when he arrived; and he turned over a $1.1-billion revenue surplus and set asides in the form of tax cuts and a Rainy Day fund to his successor. And, obviously, in his most serious fight for life—his own—he responded with a resiliency that made all Pennsylvania pleased and proud.

The governor was fond of saying in his postsurgery period that he had new pipes, a new engine, that he was ready to go. And he took full advantage of the lease he had been given on life thanks to the generosity of a humble woman from Monessen, Pennsylvania.

He lived to complete his term in office. He lived to see all twenty-eight (at the time) of his grandchildren born, more than half of them after his surgery. He had his family and they had him for seven years they otherwise would not have had together.

He even contemplated running for president in 1996. He soon abandoned the notion with the realization that his health simply would not have permitted it. While it's doubtful he could have unseated a sitting Democratic president, I do believe it would have been one helluva campaign if he were up to it. He would have made Bill Clinton squirm. More important, he would have raised the standard of the Truman Democrat—one befitting the proud heritage and tradition of the Democratic Party; a standard abandoned by the existential lifestyle and politically poll-driven philosophy of William Jefferson Clinton and his ilk.

Age sixty-eight was much too young for a man of Casey's principled drive, determination, and dedication to die. His was an important voice on important subjects and we all could have benefited from hearing from him further. But we as mere humans have no control over how long a time we spend on this earth. His time was well spent, in so many ways—as a person, a professional, and a public servant.

Toni and I went to Scranton for the viewing and the funeral Mass. That week I relived in my memory many of the events recounted here. I don't pretend to have been close to the governor—certainly not in a personal or social sense. But I did work closely with him. I know I served him ably and I served him loyally. I believe he appreciated my efforts. That was a fair return on our relationship. I am indebted to him for the opportunity he gave me to fulfill one of my life's ambitions.

There are, ultimately, two ways to judge a governor and his legacy. On the public side, there is the question, What did he do? On the private side, there is the equally important matter of what kind of a person was he?

On the public side, there was virtual unanimity that Robert Casey was a man with a passion for public service and an unwavering commitment to economic growth, opportunity (particularly for women and children), and social justice. I can only quote the public record in this regard.

The *Harrisburg Patriot-News:* "Bob Casey is the ultimate exponent of purpose and determination. In 20 years of seeking the office of governor, he never wavered from his conviction that he could fulfill the duties and lead Pennsylvania on the course to a better future."

Or this from the *Philadelphia Inquirer*, no fan of the governor during his eight-year run: "Mr. Casey gets ready to leave as an accomplished but enigmatic leader. His determination to survive—politically and personally—leaves much to be admired (though his prickly uncompromising style made him difficult to embrace)."

The *Inquirer* concluded: "His determination to continue working through his term, indeed to live . . . served as an inspiration to all Pennsylvanians. He has earned a rare and precious thing in politics: Respect."

From Allentown to Erie, there were other words of similar praise. Robert P. Casey wasn't perfect as governor. But two reporters captured the essence of his service most succinctly.

"By any measure, Casey leaves Pennsylvania a better place than it was eight years ago," wrote John Baer of the *Philadelphia Daily News*. "Casey Leaving Office to Mostly Rave Reviews" was the headline over the term-end story in the *Pittsburgh Post-Gazette* written by Tim Reeves, who, incidentally, replaced me as press secretary in the administration of Governor Tom Ridge.

On the personal side, the governor's allies were legion. His friends called him committed, principled. His critics, and they were vocal if not as legion, called him rigid, stubborn, hardheaded. But no one, friend or foe, ever called him hypocritical.

The Casey administration left town scandal free. It was no accident that it did. The governor set a high standard for proper conduct in public life and he set the model by the tone and example with which he conducted himself. Anyone who deviated to a lower bar would have done so at his or her own risk. No one that I know ever did.

So I leave it to the press, the pundits, and the political community to debate, if they wish, the pluses and minuses to his political record. No one will ever debate what kind of man he was.

Many words were said about him the week he died, trying to capture the significance of his life. Most of those who eulogized him were right on target. But two truly stand out.

Most Right Reverend Bishop Thomas Timlin of Scranton, in his remarks at the end of the funeral Mass, said that Robert Casey's life was a testimony to the virtue of family and the strength of faith. It certainly was. Eloquent, succinct, and, most important, right on.

But it was left for his oldest son and namesake, Auditor General Robert P. Casey Jr., to put an exclamation mark to the point. As a husband, as a father, as a public official, and as a human being, the son said about his dad, "He got the important things right!" He certainly did. What better epitaph, what more enduring legacy? There are none!

Index

Adams, Arlin, 143–47
Alessandroni, Walter, 143–47, 204–5
Ammerman, Senator Joseph
  (D-Clearfield), 43–50, 51–58,
  74–77
Andrezeski, Senator Anthony ("Buzz"),
  (D-Erie), 84–85
Apple, J. W., 261
Armitage, Dr. John, 261
Arrowsmith, Marvin, 36

Baer, John, 106–7, 113–14, 291
Ball, Harry W., 17, 149
Barbush, Tony, 217
Bay Area Rapid Transit (BART),
  94–100
Beagle, Ron, 15
Begler, Sam, 181–82, 184
Bell, Jack, 1
Berg, Phil, 153, 225
Bernstein, Carl, 32–33, 35
Berra, Lawrence ("Yogi"), 36
Blaik, Red, 15
Bloom, George I., 9, 131–32
Bloom, Robert, 155
Boyle, Pat, 108–9
Bower, Representative Adam
  (R-Northumberland), 48
Borea, Robert, 29
Brightbill, Senator David ("Chip")
  (R-Lebanon), 56
Broder, Dave, 36, 82
Broderick, Lieutenant Governor Raymond J., 148–58, 166–67, 171–73
Brown, James, 219, 221–23, 225–28,
  233, 250–51, 253–65, 270, 284
Brown, Governor Jerry, California, 244
Burke, Edmund, 283
Buscarini, Herman, 4
Bush, George H. W., 159, 246

Butera, Representative Robert
  (R-Montgomery), 131, 188
Bye, Joe, 146

Caliguiri, Mayor Richard (Pittsburgh),
  250–51
Camiel, Peter, 79, 103–4, 108–10
Carocci family
  Roy, 2–4, 7
  Ivo, 2, 5–7, 223
  Toni, 36, 95–96, 147, 174–75,
  204–5
Carville, James, 198–99, 219, 228–29,
  232, 238, 244
Casey Family
  Ellen, 241, 249–50, 253, 265,
  271–75
  Matt, 241, 271–73, 277
  Pat, 244
  Robert P., Jr., 244, 292
Casey, Governor Robert P., Sr., 38, 92,
  116–18, 145, 152–53, 162–65,
  170–72, 188–89, 202–92
  abortion, 223–25
  amyloidosis, 250–52
  budget fight 1991, 230–35
  national Democratic Party, 242–47
  Minnesota Democratic delegation,
  245
  prison riots, Camp Hill, 225–29
  transplant, 253–65
Catalano, Vince, 92
Cawley, James, 51
Central Intelligence Agency, 7–8
Cianfrani, Senator Henry ("Buddy")
  (D-Phila.), 47, 63–68, 71, 75,
  88–89
Childs, Marquis, 1
Clark, U.S. Congressman Frank
  (D-Butler), 187

Clark, U.S. Senator Joseph (D-Pa.), 9, 16, 128
Clinton, William Jefferson, 29, 236–47, 285–86
Coleman, Pete, 93–96
Collins, Joe, 4
Common Cause, 119
Commonwealth Media, 267
Conmy, Jack, 19, 130, 140–41, 155–56, 172, 205
Constitutional Convention, 144–47, 187
Coogan, Jim, 14
Coppersmith, Senator W. Louis (D-Cambria), 75–76
Corman, Senator J. Doyle (R-Centre), 56
Cronkite, Walter, 135–36
Cummings, John, 168
Cuomo, Mario, 134

Daily Collegian, 13–15
Davis, Lieutenant Governor John Morgan, 44, 142
Dean, Governor Howard (D-Vt.), 240
Dennis, Shirley, 193–96
Denton, Dr. Harold, 190
Dilworth, Richardson, 66, 120, 123, 127–30
Dimaggio, Joe 3
Donolow, Senator Benjamin (D-Phila.), 64, 70–71
Doran, Dick, 180–81
Dorris, Jim, 182
Duffield, Senator William (D-Fayette), 44–46, 60–61, 89, 90, 92
Dwyer, State Treasurer R. Budd, 200

Ecenbarger, Bill, 26–27, 37, 51, 171–72
Eisenhower, Dwight David, 1, 28–29, 133–34
electric chair, 158–59
Ellerbee, Linda, 34–35
Engle, Rip, 14
Erdelatz, Eddie, 14–15
Eshelman, Russ, 259
Ewing, Senator Wayne (R-Allegheny), 51

Fallows, James, 35
Fine, Governor John, 22–23
Fineman, Speaker Herbert (D-Phila.), 41–46, 54, 107
Fisher, Mike, 217
Flaherty, Hugh, 155
Flaherty, Pete 88–89, 203
Fleming, Senator R. D. (R-Allegheny), 45
Fleming, Senator Wilmot (R-Montgomery), 45
Fohl, Bob, 215
Follansbee, Dr. William, 257–58
Ford, Gerald, 141, 143
Frame, Senator Richard (R-Venango), 45, 50
Friend, Representative Stephen (R-Delaware), 183
Fumo, Senator Vincent (D-Phila.), 61, 78–86, 103–04, 106–14
Fung, Dr. John, 253–65
Furman, Lieutenant Governor Roy, 142

Gerber, Richard, 109
Glanton, Richard, 195
Goldwater, U.S. Senator Barry (R-Az.), 132–37, 162
Goodman, Jim, 215
Gore, Albert, 243–44
Graves, Dick, 13, 27, 136
Green, U.S. Congressman William, Sr. (D-Phila.), 9, 118, 121
Greenlee, Bill, 149–55
Gridiron Show, 18, 274–75
Grotevant, Bob, 221, 236

Hafer, Auditor General Barbara, 56, 282
Hager, Senator Henry (R-Lycoming), 188
Haggerty, Jim, 226–28, 252–54
Hamilton, Perrin, 171
Harris, Gene, 13, 27, 136
Harrisburg Patriot News, 291
Heinz, U.S. Senator John (R-Pa.), 238
Hershock, Mike 54, 116, 233, 279

Hill, Senator Lou (D-Phila.), 66
Hilton, Frank, 182–84
Hobbs, Senator Fred (R-Schuylkill), 45
Homer, Representative Max (D-Allegheny), 187
Honsberger, Fred, 240
Humphrey, Hubert, 1, 202

Iacocca, Lee, 284–85
income tax, state, 40–46, 144–45, 155, 157–58, 175–78
Irvis, Speaker K. Leroy (D-Allegheny), 41–46, 107

Jensen, Ed, 98
Johnson, Lyndon B., 1, 162
Johnstown Tribune Democrat, 7, 13–14
Jones, Cliff, 208
Jubelirer, Senator Bob (R-Blair), 56, 107

Kaminski, Duke, 13, 16, 27, 30, 128–30, 140
Keisling, Bill, 127–30, 208–11, 219
Kelly, Jim, 166
Kennedy, John F., 1, 28–29, 41, 121, 162
Kirk, Vicki, 103
Kline, Lieutenant Governor Ernest P., 42–46, 69–72, 117, 142, 158, 187, 203
Knoll, State Treasurer Catherine Baker, 259
Kury, Senator Franklin L. (D-Northumberland), 47–52

LaForge, Pat, 248–49
Lamb, Senator Thomas F. (D-(Allegheny), 41–46, 69–78, 179–80
Lark, Henry, 47–48
Larsen, Rolf, 56
Lawrence, Governor David L., 116, 120–24
  Pittsburgh Renaissance, 120

political polls, 120
press pool party, 123–24
Leader, Governor George, 142, 146
Lee, Speaker Ken (R-Sullivan), 107, 144
Leherr, Dave, 17
Lench, Ron, 181–82
Legislative Reference Bureau, 89–90, 105
Lewis, Senator H. Craig (D-Bucks), 52–56, 77–85, 91, 110–12
lieutenant governor reform, 166–67
Liquor Control Board, reform, 191, 212–18, 289
Lincoln, Senator William (D-Fayette), 61, 83–86, 88
Lindgren, Lindy, 13, 21–24
Lisagor, Peter, 1
Local Government Retirement Study Commission, 52
Loeper, Senator Joseph (R-Delaware), 56
lottery, state, 73, 79, 180, 190
Lucas, Michael, 265
Lynch, Jack, 13, 17, 27, 30, 134, 205–6
Lyons, Charlie, 264

Machiavelli, 89
Madigan, Charlie, 99
Madonna, G. Terry, 179, 181, 187
Manderino, Speaker James (D-Westmoreland), 43–46, 54, 107, 217
Matthews, Frank, 13, 19–21
May, Tony, 182, 219, 221, 237, 279
Maverick Restaurant, 93
Mazzei, Senator Frank (D-Allegheny), 72, 87–90, 178, 180, 187
MacArthur, Douglas, 143
McCreesh, Senator Thomas (D-Phila.), 45
McDonough, Don, 154
McGlinchey, Senator Herbert (D-Phila.), 45, 71
McGonigle, Art, 120
McGovern, George, 202
McGrory, Mary, 240–41
McIntosh, Charlie, 55, 181

McLaughlin, Mike, 63, 182, 209
McManus, Mark, 264
McSparran, J. Collins, 128
Mears, Walter, 36
Meet the Press, 133–34
Messinger, Senator Henry (D-Lehigh), 45, 53, 58–59, 63, 76–77, 100, 176
Miller, Joe, 13, 16, 19–21
Miller, Stanley, 147, 154
Mitchell, Ed, 182
Moran, Emerson, 225–26
Murphy, Bill, 130
Murray, Representative Edwin ("Erg") (D-Cameron), 131
Murray, Senator Martin L. (D-Luzerne), 41–46, 69–78, 93, 107, 179–80
Myers, Morey, 209

Napolitan, Joe, 163–65, 170
Nagle, Jack, 27
National Conference of State Legislatures, 90, 98
Nassau, Roy, 182
Nelson, Lindsey, 14
Nixon, Richard M., 32, 104, 178, 202
Nolan, Senator Thomas (D-Allegheny), 44–46, 59, 73–76, 88, 92, 105

O'Brien, Larry, 41
Oceak, Frank, 14
Owens, David, 216–18

Paterno, Joe, 14, 142
Pennsylvania Industrial Development Authority (PIDA), 179
Perot, Ross, 240
Perzel, Speaker John (R-Phila.), 107
Philadelphia Inquirer, 69–70, 72, 88, 96–97, 168–69, 172–73, 259, 291
Pittenger, John, 184
Pittsburgh Post Gazette, 256–57, 265, 288–91
Prokop, U.S. Congressman Stanley (D-Lackawanna), 25
public utility reform, 50–51

Rackley, J. Ralph, 139
Reese, Norval, 180–81
Reeves, Tim, 291
Regan, Ronald, 142
Reibman, Senator Jeanette (D-Northampton), 67
Reichley, Jim, 130
Rendell, Governor Ed, 113–14, 217
Reston, James, 1, 36
Richards, Governor Ann, 237
Ridge, Governor Tom, 106, 118, 159, 238, 286
Roche, Wally, 193
Rochelle, Lloyd, 9
Rockefeller, Nelson, 132, 157, 236
Rocks, Senator Joseph (D/R-Phila.), 80–86
Roddy, Dennis, 256–57, 263–64, 269–70
Romanelli, Senator Jim (D-Allegheny), 92
Ryan, Speaker Matthew (R-Delaware), 107, 130–31, 143, 160, 186, 196

Salvatore, Senator Frank ("Hank") (R-Phila.), 82
Sampson, Art, 155
Scalera, Judge Ralph, 171
Scanlon, Senator Gene (D-Allegheny), 59–61, 63, 83–86, 91–92
Scott, U.S. Senator Hugh, 19, 130, 154, 162, 167
Scotzin, John, 13
Schwartz, Senator Allyson (D-Phila.), 83
Scranton, City of
    Dante Literary Society, 3
    20th Ward Social and Athletic Club, 3
    Scranton Central High School, 7
Scranton, Governor William Warren, 16, 19, 116, 123, 125–41, 143, 145–46
Scranton family
    Marion Margery, 125–26
    William Jr., 137–39, 142, 188–89, 203

Scranton Tribune, 130, 140
Seaman, Bonnie, 234–35, 278
Senate Confirmation Reform, 49–50
Senate Ethics Committee, 54, 60–61
Sennett, Bill, 155–58
Seltzer, Speaker H. Jack (R-Lebanon), 66
Serwach, Joe, 249
Shafer, Governor Raymond P., 16, 22–23, 40, 47, 116–17, 142–60

Shanaman, Susan, 51
Shapp, Governor Milton, 20–22, 27, 37–38, 40, 46, 49, 117–18, 129, 148–53, 162–85, 203–5, 212
  legislative investigation, 182–84
Shelly, Judge Carl, 149–50
Shibe Park, 3
Shumaker, Senator John (R-Dauphin), 217
Siglin, Cy, 13
Sikora, Marty, 13, 140
Slinker, Ollie, 215
Singel, Lieutenant Governor Mark, 77, 234, 260–61, 264, 275–76, 280–83
Sloan, State Treasurer Grace, 202
Smith, Bill, 224–25
Smith, Senator Joe (D-Phila.), 45, 54, 61, 63, 77–78, 80–81
Smith Merriman, 1
Smith, Representative Sam (R-Jefferson), 113
Speaker, Fred, 150–51, 158–59
Specter, U.S. Senator Arlen (D-Pa.), 56, 280
Speigelman, Dick, 258, 260, 267, 278
Staisey, Senator Leonard (D-Allegheny), 165–67
Stapleton, Senator Pat (D-Indiana), 176–78
Starzel, Dr. Thomas, 253–65, 267, 270
State System of Higher Education, 138, 197, 207–8
Stevenson, Adlai, 9, 233
Stone, David, 219, 223, 227

Stroup, Senator Stanley (R-Bedford), 50
Sweeney, Senator John (D-Delaware), 53

Tabor, John, 143–47
Tate, Mayor James H. J. (Philadelphia), 47, 70, 171
Taylor, John, 17, 28, 30, 226
Taylor, Senator M. Harvey (R-Dauphin), 9, 107
Thiemann, Dennis, 181–82, 184
Thornburgh, Governor Richard, 51, 59, 73, 117, 145, 186–200, 212–13, 274
  CBS News, 199
  political fund-raising, 191–92
  Three Mile Island, 190
  U.S. Senate campaign, 198–99
  United Nations, 199
Tighe, Jack, 219, 227, 239–40, 253–65, 270
Timlin, Most Rev. Bishop Thomas, 292
Torre, Joe, 14
Truax, Craig, 131
Tullio, Mayor Louis, Erie, 250–51
Tuma, Gary, 17, 25, 27

Van Zandt, U.S. Congressman James (R-Blair), 127–28
Vathis, Paul, 28–31, 273, 276
Volavka, Marc, 217

Walters, Bob, 162
Walters, Fred, 13
Wambach, Pete, Sr., 30–122
Warner, Charles Dudley, 69
Weinrach, Jack, 93–94
Welsh, George, 15
Whalley, U.S. Congressman J. Irving (R-Somerset), 187
Whittlesey, Faith Ryan, 188
Wicker, Tom, 1, 36
Wise, Helen, 209–11
Wofford, U.S. Senator Harris (D-Pa.), 198–99, 237–38, 279, 283, 286
Wood, Senator T. Newell (R-Luzerne), 45

Woodside, Judge Robert, 127
Widoff, Mark, 76

Yeakel, Lynn, 282
Young, M Michael, 171, 181, 187

Zausner, Bob, 282
Zdinak, Paul, 146
Zemprelli, Senator Ed (D-Allegheny),
    47, 61–63

www.ingramcontent.com/pod-product-compliance
Lightning Source LLC
Chambersburg PA
CBHW021355290426
44108CB00010B/255